Luigi Nono

The anti-fascist cantata *Il canto sospeso*, the string quartet *Fragmente – Stille, an Diotima* and the 'Tragedy of Listening' *Prometeo* cemented Luigi Nono's place in music history. In this study Carola Nielinger-Vakil examines these major works in the context of Nono's amalgamation of avant-garde composition with communist political engagement. Part I discusses *Il canto sospeso* in the context of all of Nono's anti-fascist pieces, from the unfinished Fučík project (1951) to *Ricorda cosa ti hanno fatto in Auschwitz* (1966). Nielinger-Vakil explores Nono's position at the Darmstadt Music Courses, the evolution of his compositional technique, his penchant for music theatre and his use of spatial and electronic techniques to set the composer and his works against the diverging circumstances in Italy and Germany after 1945. Part II further examines these concerns and shows how they live on in Nono's work after 1975, culminating in a thorough analysis of *Prometeo*.

CAROLA NIELINGER-VAKIL is a freelance flautist and musicologist based in London. She has published widely on the music of Luigi Nono. In collaboration with Martin Brady, she has also written on film music by Paul Dessau.

Music Since 1900

GENERAL EDITOR Arnold Whittall

This series – formerly Music in the Twentieth Century – offers a wide perspective on music and musical life since the end of the nineteenth century. Books included range from historical and biographical studies, concentrating particularly on the context and circumstances in which composers were writing, to analytical and critical studies concerned with the nature of musical language and questions of compositional process. The importance given to context will also be reflected in studies dealing with, for example, the patronage, publishing and promotion of new music, and in accounts of the musical life of particular countries.

*Titles in the series*

**Jonathan Cross**
The Stravinsky Legacy

**Michael Nyman**
Experimental Music: Cage and Beyond

**Jennifer Doctor**
The BBC and Ultra-Modern Music, 1922–1936

**Robert Adlington**
The Music of Harrison Birtwistle

**Keith Potter**
Four Musical Minimalists: La Monte Young, Terry Riley, Steve Reich, Philip Glass

**Carlo Caballero**
Fauré and French Musical Aesthetics

**Peter Burt**
The Music of Toru Takemitsu

**David Clarke**
The Music and Thought of Michael Tippett: Modern Times and Metaphysics

**M. J. Grant**
Serial Music, Serial Aesthetics: Compositional Theory in Post-War Europe

**Philip Rupprecht**
Britten's Musical Language

**Mark Carroll**
Music and Ideology in Cold War Europe

**Adrian Thomas**
Polish Music since Szymanowski

**J. P. E. Harper-Scott**
Edward Elgar, Modernist

**Yayoi Uno Everett**
The Music of Louis Andriessen
**Ethan Haimo**
Schoenberg's Transformation of Musical Language
**Rachel Beckles Willson**
Ligeti, Kurtág, and Hungarian Music during the Cold War
**Michael Cherlin**
Schoenberg's Musical Imagination
**Joseph N. Straus**
Twelve-Tone Music in America
**David Metzer**
Musical Modernism at the Turn of the Twenty-First Century
**Edward Campbell**
Boulez, Music and Philosophy
**Jonathan Goldman**
The Musical Language of Pierre Boulez: Writings and Compositions
**Pieter C. van den Toorn and John McGinness**
Stravinsky and the Russian Period: Sound and Legacy of a Musical Idiom
**David Beard**
Harrison Birtwistle's Operas and Music Theatre
**Heather Wiebe**
Britten's Unquiet Pasts: Sound and Memory in Postwar Reconstruction
**Beate Kutschke and Barley Norton**
Music and Protest in 1968
**Graham Griffiths**
Stravinsky's Piano: Genesis of a Musical Language
**Martin Iddon**
John Cage and David Tudor: Correspondence on Interpretation and Performance
**Martin Iddon**
New Music at Darmstadt: Nono, Stockhausen, Cage, and Boulez
**Alastair Williams**
Music in Germany Since 1968
**Ben Earle**
Luigi Dallapiccola and Musical Modernism in Fascist Italy
**Thomas Schuttenhelm**
The Orchestral Music of Michael Tippett: Creative Development and the Compositional Process
**Marilyn Nonken**
The Spectral Piano: From Liszt, Scriabin, and Debussy to the Digital Age
**Jack Boss**
Schoenberg's Twelve-Tone Music: Symmetry and the Musical Idea

**Deborah Mawer**
French Music and Jazz in Conversation: From Debussy to Brubeck
**Philip Rupprecht**
British Musical Modernism: The Manchester Group and their Contemporaries
**Amy Lynn Wlodarski**
Musical Witness and Holocaust Representation
**Carola Nielinger-Vakil**
Luigi Nono: A Composer in Context

# Luigi Nono

## A Composer in Context

Carola Nielinger-Vakil

CAMBRIDGE
UNIVERSITY PRESS

**CAMBRIDGE**
**UNIVERSITY PRESS**

University Printing House, Cambridge CB2 8BS, United Kingdom

Cambridge University Press is part of the University of Cambridge.

It furthers the University's mission by disseminating knowledge in the pursuit of education, learning and research at the highest international levels of excellence.

www.cambridge.org
Information on this title: www.cambridge.org/9780521845342



First published 2015

Printed in the United Kingdom by TJ International Ltd. Padstow Cornwall

*A catalogue record for this publication is available from the British Library*

*Library of Congress Cataloging in Publication data*
Nielinger-Vakil, Carola, 1966– author.
Luigi Nono: A Composer in Context / Carola Nielinger-Vakil.
pages cm
Includes bibliographical references and index.
ISBN 978-0-521-84534-2 (Hardback : alk. paper)
1. Nono, Luigi. 2. Composers–Italy–Biography. I. Title.
ML410.N667N54 2015
780.92–dc23 [b] 2015020027

ISBN 978-0-521-84534-2 Hardback

*In memory of my parents, Christa and Horst, and to my musical foster parents, Elke and Reiner*

# Contents

# Figures

# Music examples

# Preface and acknowledgements

> In reality, there is not a moment that would not carry with it its revolutionary chance – provided only that it is defined in a specific way, namely as the chance for a completely new resolution of a completely new problem.
>
> Walter Benjamin, *On the Concept of History*, Thesis XVIIa (1940)

Among the most important composers to emerge from the 'Darmstadt School', Luigi Nono (1924–90) stands out for his unique combination of avant-garde composition with political commitment. With reference to Sartre's manifesto of committed writing *Qu'est-ce que la littérature?* (*What is Literature?*), Nono hailed Schoenberg's *A Survivor from Warsaw* as the 'musical aesthetic manifesto' of his epoch and, throughout his career, sought to discern the 'moral imperative' at the heart of his aesthetics in order to disclose the injustices of this world as 'abuses to be suppressed'.[1] The expressivity of his uncompromisingly avant-garde idiom is a moving testament to the sincerity with which he continued to seize his 'revolutionary chance' as a chance, too, for completely new problems and resolutions in music. Yet his fervent belief in communist ideals has also alienated many, and this, I suspect, is probably the primary reason why, despite Stephen Davismoon's invigorating attempt to stimulate 'greater awareness of Luigi Nono's massive contribution to music and to art in general',[2] Nono's work never entered the cultural consciousness in Great Britain and America in the same way as that of Karlheinz Stockhausen and Pierre Boulez.

Compared with the substantial body of secondary literature in German, Italian and French, the number of English-language articles, let alone books, on Nono is still extremely small. In part, this book is an attempt to address this gap. However, it is also an original contribution, based on more than a decade of research, to Nono studies in general. Since Nuria Schoenberg-Nono opened the Archivio Luigi Nono in Venice in 1993, scholars have been able to access a wealth of manuscript materials, much of

1 Sartre, *What is Literature?*, 46–47; cited in Nono, 'Text – Musik – Gesang' (1960), *Texte* 47; *Scritti*, I, 65.

2 Davismoon (ed.), 'Luigi Nono: the suspended song' and 'Luigi Nono: fragments and silence' (1999).

it still awaiting detailed analysis. Until then broader overarching claims must remain tentative. Having set out to write a synthesis, my focus gradually narrowed to a selection of key works. The discussion is all the richer, however, for the analytical and contextual detail made possible by these materials.

The book is structured in two parts. The first is dedicated to Nono's anti-fascist works, from the unfinished Fučík project (1951) to *Ricorda cosa ti hanno fatto in Auschwitz* (1966) with a particular focus on *Il canto sospeso* (1956). The context of anti-fascism ideally lends itself to introducing Nono's musical and political foundations. Not that he ever was the 'young partisan fighter' Taruskin imagines, who 'courageously joined the Italian Communist Party during the last days of Mussolini's dictatorship, when membership was a crime'.[3] In fact, Nono joined the PCI together with Maderna in 1952 on the condition that composition of twelve-tone music was acceptable to the party leadership.[4] Unlike Maderna, Nono remained a life-long member, was elected to the central committee in 1975, and often served as the party's 'cultural ambassador' on his many trips to the Eastern bloc and Latin America. This does not mean, however, that he uncritically subscribed to the party line. On the basis of Nono's activism, texts and letters and, above all, his music, it may be argued that, unlike so many others, he did not abandon the party precisely because he saw the need for debate and change from within. As one of his fellow Western European activists, Konrad Boehmer, repeatedly emphasised, Nono never sided with 'Stalinism or its satellites', but rather with some of Stalin's most severe Marxist critics: 'amongst others Gramsci, Merleau-Ponty and Sartre'.[5] To Boehmer, the question is therefore not whether Nono was a communist, but rather what kind of communist Nono was. What being a communist meant in practice for Nono as a composer will have to be asked anew for each piece, because, just as his compositional technique evolved in tandem with the current state of ideas and technology in music, his political and philosophical perspectives changed and developed in the context of unfolding political events: the Algerian War of Independence, the Cuban Revolution, the Vietnam War, the student

[3] Taruskin, *Music in the Late Twentieth Century*, 88.

[4] According to Nono, the PCI officially propagated 'social realism' but the party leaders in Venice replied 'if you think that this is important to you, you have to develop your struggle in this way'. Nono, 'Gespräch mit Hartmut Lück' (1972), *Texte* 289.

[5] Boehmer, 'Nono – a present future', Holland Festival 2014 (unpublished); in memory of Konrad (1941–2014) and with thanks to Robert Adlington.

revolts of 1968, Italy's 'hot autumn' of 1969, Berlinguer's 'historic compromise' and Gorbachev's Perestroika, to name but a few.

If, as a 'composer *and* citizen',[6] Nono consistently felt compelled to take a stance, he did so also in order to transcend the historical moment and shift the perspective on the future. After actively engaging with the philosophy of Walter Benjamin, Nono would speak of his particular 'nostalgia for the future'. The key works at the heart of this book were chosen precisely because they transcend their historical context in exemplary fashion and stand out as musical jewels of 'now-time' with which Nono firmly secured his place in music history: the anti-fascist cantata *Il canto sospeso*, the string quartet *Fragmente – Stille, an Diotima* (1980) and the spatial 'tragedy of listening' *Prometeo* (1985).

This book is not, however, a mere collection of studies of individual works, but aims to provide a sense of the evolution of Nono's musical thought. For this reason, the focus gradually shifts from a more contextual approach to greater analytical detail. The four chapters on Nono's anti-fascist works in Part I provide much historical and political context while also discussing various musical influences, above all the teaching of Bruno Maderna and Hermann Scherchen, the influence of the Second Viennese School and Schoenberg in particular, as well as Nono's contacts at Darmstadt. This part is based on some of my earlier published work: the analysis of *Il canto sospeso* and my contribution to *Presenza storica di Luigi Nono*.[7] The contextualisation is much extended, however, and the analysis of *Il canto sospeso* in Chapter 2 is completely new. Nono's serial techniques are no longer dealt with in such detail. Instead, I focus on the compositional freedom with which they are employed, the perceptible large-scale processes of the work and the characteristic use of instrumentation which subtly works against the 'equality' of the serial system, creating a truly disconcerting dialectics between tradition and avant-garde: the musical past and its future.

Nono first addressed the holocaust with his *Composizione per orchestra n. 2: Diario polacco '58* (1959). In Chapter 3 this orchestral work is placed in the context of Nono's controversial Darmstadt lecture 'Geschichte und Gegenwart in der Musik heute' ['History and the Present in the Music of Today' (1959)] and his subsequent falling out with Stockhausen. Not unlike Stockhausen's *Gruppen*, *Diario polacco '58* requires a specific spatial distribution of four orchestral groups. However, Nono's advanced serial

[6] Boehmer, 'Nono – a present future'.

[7] Nielinger-Vakil, 'The Song Unsung' and 'Between Memorial and Political Manifesto'.

system, his use of space and, above all, the structural concept of this work are fundamentally different. In music alone, Nono here exemplifies what he meant by historically aware composition at the time. And precisely in this sense, the piece took on a model function for further work to come. Hence, when Nono next dealt with the holocaust in his music to *Die Ermittlung* (*The Investigation*) by Peter Weiss (1965), I argue in Chapter 4 not only that he was inspired to revise and add a tape to *Diario polacco '58*, but also that this multi-layered orchestral work influenced the formation of a coherent musical discourse in the resulting solo tape piece *Ricorda cosa ti hanno fatto in Auschwitz*.

Culminating in the longest and most philosophical chapter on *Prometeo*, Part II picks up on many of the compositional characteristics exposed in Part I. Fragmentation and compositional layers are shown to be at the heart, too, of the string quartet *Fragmente – Stille, an Diotima* in which Nono first makes use of the scala enigmatica from Verdi's *Ave Maria*, pitch material to which he would repeatedly return throughout the 1980s. Precisely because the quartet is of great relevance in the context of *Prometeo*, my already published analysis is included here with minor revisions as Chapter 6.[8] Indeed, I regard this analysis as my most important, as it explains the hitherto enigmatic use of the scala enigmatica and thus also clarifies the logic behind the distribution of the Hölderlin fragments in this score. In analytical terms, this chapter is the most detailed and the reader will benefit greatly from reading it with reference to the score.

The scala enigmatica continues to be of interest in the concluding discussion of *Prometeo* in Chapter 7. However, the focus here primarily falls on the philosophical conception of this extraordinary work of spatial music theatre, its perceptible large-scale processes and the use of live electronics, in terms both of sound transformation and of the dramatic movement of sound in space. Analytical detail is provided to elucidate certain lines of thought that pervade the work as a whole and reveal the music to be as politically charged as it always was. Inspired by the philosophical thought of another unorthodox Marxist intellectual, the philosopher Massimo Cacciari, *Prometeo* is shown to integrate the political as an intrinsic element of the most abstract of musical thought. As such, this masterpiece may serve as a 'musical-aesthetic manifesto' for generations to come.

[8] Nielinger-Vakil, '*Fragmente – Stille, an Diotima*'.

To a large extent the completion of this book is due to the continued support of my family: my husband AbdoolKarim and my daughters Nuria and Sabira, who, each in their very own way, encouraged me with their love and commitment. The project was initially funded by a generous research grant from Trinity College of Music, London, and was academically supported during my research fellowship at Goldsmiths College. At the Fondazione Archivio Luigi Nono in Venice, I particularly want to thank Nuria Schoenberg-Nono for her unique readiness and determination to answer all queries, even after normal working hours, and for her boundless enthusiasm and energy devoted to keeping the archive running. Many thanks are due also to the two directors Erika Schaller and Claudia Vincis for their professional assistance over the years and to Giovanna Boscarino for dealing with all administrative issues. Thank you, too, Erika, for an unforgettable tour of San Marco without the customary herds of tourists. Research in Venice was all the more pleasant due to the hospitality of my friends Sara Gennaro and Stefano De Rossi. Besides our stimulating discussions on music and architecture, and a football game, which luckily was lost by the Germans, I will never forget our trip in the old 'Ferrari' to the Brion-Vega Cemetery designed by Carlo Scarpa. Thank you, too, to my Venetian host Renata Marzari for patiently improving my Italian by refusing to speak English. Undoubtedly, one of the most exciting events in Venice was the International Interpretation Course of Luigi Nono's Works with Live Electronics (2007) under the direction of André Richard. I here had the pleasure of being taught by Roberto Fabbriciani. Thank you, Roberto, for your excellent tuition on the 'Hölderlin' section of *Prometeo* and parts of *Das atmende Klarsein* as well as your riveting accounts of working with Nono. Thank you, too, David Ogborn for an expert 'navigation' of the tape in our performance of the Finale of *Das atmende Klarsein*. Within the Nono-research community I thank Angela Ida De Benedictis for lively discussions on *Intolleranza* and *Il canto sospeso* and countless informative e-mails. Thanks are due also to Mário Vieira de Carvalho, Christoph Neidhöfer and Erik Esterbauer for their valuable feedback. Above all, however, I want to thank three people whom I now regard as friends rather than colleagues: André Richard, Jürg Stenzl and Paulo de Assis. Thank you to all three of you for believing in my book. I would not have finished it without you!

Here in England, my editor Arnold Whittall deserves a medal for his patience and his careful critical reading of my texts when they did finally arrive. For his help with the translations from German and the illustrations, I thank my good friend and New Music companion Martin Brady.

For the Hölderlin and Heidegger translations I thank Harry Gilonis. A big thank you also goes to my editorial team at CUP: Vicki Cooper and Fleur Jones, who efficiently and patiently dealt with the submission process, my production editor, Bronte Rawlings, and my copy-editor, Steven Holt, who meticulously checked my manuscript and also much improved all translations from Italian. Thank you to all of you for your expert assistance.

Various institutions and individuals kindly granted me permission to publish extracts of Nono's correspondence and other previously unpublished material:

Luigi Nono, letters to Alfred Andersch, courtesy of the heirs of Luigi Nono and by permission of the Literaturarchiv Marbach

Luigi Nono, letters to Paul Dessau, courtesy of the heirs of Luigi Nono and by permission of Maxim Dessau and the Archiv der Akademie der Künste Berlin

Luigi Nono, correspondence with Erwin Piscator, Erwin Piscator Papers, courtesy of the heirs of Luigi Nono and by kind permission of Karl-Heinz Piscator and the Special Collection Research Center Southern Illinois University Carbondale

Luigi Nono, letters to Wolfgang Steinecke, courtesy of the heirs of Luigi Nono and by permission of the Archive of the International Music Institute Darmstadt (IMD)

Luigi Nono, correspondence with Karlheinz Stockhausen, courtesy of the heirs of Luigi Nono and by permission of the Stockhausen-Foundation Kürten

Massimo Cacciari, letters to Luigi Nono and material for the libretto of *Prometeo*, courtesy of the heirs of Luigi Nono and by kind permission of Massimo Cacciari

Italo Calvino, letters to Luigi Nono and Matthias Theodor Vogt, by kind permission of Giovanna Calvino and The Wylie Agency

Bruno Maderna, letter to Luigi Nono, by kind permission of Catarina Maderna and Claudia Maderna-Sieben

Luigi Nono's writings and interviews have been published in the following editions:

Jürg Stenzl (ed.), *Luigi Nono: Texte, Studien zu seiner Musik* (Zurich: Atlantis, 1975)

Laurent Feneyrou (ed.), *Luigi Nono: Écrits* (Paris: Editions Bourgois, 1993)

Angela Ida De Benedictis and Veniero Rizzardi (eds.), *Luigi Nono: Scritti e colloqui*, Le Sfere, 2 vols (Milan: Ricordi and LIM, 2001)

Matteo Nanni and Rainer Schmusch (eds.), *Incontri: Luigi Nono im Gespräch mit Enzo Restagno* (Hofheim: Wolke, 2004)

Angela Ida De Benedictis and Veniero Rizzardi (eds.), *Luigi Nono: La nostalgia del futuro. Scritti scelti 1948–1986* (Milan: Il Saggiatore, 2007)

Paulo de Assis (ed.), *Luigi Nono – Escritos e Entrevistas*, trans. A. Morão, Casa da Música, Centro de Estudos de Sociologia e Estética Musical (Porto: Empresa Diário, 2014)

Angela Ida De Benedictis and Veniero Rizzardi (eds.), *Nostalgia for the Future: Selected Writings and Interviews of Luigi Nono* [working title], trans. J. O'Donnell (Oakland, CA: University of California Press, 2016)

I generally refer to the complete Italian edition of 2001, henceforth abbreviated as *Scritti*. However, whenever the source texts are translated from German or French, I also refer to the German and French editions (abbreviated as *Texte* and *Écrits*).

PART I

# Music and Memory

# 1 Political and musical premises

A remarkably bold story, 'Impiccagione di un giudice' ('The Hanging of a Judge') by Italo Calvino, was first published in 1948 on the condition that its title be changed to 'Il sogno di un giudice' ('The Dream of a Judge').[1] The story describes the trial of a fascist accused of participation in one of the brutal reprisal actions that shook northern Italy throughout the partisan war. The crime is mentioned only in passing, however, as the story is told from the perspective of the judge Onofrio Clerici, whose sympathy for the former fascist regime is made clear from the outset. Within the realms of the judicial system the judge feels completely at ease, confident in the knowledge that the law was written by people like him and may be turned in any direction. But gallows are being constructed in the courtyard, and Onofrio's confidence is undermined further by three characters hitherto unknown to the court: a clerk and two guards. The mob at the back of the court room, too, is unusually silent. 'Stupid and ignorant people, – thought judge Onofrio, – they believe the accused will be condemned to death. That's why they have erected gallows.'[2] And to teach them a lesson the judge proposes that the accused be absolved, a sentence that is unanimously approved by the magistrates of the court. Onofrio then signs the acquittal and another document, slipped in by the clerk: his own death sentence, condemning him to die 'like a dog'.[3] Without protest, the judge succumbs to this sentence and, following the orders of the two guards, hangs himself on the gallows in the now deserted courtyard.

Calvino's references to Kafka are obvious: gallows of dimensions just as intimidating as those of the apparatus in *The Penal Colony*, the Kafkaesque clerk and the two 'door keepers' and the allusion to *The Trial*, in which Josef K., too, is condemned to die like a dog. Recourse to Kafka's modernist world of abstraction and its recurring theme of inescapable dependence on a higher law not only transcends the neo-realist setting, but also emphasises Calvino's biting social critique, the complete loss

[1] Calvino, 'Il sogno di un giudice', *Rinascita*, 5:2 (1948).

[2] Calvino, 'Impiccagione di un giudice', in *Ultimo viene il corvo*, 231; unless stated otherwise, translations are my own.

[3] *Ibid.*, 232.

of faith in the judicial system in the given historical context. Without doubt Bruno Maderna drew on *The Trial* for his *Studi per "Il processo" di F. Kafka* (1950) for similar reasons.[4]

Such modernist social critique has to be understood in the context of the Italian amnesty laws after WWII. The first amnesty was passed in 1946 by none other than Palmiro Togliatti, the leader of the Communist Party and Minister of Justice of the newly founded Republic.[5] Approved in the name of 'national pacification' but perceived by many as a first betrayal of the Resistance, this amnesty was primarily aimed at the large number of citizens who had served the fascist regime in administration and public services. Excluded were those who had held positions of higher command and those involved in war crimes. The amnesty was applied with greatest leniency, however, especially by the appeal courts which, according to Woller, had hardly been affected by the half-hearted purge under Marshal Badoglio.[6] Doors thus opened for fascist ministers, state officials, chief editors and judges alike. Of the 12,000 fascists under arrest in 1946, only 2,000 were still in prison the following year. By 1952 this figure had dropped to just 266. In 1953, a further amnesty extended the benefits to fascists who had been forced to leave the country and by the mid fifties virtually everybody had been absolved.[7]

A wave of releases of high-ranking fascists occurred almost immediately after the Communists and Socialists had been ousted from government by the Christian Democrats under De Gasperi in 1948. Prince Junio Valerio Borghese, for example, ex-commander of the infamous X[a] MAS division, accused of ferocious attacks during the partisan war and personally responsible for forty-three murders, was initially sentenced to twelve years' imprisonment in February 1949.[8] With support from the Vatican, the prince was absolved, however, and immediately released. Behan describes a courthouse scene not dissimilar to that in Calvino's story:

[4] On Maderna's *Studi per "Il processo" di F. Kafka* (1950) see Borio, 'La tecnica seriale'; and Dalmonte, 'Letture maderniane'. Nono himself would later turn to Kafka in the context of *Fragmente – Stille, an Diotima* (1979–80).

[5] See Cooke, *Legacy of the Italian Resistance*, 19–28; and Behan, *Italian Resistance*, 114–18.

[6] Woller, '"Ausgebliebene Säuberung"?', 148–91.

[7] Focardi, *La guerra della memoria*, 29.

[8] Focardi, *La guerra della memoria*, 29. The X[a] MAS division, which was 'deployed specifically to combat partisan actions', 'had 800 documented murders to its name, as well as the looting and burning of entire villages, and the torture of hundreds of partisans'; Behan, *Italian Resistance*, 118.

> The appeal court that released Borghese was presided over by a family friend and ex-fascist, and many jurors were known to be former fascists too. When the decision to release him was announced, it was greeted in the courthouse by fascist salutes.[9]

Borghese went on to become a member of the neo-fascist Movimento Sociale Italiano (MSI) and later joined the clandestine 'Gladio' army, secret military units funded by the CIA and trained by the British Intelligence Service to overthrow the Communists, should they take power.[10] In 1970, just after the 'hot autumn' of student and workers protests, Borghese even attempted a military coup, with fifty former parachute regiment members invading the armoury of the Ministry of the Interior. The coup was swiftly aborted, however, due to there being insufficient support within the state machinery.[11]

Another extremely high-profile trial was that of Field-Marshal Graziani (1882–1955), commander-in-chief of the armed forces of Mussolini's Italian Social Republic (RSI), also known as the Republic of Salò. Graziani, who had initially been named by the British to be tried by the Allies, stood trial in Rome (1948–50).[12] He was sentenced to nineteen years of imprisonment but remained in prison for only a few months. After his release he was made honorary president of the MSI and his autobiographical *Ho difeso la patria* (1948) was a bestseller.[13] Primo Levi, on the other hand, was struggling to find a publisher for his now famous Auschwitz account *Se questo è un uomo*, which first appeared with a print run of just 2,500 in 1947.

At the same time another important case was being heard at the courts in Rome: the trial of the partisans responsible for the attack on the Via Rasella that killed 33 Germans and led to the brutal reprisal shooting of 335 Italians at the Fosse Ardeatine in 1944. Although they were acquitted,

[9] Behan, *Italian Resistance*, 118. Borghese was initially saved from execution by the US Proconsul in occupied Italy. Other former X$^a$ MAS officers were trained in the USA for the so-called Office of Strategic Services, the forerunner of the CIA. *Ibid.*, 138–39.

[10] The earliest official reference to 'Gladio' is found in a US National Security Council document of 1954. A formal agreement with the USA was signed by the head of the Italian secret service, Giovanni De Lorenzo, but kept secret from parliament in 1956. De Lorenzo, too, was an ex-fascist of the highest rank, having served as a career officer under Mussolini. The existence of 'Gladio' (with 139 arms caches) was finally admitted in 1990. Behan, *Italian Resistance*, 141.

[11] See Behan, *Italian Resistance*, 144–45.

[12] Overy, *Interrogations*, 29. 'Graziani had been sentenced to death by a partisan court in 1945, but luckily for him surrendered to the Allies'; Behan, *Italian Resistance*, 140.

[13] Focardi, *La guerra della memoria*, 20–21.

the fact that partisans, the liberators of the country, were being tried and held responsible for such reprisal actions left an indelible stain on the Resistenza. As both Behan and Cooke have shown, trials of partisans increased sharply after the Togliatti amnesty and continued throughout the 1950s.[14] Especially after the Communists and Socialists had been ousted from government, increasing numbers of partisans were questioned and subjected to months, in some cases years, of preventative detention, while ever more fascists were absolved of their crimes. Understandably, the morale among former resistance fighters was such that the partisans from the Veneto, for example, staged a demonstration and publicly burnt the Alexander award they had each received for their service to the country.[15] Long before the Tambroni affair in 1960, when the Christian Democrats relied on MSI support to stay in government, Nono wrote to Alfred Andersch: 'Attempt by the Christian Democratic Party to form a government of our republic together with Nazis and Monarchists?????? . . . restoration is everywhere!!!!!!! today the Resistenza is increasingly portrayed as a criminal deed! by permission of the government (???) and not too much reaction from the public!'[16]

Throughout the years of the Cold War, the legacy of the Resistenza with its undeniable roots in the predominantly communist anti-fascist movement was centre stage to the growing rift between right and left. Naturally, the Christian Democrats tried to play down the significance of the Resistenza and even attempted to criminalise it. The political left, on the other hand, mobilised the memory of the Resistenza, its immense sacrifices and loss of life in support of the liberation, to demand a progressive kind of socialism modelled on the ideas of Antonio Gramsci, whose prison notebooks and letters took Italy by storm at this time. To the left, the Resistenza signified not only the heroic anti-fascist partisan movement, but also the ongoing struggle for a democratic and just, socialist society, and this understanding would later be shared by Nono.[17] The socialist dream, however, suffered a hard blow with the election defeat of the

[14] Behan, *Italian Resistance*, 114–18; Cooke, *Legacy*, 22–23.

[15] Behan, *Italian Resistance*, 115.

[16] Nono, letter to Andersch, 11 June 1957 (Deutsches Literaturarchiv Marbach; copy at ALN, Andersch/A 57-06-11 d): 'Versuch von demo-christliche Partei hier zusammen mit Nazi und Monarchisten eine Regierung von unsere Republik zu bilden?????? [. . .] es ist überall Restaurationszeit!!!!!!! heute und immer mehr wird hier die Resistenza als Banditentat gezeigt! mit Erlaubnis von Regierung (???) und nicht so starke Reaktion von Opinion!' On the Tambroni affair see Cooke, *Legacy*, 84–93. The MSI joined Berlusconi's coalition government in 1994.

[17] Nono, 'Musica e Resistenza' (1963), *Scritti*, I, 144.

Communist and Socialist alliance in 1948. That year the parliamentary decision was taken to join NATO and the papal 'avviso sacro' decreed that Communists and all members of Communist organisations such as trade unions or youth clubs be excommunicated from the Catholic Church. A further attempt to incapacitate the political left was the introduction of a new electoral law, according to which any alliance of parties that gained more than 50% of the votes would receive two thirds of the seats in the Chamber of Deputies. Communists and Socialists immediately dubbed this law of 1952 'la legge truffa' ('the swindle law') and saw in it a dangerous parallel to Mussolini's 'Acerbo Law' which had consolidated the fascists in power in 1923. As it happened, the centre coalition missed the 50% mark by a fraction in 1953 (49.85%) and the law was annulled a year later.

It was precisely during these 'hard years' of Cold War persecution that Nono and Maderna decided to join the PCI in 1952. Both composers grew up under Mussolini and both had supported the Resistance. Maderna was twenty-three years old when he was conscripted in 1942, but lucky to serve a colonel who allowed him to take occasional leave for concerts and study. After 8 September 1943, Maderna joined the anti-fascist 'Fronte di liberazione' in Verona. Escaping arrest by the SS in February 1945, he subsequently joined partisans in the Veneto.[18] Nono was lucky not to be conscripted. The Socialist radiologist Vespignani (whose sons attended the Liceo Marco Polo with Nono) intervened on his behalf and 'emphasised' a minor medical condition.[19] Bowing to his father's wishes, Nono thus began to study law at Padua University in 1942, while continuing his external studies with Gian Francesco Malipiero and Raffaele Cumar at the Venice Conservatoire.[20] In Venice, Nono had been in contact with anti-fascist circles since his late teens. At Vespignani's house he met the writer and music critic Massimo Bontempelli and the sculptor Arturo Martini, who provided the Resistance with clay for counterfeit stamps. Carlo Cardazzo's gallery Il Cavallino was another cultural haven free of fascist ideology. Equally formative was the encounter with the painter and

[18] See 'Guerra e Dopoguerra' in Baroni and Dalmonte (eds.), *Bruno Maderna: documenti*, 49–61; and Stenzl, *Von Giacomo Puccini zu Luigi Nono*, 194.

[19] Gennaro, 'Per un ritratto', 6.

[20] Malipiero introduced Nono to the music of the sixteenth and seventeenth centuries up to Monteverdi and theoretical works by Zarlino, Vicentino, Gaffurio and Doni. During their customary walks, Nono also first heard of the Second Viennese School and Béla Bartók. Cumar, a student of Malipiero, taught Nono counterpoint. Nono, 'Un'autobiografia', *Scritti*, II, 477, 483–84.

life-long 'comrade' Emilio Vedova.[21] Padua University, too, was remarkably liberal. As Nono himself recounts in conversation with Restagno,

> I have good memories of those years at Padua University because there was a very stimulating intellectual environment: just imagine, I studied philosophy of justice with Norberto Bobbio. I would have liked to write my final dissertation with him: I went and proposed one on Berdyaev, but he refused. He asked me why this choice, but evidently my reasons were not sufficiently convincing. Berdyaev, alongside other Russian works translated into Italian, fascinated me enormously: for me they were voices from afar, expressions of a different reality.[22]

In the autumn of 1943, the Vice Chancellor of Padua University publicly encouraged students to take up arms against the government.[23] Nono chose not to follow this call and later insisted that he did not play an important role in the Resistance. His future brother in law, Albano Pivato, however, was an important liaison, and Nono and his sister Rina supported him in various ways: they helped to print and disseminate the clandestine publication *Fedeltà all'Italia*, hid arms inside a disused boat and once enabled 'The Red Count' of the Venetian Liberation Committee, Giovanni Tonetti, to escape Venice. Under Pivato's leadership, Nono further assisted in the occupation of a hotel and a commissariat on the day of the liberation of Venice (28 April 1945).[24]

Nono's and Maderna's paths first crossed in 1946. On expressing the wish to study Hindemith's *Unterweisung im Tonsatz* (*The Craft of Musical Composition*), Malipiero referred Nono to the 'young musician' who had just arrived for a concert at La Fenice.[25] Their first encounter that evening was the beginning of Nono's most formative musical education, Maderna's 'totally different manner' of 'living music':

[21] Nono, 'Un'autobiografia', *Scritti*, II, 482, 484.

[22] Nono, 'Un'autobiografia', *Scritti*, II, 484–85. On Nono's studies in Padua (1942–47) further see Pellegrini, 'Musica o diritto?'.

[23] Welcoming first-year students, Vice-Chancellor Concetto Marchesi spoke out in support of the Resistance. 'The effect of this speech was electrifying' and 'students threw out the armed fascist students who had also been in the main hall'. Marchesi was subsequently forced to resign and went into hiding; a hundred students from Padua University were killed in the Resistance. Behan, *Italian Resistance*, 53.

[24] See Gennaro, 'Per un ritratto', 6–8. Gennaro also discusses the anti-fascist roots in the family of Nono's mother, Maria Manetti (1891–1976). One of Nono's uncles was the former Socialist mayor of Limena and a friend of Matteotti, the Socialist deputy murdered by the fascists in June 1924.

[25] The programme included Maderna's *Serenata per undici strumenti*, Riccardo Malipiero's *Piccolo concerto* and Togni's *Variazioni* for piano and orchestra (21 September 1946).

> He did not teach recipes, he did not hand out catalogues of methods, above all he avoided teaching his own ideas or an aesthetic; his fundamental concern was to teach musical thought, in particular about music in different, combined tempi, like the enigmatic canons of the Flemish Renaissance, for example. Following this procedure, one already had to know what the last note would be while writing the first; that is to say, one knew that the same sound read with different prolations would have had different durations, and thus different harmonic and melodic relationships. This was not the mentality of *Gradus ad Parnassum*, of setting note against note, two notes against one note, three notes against one note, in which we find an undoubtedly important, but very academicised, historical mechanism.[26]

Maderna's tuition further included prolonged periods of study at the Biblioteca Marciana:

> Bruno read one theorist, I read another. We then exchanged the information acquired and our reflections. Then we took up scores, for example Ottaviano Petrucci's *Odhecaton*, with its collection of two- and three-part Chansons by the great Flemish masters, which we would transcribe, comparing the compositional practice with the theoretical discussion contained in the various treatises. [. . .] Other habitual reading for us was Zarlino's *Istitutioni harmoniche* and *Dimostrationi harmoniche*, in which the debates which evolved in the semi-darkness of the church of San Marco among Zarlino, Francesco della Viola, who was a composer from Ferrara, Claudio Merulo and Adrian Willaert were reported.[27]

Not unlike these Renaissance composers, Maderna taught a way of life:

> We remained shut up in the attic to study, copy and write music for hours on end, then we went out to walk and eat. Bruno, I and the other students (Gastone Fabris and Renzo Dall'Oglio, who are nowadays working in the management of the RAI) went to the Lido together to swim with our girlfriends. We got totally plastered and had the most euphoric escapades. We moved with great ease from the most rigorous discipline of our studies to this incredibly entertaining atmosphere, and in every circumstance the same desire to participate in life affirmed itself in us.[28]

Maderna, in turn, later praised Nono's commitment:

> Nono [. . .] realised that he had studied music badly and began all over again, literally with the bass-lines and chords in thirds and fifths. But he applied

[26] Nono, 'Un'autobiografia', *Scritti*, II, 477–78.
[27] Nono, 'Un'autobiografia', *Scritti*, II, 478–79.
[28] Nono, 'Un'autobiografia', *Scritti*, II, 487–88.

> himself with such rigour [. . .] that in a few years he had covered all aspects of counterpoint with me and was in possession of a fabulous technique.[29]

As shown by Schaller, Nono covered modal, tonal, atonal and dodecaphonic counterpoint. In addition, Maderna would engage his students in the comparative study of music of all ages with a specific compositional problem and its contemporary solutions in mind. On the topic of song Nono recalls that they began with Francesco Landini, studied the function of the tenor in *L'Homme armé* and Ockeghem's masses and then moved on to songs by Schubert, Schumann, Wolf, Webern and Dallapiccola.[30]

Dallapiccola, who had witnessed the first Italian performance of *Pierrot lunaire* under Schoenberg in Florence (1924) and had also met Berg and Webern in person, was another decisive influence.[31] As early as 1946 or 1947, Nono sent Dallapiccola the now lost score of his first work, *La discesa di Cristo agli inferi* (1945). Dallapiccola, who was working on his opera *Il prigioniero* at the time, replied 'I understand that here you have a lot in your heart you wish to express, but you still have to study a great deal in order to be able to do so'.[32] The study and adoption of dodecaphonic techniques attained further musical and political impetus in the summer of 1948, when Nono and Maderna both attended Hermann Scherchen's influential conducting course in Venice. More than thirty years later, Nono still attested that 'the new "rhetoric" of Luigi Dallapiccola's musical thought' was first introduced to him by Scherchen.[33] Indeed, Nono and Maderna both began to compose their own *Liriche greche* during or soon after this course.[34] Also Nono's first musicological essay, 'Luigi Dallapiccola e i *Sex Carmina Alcæi*', attests to the importance of Dallapiccola's dodecaphony at this time.[35]

[29] Maderna, interview with Leonardo Pinzauti (1972), in Schaller, 'L'insegnamento di Bruno Maderna', 109. On Nono's courses at the conservatoire (1947–49) also see Pellegrini, 'Musica o diritto?'.

[30] Nono, 'Un'autobiografia', *Scritti*, II, 489. On Maderna's teaching also see de Assis, *Luigi Nonos Wende*, 150–52.

[31] Borio, 'L'influenza di Dallapiccola', 357–87. On the adoption and dissemination of dodecaphony in Italy also see Stenzl, *Von Giacomo Puccini zu Luigi Nono*, 183–91.

[32] Dallapiccola, letter to Nono, cited in De Benedictis, 'Nono', ALN website.

[33] Nono, 'Con Luigi Dallapiccola', *Scritti*, I, 483.

[34] A facsimile of Nono's *Due liriche greche* (1948–49) has only recently been published by Edizioni RAI Trade. The work is the first surviving composition by Nono. On Nono's and Maderna's *Liriche greche* see Borio, 'L'influenza di Dallapiccola', 358–69. On Maderna's *Tre liriche greche* see the critical edition by Caprioli (Milan: Zerboni, 2002) and Conti, 'Le *Tre liriche greche* di Maderna', in Dalmonte and Russo (eds.), *Bruno Maderna*, 275–86. Like Dallapiccola, Nono and Maderna used the Salvatore Quasimodo translation of 1944.

[35] Nono, 'Luigi Dallapiccola e i *Sex Carmina Alcæi*' (*ca.* 1948), *Scritti*, I, 3–5.

Scherchen's course further covered Verdi's *Ave Maria* with the enigmatic scale that was to take on an intriguing role in Nono's oeuvre after 1975.[36] The conductor's discussion of the *Art of the Fugue*, too, seems to have had seminal impact. A year later Maderna made his Darmstadt debut with his own variations on B.A.C.H., the *Fantasia per due pianoforti* (1949).[37] The motif was later of interest also to Nono, in his analysis of Schoenberg's *Variations for Orchestra* op. 31 (Darmstadt, 1957).[38] Above all, however, Scherchen must have impressed the young generation as a committed artist *par excellence* who combined his experience of the Weimar Republic and the works of the Second Viennese School with a total commitment to the promotion of the musical avant-garde. Moreover, Scherchen remained true to the socialist convictions he had adopted in Russia during WWI. Right up to the onset of the Third Reich, he performed with workers' choral societies for which he had translated and arranged the Russian revolutionary songs *Unsterbliche Opfer* and *Brüder, zur Sonne, zur Freiheit*.[39] Such engagements went hand in hand with performances of works by the leading composers of the day, not only Schoenberg, whose career Scherchen had followed ever since their joint tour of *Pierrot lunaire* in 1912, but also Berg, Webern, Stravinsky, Bartók, Weill and Hindemith. At the Bauhaus, Scherchen produced Stravinsky's *Soldier's Tale* (1923) and collaborated with Oskar Schlemmer on a production of *Les Noces*.[40] Excerpts from Berg's *Wozzeck* were first heard under Scherchen in 1924, as were Brecht's *Lindberghflug* (1929) with music by Weill and Hindemith and Hába's experimental quarter-tone opera *Die Mutter* (1931). While married to the actress Gerda Müller, Scherchen further experienced some of the ground-breaking productions of Erwin Piscator's avant-garde political theatre at the Volksbühne in Berlin.

36 On the repertoire studied at Scherchen's course, including a reproduction of Nono's transcription of Verdi's *Ave Maria*, see Pellegrini, 'Musica o diritto?', 20–23.

37 Maderna's *Fantasia per due pianoforte* was premiered by Carl Seeman and Peter Stadlen (Darmstadt, 9 July 1949).

38 Nono, 'Die Entwicklung der Reihentechnik' (Darmstadt, 23 July 1957), *Texte*, 24; *Scritti*, I, 22–24. A facsimile edition of Nono's annotations to Schoenberg's *Variations for Orchestra* op. 31 is available through the ALN.

39 Scherchen was accused of conducting his Deutscher Arbeiter Sängerbund in a 'red sweater' at an election event in 1932. The press was subsequently banned from reviewing Scherchen's concerts; Scherchen, *Aus meinem Leben*, 52. On Scherchen's workers' song arrangements see Lammel, *Das Arbeiterlied*, 118–21, and 'Die beiden Berliner "Scherchen Chöre"'. The Nazis later appropriated these arrangements; Scherchen, *Aus meinem Leben*, 51.

40 See Marbach, 'Schlemmers Begegnungen', 531–34. For illustrations of Schlemmer's coloured projections see Maur, *Oskar Schlemmer*, II, 271–77.

After the war, Scherchen was one of the first to premiere works by Hans Werner Henze, Rolf Liebermann and Karl Amadeus Hartmann (for whom he had written the libretto of *Simplicius Simplicissimus* in 1934–35). In 1949, he directed the first concert performance of *Il prigioniero*, and, together with René Leibowitz, was among the first to promote Schoenberg's *A Survivor from Warsaw* (1947) in Europe.[41] Many important performances of Schoenberg's stage works in particular were to follow: the premiere of the 'Dance Around the Golden Calf' from *Moses und Aron* (Darmstadt, 1951), *Von heute auf morgen* (Naples, 1952), and *Moses und Aron* in Berlin (1959), Milan (1961) and Rome (1966). Whatever the cause, Scherchen pursued it with remarkable integrity. His participation at the Prague Spring Music Festival in 1950 (with a performance of Beethoven's Ninth Symphony) cost him two lucrative contracts with the Swiss Broadcasting Corporation (SRG SSR) and the Music College Winterthur. In addition, he risked losing the opportunity of being the first to publish and conduct the 'Dance Around the Golden Calf' by answering Schoenberg's rather awkward query about his political convictions with the utmost honesty.[42] With an equally uncompromising attitude, he went ahead with the 1951 premiere of the Brecht–Dessau collaboration, the opera *Das Verhör des Lukullus*, despite the official ban imposed by the Central Committee of the East German SED in the course of its 'Fight against Formalism in Art and Literature'.[43]

Scherchen no doubt made a profound impression on the young Nono, to the extent that he became his adopted 'musical father'.[44] Nono later spoke of his 'continuous lessons' on

> Premieres of Schoenberg and Webern, of Stravinsky, of Bartók, the cultural life at the time of the Weimar Republic, of Berlin before Nazism and above all

[41] Leibowitz conducted the first European performance (Paris, November 1949); Scherchen directed the first German performance (Darmstadt, 20 August 1950). Also see Calico, *Arnold Schoenberg's* A Survivor, 22–31.

[42] See Schmidt (ed.), *Arnold Schönberg: Sämtliche Werke*, III: 8,2b, 'Briefdokumente', 17–33. In a letter of 31 August 1950 Schoenberg asks 'I have been told on several occasions that you are a communist. Is this true or not?' Scherchen replied 'I have always been, since my early youth, a dedicated socialist. Every dedicated socialist knows only the communistic as the true socialist structure of society'; trans. in Spangemacher, 'Schönberg as Role Model', 36 (amended).

[43] On the 'Formalism–Realism' debate in the context of Dessau's *Lukullus* see Lucchesi (ed.), *Das Verhör in der Oper*.

[44] Nono lived with Scherchen in Zurich and Rapallo after Malipiero had told Nono's father of his son's 'regrettable' decision to adopt the twelve-tone technique. Malipiero later apologised and Nono never again mentioned the matter; see Stenzl, *Luigi Nono*, 15.

> the research on the transformation of sound which took place when it was broadcast on the radio.[45]

Scherchen is further remembered for his political education:

> Through him, I was entrusted with the historical, cultural and political importance of Berlin in the years before 1933, the world meeting point and centre for exchange between the new Soviet culture and the progressive intelligentsia of the West. But he also revealed the Munich of the Spartacus Revolt to me, with its great political and cultural charisma. Last but not least, I discovered through Hermann Scherchen the Soviet Union, a country he knew very well.[46]

When Nono first attended Darmstadt in 1950 for the rather scandalous premiere of his *Variazioni canoniche sulla serie dell'op. 41 di Arnold Schönberg* (1949),[47] his musical outlook was thus already firmly grounded in political and historical awareness. Hence the choice of the series of Schoenberg's anti-fascist *Ode to Napoleon* op. 41 (1942), this most sarcastic of twelve-tone works, which audaciously ends in E♭ major, the key of Beethoven's *Eroica*.[48] Hence Nono's repeated insistence on serialism as a logical and necessary historical development in his first lectures at Gravesano (1956) and Darmstadt (1957) and his understanding of Darmstadt as a school comparable to the Bauhaus.[49] Hence his continued interest in the works of Schoenberg alongside those of Webern, and Schoenberg's stage works in particular, at a time when Schoenberg had

45 Nono, 'Un'autobiografia', *Scritti*, II, 495.

46 Nono, 'Gespräch mit Jean Villain', *Texte*, 301; trans. in Spangemacher, 'Schönberg as Role Model', 34 (amended).

47 According to Nono, 'there is a recording of this concert on which one hears the voice of Scherchen, who turned to the grumbling audience and said: 'Schweinebande' (pack of pigs)'. Nono, 'Un'autobiografia', *Scritti*, II, 495. Also see Iddon, *New Music at Darmstadt*, 37–38.

48 Nono first considered the series of Schoenberg's *Piano Concerto* op. 42 and the *Piano Piece* op. 33a (as suggested by Togni), but then decided on the series of *The Ode to Napoleon*; Rizzardi 'Nono e la "presenza storica" di Schönberg', 232. In the tradition of Renaissance puzzle canons, Nono deliberately disguises the series, but reveals it in full in the last section. On the *Variazioni canoniche* see Aragona, '*Variazioni canoniche*', Iddon, 'Serial Canon(s)'; Rizzardi, 'La "nuova scuola veneziana"', 10–14; Spangemacher, 'Schönberg as Role Model', 36–39; and Vieira de Carvalho, 'Towards Dialectic Listening', 38–39.

49 Nono, 'Zur Entwicklung der Serientechnik' (1956), *Texte*, 16–20, *Scritti*, I, 9–14; 'Die Entwicklung der Reihentechnik' (1957), *Texte*, 21–33 (comparison with the Bauhaus, 30); *Scritti*, I, 19–42. The bond between the young serialists was not to last. Unbridgeable fissures opened up with Cage's appearance on the scene in 1958; see Iddon, *New Music at Darmstadt*.

long been declared 'dead'.[50] Hence also the committed declaration on *A Survivor from Warsaw*, a decade after Scherchen's first German performance, as Nono was about to leave Darmstadt behind:

> This masterpiece is, by virtue of its creative necessity and the text–music and music–listener relationships, the musical aesthetic manifesto of our epoch. In a completely authentic way Schoenberg's creative necessity attests to that which Jean-Paul Sartre writes in his fundamental essay *Qu'est-ce que la littérature?* on the problem *Why does one write?*: 'And if I am given this world with its injustices, it is not so that I may contemplate them coldly, but that I may animate them with my indignation, that I may disclose them and create them with their nature as injustices, that is, as abuses to be suppressed [. . .] Although literature is one thing and morality a quite different one, at the heart of the aesthetic imperative we discern the moral imperative.'[51]

Nono's politicised, humanist outlook on Schoenberg was undoubtedly shaped by Scherchen whose appropriation of the twelve-tone technique for the committed avant-garde at the end of the 1940s was of course also a reaction against the socialist-realist manifesto issued at the Second International Congress of Composers and Music Critics in Prague (1948). As Rizzardi has shown, the compatibility of dodecaphony with socialist-realist aesthetics was also a matter of great debate between Nono and the Brazilian pianist Eunice Katunda, who, with a group of students of Hans-Joachim Koellreutter, had also attended Scherchen's conducting course and remained in Venice until 1949. Katunda sent Nono a copy of Serge Nigg's 'Vers des nouvelles sources d'inspiration' (*La critique marxiste*, 1949) and Nono's annotations show that he, like Scherchen and Leibowitz, was from the very outset firmly opposed to the stifling, anti-progressive resolutions of the Prague Manifesto.[52]

Scherchen, Leibowitz, Dallapiccola, Maderna, Togni and Katunda are all known to have participated in the first International Twelve-tone Congress in Milan (1949), which was organised by Riccardo Malipiero and Vladimir Vogel.[53] Nono, who had yet to establish himself as a

[50] Boulez, 'Schoenberg is dead' (1952).

[51] Nono, 'Testo – musica – canto' (1960), *Scritti*, I, 65; quotation from Sartre, *What is Literature?*, 46–47.

[52] Rizzardi, 'Nono e la "presenza storica" di Schönberg', 231. On Leibowitz's political appropriation of Schoenberg see Carroll, *Music and Ideology*, 116–31.

[53] Rizzardi, 'Nono e la "presenza storica" di Schönberg', 231–32; Borio and Danuser (eds.), *Im Zenit der Moderne*, I, 176–81. Scherchen conducted the opening concert with works by Riegger, Dallapiccola and Liebermann. A second congress took place in Darmstadt in 1951; *ibid.*, 183–87.

composer, was not directly involved, but may have attended the event.[54] Scherchen reacted with an article in *Melos*, in which he argues that the congress resolution to maintain personal and artistic freedom, and to solve questions of conscience and social responsibility individually, fundamentally failed to address the aesthetic and ideological issues of the Prague Manifesto.[55] 'Precisely because most of the so-called art-revolutionist composers sympathised with the Marxist Left', Scherchen points out, 'an attempt should have been made [. . .] to re-examine the alleged formalistic and reactionary tendencies of twelve-note composition and to compare them with the results of the politically aware art of the East.'[56] 'Without the intervention of Marxist theorists', the conductor continues, 'not one outstanding musician would have attempted to [. . .] refer back to earlier developmental stages of the musical idiom.'[57] In view of the 'present situation of modern music', Scherchen leaves no doubt, 'only the twelve-tone composers did not shy away from the task that befalls each truly creative artist: to consciously develop new, more advanced ways of human expression'. Not unlike Adorno in his *Philosophy of New Music*, also published in 1949, and Leibowitz in his publications on Schoenberg and the Second Viennese School (and in his dispute over Schoenberg and Stravinsky with Nabokov), Scherchen thus unequivocally advocates serialism as the way forward, whereas Stravinsky's *Les Noces* and the *Concerto for Strings* are explicitly named as works of a composer who is willing to make concessions to external circumstances such as audience expectations and state regulations.[58]

Sartre's appeal for committed literature, too, would have been known to Nono before his Darmstadt debut in 1950, though not through Leibowitz's *L'artiste et sa conscience* (1950) but via the hugely influential journal *Il Politecnico* (1945–47).[59] This cultural journal, which was modelled on Sartre's *Les Temps Modernes*, was edited by Elio Vittorini,

[54] Spangemacher speculates that Nono would have met Leibowitz at this congress; Spangemacher, 'Schönberg as Role Model', 35.

[55] Scherchen, 'Die gegenwärtige Situation' (1949), 142. The resolution is quoted in full in Rufer, 'Arnold Schoenberg [1949]', 45.

[56] Scherchen, 'Die gegenwärtige Situation'; trans. in Spangemacher, 'Schönberg as Role Model', 36.

[57] Scherchen, 'Die gegenwärtige Situation', 143.

[58] Scherchen, 'Die gegenwärtige Situation', 143.

[59] *Il Politecnico* was founded in 1945 with financial support from the PCI. It started as a weekly and was published monthly from May 1946. Nono mentions *Il Politecnico* in 'Un'autobiografia', 506. Togni advised Nono to read *Schoenberg et son école* (1947) as soon as it was published; Rizzardi, 'Nono e la "presenza storica" di Schönberg', 230. An annotated copy is at the ALN and Nono acknowledges the book's importance in

author of *Uomini e no* (1945), the first Resistenza novel to be published in Italy after the war.[60] Vittorini published *Présentation* (1945), Sartre's introductory appeal to committed writing in *Les Temps Modernes*, and *Qu'est-ce que la littérature* in *Il Politecnico*.[61] Nono was to refer to *Qu'est-ce que la littérature* repeatedly between 1960 and 1972, the period of his most overtly political works. In his Darmstadt lecture of 1960, the reference was clearly meant to warn once more against the use of aleatoric procedures in music, reinforcing the views expressed in his controversial lecture 'History and the Present in the Music of Today' the year before.[62] More importantly, however, Nono took particular interest in Sartre in the wake of his first 'azione scenica', *Intolleranza 1960* (1961), which he dedicated to none other than Arnold Schoenberg.

In terms of the concept of music theatre, Nono repeatedly acknowledged Schoenberg's expressionist opera *Die glückliche Hand* as a pivotal model.[63] With 'Man' and 'Woman' socially reconceived as the 'Emigrant' and his female 'Comrade', *Intolleranza 1960* responds to Schoenberg's haunting expressionist vision with an existentialist journey towards political consciousness, the production of which is to be adapted to current political affairs. Sartre was of particular interest in this context for his 'théâtre de situations', which, together with the theatre of the Russian avant-garde (that of Meyerhold in particular) and Piscator's and Brecht's epic theatre, influenced Nono's concept of the 'azione scenica'. The French philosopher was further of importance for his outspoken support for the freedom fighters in the Algerian War of Independence.[64] The torture of political prisoners in Algeria is undoubtedly the most hard-hitting 'situation' in

'Intervista di Philippe Albèra' (1987), *Scritti*, II, 415. *L'artiste et sa conscience* (1950) is not at the ALN.

60 Vittorini, *Uomini e no* (1945); *Men and not Men* (1985).

61 Simone de Beauvoir describes meeting Vittorini (Paris, 1946) in *Force of Circumstance*, 79. Vittorini published Sartre's *Présentation* and serialised *Qu'est-ce que la littérature?* in 1947. *Les Temps Modernes*, in turn, published a special issue on Italy with a particular focus on Gramsci and Gobetti, and the anti-fascist writers Moravia, Carlo Levi, Silone, Brancati and Pratolini. *Les temps modernes*, 23/24 (1947). Levi's *Cristo si è fermato a Eboli* (1946) was serialised in *Les Temps Modernes*. On Sartre's influence in Italy further see Verzina, 'Musica e impegno nella *Kranichsteiner Kammerkantate* (1953)', 199–225.

62 On the reception of 'Geschichte und Gegenwart in der Musik heute' (1959), ghostwritten by Lachenmann, see Iddon, *New Music at Darmstadt*, 255–74.

63 See, for example, Nono, 'Appunti per un teatro musicale attuale' (1961), *Scritti*, I, 89/91; and 'Possibilità e necessità di un nuovo teatro musicale' (1962), *ibid.*, 123/26.

64 Nono repeatedly acknowledged the influence of Sartre's 'théâtre de situations', most prominently in 'Possibilità e necessità di un nuovo teatro musicale' (1962), *Scritti*, I, 122; also see Stenzl, 'Drammaturgia musicale', 171; and Rizzardi, 'Verso un nuovo stile rappresentivo', 41.

*Intolleranza*.[65] Before Nono's rather ill-fated collaboration with Angelo Maria Ripellino (which meant that the work was eventually composed in just three months), the composer had already decided to use *La question* by Henri Alleg, a harrowing account of torture in Algeria to which Sartre wrote the preface.[66] As Calvino later recalled, a librettist for subjects of this nature was not easily found:

> I remember that Luigi Nono wrote to me in 1958 or 1959 and then came to Turin [. . .] to convince me to write an opera libretto for him. [. . .] I admired Nono for his innovative enthusiasm and his personal qualities but I felt far removed from his dramatic world and particularly from the political passion he wanted to express in his music and in the action on stage. Nevertheless, Nono continued to believe that I was the right writer for the job. A dear mutual friend, the critic Massimo Mila, explained to him that I tended towards humour, irony, the grotesque, and that I definitely would not be able to express the gravity and tension that animated his inspiration. But Nono still insisted. I remember that it occurred to him to ask me for a libretto derived from a book on torture in Algeria that had just been published: *La question* by Alleg. With great regret I told him that I was incapable of dealing with such a dreadful and bleak subject.[67]

In the end, Nono himself compiled the libretto 'after an idea by Angelo Maria Ripellino', giving both Alleg and Sartre a 'voice', as also the Czech resistance fighter Julius Fučík. Also included are slogans of various liberation movements, as well as poems by Ripellino, Éluard, Mayakovsky and Brecht.[68] The topical issue of colonial oppression in Algeria is thus firmly anchored in the historical context of fascist oppression in Europe, while

65 On *Intolleranza 1960* see De Benedictis, 'The Dramaturgical and Compositional Genesis', 101–41; and De Benedictis and Mastinu (eds.), *Intolleranza 1960 a cinquant'anni*. On the libretto see De Benedictis, 'Gli equivoci del sembiante' (including Ripellino's original libretto) and '*Intolleranza 1960* von Luigi Nono', 305–27.

66 Alleg's *La question* (1958) is a personal account of the torture practiced by the French in Algerian detention camps. The book was seized by French police as soon as it was published. Nono quotes Alleg in *Intolleranza* at the end of the 'Interrogation' scene (I.4); Sartre's preface is cited in the following 'Torture' scene (I.5).

67 Calvino, letter to Matthias Theodor Vogt (1984), in Calvino, *Lettere 1940–1985*, 1524–25.

68 Nono sets the following slogans: the pacifist *Nie wieder!* for which Käthe Kollwitz designed the poster *Nie wieder Krieg!* (1924), *No pasarán!* from the Spanish Civil War (1936), the slogan *Morte al fascismo. Libertà ai popoli!* of the anti-fascist resistance, *La sale guerre!* against the French Colonial War in Indochina (1946–1954) and *Down with discrimination!* from the African-American civil rights movement. The poems cover an equally wide time span: Vladimir Mayakovsky, *Our March* (1917), Bertolt Brecht, *An die Nachgeborenen* (1938), Paul Éluard, *La liberté* (1942) and Angelo Maria Ripellino, *Vivere è stare svegli* (1960).

related historical moments provide the political and sociological framework for the more abstract and adaptable themes of worker exploitation, unemployment, protest and resistance, as well as the exacerbation of natural disaster through greed for profit and human negligence. In this highly abstract 'theatre of situations', torture is not staged. Instead, the fact that torture was practiced by the French, who had themselves only recently been liberated from Nazi rule, is exploited for a Brechtian alienation effect: the 'chorus of tortured prisoners' suddenly turns to the audience with the words

| | |
|---|---|
| E voi?<br>Siete sordi?<br>Complici nel gregge?<br>Nella turpe vergogna?<br>Non si scuote il lamento<br>dei nostri fratelli?<br>Megafoni! Amplificate quest'urlo!<br>Prima che la colunnia lo deformi<br>e l'indifferenza lo strozzi! | And what about you?<br>Are you deaf?<br>Following the herd,<br>in its wicked shame?<br>Doesn't the wailing<br>of our brothers rouse you?<br>Megaphones! Amplify this shout!<br>Before slander twists it<br>and indifference chokes it![69] |

Like a radio commentary, the 'Voice of Sartre' is then tuned in through loudspeakers to quote from the preface of *La question*:

> At no time has the wish to be free
> been more urgent or stronger.
> At no time has oppression been
> more violent or better armed.[70]

Pictures of rehearsals for the premiere at La Fenice (13 April 1961) show that the avant-garde projection techniques of Josef Svoboda and Václav Kašlík from the Laterna Magika in Prague were momentarily reversed and the audience itself was put into the spotlight.[71] By a twist of fate, these merciless beams of light would have exposed not only the audience, but also the neo-fascist rioters who disrupted the premiere.

Nono's engagement with Sartre continued well into the 1960s. For a theatre project with Emilio Jona (1963), he annotated the essay *Anti-Semite*

[69] Nono, *Intolleranza 1960*, I.5, trans. Graham, CD booklet, Staatsoper Stuttgart, Bernhard Kontarsky (Teldec, 1993), 125/27.

[70] *Ibid.*, 127.

[71] See De Benedictis and Mastinu (eds.), *Intolleranza 1960 a cinquant'anni*, 280–81.

*and Jew* (1945).[72] At the time of the colonial wars in Africa and Black freedom movements in the USA, the Jew had become exchangeable with 'the Other'. While *Intolleranza 1960* exposes this in the context of Algeria, the focus shifts to the USA and the case of Robert Oppenheimer with Jona. *Un diario italiano* (1963–64), another unrealised theatre project with Giuliano Scabia, was to home in on the Italian situation. *La fabbrica illuminata* (1964) is the only complete composition to emerge from this project.[73] Fascist oppression – and with it, economic exploitation – is here first equated with the contemporary situation of the worker: 'fabbrica come lager'. As is well known, Nono recorded a large part of the material for this piece at the metallurgy plant Italsider in Genoa, including production noises (from the furnace in particular) as well as recorded speech. Some of the slogans used, including 'fabbrica dei morti la chiamavano' (factory of the dead they called it) and 'fabbrica come lager', stem from the workers themselves.[74] A delegation of the workers who had participated in the recordings later travelled to Venice to attend the premiere. Sartre, too, was a guest of honour, and the performance provoked intense discussion. Following its initial success with the workers, the piece was subsequently introduced and discussed by Nono and Luigi Pestalozza in communist workers' societies throughout the Reggio Emilia Romagna, as a core event of Pestalozza's Musica/Realtà project in Italy's so-called 'Red Belt', which was also actively supported by Maurizio Pollini and Claudio Abbado.

Political and cultural activism also took Nono much further afield. Apart from two inspirational journeys to Latin America (in 1967 and 1968), a context too vast to deal with here, Nono travelled to the European Eastern Bloc and first visited the Soviet Union together with Pestalozza in 1963. Nono recorded his experience of the USSR in all honesty for the Communist paper *L'Unità* and sent an extremely indignant complaint to the paper's director when he saw that his critique of the Soviet 'socialist-realist'

[72] 'The Jew only serves him as a pretext, elsewhere his counterpart will make use of the Negro or the man of yellow skin' is marked '*per Jona prigionieri*' by Nono in *L'antisemitismo: riflessioni sulla questione ebraica* (1960), ALN; Sartre, *Anti-Semite and Jew*, 54.

[73] Secondary literature on *La fabbrica illuminata* includes Jozefowicz, *Das alltägliche Drama*; Henius, *Carla Carissima*; Riede, *Luigi Nonos Kompositionen mit Tonband*; and Spangemacher, *Luigi Nono. Die elektronische Musik*. On *Diario italiano* see Noller, '*Diario italiano* und *La fabbrica illuminata*'.

[74] Nono, 'Gespräch mit Hartmut Lück' (1972), *Texte*, 280–90; *Scritti*, II, 100–112.

party line had been glossed over.[75] On a regular basis, Nono travelled to East Germany, for performances of his own works and important premieres of works by his friend Paul Dessau (operas in particular), and as a socialist ambassador for the musical avant-garde.[76] Nono's experiences of East Germany, too, are recorded in various texts.[77] These testimonies make clear that Nono actively sought contact with intellectuals of the Socialist East in order to work against an all too dogmatic and bureaucratic form of socialism, while the contact with the intelligentsia of the West was increasingly fraught with tension due to his own 'all too dogmatic' belief in socialist society, which, at the height of his political activism in the late sixties and early seventies, even alienated friends such as Maderna and Helmut Lachenmann.[78]

Nono's music would not be what it is without this existential conflict between his belief in communist ideals and the ever more disappointing real-life experience of bureaucratic narrow-mindedness and petty power struggles that prevented their realisation. Time and time again, this 'constellation saturated with tension' (to echo Walter Benjamin, whose philosophy would later offer glimpses of a resolution) prompted Nono to confront some of the boldest questions of his time in an expressive and arresting way. The following case studies attempt to capture this unique amalgamation of political and musical consciousness for a historically contextualised understanding of Nono's musical thought and expressivity.

[75] Nono, 'Viaggio attraverso la musica nell'URSS' (1963), with Nono's letter of complaint, *Scritti*, I, 150–57.

[76] See Pommer and Wagner, 'Begegnungen mit Nono in der DDR', 149–55.

[77] Nono, 'Emigranti a Berlino' (1969), *Scritti*, I, 256–60; 'Come si fa musica nella RDT' (1974), *ibid.*, 316–19; 'Note di viaggio a Berlino, Dresda e Lipsia' (1978), *ibid.*, 346–50; 'La terra di Paul Dessau e Bertolt Brecht' (1979), *ibid.*, 364–65.

[78] On the eleven-year break in the friendship with Lachenmann see Nonnenmann, *Der Gang durch die Klippen*. Nono was ultimately reconciled with both Maderna and Lachenmann.

# 2 *Il canto sospeso* (1955–56)

> A cry of grief is a sign of the grief which provokes it, but a song of grief is both grief itself and something other than grief. Or if one wishes to adopt existentialist vocabulary, it is a grief which does not exist any more, which is.
>
> Jean-Paul Sartre, *Qu'est-ce que la littérature?*[1]

A work by a committed communist who dared to address Nazi crimes at a time when they were still largely taboo in West Germany was bound to cause controversy. At the height of the Cold War, *Il canto sospeso* was first performed to great acclaim under Scherchen (Cologne, 24 October 1956). The work's reception, however, was soon overshadowed by Adorno's distorting association of integral serialism with totalitarian regimes (fascist as well as Stalinist).[2] In addition, Stockhausen's critique of the use of text did Nono few favours.[3] To the composer himself, however, the work was of such importance that he later integrated the entire fourth movement into *Intolleranza 1960*.[4] Given the chaotic genesis of *Intolleranza*, this self-quotation may have been a last-minute decision. Within the montage of texts and situations through which we are to attain greater political consciousness, the music of *Il canto sospeso* is nevertheless utterly appropriate, in terms both of subject matter and of emotional impact.

At the time of the first Italian performance in 1960, Massimo Mila admired this complex work for its unique expressivity:

> The emotional response which *Il canto sospeso* produces even with non-musicians is a fact which is rarely experienced but continuously sought: it is the elimination of that much deprecated chasm which divides modern art from the common man, an elimination obtained

1 Sartre, *What is Literature?*, 3.

2 Adorno, 'Das Altern der neuen Musik', broadcast 1954, first published in *Der Monat*, 80 (1955); expanded in *Dissonanzen* (1956).

3 Stockhausen, 'Musik und Sprache' (1957), in *Darmstädter Beiträge*, 1 (1958), revised for *die Reihe*, 6 (1960), 36–58, and *Texte*, II, 58–68, 149–66. Despite this criticism, the correspondence shows that Stockhausen thought very highly of *Il canto sospeso*.

4 In *Intolleranza 1960* the fourth movement of *Il canto sospeso* links the 'Interrogation' and 'Torture' scenes (I:4, I:5).

> without the shadow of a concession and without compromising strict adherence to idiomatic originality.[5]

Four years earlier, *Il canto sospeso* had had a similar effect in Germany. 'Never before did I experience such tension in the audience with my work!', Nono wrote to Paul Dessau after the premiere, 'Tension as total *silenzio*, no noise throughout the performance, nothing.'[6] Herbert Eimert, too, responded with great admiration: '*Il canto sospeso* [. . .] probably left the most significant impression to date of any concert work of the young generation of composers today [. . .] This one work would suffice to legitimise the enigmatic "legacy of Webern" once and for all.'[7] Adorno's view that 'no one is actually challenged' by integral serialism, 'no one recognizes himself in it, or senses in it any binding claim to truth', could not have been disputed with greater poignancy.[8] But what exactly is it about *Il canto sospeso* that left and continues to leave such a strong impression? One reason, certainly, is the choice of text from letters of European resistance fighters about to be executed. Nono selected these from the anthology *Lettere di condannati a morte della Resistenza europea*.[9] The score is dedicated 'a tutti loro' (to all of them) and cites the following passage from the preface by Thomas Mann:

> [. . .] the faith, the hope, the readiness for sacrifice of a young European generation, which bore the fine name of the 'résistance', of internationally unanimous resistance against the disgrace of their country, against the shame of a Hitlerite Europe and the horror of a Hitlerite world, though who wanted more than simply to resist, feeling themselves to be the vanguard of a better human society [. . .][10]

Some of the letters selected by Nono do indeed focus on this aspect of hope and sacrifice for a better world: 'I am dying for a world which will shine

5 Mila, 'La linea Nono', 311. The first Italian performance took place in Venice (17 September 1960, Maderna, Cologne Radio Symphony Orchestra and Chorus, with Hartmann's *Symphony* no. 7, Fortner's *Aulodia* and Dallapiccola's *Dialoghi*, broadcast live on RAI 3).

6 Nono, letter to Dessau, 24 November 1956 (Akademie der Künste, Berlin, Paul-Dessau-Archiv 2140; copy at ALN, Dessau/P 56–11–24 d): 'in meinem Werk nie von Publikum eine solche Spannung gehört! Spannung als totale silenzio, während der Aufführung kein Lärm, nichts.'

7 Eimert, 'Uraufführung von Nonos *Canto sospeso*', 354.

8 Adorno, 'The Aging of the New Music', 185.

9 Malvezzi and Pirelli (eds.), *Lettere di condannati a morte della Resistenza europea*, with a preface by Thomas Mann (1954). An anthology of letters from the Italian resistance was compiled by the same editors in 1952.

10 Mann, 'Preface', trans. Owens, in Nono, *Il canto sospeso*, 'Appendix', 89.

with light of such strength and beauty that my own sacrifice is nothing [...] I am dying for justice. Our ideas will triumph' (Anton Popov, 26, Bulgaria), 'I am dying for freedom' (Andreas Likourinos, 14, Greece) and 'I go in the belief of a better life for you' (Ellie Voigt, 32, Germany). Others simply deal with the difficulty of saying 'goodbye for ever to life which is so beautiful' (Esther Srul, Poland).[11] Most of the texts are extracts. The first text to appear in the sketches, however, is the aphoristic note 'Goodbye mother, your daughter Lyubka is going into the moist earth'.[12] Lyubov Shevtsova was a member of the Russian resistance movement known as the Young Guard and among those captured in December 1942 for helping seventy-five prisoners escape from German concentration camps. She was tortured and finally beaten to death under the eyes of a *Rotenführer* of the SS on 7 February 1943. Her short testimony, representative of the fate of so many, lies at the heart of Nono's conception and was later used for movement no. 7, the lyrical apotheosis of the work.

Nono himself referred to *Il canto sospeso* as a cantata, and Mila later coined the term 'freedom mass'.[13] None of the chosen letters seeks refuge in religion, however. Nono most probably agreed with Mann that 'those who do not speak of God and Heaven, find much higher, more spiritual, and more poetic expression for the idea of living on'.[14] Furthermore, *Il canto sospeso* was written during the time when Italian Communists were publicly denounced and officially excommunicated from the Catholic Church, and this religious institution was also not exactly known for its role in the European resistance.[15] Unlike Maderna and Calvino, Nono remained an active member of the PCI and could not but write a secular cantata.[16] Had the work not been a West German commission, its political message might have been voiced in stronger terms. Under the circumstances, contemporary politics could only be alluded to. The passage Nono quotes from Mann is in fact part of a vicious attack on the deadlock situation of the then

[11] *Ibid.*, 90–91. Communist ideals are articulated in some of the later discarded texts: the Bulgarian communist Nikola Botušev, for example, encourages his family to 'search for the meaning of life in the struggle'; Malvezzi and Pirelli (eds.), *Lettere*, 61.

[12] *Ibid.*, 794. The diminutive form Любка, derived from the first name Любовь, used in the letter, has variously been transliterated as Lyubka, Ljubka and Liubka in English, German and Italian texts.

[13] ALN 14.02.01/04; Mila, 'La linea Nono', 302–307.

[14] Mann, 'Vorwort', 816.

[15] Card-carrying Communists were excommunicated by Pope Pius XII after his *Avviso sacro* declaration in 1949. The PCI, however, never defined itself as anticlerical; see Shore, *Italian Communism*, 38.

[16] The brutally crushed Hungarian uprising in 1956 prompted many Italian intellectuals, including Maderna and Calvino, to leave the PCI.

divided world: 'a world of evil regression' ruled by superstitious hate and persecution mania, a world where weapons of mass destruction are entrusted to those who are intellectually and morally incompetent, and a world in which 'the sinking level of culture, the atrophy of education, the mindless acceptance of atrocities committed by a politicised judiciary, bigwigs, blind greed for profit, the decay of loyalty and faith' seemed to offer 'poor protection' against the threat of a third world war.[17]

Nono alludes to this deplorable state of affairs not only by quoting Mann (whose preface may well have been known to German readers at the time),[18] but also by means of the work's title. As shown by De Benedictis, the title *Il canto sospeso* (*The Suspended Song*) stems from the Italian translation of the poem *If We Die* by Ethel Rosenberg:

> You shall know, my sons, shall know
> why we leave the song unsung,
> the book unread, the work undone
> to rest beneath the sod.
>
> Mourn no more, my sons, no more
> why the lies and smears were framed,
> the tears we shed, the hurt we bore
> to all shall be proclaimed.
>
> Earth shall smile, my sons, shall smile
> and green above our resting place,
> the killing end, the world rejoice
> in brotherhood and peace.
>
> Work and build, my sons, and build
> a monument to love and joy,
> to human worth, to faith we kept
> for you, my sons, for you.[19]

Nono would have chosen the fragment 'il canto sospeso' (the song unsung) for the poetic ambiguity of the word 'sospeso', meaning suspended in the sense of both 'floating' and 'interrupted'. However, the allusion to the Rosenberg affair was surely also deliberate. The Jewish couple Julius

[17] Mann, 'Vorwort', 817–18.

[18] The German edition, *Und die Flamme soll euch nicht versengen*, was published in 1955.

[19] Ethel Rosenberg, *If We Die* (24 January 1953), in Ethel and Julius Rosenberg, *The Rosenberg Letters*, 6. Nono owned the Italian edition, *Lettere dalla casa della morte*. Nono later reconsidered the poem for *Intolleranza 1960*; see De Benedictis, 'The Dramaturgical and Compositional Genesis', 113/116–17.

and Ethel Rosenberg stood trial in 1951, charged with conspiracy for passing secret information on nuclear weapons research to the Soviet Union. The alleged dealings took place in 1944 and 1945, at a time when the USSR and the USA were still allies. In the surge of American anti-communist hysteria the Rosenbergs were sentenced to death. This sentence caused an outcry within the European political left, especially in France. Many intellectuals, including Sartre and Aragon, and religious leaders of all denominations appealed for clemency, to no avail.[20] After two years of 'torture by hope' the Rosenbergs were electrocuted on 19 June 1953, and their case may well have been one of the 'atrocities' Mann had in mind when attacking a politicised judiciary in 1954.

Given the high degree of public interest in the Rosenberg affair, Nono's reference to the poem would not have gone unnoticed. The connection was certainly known to Mila, who drew an analogy between the Rosenbergs' execution and that of the resistance fighters whose words are set in *Il canto sospeso* – a clear hint that these words should not merely be regarded as a matter of the past.[21] Moreover, as a personal tribute to the Rosenbergs' sons (aged 6 and 10 at the time), this poem, too, does not claim to be high art, but is yet another moving testimony of the sort found in the letters of the European resistance. Mann describes the peculiar effect of such documentary 'poetry': 'One admires poetry because it can express itself like real life. One is doubly affected by life itself, because unintentionally it expresses itself as poetry.'[22]

Notably, Adorno's 'The Aging of the New Music' cites a document of similar nature: the title-page illustration from the first edition of Karl Kraus's apocalyptic drama *The Last Days of Mankind* (1921). The picture shows 'the execution of the deputy Battisti, accused by the Austrians of spying', with 'a merrily laughing hangman' at its centre. The fact that this image, 'along with another that was, if possible, even more shocking', was omitted from the drama's first post-WWII edition prompts Adorno to argue as follows:

> As a result of this seemingly superficial change something decisive was transformed in the work. A similar transformation, a little less crass, occurred in New Music. The sounds remain the same. But the anxiety that gave shape to its great founding works has been repressed. Perhaps that anxiety has become so overwhelming in reality that its undisguised image would scarcely

[20] The British edition of the Rosenberg correspondence includes letters of protest by Einstein, Sartre and Aragon among others.

[21] Mila, 'La linea Nono', 306. [22] Mann, 'Vorwort', 814.

> be bearable: to recognize the aging of the New Music does not mean to misjudge this aging as something accidental. But art that unconsciously obeys such repression and makes itself a game, because it has become too weak for seriousness, renounces its claim to truth, which is its only raison d'être.[23]

In setting text that no longer merely conjures up the image of a 'merrily laughing hangman' but evokes Nazi-style executions and, ultimately, the extermination camps, Nono, among very few other composers of his time, took the bold step demanded by Adorno and addressed his European contemporaries with a work that forced them to confront their recent past. Moreover, he did so with compositional means of the most advanced kind. While retaining the traditional line up of soloists, chorus and orchestra, as well as the movement structure of established genres such as oratorio or cantata, each of the nine movements of *Il canto sospeso* is also an extremely refined example of serial technique. Nono later described the work as a '*Divertimento* of different compositional ideas'[24] and the variety with which serial technique is employed in *Il canto sospeso* is hardly surpassed in later works of this period and certainly justifies the attention this masterpiece has been given in purely analytical terms.[25] However, one question does impose itself: are these adequate means for the expression of such content – if, indeed, any such means can be said to exist? This question has been asked time and again, especially in German criticism, ever since Adorno first formulated his most heatedly debated dictum: 'to write poetry after Auschwitz is barbaric'. Precisely this question is also at the heart of Matteo Nanni's book *Auschwitz – Adorno und Nono*, though not in relation to *Il canto sospeso*.[26] In the context of Adorno's bold assertion of 1951 (more widely disseminated with the publication of *Prismen* in 1955),[27] Eimert voiced similar concern regarding Nono's choice of text: 'Can one "set" this

[23] Adorno, 'Aging', 183.

[24] Nono, 'Un'autobiografia', *Scritti* II, 511.

[25] On *Il canto sospeso* as a whole see Bailey, 'Work in Progress' (1992); Motz, *Konstruktion und Ausdruck* (1996); Feneyrou, *Il canto sospeso* (2002); Nielinger, 'The Song Unsung' (2006). On individual movements see, re no. 1, Motz, 'Konstruktive Strenge' (1999); re no. 2, Stockhausen, 'Musik und Sprache' (1957); Kramer, 'The Fibonacci Series' (1973); Schaller, *Klang und Zahl* (1997), 112–25; re no. 4, Borio, 'Sull'interazione' (1999); Herrmann, 'Das Zeitnetz als serielles Mittel' (2000); re no. 6, Huber, 'Il canto sospeso VI a, b' (1981), re no. 8, Borio, 'Tempo e ritmo nelle composizioni seriali' (2004), 112–14; re no. 9, De Benedictis, 'Gruppo, linea e proiezioni armoniche' (2004), 204–5; re nos. 1, 4 and 8, Gerrero, 'Serial Intervention' (2006).

[26] Nanni, *Auschwitz – Adorno und Nono.*

[27] Adorno, 'Kulturkritik und Gesellschaft' (1949), first published in *Soziologische Forschung in unserer Zeit* (1951), later included in *Prismen*, 7–31; 'Cultural Criticism and Society', 34.

to music? Embarrassing to think that this may have been done with traditional means of expression, descriptive narrative or sensational reportage with large-scale magazine reproductions.'[28] Eimert's response to Nono's treatment of the text, however, is essentially positive:

> Nono does not interpret the words, nor does he cover them up. Instead the word is incorporated into the structure – not just words, but syllables, too, meander through the voices. The phonetic thus becomes part of the 'serial' – this happens here for the first time outside the field of electronic music. And it happens so convincingly that the 'composed' vocal colour merges into a vibrating image of sound, an objectified music of metallic plasticism and greatest intensity.[29]

As is well known, Stockhausen responded with much greater uneasiness. His analysis of the second movement of *Il canto sospeso* begins with the following reflections on the music–text relationship:

> In certain pieces of the 'Canto', Nono composed the text as if to withdraw it from the public eye where it has no place [. . .] The texts are not delivered, but rather concealed in such a regardlessly strict and dense musical form that they are hardly comprehensible when performed. To what end, then, text, and particularly this one? One can explain it as follows: particularly when setting those passages from the letters where one is most ashamed that they had to be written, the musician acts purely as a composer [. . .] he does not interpret, he does not comment. Instead, he reduces language to its syllables [. . .] permutations of vowel-sounds, a, ä, e, i, o, u; serial structure. Should he not have chosen texts so rich in meaning in the first place, but rather sounds? At least for the sections where only the phonetic properties of language are dealt with?[30]

In part, Stockhausen's stern critique of the text–music relationship in *Il canto sospeso* can be understood as a self-defence against similar attacks on the deconstruction of text and structural use of phonetics in *Gesang der Jünglinge* (also premiered in 1956).[31] Such deconstruction is here justified, Stockhausen argues, because the text – 'a sequence of acclamations from the Apocrypha to the Book of Daniel' – is not only extremely repetitive, but, to a great extent, 'general knowledge'.[32] Stockhausen's critique of *Il canto sospeso* thus fundamentally concerns the nature of the text itself.

[28] Eimert, '*Canto sospeso*', 354. [29] *Ibid.*, 354.

[30] Stockhausen, 'Music and Speech', 48–49; and Grant, *Serial Music*, 203.

[31] Wismeyer, 'Wider die Natur!', 136–37; Grant, *Serial Music*, 198. For further reviews in this vein see Wagner (ed.), *Karl Amadeus Hartmann*, 136–37.

[32] Stockhausen, 'Music and Speech', 57.

Not only are these testimonies felt to be too personal to be placed in the public eye, but, to the ordinary German who endured the Nazi regime without much resistance, they will have evoked an overpowering sensation of shame and guilt.[33] Precisely this feeling of disgrace prevailed in the radio broadcast of 8 May 1945 with which Thomas Mann laid bare the truth of the camps:

> The thick walls of the torture chamber Germany was turned into under Hitler have been forced open. Our disgrace is revealed to the eyes of the world, to the foreign commissions, to whom these unbelievable images are now shown and who report at home that this exceeds all dreadfulness that any human being can imagine. 'Our disgrace', German readers and listeners! Because everything German, everybody who speaks German, writes in German, and has lived the German way, is affected by this degrading revelation.[34]

German culture had been severely dislocated. Adorno's incessant reliance on negative dialectics, too, is inseparable from the watershed event encapsulated in the name Auschwitz. Time and again Adorno reflects on the dilemma of the impossibility of representing Auschwitz and the imperative of having to address it. *In nuce* the topic is already present in *Minima Moralia*, written in exile but published only in 1951:

> *All the world's not a stage.* – The coming extinction of art is prefigured in the increasing impossibility of representing historical events. That there is no adequate drama about Fascism is not due to lack of talent; talent is withering through the insolubility of the writer's most urgent task. [...] The impossibility of portraying Fascism springs from the fact that in it, as in its contemplation, subjective freedom no longer exists. Total unfreedom can be recognized, but not represented. Where freedom occurs as a motif in political narratives today, as in the praise of heroic resistance, it has the embarrassing quality of impotent reassurance.[35]

[33] Stockhausen himself is a typical example. His own mother, a victim of the Nazi euthanasia programme, had been 'officially put to death' in 1941. His father was shot in battle in April 1945. Yet Stockhausen states 'I simply accepted it as given, not as an injustice, a challenge, that's my way'. Stockhausen, 'About my Childhood' (1971), 20–21.

[34] Mann, 'Die Lager' (1945), 699. Throughout the 1940s Mann addressed the German people with appeals to resist. Once a month an 8-minute-long message was transmitted by telephone to London and broadcast by the BBC. The broadcasts were published under the title 'Deutsche Hörer!'. Mann's broadcast on the camps is mentioned in Levi, *The Drowned and the Saved*, 161.

[35] Adorno, *Minima Moralia*, 143–45; Nono owned the first Italian edition of 1954.

The much debated dictum on poetry after Auschwitz, however, is later put into question by the author himself: 'Perennial suffering has as much right to expression as a tortured man has to scream; hence it may have been wrong to say that after Auschwitz you could no longer write poems.'[36] Adorno here clearly moves on from his original statement in 'Cultural Criticism and Society' and adds that 'A new categorical imperative has been imposed by Hitler upon unfree mankind: to arrange their thoughts and actions so that Auschwitz will not repeat itself, so that nothing similar will happen.'[37] Despite this concession, written at the time of the Frankfurt Auschwitz trial and published just after the production of Peter Weiss's documentary drama *Die Ermittlung* (*The Investigation*), for which Nono wrote music in 1965, Adorno never fully embraced art that addressed the topic of Auschwitz, however modernist or conscious of its function in society. One reason for this, in regard to music, was Adorno's modernist belief in the inherent historicity of the musical material itself. Politics, however, was clearly also at stake, and most certainly so in the case of Nono. As is evident from Hans Werner Henze's autobiography, Adorno refused outright to align with intellectuals in communist alliances. When Henze asked for a letter of support in the context of the ill-fated premiere of *Das Floß der Medusa* (*The Raft of the Medusa*) in 1968, Adorno responded positively at first but changed his mind after having heard that such letters had already been written by Nono and Weiss.[38]

Such were the political frontiers in West Germany at the time that Heinz-Klaus Metzger's defence of integral serialism in response to Adorno's 'Aging of the New Music' not only excluded Nono, but explicitly accused him of serialist composition of the sort which, 'stagnant' and 'without a sense of history', could only serve to justify Adorno's critique of this technique. *Il canto sospeso*, even Metzger is forced to concede, is 'perhaps the most impressive' of Nono's serial works, but

> Partisans in the struggle against reactionary oppression can no longer write one last line to their mother before being executed without becoming the subject of one of the masterpieces by composers who specialise in these matters. The war in Algeria had not even ended by the time Nono prepared himself to musically process the screams of those who were tortured there, with the usual twelve notes, in order to present them at the next important festival to the applause of a delighted bourgeoisie. Of all the well-known

[36] Adorno, *Negative Dialectics* (1966), 362. [37] *Ibid.*, 365.

[38] Henze, *Bohemian Fifths*, 244. Nono, letter of support, 'Saluto a Henze' (1968), *Scritti*, I, 254–55.

> composers of his generation, however, the author of *Intolleranza 1960* resists musical progress with the greatest intolerance – a serial Pfitzner.[39]

In marked contrast, Mila argued that, precisely because *Il canto sospeso* successfully defies Adorno's historical pessimism in 'The Aging of the New Music', its significance 'surpasses the usual satisfaction with an accomplished work of art'.[40] Well aware of the political implications of Adorno's polemic, Mila (himself an ex-partisan) not only defends Nono against Metzger, but specifically homes in on the Italian context:

> In *Il canto sospeso* there is nothing of that cheap sentimental blackmail which has prompted surviving partisans more than once to paraphrase Leconte de Lisle: 'It is forbidden to lay music on the tombs of our dead'. On the contrary, the most rewarding praise one can possibly write for *Il canto sospeso* is that the music is worthy of its texts and that, within its own sphere, it manages to recreate the dramatic moral depth of the letters of the Resistance fighters condemned to death – of words, that is, the validity of which has been affirmed by the most decisive of proofs.[41]

The difference between the West German and Italian appreciations could not be clearer. While Germans received the work in the context of the unspeakably shameful, all too recent history of the holocaust, *Il canto sospeso* was part of the legacy of the Resistance in Italy, where the two anthologies of letters by Italian and European resistance fighters were simply known as the *Lettere* and soon took their place among the 'sacred' and most widely read texts of the Resistance. They were published in many different formats and regularly read in schools on or before the April 25 commemorations (often by former partisans). Even before publication, the typescript of the first anthology, *Lettere di condannati a morte della Resistenza italiana*, won the Premio Venezia della Resistenza (1951), and it was 'nothing short of a publishing sensation' when first released by Einaudi in 1952.[42] The second anthology, *Lettere di condannati a morte della Resistenza europea*, with its outspoken preface by Mann followed suit in 1954. As Cooke explains, these last letters were of such popular appeal precisely because they revealed and acknowledged the broad ideological span and political plurality within the Italian and European resistance movements and thus encouraged people of all political persuasions, including the Christian Democrats, to engage with the history and ideals of the

[39] Metzger, 'Das Altern der jüngsten Musik', 120–21.
[40] Mila, 'La linea Nono', 300–301.
[41] Mila, 'La linea Nono', 310–11.
[42] Cooke, *Legacy of the Italian Resistance*, 51–52. Nono also possessed a version on vinyl.

Resistance.[43] In the tense political climate during the 'hard years' of Cold War persecution, the *Lettere* consciously went beyond party politics to redeem the image of the Resistenza, and in this vein they also left their mark in the music of the younger generation.

Vittorio Fellegara (1927–2011), who attended the Darmstadt courses (1955/56) and briefly adopted serial practices in the late fifties, composed the cantata *Lettere di condannati a morte della Resistenza italiana* (1954) for orchestra, reciting voices and chorus.[44] Maderna, who had been among the first to write music for a radio broadcast on poetry of the Resistance in 1946, also chose one of the letters for his *Quattro lettere* (*Kranichsteiner Kammerkantate*) in 1953.[45] Maderna, however, clearly regarded the *Lettere* as part of the Communist legacy of the Resistance and therefore treated them with caution. Early in 1953 he wrote to Nono 'The letters on the *Resistenza* are very beautiful but I don't want to cause speculation.'[46] One reason for this more cautious approach may have been the increasingly anti-communist climate in West Germany, where the piece was to receive its first performance.[47] Apart from Kafka's love letter to Milena, however, the other letters of Maderna's *Quattro lettere* – a business letter to demonstrate 'how a large capitalist *Trust* can damage a small business' and one of Gramsci's prison letters – are hardly less political.[48] In addition, the work's pitch material derives from one of the most famous Resistance songs, *Fischia il vento*.[49] This popular base material is well disguised,

43 The neo-fascists 'retaliated' with *Lettere di caduti della Repubblica Sociale Italiana* (1960); Cooke, *Legacy of the Italian Resistance*, 52.

44 See Pestalozza, 'Musica ispirata dalla Resistenza' (1955), 687–95. Fellegara further composed an *Epigrafe per Ethel e Julius Rosenberg* (1955), Lorca is set in his *Requiem di Madrid* (1958) and *Dies irae* (1959), and the chamber works *Epitaphe* (1964) and *Chanson* (1974) set poetry by Éluard.

45 On the broadcast 'Poesia della Resistenza' (17 November 1946) with music by Maderna see De Benedictis, *Radiodramma e arte radiofonica*, 15; and Romito, 'I commenti musicali di Bruno Maderna', 79. Maderna's *Quattro lettere* (*Kranichsteiner Kammerkantate*) for soprano, bass and chamber orchestra was premiered under Maderna together with Fortner's cantata *Mitte des Lebens* and Milhaud's *La mort d'un tyran* (Darmstadt, 30 July 1953).

46 Maderna, letter to Nono, February/March 1953 (Maderna/B 53–02/03-?? m, ALN): 'le lettere sulla Resistenza sono bellissime ma non vorrei farne una speculazione'.

47 In West Germany the Communist Party was banned in 1956; in Italy the PCI attained more than 22% of the vote in the 1953 elections and consistently remained the second largest party until its demise in 1990; Ginsborg, *A History of Contemporary Italy*, 442.

48 Maderna, letter to Nono (Maderna/B 53–02/03-?? m, ALN).

49 The song *Fischia il vento* (*The Wind Whistles*) uses the melody of the Soviet song *Katyusha* known to many Italian soldiers who had fought on the Eastern Front. The Italian version, of which there are many variations, was written by Felice Cascione,

however: pitch permutation techniques ensure that the song remains completely unrecognisable.[50] As in Calvino's story 'Impiccagione di un giudice', neo-realist elements provide the ideological basis for the work but do not predominate. Combined with an uncompromisingly avant-garde idiom, the work's underlying ideological content is raised to a modernist level of abstraction. During Maderna's lifetime the work was never heard in Italy, however, while the much more conventional rendition of *Fischia il vento* which triumphantly concludes Mario Zafred's fourth symphony 'In onore della Resistenza' (1950) repeatedly resounded over the tombs of Italy's dead up to 1960, producing precisely that nausea of inadequacy Mila was to refer to in his defence of *Il canto sospeso*.[51]

Nono himself later singled out Maderna's *Quattro lettere* for the composer's exemplary ideological engagement and commitment to the musical avant-garde:

> In post-war Italy musical research and creativity developed in a very different way from elsewhere. The urgency of a new idealism, provoked by the Resistenza, was coupled with the search for adequate technical means and new possibilities, including electronic music. Ideological commitment went hand in hand with commitment to language. Bruno Maderna, the fundamental pivot of the new musical situation in Italy, showed the way. In 1951 [*sic.*] he composed a chamber cantata, *Quattro lettere* [. . .] In this composition there is a reciprocal interaction between new and complex conceptual content and the novel projection of musical conception and invention. (It has never been performed in Italy.) There were only a few of us around Maderna at the time who spoke of total engagement, both ideological and technical.[52]

With such idealist engagement Nono, too, repeatedly turned to political song. Particularly in the surge of the 'hot autumn' (1969), when Resistance songs regained huge popularity and thousands gathered for the largest ever performance of 'Bella ciao', Nono did not hesitate to make overt use of political song with all its historical and political connotations.[53]

a partisan commander in the region of Imperia. The song was sung by almost every brigade; see Solza and Michelis (eds.), *Canti della Resistenza italiana*, 163, ALN; and Cooke, 'The Resistance movement: 1943–1945', 9. On Maderna's version of the song and a translation of the text see Earle, 'Mario Zafred and Symphonic Neorealism', 152.

50 See Verzina, 'Tecnica della mutazione', *Bruno Maderna: Étude historique et critique*, and 'Musica e impegno'. The concealment of this song prompts Earle to question its use in defence of Zafred's heroic, neo-realist rendition in the Finale of his symphony 'In onore della Resistenza' (1950); Earle, 'Zafred and Symphonic Neorealism', 153.

51 'History was not on Zafred's side', even Earle is forced to concede; *ibid.*, 171.

52 Nono, 'Musica e Resistenza' (1963), *Scritti*, I, 145.

53 On the renaissance of Resistance song in the early 1970s see Cooke, *Legacy*, 113.

The use of such politically charged base material culminates in Nono's second 'azione scenica' *Al gran sole carico d'amore* (1972–74). Spanning a century of brutally crushed revolutions from the Paris Commune (1871) to the Vietnam War, this swan song of the socialist revolution integrates and is possibly entirely derived from characteristic motifs, rhythms and melodic particles of the revolutionary songs *Non siam più la Comune di Parigi*, the *Internationale*, *Bandiera rossa*, the Russian songs *O fucile, vecchio mio compagno* and *Dubinushka*, the Cuban *March of the 26th of July* and *The East is Red* from the Cultural Revolution.[54] In contrast to the politically 'suspicious' melting pot of anthems in Stockhausen's *Hymnen* (1965–69) – 'imagine: the fascist anthem of Franco Spain next to that of the People's Republic of Albania, and *Bandiera rossa* next to the *Deutschlandlied*', Nono exclaims in conversation with Hansjörg Pauli[55] – this choice of revolutionary song adds a congruent musical layer of historical reference to the equally diverse montage of literary and documentary texts.

The Russian song *Dubinushka*, for example, was originally sung to goad manual labour with a wooden cudgel. In peasant rebellions of the late nineteenth century and the Russian revolution of 1905 the song came to symbolise the people's struggle against injustice and exploitation. A legendary recording by the Russian bass Fedor Shalyapin also greatly popularised the song with the elite. In *Al gran sole* the song is associated with Maxim Gorky's novel *The Mother* (1906) in Brecht's version of 1933/38 and Yuri Lyubimov's stage adaptation of 1969. In the contemporary context of workers' strikes in Italy, the use of *The Mother* and also the song *Dubinushka* was probably suggested by Lyubimov (the director of the Taganka Theatre in Moscow) when Nono first asked him to collaborate

54 Sketches further make reference to *La guardia rossa*, a song from the 1919 Spartacus revolt, *Auf, auf zum Kampf*, also known as the *Karl Liebknecht Lied*, Eisler's *Solidaritätslied* and Scherchen's *Unsterbliche Opfer*. How Nono derived his material from these songs remains to be studied in detail.

55 Nono, 'Gespräch mit Hansjörg Pauli' (1969), *Texte*, 206. Nono's reflection on *Hymnen* continues as follows: 'the purest Social Democracy: all adversaries are invited to one round-table in order to gain as much capital as possible from the conflict. Fundamentally this is not any better than the widespread tendency to integrate quotations from different periods of music history in pastiche manner into music of our own, without taking the function and the historical meaning of this material into account. This is restoration. Such methods do not achieve development, create no openings, no new perspectives, precisely because there is no dialectical process between technique and material. The quotations in these works take on the function of consumer goods. Likewise, the works themselves are turned into neutralised consumer goods of the music industry of the capitalist West.'

on *Al gran sole* in 1973. Just a year after the occupation of the central square in Prague by Russian tanks, Lyubimov had produced Gorky's *Mother* with 'real live soldiers standing with fixed bayonets round the edge of the stage' and the entire drama unfolding 'inside this square'.[56] With a passion rarely found in academic literature, Smeliansky describes the production's culminating rendition of *Dubinushka*:

> In Russia everyone knows the song about the 'cudgel' (*dubinushka*), if only because of the superb rendition by Shalyapin. Nowhere will you find a better expression of the spirit of the workers' artel [a rudimentary form of collective organisation], of Russian oppression and Russian rebellion, than in this song of the people [. . .] In Lyubimov's production this song of the workers' artel grew into a musical image of an enslaved country threatening one day to straighten its back and to lash out with this 'cudgel'. The dark expanse of the stage was filled with human faces slightly lit from below. The actors were standing on fly beams at different heights, so that not only the horizontal stage space, but the vertical space was filled. The effect was as if the air of the stage itself was thick with anger. And these faces, suspended in air, this Taganka artel, began to sing 'Dubinushka'. They began softly, not articulating the words, just intoning the stresses, winding the theatre up with sheer energy . . . Then, at the refrain, the faces swam through the air and this movement caught up the tune, intensified it a hundredfold . . . Suddenly Shalyapin's incomparable bass wove itself into the tumult of modern voices. It was as though the great Russian art of the past was experiencing with them what they were doing on the Taganka stage, echoing this movement, this heaving towards liberation. It is difficult to describe the impact it had on the audience. Probably it was one of the most sublime moments of sixties Soviet theatre.[57]

*Dubinushka* takes on a far less triumphant guise in *Al gran sole*. Like all other remnants of socialist workers' song, it cuts through twelve-tone and microtonal textures like an echo of the revolutionary past. The song is introduced on timpani, then fragments of the melody are interwoven with a dramatic recitativo dialogue from *The Mother* before it is vocalised in full by a male chorus. Yet even this final vocal rendition is far removed from emphatic, 'popular' workers' song: its repetitive structure is essentially exploited for echo formation with maximum dynamic contrast. Lyrical echoes of the tonal revolutionary past are thus quietly shrouded in atonal textures through which the consistently wordless origin shines like a

[56] Smeliansky, *Russian Theatre after Stalin*, 45.

[57] Smeliansky, *Russian Theatre*, 45–46. On Lyubimov's *Mother* also see Beumers, *Yuri Lyubimov*, 73–76.

reminder for generations to come and convincingly gives rise to the scene's lyrical apotheosis for high solo soprano and tape setting poetry by Cesare Pavese.[58]

Back in the 1950s, such overt references to socialist song were as yet unthinkable, especially in view of performance in Germany. However, this did not prevent the young Italians from making use of such politically charged material. On the contrary, it seems to have been all the more attractive to disguise such references without necessarily being found out. In Nono's works up to 1954, the middle movement of the first *Epitaffio per Federico García Lorca* (1952), for example, makes use of rhythmic material from the communist 'hymn' *Bandiera rossa*, which was sung by the International Brigades in the Spanish Civil War and by partisans in WWII.[59] Again in the context of the Spanish Civil War and the continuing political oppression under Franco, *La victoire de Guernica* (1954), Nono's first setting of poetry by Paul Éluard, makes use of the *Internationale* and *Mamita mia*.[60] While the rhythmic motifs from the *Internationale* are barely disguised, the pitch derivation from these songs is much more complex: six pitches from *Mamita mia* and three pitches from the *Internationale* are combined to form a new nine-pitch series.[61] Similarly to Maderna's serial deconstruction of *Fischia il vento*, this procedure transforms the pre-existent origin beyond recognition.

In addition to workers' songs, Nono also turned to non-political source material. This material from aural folk traditions, too, is very much in line with the 'neo-realist' trends that dominated Italian literature and film at the time. The first movement of *Polifonica – Monodia – Ritmica* (1950) incorporates a rhythmic motif from the ceremonial song *Yemanjá*, which is sung by indigenous Indians in Brazil during the offering of

58 Nono here sets the first stanza of *In the morning you always come back* from *Verrà la morte e avrà i tuoi occhi* (1950), in Pavese, *Disaffections*, 340/41. Pavese, who committed suicide in 1950, was one of Nono's favourite authors. His poetry is also set in *La terra e la compagna* (1957), *Sarà dolce tacere* (1960), *Canti di vita e d'amore* (1962), *La fabbrica illuminata* (1964) and *Musica-Manifesto n. 1* (1969). On Nono's Pavese settings see Stenzl, 'Luigi Nono und Cesare Pavese'; Breuning, *Luigi Nonos Vertonungen von Texten Cesare Paveses* and De Benedictis, 'Luigi Nono et Cesare Pavese'.

59 On the use of *Bandiera rossa* in 'La Guerra' (Neruda), and the 'Lenin' (Mayakovsky) movement which it replaces, see Borio, 'Tempo e ritmo nelle composizioni seriali', 71–73.

60 *Mamita mia*, an ironic song about four fascist generals, was written by Ernst Busch to a Spanish folk tune (1937). The title 'my dear mother' refers to Madrid. On the anti-fascist struggle under Franco and its impact on Italian post-war composers see Pestalozza, 'La guerra civile spagnola'. Éluard's resistance poem *Liberté* (1942) is set in *Intolleranza*.

61 ALN 08.03/10v.

**Example 2.1** Nono's all-interval series on A (1955–59)

wreaths to Yemanjá, the goddess of the sea.[62] In a similar vein, the final part of Nono's *Epitaffio per Federico García Lorca n. 2: Y su sangre ya viene cantando* (1952) combines rhythms from various Gypsy songs of Andalucía. And the second of the *Due espressioni* (1953) for orchestra (one of the pieces reused in *Intolleranza*) assimilates rhythmic elements of the 'Furlana', a popular Italian folk dance.[63]

Nono abruptly abandoned the use of such pre-existent material after 1954. '*La victoire de Guernica* was a diversion', he later told Restagno, 'born in reaction to what was happening in Darmstadt: ever more repetitive sterile formulas, supreme exaltation of unifying "rationality".'[64] And yet, from 1955 to 1959, Nono himself embraced this 'unifying rationality' and worked almost exclusively with a textbook twelve-tone row: the 'basic chromatic form' of the all-interval series according to Eimert's *Lehrbuch der Zwölftontechnik* of 1950.[65] In stark contrast to the politically suggestive materials of previous works, the nature of this series is extremely objectified. Similarly to the chromatic series of Stockhausen's *Klavierstück* no. 1 (a piece Nono discussed at Gravesano in 1956),[66] it is simply constructed of two chromatic hexachords and the full interval reservoir is attained by means of interlocking chromatic expansion (see Example 2.1). The first work to make use of this series was *Canti per 13* (1955).[67] With the exception of *Incontri* (1955), the series is

62 Nono, 'Un'autobiografia', *Scritti*, II, 501. Nono was introduced to Brazilian folk traditions and the work of García Lorca by Katunda. On Katunda's influence and Scherchen's controversial cropping of *Polifonica – Monodia – Ritmica* see Rizzardi, 'La «Nuova Scuola Veneziana»', 15–31; and Iddon, *New Music at Darmstadt*, 43–44.

63 As De Benedictis explained to me, 'Furlana' or 'Friulana' is a dance of courtship from the region of Friuli. The second of Nono's *Due espressioni* is cited with a different ending in *Intolleranza 1960*, II:3 (bars 294–313).

64 Nono, 'Un'autobiografia', *Scritti*, II, 514.

65 Eimert, *Lehrbuch der Zwölftontechnik*, 25; Nono annotated the Italian edition of 1954 and briefly discusses this row in 'Zur Entwicklung der Serientechnik' (1956), *Texte*, 20; *Scritti*, I, 14. Further see Bailey, 'Work in Progress', 281; De Benedictis, 'Gruppo, linea e proiezioni armoniche', 204; Motz, *Konstruktion und Ausdruck*, 22–28, and Schaller, *Klang und Zahl*, 89–93.

66 Nono, 'Zur Entwicklung der Serientechnik', *Texte*, 20; *Scritti*, I, 13–14. Nono's score of Stockhausen's *Klavierstücke I–IV* is annotated.

67 *Canti per 13* was written for Boulez's Domaine musical and premiered under Boulez (Paris, 26 March 1955).

used for all subsequent works up to *Composizione per orchestra n. 2: Diario polacco '58* (1959). Apart from in *Diario polacco '58*, Nono refrains from transposition and works with the basic form of the series (on A or C) throughout.

My earlier analysis of *Il canto sospeso* focuses primarily on the serial organisation and explains how the all-interval series on A comes into use in each of the nine movements, along with detailed information on the serialisation of dynamics, duration factors and even instrumentation.[68] However, Nono himself stubbornly refrained from disclosing such inner secrets of his compositional technique. When approached by Stockhausen, in October 1955, to contribute an article for *die Reihe* 'on technical problems he had solved and dealt with in the past', he replied jokingly, but also with great seriousness:

> Esteemed Professor!
> I was very pleased, because you, esteemed Prof, asked me for something for your noble journal, which means that you, esteemed Prof, believe or think that I have something to write or say, other than my music?
> What to do????????????????????
> You say too many things I do not agree with.
> [. . .] my technical problems and solutions are for me and to be discussed between friends.
> But, and I STRONGLY believe this, they are not for journals. Because there is no recipe!!!!! Today, as ever. And there are too many people waiting for recipes or who already have them.
> And one delivers them all too light-heartedly.
> [. . .] the true 'solutions' and techniques are found on the way!
> They can only come into being.
> I am and always have been against writing about oneself and speaking and writing about one's own technique in analytical terms.[69]

With this stark warning in mind, I now focus on the perceptible large-scale features which tie this 'divertimento of different compositional ideas' into an expressive whole.

'The explosive charge of freedom that animated the young writer was not so much his wish to document or to inform as it was his desire to *express*', Calvino wrote in one of the most interesting documents on 'neo-realism' in Italian post-war literature, the 1964 preface to his first

68 Nielinger, 'The Song Unsung'.

69 Nono, letter to Stockhausen, 26 November 1955 (Stockhausen Foundation, Kürten; copy at ALN Stockhausen/K 55-11-26 d).

novel *The Path to the Nest of Spiders* (1947), which Nono owned and annotated. 'Express what?' Calvino continues,

> Characters, landscapes, shooting, political slogans, jargon, curses, lyric flights, weapons, love-making were only colours on the palette, notes of the scale; we all knew too well that what counted was the music and not the libretto. Though we were supposed to be concerned with content, there were never more dogged formalists than we; and never were lyric poets as effusive as those objective reporters we were supposed to be [. . .] Actually the extra-literary elements stood there so massive and so indisputable that they seemed a fact of nature; to us the whole problem was one of poetics; how to transform into a literary work that world which for us was *the* world.[70]

The extra-literary texts of *Il canto sospeso* certainly formed part of this world and its challenging problem of poetics. And precisely for these texts, Nono turns away from pre-existent source material and fully adopts the 'unifying rationality' he critically engaged with at Darmstadt. New serial rigour first manifested itself in the purely instrumental *Canti per 13* and *Incontri* (1955), and this rigour, it seems, finally allowed Nono to arrive at an appropriate musical idiom for the hard-hitting, emotionally charged, anti-fascist subject matter after his first large-scale project on the Czech resistance fighter Julius Fučík (1951) remained unfinished. In introductory notes for *Il canto sospeso*, Nono himself recognises this idiomatic turning point:

> After the *canti per 13* and *incontri per 24 str*[*umenti*], a new compositional technique is developed in this work (for example in the use of the chorus, where the word acquires a new flexibility through the simultaneous melodic and harmonic projection of the syllables, as in No. 9). The problems of composition and the text are equally reciprocal, in that the text is directly about our present and our future, rejecting all archaisms [. . .], which, today more than ever, are mere 'plaisanteries à la Louis XVI'.[71]

The reflection continues in Nono's introduction to his *Diario polacco '58* (1959), again with reference to choral writing:

> Recently, my interests have increasingly focused on compositions with chorus and vocal soloists, one reason being that the human voice is not constrained to the historic functional limits of melodic instruments: these instruments were invented at a specific time for a specific technique of expression.

70 Calvino, *Il sentiero dei nidi di ragno*, ALN, highlighted by Nono; *The Path to the Nest of Spiders*, vi–vii.

71 Nono, introductory remarks on *Il canto sospeso*, in Flamm, 'Preface', score, vii.

> Melody is no longer to be understood from the point of view of the perspective succession that is typical of tonal music. [. . .] Melody results from simultaneity within a differentiated spectrum of unified rhythmic values, their duration and interrelationship.
>
> I began such melodic development in the second and ninth part of *Il canto sospeso* (for a cappella chorus), and continued it in *La terra e la compagna* and *Cori di Didone* – always with the chorus – and now I have also introduced it on instruments in *Diario polacco*.
>
> To the listener who, out of tradition and inertia, has become accustomed to a unified rhythmic-metric pulse, this concept will falsely seem static, just as Indian music seems monotonous to the European ear, though it is based on a far richer differentiation of intervals than traditional European music. The capacity to create and to explore, to attain new levels of spirituality, sentiment and consciousness, of understanding and explanation is without limits. Those who try to crush and restrict it in an arrogant, authoritarian and malicious way voluntarily place themselves outside of history.[72]

## Choral pillars

The 'new compositional technique' with which Nono meant to liberate himself of all 'archaisms' and mere 'plaisanteries à la Louis XVI' takes on its most radical form in the choral movements, nos. 2 and 9. The 'structuralist cleansing of a succinct' and 'quasi-archaically renewed expressivity' Lachenmann speaks of in regard to Nono's works of this period[73] finds one of its most striking manifestations in these 'naked' choral statements without (or almost without) the ballast of instrumental historicity. In both movements the untransposed all-interval series runs through fifteen times and gives rise to a great variety of constellations of pitch, duration, dynamics and density, before it is drawn into a concluding prolation canon, the more directional nature of which gives the episodic progression a distinct final focus. 'I wanted a horizontal melodic construction encompassing all registers,' Nono later told Pauli, 'floating from sound to sound, from syllable to syllable: a line which sometimes consists of individual tones or pitches, and sometimes thickens into chords.' More significant than pitch, Nono emphasises, are the intervals and 'the relationship with surrounding musical figures; and these relationships are not confined

72 Nono, '*Composizione per orchestra n. 2 – Diario polacco '58* ' (1959), *Texte*, 125; *Scritti*, I, 436. The development continues in the choral works *Sarà dolce tacere* and «*Ha venido*» *Canciones para Silvia* (1960); see De Benedictis, 'Gruppo, linea e proiezioni armoniche'.

73 Lachenmann, 'Von Nono berührt' (1990), 298.

to what is called the vertical and the horizontal, but affect all levels of the composition, like a net which extends in all directions'.[74] Rigorous serial organisation thus served as a safety net: a new basis for pitch and interval relationships which prevented regression into tonal modes of thought at all times. As Lachenmann argues, Nono's incessant use of one and the same row is fundamentally grounded in the necessity 'to extinguish a material and to a certain extent force it into line, because its tendency to form premature interval relationships or even thematic figures was all too great'. However, Lachenmann also leaves no doubt that, within this 'serially manipulated process of extinction', traces of 'unbroken, merely reduced harmonic thematicism which are inevitably present in permanent chromaticism' not only remain in Nono's music, but lie at the very heart of its expressivity.[75]

A comparative look at movements nos. 2 and 9 will demonstrate how freely Nono composed within systematic limits, how subtle differences between the predetermined parametric settings open up totally different possibilities, and how they form the basis for new, expressive content. In movement no. 2, the series is consistently used in its original form. In no. 9, it is first read in retrograde but returns to its original form on its sixth run. The duration factors, too, are similar. For no. 2, Nono makes use of the first six numbers of the Fibonacci series: 1 2 3 5 8 13/13 8 5 3 2 1. This gradual progression from short to long and from long to short durations is further maintained with the applied permutation (first number to end) which ensures that the twelve pitches of the series are always coupled with a different set of duration factors. Additional differentiation results from the use of four duration values (crotchet divided by 2, 3, 4 and 5). Actual durations thus range between one quintuplet and thirteen quavers, whereby the choice of values allows for both contrast and assimilation (five quintuplets, for example, equal two quavers and thirteen quintuplets are shorter than five quavers).

For no. 9, Nono makes use of similar duration factors, but sets them up in a different manner. The first six odd prime numbers are polarised in pairs, moving from maximum to minimum contrast: 1 13 3 11 5 7/13 1 11 3 7 5. The distinct polarisation, however, is lost with the applied permutation. The distribution of long and short values is therefore much more irregular. The factors are applied to three duration values (crotchet divided by 3, 4 and 5) and also this choice allows for contrast and assimilation.

[74] Nono, 'Gespräch mit Hansjörg Pauli' (1969), trans. in Flamm, 'Preface', score, ix.

[75] Lachenmann, 'Luigi Nono oder Rückblick auf die serielle Musik' (1969), 250–52, 256.

Table 2.1 *Dynamics for movements nos. 2 and 9*

| | 1 | 2 | 3 | 4 | 5 | 6 | 7 | 8 | 9 | 10 | 11 | 12 |
|---|---|---|---|---|---|---|---|---|---|---|---|---|
| **No. 2** | *ppp* | *p* | *mp* | *mf* | *f* | *ppp* | *ppp–f* | *f–ppp* | *ppp–mf* | *mf–ppp* | *p–f* | *f–p* |
| **No. 9** | *ppp* | *pp* | *p* | *mp* | *mf* | *f* | *ppp–f* | *f–ppp* | *pp–mf* | *mf–pp* | *p–mp* | *mp–p* |

Dynamics, too, are organised serially. As shown in Table 2.1, Nono makes use of six simple and six compound dynamics for both movements. In both movements the quiet dynamics outnumber the loud dynamics and these series, too, are permutated. The application, however, is different: whereas each pitch is assigned its own series of dynamics in movement no. 2, the dynamics are linked to the duration-factor series in no. 9. Since each duration factor occurs twice per series, the composer is thus given the choice of two possible dynamics. Without abandoning the principle of constant change, this additional choice greatly benefits the dynamic balance.

Movement no. 2 is set for mixed chorus in eight parts, but the density of the vocal texture rarely goes beyond five parts. Melodic units are conditioned by the series constellations, though they generally exceed them in duration. The desired effect of 'floating from sound to sound, from syllable to syllable' is achieved by means of the sustained and carefully interwoven long durations (the inner symmetry of the duration-factor series is here fully exploited), while inner differentiation results from the always varied articulation of the shorter values. The relation between sustained chords and articulated figures constantly changes. In the first series constellation (bars 108–10), for example, the sustained durations are concentrated in the lower and middle voices, while the highest and lowest voice are assigned melodic figures in contrary motion: a falling diminished tenth in the first soprano answered by an ascending major sixth in the second bass. Contrary to Stockhausen's accusations, these two voices do articulate the text and the phrase continues with equally wide intervals in the first soprano ('muoio/ per un/ mondo', P1(12)–P2, bars 110–11).

The use of register is completely different at the end of the first part (P15, bars 139–42). The long durations are here sustained in a much higher register by the tenors, the first altos and the second sopranos. The C in the second soprano is in fact the highest note of the entire movement and occurs just once previously, in the expressive rendition of the word 'milioni' by the first soprano (P10–P12; bars 129–32). With this second high C comes the falling semitone progression G–F♯ in the first soprano.

From the sopranos' unison G thus emerges a setting of the word 'morti' (the dead) that is as much the result of the underlying serial system as it is a combination of the traditional semitone 'sigh' and the 'devil's interval' of the tritone. In the firm grip of Nono's serial organisation, such allusive pitch constellations are never experienced as 'mere plaisanteries à la Louis XVI' but, rather, the traditional affect is given new idiomatic rigour and expressiveness. With such structurally 'controlled de-construction', Lachenmann argues, 'music is driven into the space in which the archetype, ossified in conventional expression, [. . .] is liberated'.[76]

> [. . .] muoio per un mondo che splenderà con luce tanto forte con tale bellezza che il mio stesso sacrificio non è nulla. Per esso sono morti milioni di uomini sulle barricate e in guerra. Muoio per la giustizia. Le nostre idee vinceranno [. . .]
>
> [. . .] I am dying for a world which will shine with light of such strength and beauty that my own sacrifice is nothing. Millions of men have died for this on the barricades and in war. I am dying for justice. Our ideas will triumph [. . .][77]

Of the ten texts in *Il canto sospeso*, this opening text by the Bulgarian teacher and journalist Anton Popov (arrested for clandestine communist resistance in 1941, interrogated, tortured, and shot in the central prison of Sofia in July 1942 at the age of 26) is the only one which openly alludes to the communist cause and its importance to the European anti-fascist resistance. And the way it is set leaves no doubt that this movement is indeed, as Mila argues, the 'Credo' of this 'Messa di libertà'.[78] The highly idealistic statement is at first compressed into a constantly shifting and mutating choral texture. The density remains more or less constant and the focus falls on maximum inner differentiation. The concluding prolation canon then effectively homes in on the last two phrases: 'muoio per la giustizia' (I am dying for justice) and 'Le nostre idee vinceranno' (Our ideas will triumph). It is here that the choral collective suddenly thins down to a single pitch. The canon's four duration layers (one per duration value) evolve from the pitch A in middle register (second alto) and similarly thin down to the concluding pitch E♭ (first alto). In all four layers the duration factors move from the largest to the smallest number and back, and the layers are stacked symmetrically. The final two phrases of the text are thus drawn into an audible process of contraction and expansion, at the centre of which the

[76] Lachenmann, 'Von Nono berührt', 298. [77] Nono, *Il canto sospeso*, 'Appendix', 90.
[78] Mila, 'La linea Nono', 302.

words 'giustizia' and 'vinceranno' fall together, so that there is absolutely no misunderstanding: justice will prevail.

The main difference between movements nos. 2 and 9 is one of proportion. In the second movement, the concluding prolation canon is approximately half as long as the preceding fifteen constellations of the all-interval series (thirty-four versus fifteen 2/4 bars at the constant speed of ♩ = 60–66). In movement no. 9, this proportion is extended to an approximate 4:1 relationship. With a length of forty-nine bars (2/4, ♩ = *ca.* 54), Part I is significantly more drawn out, while the concluding prolation canon is given a similar time frame to that in no. 2 (eleven 2/4 bars, ♩ = 44). In other words, the fifteen runs of the series which took thirty-four bars to complete in no. 2 require an additional fifteen bars in no. 9. The prolation canon is further audibly separated by a pause, the mentioned speed change and a complete shift in sound colour as this last section is sung 'bocca chiusa' throughout.

> ... non ho paura della morte ...
>
> ... I am not afraid of death ...
>
> ... sarò calmo e tranquillo di fronte al plotone di esecuzione. Sono così tranquilli coloro che ci hanno condannato? ...
>
> ... I will be calm and at peace facing the firing squad. Are those who have condemned us equally at peace? ...
>
> ... vado con la fede in una vita migliore per voi ...
>
> ... I go in the belief of a better life for you ...

Unlike the texts of the three Greek resistance fighters in movement no. 3, these texts by Irina Maložon, Eusebio Giambone and Ellie Voigt do not stem from one country, and Nono does not layer or distinguish them in compositional terms. Instead, they are rendered one after another in a similar form to the opening text by Popov. Likewise, Maložon, Giambone and Voigt all actively supported the communist resistance, though this is not conveyed in the chosen texts. Irina Maložon, a member of the Russian youth organisation 'Komsomol', helped to print and disseminate pamphlets for the clandestine communist resistance. She was captured and shot by the Germans. The Italian typesetter Eusebio Giambone (1904–44), a contemporary of Gramsci, took part in the socialist experiment of the 'Ordine nuovo', progressive Soviet workers' councils in Turin (1920–21). As a militant communist, he was exiled to France in 1923. He was arrested and sent to the Vernay camp under the Vichy government in 1942, but expelled from France in 1943. On his return to Italy, Giambone joined the

Table 2.2 *Series and text distribution in movement no. 9*

| Author | Series | Text | Parts | Length | DFS |
|---|---|---|---|---|---|
| Maložon | R1 | *Non ho paura della morte* | 4 + timp | 6 bars (545–50) | ← 5 |
| Giambone | R2 | *Sarò calmo* | 8 + timp | 5 bars (551–55) | ← 4 |
| | R3 | *e tranquillo* | 8 + timp | 4 bars (555–59) | ← 3 |
| | R4 | *di fronte* | 7 + timp | 3 bars (559–62) | ← 2 |
| | R5 | *al plotone* | 9 + timp | 3 bars (562–64) | ← 1 |
| | R6 | *d'esecuzione* | 8 + timp | 4 bars (564–67) | 10 → |
| | R7 | *Sono tranquilli* | 8 + timp | 5 bars (566–70) | 9 → |
| | R8 | *coloro che ci hanno* | 7 + timp | 4 bars (569–72) | 8 → |
| + Voigt | R9 | *condannato/ Vado* | 9 + timp | 4 bars (572–75) | 7 → |
| Voigt | R10 | *vado con* | 6 + timp | 4 bars (574–77) | 6 → |
| | R11 | *la fede in* | 7 + timp | 6 bars (575–80) | 5 → |
| | R12 | *una vita* | 6 + timp | 5 bars (579–83) | 4 → |
| | R13 | *vita migliore* | 7 + timp | 5 bars (582–87) | 3 → |
| | R14 | *vita migliore* | 8 + timp | 5 bars (586–90) | 2 → |
| | R15 | *migliore per voi* | 6 + timp | 6 bars (589–94) | 1 → |

Resistance in Turin. On 31 March 1944, Italian fascists uncovered a committee meeting in the sacristy of San Giovanni, and Giambone was shot with four others on 5 April 1944. The German worker Ellie Voigt (32) was married to the communist Fritz Voigt. Like Maložon, she was arrested for dissemination of anti-fascist leaflets, and was decapitated by the Nazis on 8 December 1944.

Table 2.2 specifies the text, density, length and duration-factor series (DFS) for each of the fifteen series constellations in the first part of no. 9. In contrast to the first part of no. 2, in which the series constellations are consistently spread over 3 bars, those of no. 9 vary considerably in length, density and overlap. If the long values are constantly grouped together in no. 2 to give the choral texture body, this is not always the case in no. 9. Expansion and spaciousness are gained by lightening the choral texture. The four-part opening with its text by Maložon is an example in point. With a maximum overlap of just three parts, this statement is far more linear than any in movement no. 2. Nono begins with a single soprano voice. With values of medium length the line thickens and gradually moves into lower regions to settle on the longest value in the bass (C: 13 × 3). The first hexachord of the series (read in retrograde at this point) follows with similar transparency. Precisely because the longest durations are not superimposed but instead succeed each other, this pronouncedly linear opening is drawn out to maximum length. Similar transparency is regained only at the very end of the first part. R15 also spreads over 6 bars, begins with a single soprano voice, gradually thickens into a three-part texture and breaks off with the soft articulation of the short last pitch on timpani.

Between these exceedingly transparent series constellations, the choral texture gradually contracts and expands. The densest pitch constellations are reached fairly soon: R4 and R5 (bars 559–64) form the densest textures, and Nono makes use of the maximum number of nine vocal parts. Precisely at this moment of greatest density, the text refers to the firing squad. Up to this point the duration-factor series is read in retrograde (as is the all-interval series). In construction, though hardly in terms of audible perception, Nono thus makes use of compositional devices similar to those in the only other choral movement, no. 6. This is surely no coincidence, for the dramatic climax of no. 6a, too, directly addresses the issue of coming face to face with the executioners. The haunting image is here dramatically voiced in conjunction with the lowest instruments (bassoons, horns, trombones, cellos and double basses) and accompanied by evocative rolls on timpani. In no. 9, the image is set with a much greater degree of abstraction. The instrumental layer is no longer a confrontational force of equal strength to the choral collective, but radically reduced to delicate punctuation on timpani. In other words, the historicity of the instrumental layer that was so clearly exploited for the central confrontation between victims and aggressors is now deliberately reduced to the core in order to go beyond the archetype and give rise to maximum ambiguity. The association of the timpani with the military drum roll may still be at the back of the listener's mind, also on account of its prominent use in the preceding instrumental movement no. 8, but this role is now clearly overcome. Like the text itself, the extremely sparse punctuation of the contracting and expanding choral texture points both to the past and to the future. Motz, too, regards the short timpani beats as both 'a "memento" of the representation of brutal extermination in VIa' and 'a reminder not to forget'.[79] In view of the timpani's later role in *Al gran sole* as a herald of the revolutionary working class, not to mention its prominent use in the preceding *Liebeslied* (1954) and *Incontri* (1955), this most dominant percussion instrument here goes far beyond the connotations of the untuned military drums Nono favoured in earlier works. Subtly subversive, as in Beethoven's violin concerto, these timpani strokes ultimately carry a much more universal appeal and significance.

[79] Motz, *Konstruktion und Ausdruck*, 132.

## Looking back to *Fučík*

Shortly after the composer's death in 1990, Lachenmann wrote of the stringent urgency and expressive intensity of Nono's serial structuralism, in the light of which 'the seemingly familiar gesture is constantly refracted and transformed'.[80] It is precisely this structural rigour that distinguishes *Il canto sospeso* from the earlier *Fučík* project, the influence of which is evident from the annotations on form and forces in Nono's initial text compilation from the *Lettere*.[81] In terms of content, the connection is obvious. Julius Fučík (1903–43), a journalist by profession and one of the leaders of the Czech communist Resistance, was arrested by the Gestapo in 1942. Imprisoned in Prague, Fučík wrote his *Report from the Gallows*, a moving testimony to the communist struggle in Czechoslovakia, the belief in its final victory and a personal farewell to comrades and family. The script was smuggled out, page by page, by a prison guard, who handed it to Fučík's wife after the liberation. Fučík was transferred from Prague to Berlin-Plötzensee in August 1943 and executed on 8 September.

Fučík's 'prison notebook' was first published in Zagreb in 1946.[82] The first German translation came out in East Berlin in 1948.[83] The Italian edition, which immediately aroused Nono's interest, followed in 1951.[84] Nono's library also contains the programme for a Czech documentary drama on Fučík, produced at the Deutsches Theater (East Berlin) during the 1951/52 season. Nono may have attended this production or known of it through Paul Dessau.[85] In 1954, Sartre, too, spoke of Fučík. Addressing an assembly of workers in a factory outside Paris, he posed a question that had already concerned him in *Morts sans sépulture* (1946): 'And what about us; would we have resisted if we were tortured?'[86] With reference to Sartre and in the context of torture in Algeria, the figure of Fučík would later resurface in *Intolleranza*.

Back in 1951, Nono began his project with Fučík's arrest, torture and subsequent state of agony.[87] However, the vocal line that was to distinguish the figure of Fučík from the aggressive speech of the commanding Nazi was never completed. Furthermore, despite the use of distinct materials,

[80] Lachenmann, 'Nachruf', 293. [81] ALN 14.01.01/06–07.

[82] Fučík, *Reportáž psaná na oprátce* (Zagreb, 1946); *Report from the Gallows* (London, 1957).

[83] Fučík, *Reportage von unter dem Strang* (East Berlin, 1948).

[84] Fučík, *Scritto sotto la forca* (Milan, 1951).

[85] Buryakowsky, *Julius Fučík*, produced by Langhoff, scenography by the brothers Heartfield/Herzfelde, Deutsches Theater (East Berlin, 1951/52).

[86] Sartre, 'Julius Fucik', in Contat and Rybalka (eds.), *The Writings of Jean-Paul Sartre*, 301. Nono owned the first Italian edition of *Morts sans sépulture* (1949).

[87] A performance edition of the first episode was edited and premiered by Peter Hirsch (Munich, 6 May 2006).

a 'serie melodica' for Fučík and a 'serie armonica' for the Nazi, plus characteristic rhythmic cells derived from the spoken interrogation, the music is generally not marked by extreme contrast, but instead amounts to a typically slow moving, reflective and beautifully orchestrated arch form. This, it seems, is not yet the music of extremes with which Nono would later tackle situations of violent oppression: long floating lines and textures disrupted by dramatic thrusts of sound, orchestral and/or electronic gestures of utmost violence. Perhaps not for political reasons alone, the second and third episodes of Nono's *Fučík* were thus never written. Their content, however, was outlined in a letter to Scherchen. The second episode was to reflect Fučík's account of the Czechoslovakian class struggle and the third was to convey his certainty that the struggle will continue.[88] In affirmation of this belief, the work was to conclude with a quotation from Karl Liebknecht's last article 'Trotz alledem!' ['Despite Everything!' (1919)], published the day Liebknecht and Rosa Luxemburg were murdered: 'And if we are still alive when it is achieved – our programme is alive; it will rule the world of redeemed humanity.'[89] All this, as Rizzardi has shown, was planned on a much larger scale than is evident from the first episode: *Fučík* was to include several spoken parts, one or two soloists, chorus and large orchestra.[90]

Nono's initial notes on the form and forces of *Il canto sospeso* show that the work was at first envisaged in four parts. Bulgarian and Greek resistance was to feature in Part I, the resistance of Polish Jews in Part II, the Italian and French resistance in Part III, and the Russian and Austrian resistance in Part IV. Except for the three texts set in no. 9, all of the texts included in the finished work are already present in this initial compilation. Most were written by members of the communist resistance. Most striking in regard to the preliminary musical annotations is that Nono was still considering using recited speech. If Schoenberg's *A Survivor from Warsaw* always served as *the* model of anti-fascist music, the use of recited speech is also specifically linked to the earlier *Fučík* project. An additional text by the Greek communist Kostas Manolòpoulos is found at the end of Part I.

[88] Nono, letter to Scherchen, 2 June 1951 (ALN Scherchen/H 51–06–02 d), in Rizzardi, 'Verso un nuovo stile rappresentativo', 38; German in Stenzl, *Luigi Nono*, 23.

[89] Liebknecht, 'Trotz alledem!', *Die Rote Fahne* (15 January 1919), in *Gesammelte Reden und Schriften*, 676; as cited in Nono, letter to Scherchen (ALN Scherchen/H 51–06–02 d); Nono owned the following editions: Liebknecht, *Ausgewählte Reden, Briefe und Aufsätze* (Berlin, 1952); *Scritti politici* (Milan, 1971). Nono also read Piscator's political revue *Trotz alledem!* (1925), though he had not yet done so in 1951. Liebknecht was later reconsidered for *Al gran sole carico d'amore*.

[90] Rizzardi, 'Verso un nuovo stile rappresentativo', 39–42. In 1953, Nono further planned a work with texts by Fučík, Éluard, Rosenberg and an Italian resistance fighter; see Rizzardi, *ibid.*, 44.

Central to this text is the agony of waiting to be executed. As in *Fučík*, the first part of *Il canto sospeso* was thus initially envisaged to conclude with a state of agony. Next to this text by Manolòpoulos Nono notes 'CHORUS/ spoken and sung/ in rhythmic unison'.[91] Both the text and the idea of recited speech were later discarded, but one wonders whether the idea of a state of agony still found its way into the purely instrumental no. 4 which now concludes the first part.

The quotation of Liebknecht's 'Trotz alledem!', too, with its faith in the victory of the class struggle finds its equivalent in this first draft of *Il canto sospeso*. The final text of the compilation stems from a letter by the Austrian communist Oskar Klekner, written to his brother Rudolf shortly before their decapitation at the 'Landesgericht' in Vienna on 2 November 1943. It reads as follows: 'Now [. . .] it is our turn. We, too, will go to the gallows with our heads held high and hand over the flag of liberty to those still fortunate enough to experience the hour of freedom.'[92] If the *Bandiera rossa* was no longer considered adequate musical source material, it is all the more striking that Nono at first toyed with the idea of this final image of passing on the 'flag of liberty' to future generations such as his own. Klekner's text is marked 'FINALE' and allocated the forces 'S/A/T' and 'Coro'. In the margin Nono further notes 'Corale 4 parti' and, later, 'con coro come inizio'.[93] Other sketches show that Nono must for a while have adhered to the idea of a finale with text by Klekner (indicated by its country of origin, 'Austria'). Klekner was eventually replaced by Maložon, Giambone and Voigt. Although the communist cause is left unmentioned in this final choice of text, again there is hope for a better society: 'Vado con la fede in una vita migliore per voi' (I go in the belief of a better life for you). Not only are these last words repeated several times, but also the choral collective continues, 'bocca chiusa', and renders a prolation canon very similar to that with which Nono homes in on Popov's faith in social justice at the end of no. 2. The point of maximum intensity is now marked, not by words, but by three short beats on timpani (*pp–f–pp*). Perhaps the image of handing over the 'bandiera rossa' to future generations thus also subtly reverberates in these last notes of *Il canto sospeso*.

After this initial choice of text, Nono soon decided on three parts instead of four, and envisaged the work in twelve movements

[91] 'CORO/ parlato e cantato/ insieme stesso ritmo!', ALN 14.01.01/06.

[92] 'Ora [. . .] tocca a noi. Anche noi ci avviamo al capestro a testa alta e consegnamo la bandiera della libertà a quelli che avranno ancora la fortuna di vivere l'ora della libertà'; Klekner, letter to his brother (2 November 1943), *Lettere*, 61.

[93] ALN 14.01.01/06.

(4 + 3 + 5).[94] As it became more and more apparent that this 'freedom Mass [. . .] did not allow the radiant joy of a Gloria',[95] the idea of a grand finale was discarded and Nono eventually settled for nine movements in three parts, each with fewer constituent movements (4 + 3 + 2). Table 2.3 specifies the forces, duration values and use of the series for each movement.

The following movement-by-movement analysis focuses on the application of serial technique in conjunction with the 'historically conditioned' instrumental forces. If its integral serialism consistently places the work at the forefront of the avant-garde, the instrumentation is often deliberately exploited for its traditional associations: the 'domesticated' musical archetypes Lachenmann identifies as 'noble Belcanto figure, the fanfare, gestures of violence, gestures of protest and appeal, but also inner depth [Innigkeit] and mourning'.[96]

## Movement no. 1

Throughout *Il canto sospeso*, Nono pitches the diverse colour spectrum of woodwind, brass and percussion against the much more homogeneous – 'noble' – sonorities of the strings and the vocal forces. This fundamental dichotomy is effectively introduced in the purely instrumental opening movement. As discussed in my 2006 analysis, the all-interval series is here permutated by means of the so-called 'tecnica degli spostamenti' (technique of displacement), which allows much more flexible and continuously mutating pitch constellations.[97] The movement's overall form has been

[94] Drafts of the overall form are found in sketches ALN 14.02.01/01–04; two are reproduced in Motz, *Konstruktion und Ausdruck*, 187–88. An initial selection of text indicates up to fifteen movements (ALN 14.01.01/06–07).

[95] Mila, 'La linea Nono', 302. [96] Lachenmann, 'Von Nono berührt', 298.

[97] The technique was first identified by Borio and Rizzardi in the early 1990s in sketches of Maderna's *Improvvisazione n. 1* (1951) and Nono's *Composizione per orchestra* (1951). Its use in *Il canto sospeso* was only fully understood by Borio and Motz in 1997, just after the publication of Motz's *Konstruktion und Ausdruck*. Motz subsequently published a revised analysis of the first movement, while Borio explained the pitch structure of movement no. 4; Motz, 'Konstruktive Strenge'; Borio, 'Sull'interazione'. On the 'tecnica degli spostamenti' further see Rizzardi, 'La «Nuova Scuola Veneziana»'. Verzina uses the term 'tecnica della mutazione'. Maderna's use of this technique is further explained in Neidhöfer, 'Bruno Madernas flexibler Materialbegriff' and 'Bruno Maderna's Serial Arrays'. Considering this substantial body of research, I think Iddon is wrong to view Maderna's *Quartetto per archi in due tempi* (1955) as his 'only excursion into a more fully fledged serial world' and to claim 'that Nono was doing his best to bring Maderna into a serial fold where he had no place'; Iddon, *New Music at Darmstadt*, 121/144.

Table 2.3 *Formal overview*

| Part | I | | | | II | | | | III | |
|---|---|---|---|---|---|---|---|---|---|---|
| Mvt. | 1 | 2 | 3 | 4 | 5 | 6a | 6b | 7 | 8 | 9 |
| Forces | wind<br>brass<br>timp.<br>strings | chor. | T/A/S<br>wind<br>brass<br>strings | wind<br>brass<br>perc.<br>strings | T<br>solo<br>instr. | chor.<br>low<br>instr.<br>timp. | chor.<br>high<br>strings | S/S/A<br>solo<br>instr. | wind<br>brass<br>timp. | chor.<br>timp. |
| DV | 2<br>3<br>4<br>5<br>7 | 2<br>3<br>4<br>5 | 4 | 3<br>4<br>5<br>7 | 4<br>5<br>6 | 3<br>4<br>5 | 3<br>5 | 4 | 3<br>4<br>5<br>7 | 3<br>4<br>5 |
| Series | pitch<br>perm. | P | pitch perm.. | pitch<br>perm. | P + 4<br>add.<br>series | P/R<br>reduced<br>pitch | P | 12<br>add.<br>series | P | R/P |

outlined by Motz.[98] The length of the thirteen sections ranges from one to twenty bars. Up to bar 68, which breaks off with a single beat on timpani over a sustained E♭ in the first violins, the two instrumental factions are essentially assigned different compositional processes and only come together in a final *tutti* section of fifteen bars (53–67) plus one (68). Throughout this first part, the duration layers of the wind and timpani include rests, while those of the strings progress seamlessly. The pitch constellations in the wind are further drawn out by a slower speed. Their 4/8 bars are conducted in quavers and the speed stays more or less constant at ♪ = 92 (♩ = 46). In contrast, the 3/4 bars of the strings are conducted in crotchets with the speed ♩ = 60 gradually accelerating to ♩ = 82.

Wind and timpani begin the movement with a falling semitone motif in the trumpets over a chromatic block in the lower brass, followed by a higher, less dissonant and more sustained pitch constellation in the flutes and trumpets, accompanied by a fading roll on timpani. The trumpets are clearly the protagonists of this opening, while the overall decrescendo of the accompanying instruments prepares the ear for the exceedingly quiet first string entry. After the combination of all five duration layers in the opening wind section, the muted violins emerge with quasi-tonal simplicity: a descending G-major arpeggio combined with the most straightforward duration layer of the quaver. This brief moment of 'tonality' is, as I have shown, not at odds with the underlying serial system, but in fact a result of the strict application of its rules.[99] Not unlike Alban Berg, Nono here momentarily exploits the predetermined serial system for its tonal possibilities (though it was probably not set up with these possibilities in mind) and begins the emerging string layer with a fleeting memento of the musical past.

As the two factions alternate, the seamless lines of the strings gradually gain in momentum: up to bar 48 they steadily increase in length, density (number of duration layers), ambitus and dynamic contrast. Greater presence of sound is further attained by a combination of muted and normal sound in the fourth and last of the string sections. Meanwhile, the wind and timpani gradually mellow and dwindle down to an exceedingly quiet combination of just two duration layers in lower and middle register (bars 34–40: quavers, quintuplets, *ppp–p*). This section does not include the timpani and is almost exclusively scored for woodwind. Brass and timpani reassert themselves in full force after the last string section. With another 'fanfare' and a dramatic roll on timpani (now marked *ppp–f*), they lead into the first *tutti* passage. The strings adopt the speed of the wind

98 Motz, *Konstruktion und Ausdruck*, 35.

99 'The Song Unsung', 109–10.

instruments, and both instrumental groups now make use of all five duration layers. Owing to the continued division between seamless pitch progression and the inclusion of rests, however, this dense *tutti* is clearly led by the traditional protagonists of the symphony orchestra, and the opening brass interventions are gradually superseded by the much less strident sound of the woodwind.

The opening of Part II (bar 69) radically reverses this traditional relationship. Now the pitches of the wind progress seamlessly while the string layer is much less prominent and porous with rests. Another striking contrast is the basic level of dynamics. Whereas the whole of Part I was predominantly quiet with occasional outbursts into *f*, the basic dynamic is now *fff*. With maximum density in both instrumental groups, this dramatic climax of the movement clearly puts the traditional supremacy of the strings into question. However, the raucous thrusts of sound in the wind and timpani do not last, and typically make way for a concluding lyrical apotheosis: woodwind and strings join forces, ascend into hitherto unheard heights and bring the movement to a close in the upper-registral stratosphere.

## Movement no. 3

While the compositional system advocates equality on all levels, the hierarchical tradition of instrumentation is exploited to subtly undermine this ideal. In this sense Nono's serialism reveals itself as intrinsically dialectical and indeed immensely political in musical terms alone. This 'politics' of instrumentation pervades the whole of *Il canto sospeso* and becomes ever more apparent in the movements with text. After the truly 'equal' choral movement no. 2, the three vocal soloists make their first appearance together with the orchestra. As Nono himself explains, three texts of Greek resistance fighters are here merged in order to 'formulate that which all three situations have in common with heightened intensity'.[100] The three texts are assigned a compositional layer each. All three layers are generated by means of the 'tecnica degli spostamenti' and assigned a vocal soloist and a matching set of wind instruments:

| | | |
|---|---|---|
| Layer 1 | Tenor; oboe, bassoon, trombone | $c–c^3$ |
| Layer 2 | Alto; clarinet, bass clarinet, horn | $f–f^3$ |
| Layer 3 | Soprano; flute, trumpet | $c^1–c^4$ |

[100] Nono, 'Text – Musik – Gesang', II (1960), in *Texte*, 53.

The three layers are generated with different, yet similar, parameter settings, and unification is further guaranteed by the use of a common duration value (semiquavers).[101] Not one but three simultaneous projections of the all-interval series create a sense of 'heightened intensity' throughout. Compared with the first movement, there are thus three times as many pitches at play at any one time. Such amassing of pitch, however, never just allows an increase in sound, but also, as Lachenmann acutely observes, permits 'a refraction of this potential of rhetorical force by means of a sometimes utopian concept of differentiation within'.[102] In this movement, the layered pitch structure is essentially the basis for a play with background and foreground textures, and the dialectic between instrumentation and serial organisation is exploited for this purpose.

The movement evolves in three sections: a prelude for wind and brass (bars 158–76), a central part, in which fragments of each of the three texts are led by the respective soloists and additional strings (Part A: bars 177–219), and a joint rendition of the tenor's final phrase, accompanied by wind and brass only (Part B: bars 219–39). With just five actual durations and a comparatively fast speed (♪ = 152), Nono sets an unusually clear pulse, the urgency of which is immediately felt in the opening wind prelude.[103] Precisely because of the single duration value and the extremely limited range of durations (1, 3, 5, 7 and 9 semiquavers), this passage is actually perceived not as a polyphony of instrumental layers (which it is in compositional terms), but rather, like the concluding prolation canon of the preceding choral movement, as an increasing and decreasing mass of pitches that contracts and intensifies with the addition of ever shorter and higher pitches and then expands and recedes into lower registers once more as the upper soprano and alto layers gradually fade out.

The entry of the female soloists and first violins marks the beginning of Part I. The stark contrast in colour immediately reinforces the fundamental divide between wind and strings set up in movement no. 1. Throughout this part the soloists create an almost entirely seamless vocal band and provide the music with a strong focus in the middle register. This vocal band is led in alternation by the solo singer whose text is being interpreted. Table 2.4 lists the texts, their compositional layers and the series elements used for the sung passages.

The act of composition lies not only in the combination of the three layers (which basically run through in their predetermined form, with some

101 For the serial generation of the three layers see 'The Song Unsung', 102–109.
102 Lachenmann, 'Von Nono berührt', 302.
103 On the duration structure see 'The Song Unsung', 103–105.

Table 2.4 *Movement no. 3, Part I (bars 177–219)*

| Bars | Layer | Text (soloists & strings) | Series elements |
|---|---|---|---|
| 177–81 | S | *mi portano a Kessariani*<br>they are taking me to Kessariani | S3 (1–10) |
| 181–85 | T | *m'impiccheranno*<br>they are hanging me | T3 (2–6) |
| 185–90 | A | *oggi ci fucileranno*<br>today they will shoot us | A3 (1–8) |
| 190–96 | S | *insieme ad altri sette*<br>together with seven others | S5 (6–12)<br>S6 (1–4) |
| 195–97 | T | *Perchè*<br>Because | T4 (9–10) |
| 197–99 | | [wind only] | [S1, A4, T4] |
| 199–205 | T | *sono patriota*<br>I am a patriot | T5 (2–8) |
| 202–14 | A | *moriamo da uomini per la patria*<br>we die as men for our homeland | A5 (1–12)<br>A6 (1–5) |
| 214–19 | | [wind only] | [A6] |

exceptions in the soprano layer), but also in the determination of the leading voice which governs the choice of pitch for the vocal band and its embedding string sonorities.[104] The vocal band begins with S3 of the soprano layer. This particular series contains pitch sets of two to four pitches. Example 2.2 demonstrates how Nono allocates these pitch sets to the leading solo soprano part, the supporting vocal parts and strings (in this case the first violins). The first ten sets of S3 are used for the nine syllables of this almost continuous opening vocal statement. When the solo tenor continues the vocal line with pitch sets 2–6 of T3 at the end of bar 199, the soprano layer continues in the wind (flutes and trumpets, S3–S5), though selected pitches are also assigned to the strings. Only when the vocal band is once again led by the solo soprano (bars 190–96) does the soprano layer move back into the foreground and become entirely embedded in violin sonorities while the other layers recede into the wind. The instrumentation thus highlights the leading compositional layer, but also subtly overrides the pitch predisposition, insofar as the string sonorities are not always layer-bound. With a reflected combination of pitch from the reservoir as a whole, Nono makes use of the pre-generated layers to play with foreground and background

[104] The overlap of layers is shown in 'The Song Unsung', 103–109.

(a)

**Example 2.2** (a) *Il canto sospeso* no. 3, reduction of mm 177–82. (b) S3 as generated by the 'tecnica degli spostamenti'.

textures. Apart from a brief rhetorical pause after the word 'perchè' (because), the solo voices and strings seamlessly interweave the chosen texts. The last two overlap slightly (bars 202–5) and thus intensify the homogeneous linearity and pronounced lyricism that lifts this central vocal band out of the much more jagged background texture of the wind. As song comes to an end in the alto layer, series A6 continues in the five trumpets with a subtle increase in dynamics (from *ppp–p–mf* to *p–mf–f* ) emphasised by a menacing final crescendo.

Part II begins with the voices alone. Together they render the tenor's last phrase 'Tuo figlio se ne va, non sentirà le campane della libertà' (Your son is leaving, he will not hear the freedom bells). Without the strings, the 'naked' vocal sound attains a new state of unity and clarity. The text is no longer assigned to the leading voice alone, but articulated in rhythmic unison by all three singers. At first the soloists are mostly coupled in pairs, but the final words 'della libertà' are sung by all. Throughout this final phrase it is impossible to perceive who leads, though again the pitches stem from alternate compositional layers. Example 2.3 explains the serial structure of this last vocal phrase and indicates which compositional layers run on in the wind before all of the remaining pitches are compressed into an evocative final outburst of flutter-tonguing in wind and brass, which, in the context of the finality of these particular texts, takes on truly sinister connotations.

(a)

**Example 2.3** (a) *Il canto sospeso* no. 3: reduction of mm 219–35. (b) S3–4, A7 and T6 as generated by the 'tecnica degli spostamenti'.

(b)

**Example 2.3** (*cont.*)

## Movement no. 4

The three texts of the Greek resistance set in movement no. 3 were initially to be followed by a choral setting of the last words of the Greek communist headteacher Kostas Manolòpoulos (1905–44). Manolòpoulos was arrested by the Germans on 15 January 1944, tortured, and shot without trial on 17 May 1944. Written in blood, the following text was left behind on the wooden panels of his cell:

> 12 hours of agony 7am to 6pm for the shooting of Kostas Manolòpoulos, headteacher of the primary school Kallithea IX, 16.5.44. Should my family be informed I am dying for Freedom.

The circumstances of this testimony remind me of the choice of text for the middle movement of Górecki's Third Symphony (1976): a prayer inscribed on the walls of a Gestapo jail in 1944 by an eighteen-year-old girl from the Polish highlands. Though Górecki's unabashedly tonal setting of this prayer has moved millions, to me it verges on that 'cheap sentimentality' which, according to Mila, forbids surviving partisans to lay music on the tombs of their dead.[105] Nono's sinuous modernism and the emotionally assured decision to discard texts such as that by Manolòpoulos set *Il canto sospeso* worlds apart from the garish poster colours of Górecki's postmodern symphony.

The purely instrumental movement no. 4 which follows the testimonies of the Greek resistance (and was later reused to link the interrogation and

105 Mila, 'La linea Nono', 311.

torture scenes in the first act of *Intolleranza*) is a prime example of the use of the 'tecnica degli spostamenti'.[106] The underlying pitch structure is the same as that of the first movement, but its application is much more straightforward. The movement thus lends itself to explaining the permutation technique practiced by Maderna and his disciples in the early to mid fifties.[107] It is also an example of extreme compositional restraint. The predetermined pitch structure runs through once, the register is confined to a single octave, and even the use of wind and percussion is serialised. Yet this strictest of movements is also one of the most moving – a musical manifestation of Mies van der Rohe's modernist dictum 'less is more'. What evolves here is a simple, slow-moving arch form, the gradual contraction and expansion of which is emphasised by means of increasing and decreasing dynamics covering the whole range from *ppp* to *fff*. Flutter-tonguing in the wind and tremolo on percussion subtly internalise the violent gesture which concluded movement no. 3 and add to the anxiety and tension that build up in this instrumental afterthought. As the densest point is reached, flutter-tonguing is abandoned and the music recedes into purer regions. Tremolo on percussion is maintained throughout, however, and adds much to the poetry of the evolving texture. The tuned percussion instruments (vibraphone, xylophone, marimba and bells) make up a third of the twelve instruments which realise this serial structure. In addition, Nono makes use of untuned percussion (cymbals and drums of different sizes) for the sixteen elements of the pitch structure which happen to contain no pitch.[108] Of all the movements in *Il canto sospeso*, no. 4 thus has the largest percussion section and also uniquely makes use of tubular bells, no doubt with reference to the last words sung in no. 3: 'Your son is leaving, he will not hear the freedom bells.'[109]

This allusive layer of wind and percussion is unobtrusively driven by the string sound that envelops it. The strings double each pitch, hold it until the end of its next occurrence, pause and then sustain the same pitch again from its next entry. Marked *crescendo* and *decrescendo*, these sustained string pitches gradually increase and decrease in dynamics and, on a much larger scale, translate into sound (and silence) the proportions of the number square which determines the pointillist structure in the wind and percussion. Once again, the compositional act is thus intrinsically

106 See Borio, 'Sull'interazione', 15–17. 107 See 'The Song Unsung', 99–102.

108 See Example 1 in 'The Song Unsung', 137.

109 With similar connotations, tubular bells later also feature in Nono's settings of Éluard's *La liberté* (1942) in *Intolleranza 1960* (I:6) and of Pavese's *In the morning you always come back* in *Al gran sole carico d'amore* (II:4).

linked to the fundamental dichotomy between the wind and percussion on the one hand and the strings on the other. Within the strictest of limits, freedom manifests itself in the subtle differentiation of these layers, and it is in their constantly mutating interaction that lyrical expression takes hold. The extreme reduction of means, the exceptionally clear formal layout and the fundamental concern with envelopment and purity of sound in this movement are among the compositional issues which are later also at the very heart of *Prometeo.*

## Movement no. 6a/b

The fundamental division between wind and strings is brought to a head in the central part of *Il canto sospeso*. Between the emotional outcry of the young Polish shepherd Chaim (no. 5) and the measured farewell of the Russian resistance fighter Lyubov Shevtsova (no. 7), the sixth movement sets the following text by Esther Srul:

> . . . le porte s'aprono. Eccoli i nostri assassini. Vestiti di nero. Ci cacciano dalla sinagoga. Com'è duro dire addio per sempre alla vita così bella . . .

> . . . the doors open. Here are our murderers. Dressed in black. They drive us out of the synagogue. How hard it is to say goodbye for ever to life which is so beautiful . . .

This text is unique in that it names and points directly at the executioners. The testimony is one of about 100 inscriptions on the wall of the Great Synagogue of Kovel. In this rural town (now part of the Ukraine) the Nazis wiped out 18,000 Jews in less than two months (August–September 1942). They were herded into the main synagogue, held without food and water, and eventually driven out to face mass execution. Esther Srul was among those shot on 15 September 1942, before the synagogue itself was set on fire.

Nono's setting of this text is the dramatic climax of the work and indeed one of the most gripping pieces of integral serialism.[110] The scenario of a community coming face to face with their executioners is aptly set for the choral collective. With tone repetition on extremely few pitches, the most expansive range of duration factors (2–17) and dynamics ranging from *ppp* to *fff*, the first four phrases of the text are cast into four internally fluctuating vocal blocks. For the chorus, 'the doors open' on the last pitch of the series in the lower middle register. This unison E♭ gradually thickens into a six-part choral texture (split inner voices) and breaks off simultaneously after nine

[110] Time and again this was confirmed to me by the reactions of my students.

bars (bar 327). The extreme pitch reduction conveys both a sense of confinement and unity. With loud dynamics accumulating towards the end of the phrase, it seems that the voices increasingly brace themselves against the orchestral forces. This is a battle, however, that is unlikely to be won, given that the consortium of low instruments is led by four trombones, four horns and two timpani – instrumental forces easily able to overpower a chorus, especially with dynamics branching out to *fff* and emphatic tremolo on the timpani. With maximum semitone friction, all instruments begin simultaneously on the first four pitches of the series (A, B♭, A♭ and B). The clash between the vocal unison and the chromatic cluster in the low orchestra is greatly enhanced by the serially differentiated articulation and dynamics, and it is on this level that the struggle between the human voice and the instrumental 'machinery of repression' attains its true *raison d'être* in performance.

The next phrase in the chorus – 'Here are our murderers' – is almost twice as long as the first (seventeen bars) and far less dense. The chorus continues to render the series in retrograde and is now assigned the pitches E and D. The female voices are consistently assigned the pitch E, the male voices the pitch D; and both are sung in the same lower middle register as the preceding E♭. The chorus is once again notated in six parts (split outer voices), but the vocal density of the phrase does not go beyond five parts (three female and two male voices). This second phrase of the chorus begins two bars before the end of the first orchestral block, which has gradually been reduced to one bassoon, two horns and two trombones. As the choral phrase intensifies, the orchestra, too, resumes in force. The second instrumental block gradually exposes the next three pitches of the series (G, C and F♯) in wind and timpani, and breaks off almost simultaneously in bar 337. The chorus, however, has not yet completed its second phrase, and the key word 'assassini' (murderers) is now eerily combined with the series-framing tritone E♭–A, or 'SA' in its German transliteration. This tone-symbolism prompted Huber to identify the orchestra as 'the voice of the murderers'.[111] While the allusion to SS and SA may well have been intended, the music is surely much more ambiguous. After all, also the chorus begins with the repeated rendition of E♭ – SS. If the vocal forces represent the 'human' voice of the victims and those who resisted, is it not particularly significant that, at the very moment at which the murderers are named, the instruments take on the first sung pitch of this movement, i.e. a human dimension of their own, albeit as part of the traditional 'devil's

[111] Huber, 'Luigi Nono: Il canto sospeso VIa, b', 66.

interval'? The dominant layer, at this moment in time, is that of the five-part chorus (SSATB). The quiet entry of the tritone 'SA' on just two trombones and the double basses is almost effaced, though the harmony is then sustained for seventeen bars (up to bar 349; A only up to bar 354) and soon dramatically intensifies with the tremolo on timpani.

As Huber has shown, the four blocks of the chorus and the orchestra are mirrored in terms of form, density and timing and combined in contrary motion (resulting in a slightly displaced overlap of the pitch sets).[112] The pitches of the series, too, are at first combined in contrary motion, with sets from one to four pitches in each layer and each combined set adding up to five pitches. This progression is deviated from, however, with the introduction of the tritone E♭–A in the orchestra. Thereafter, the last pitch in the orchestral layer (B♭) is most logically regarded as part of the pitch set of the vocal layer (pitch 11 of the series in retrograde). In the end, it is thus the chorus which emerges stronger from this dramatic confrontation between the 'voice that names' and that of violent repression. While the final choral block builds up a dense eight-part texture and breaks off simultaneously, the instrumental layer is gradually reduced to a single *ppp* beat on timpani that briefly anticipates the poignant reuse of this instrument at the very end of the work.

From this last block of movement no. 6a emerges one of the most magical moments of the piece as a whole: the last and first pitch of the series R and O is sung *ppp* and *bocca chiusa* by the tenors and sustained without any accompaniment at all until the altos subtly resume semitone friction two bars (about 4″) later. The unprecedented purity of this single, wordless vocal A and the extreme restraint with which it is rendered in the high register of the tenors anticipate the clarity of Nono's late vocal writing of the 1980s. In this brief moment of absolute 'Klarsein' (clarity), the movement changes into its total opposite. As observed by Huber, low register becomes high register, dissonant blocks become soaring melodic lines, syllabic articulation turns melismatic or is altogether abolished with 'bocca chiusa' and the 'quasi bocca chiusa' intonation of vowels, the wide dynamic range is reduced to six simple dynamics (*ppp*, *pp*, *p*, *mp*, *mf*, *f*) and the heterogeneous sound of low wind, strings and percussion is replaced by the warm, homogeneous sound of the strings.[113] Extrovert drama is effectively replaced by introvert reflection for the final phrase 'How hard it is to say goodbye for ever to life which is so beautiful!'

[112] *Ibid.*, 68. [113] *Ibid.*, 72.

As in the choral movements nos. 2 and 9, the series here simply runs through in succession (eleven times, plus an additional A in vln 1). In this case, however, the pitch reservoir is shared between the chorus and the strings.[114] Consequently, the vocal phrases are markedly more linear and hardly involve more than three parts. Embedded in the high string sound (viola and cello are consistently notated in the treble clef), it is as if the solo voices of the Greek resistance multiplied and lifted themselves out of the firm grip of the wind. To the words 'addio per sempre', however, a high trumpet breaks in with the falling semitone D–C♯, sustained over seven bars. Despite the extremely high degree of abstraction of this single wind intervention (Nono refrains from any rhythmic characterisation and keeps the dynamic at a constant *f*), the mere sound of the high trumpet – with its historical baggage of military association – serves as a potent reminder of the by now clearly established association of wind and percussion with violence and oppression.

In the context of *Prometeo*, Massimo Cacciari would later speak of 'the memory of an atemporal – insoluble – grief' in *Il canto sospeso* as a 'memory of what we have not experienced' and 'a memory of a path *not* taken'.[115] This concept of looking back into the past in order to turn our gaze into the future is perhaps most keenly felt in this second part of movement no. 6, in which the traditional 'beauty' of the string sound carries and lifts the voices into utopian heights. Out of the dramatic, yet also distinctly static, blocks of sound in the first half, the memory of 'life which is so beautiful' emerges as the truly moving component, and this 'moving' quality is furthermore enhanced by the unusually static entry of the trumpet. By now the dialectics of instrumentation has been established to such a degree that both the strings and the abstract intervention of the trumpet take on the function of sound symbols. The bold association of the phrase 'How hard it is to say goodbye for ever to life which is so beautiful!' with the traditional 'beauty' of the high string sound is a particularly poignant example of Nono's awareness of the 'historic functional limits of melodic instruments' and their deliberate exploitation for maximum emotional impact. Were it not for the 'safety net' of serial organisation, the combination of high strings with such drawn-out, melismatic choral lyricism could easily verge on sentimentality. As it is, the instrumentation potently symbolises the beautiful life which is left behind for ever. In this

[114] Each vocal part is assigned a string instrument: S/vln I, A/vln II, T/vla, B/vcl; 'The Song Unsung', 121.

[115] Cacciari, letter to Nono, 22 June 1980 (Cacciari/M 80–06–22 m; ALN 51.07.02/07); see Chapter 7.

daring compositional glimpse of the musical past, this music is truly 'memory of a path not yet taken'.

## Webernian lyricism

The dramatic contrast between movements nos. 6a and 6b is greatly enhanced by the pronounced lyricism of the two adjacent movements. With the orchestra stripped down to a transparent chamber ensemble, solo song comes into true being in these two movements. And, precisely for this pinnacle of vocal lyricism, Nono decides to go beyond the unifying all-interval series on A and makes use of several additional rows and strict canonic procedures. At the peak of serial rationalisation, few of Nono's colleagues would have used such an array of rows in such Webernian fashion. Though he was reprimanded by Stockhausen for not paying tribute on the tenth anniversary of Webern's death,[116] Nono's compositional practice was, in fact, much more indebted to Webern at the time than Stockhausen's own. With *Gruppen* (1955–57), Stockhausen was moving on to series substitution, meaning that the twelve all-interval series which structure this work are no longer actually heard. Instead, the register and interval relationship of each pitch is used to determine the time- and pitch-spectrum of an entire 'group'.[117] While Stockhausen thus breaks with the relentless repetition of all twelve notes, Nono deliberately turns to the tried and tested methods of the Second Viennese School to attain new levels of expression in his own music.

Although Webern generally features far less in Nono's texts and interviews than Schoenberg, the dedicatee of *Intolleranza 1960* whose oeuvre (music theatre above all) remained of huge importance throughout Nono's entire career, I believe that Webern was of great significance to Nono and not quite as secondary to his compositional thought in the early and mid fifties as Iddon argues.[118] Though Nono mostly avoided theoretical discourse, two fairly rudimentary lectures on the 'Development of the Serial

116 'Heute wollte ich Dir nur sagen, daß ich Dich sehr blöd finde! Wie kannst Du zum 10. Todestag Weberns so unbeteiligt sein! Und wenn es nur ein ganz kurzes Bekenntnis gewesen wäre. Schaf! Grüße an Nuria (nicht an Dich): sie ist immer viel lieber als Du!!' (Today I just wanted to tell you that I think you are very stupid! How can you be so detached on the 10th anniversary of Webern's death! If it were only a very short tribute. Sheep! Greetings to Nuria (not to you): she is always much kinder than you!!) Stockhausen, postcard to Nono, 3 August 1955 (Stockhausen/K 55–08–03 m, ALN).

117 For a detailed analysis of the serial structure of *Gruppen* see Misch, *Zur Kompositionstechnik Karlheinz Stockhausens.*

118 Iddon, *New Music at Darmstadt.*

Technique' (presented at Gravesano in 1956 and Darmstadt in 1957) give insight into his understanding of the music of the Second Viennese School. The first lecture focuses on the characteristic traits of the series of Schoenberg's *Serenade* op. 24 and the *Variations for Orchestra* op. 31 as well as Webern's *Chamber Symphony* op. 21 before moving on to their 'logical extension' in works by Boulez (*Structures* I) and Stockhausen (*Piano Piece* No. 1) and in works of his own (*Il canto sospeso*).[119] The second lecture discusses Schoenberg's *Variations for Orchestra* op. 31 and Webern's *Variations* op. 30 in much greater detail than any of the works of Nono's own generation (Boulez's *Structures* I, Maderna's String Quartet, Stockhausen's *Studie II* and *Zeitmaße*, as well as his own *Incontri*).[120] In this second lecture Nono distinguishes three historical stages of serialism: Schoenberg's thematic use of the row, the 'new structural function' of the row independently of 'characteristic thematic figuration (*Gestalt*)' in Webern's music and the extension of serial principles to elements other than pitch and series projection by means of permutation in the music of the young generation. Both lectures show that Nono was particularly interested in the reduced interval content and the inner symmetries of Webern's rows which result in overlap and radical reduction of the basic material. In contrast to the thematic exposition and use of all four forms of the row (O, R, I, RI) in Schoenberg's *Variations for Orchestra*, within which the four-tone motif B–A–C–H functions as an 'independent thematic–formal element', Nono repeatedly homes in on the characteristic 'ambiguity' of Webern's series, and his analysis of the *Variations* op. 30 largely focuses on the exploitation of this structural ambiguity. Selected examples show how the varied combinations of the overlapping 'four-tone motifs' result in new pitch configurations that essentially break with the row's 'characteristic thematic figuration' and thereby take on a 'new structural function'.

As with Schoenberg, however, Nono did not consider Webern's music solely in terms of technique. When invited to co-host the Darmstadt seventieth-anniversary tribute to Webern in 1953 (an event discussed in detail by Iddon), Nono accepted enthusiastically and immediately expressed his intention 'to say something new' against those who regarded Webern's music solely 'as high abstract mathematics'.[121] In the midst of praise for Webern's technical innovations, Nono thus warned of an all too

[119] Nono, 'Zur Entwicklung der Serientechnik' (1956), *Texte*, 16–20; *Scritti*, I, 9–14.

[120] Nono, 'Die Entwicklung der Reihentechnik' (1957), *Texte*, 21–33; *Scritti*, I, 19–42.

[121] Nono, letter to Steinecke, 22 June 1953, in Borio and Danuser (eds.), *Im Zenit der Moderne*, I, 216; in Iddon, *New Music at Darmstadt*, 89–102 (90).

schematic understanding of his music. 'Webern's artistic consciousness', he argued, 'clearly understood the demands of our time [. . .] Expression and form in Webern are a compressed synthesis, in which the essential human qualities of today may be recognised.'[122] Such emphasis on the human qualities, on music as a 'sounding experience' rather than an object of mechanical construction, is typical of Nono but was merely shrugged off with bemused irony at the time.[123] Movements nos. 5 and 7 of *Il canto sospeso*, however, are a sounding reaffirmation of this historically aware, uncompromisingly humanist attitude which essentially had its roots in Maderna's equally humanist teaching of music of all ages. With Maderna, Nono later recalled, Webern's music was encountered and studied comparatively, in view of specific compositional problems:

> I have been asked many times: 'why is there C♯ after C?' I don't know: after C there could be an eighth of a tone, or any other sound. These are the mysteries of composition, and Bruno knew how to introduce them to me in incomparable fashion. Bruno also got me to approach such secrets through the study of Webern. I remember that we compared Webern to Schubert, to Schumann, to Wolf, to Heinrich Isaac and to Haydn. [. . .] In Webern a single pitch is often like an entire melody by Schubert. The sound quality, the articulation, and the way it develops and fades out contain an entire melodic arch in the most concentrated synthesis. Thus it is not a matter of this or that individual sound being placed like a stone in a mosaic, and this concept of sound was, as you know, the great strength of Maderna as a conductor. [. . .] The comparison to Haydn is clearer if one takes into consideration Webern's quartet, in which one finds a construction of pulsations within the rhythms and ritornellos that is reminiscent of that in Haydn's quartets. Webern is often accused of rhythmic poverty, but actually with this inner pulsation within an apparently simple movement recollection of Haydn explodes into one's mind. I am telling you these things because it was precisely on this terrain that the dispute regarding interpretations of Webern at Darmstadt flared up. On the one hand, there were Bruno and I, who thought in this way, on the other, Henri Pousseur and Stockhausen, who produced their statistical analyses of Webern's *Concerto for Nine Instruments*.[124]

[122] Nono, 'Über Anton Webern', in Borio and Danuser (eds.), *Im Zenit der Moderne*, III, 63–64; *Scritti*, I, 7.

[123] Eimert envisaged the event as follows: 'I thought that I would start off and, for a couple of minutes, present the general situation from the perspective of the young composers. Then Nono would say something about the hu-uman ['das Määnschliche'] for 5 to 6 minutes, followed by Stockhausen talking shop for *ca*. 15 minutes. I would then include Boulez's contribution in my conclusion.' Eimert, letter to Steinecke (22 June 1953), in Borio and Danuser (eds.), *Im Zenit der Moderne*, I, 216.

[124] Nono, 'Un'autobiografia', *Scritti*, II, 490–92.

The series dispositions in movements nos. 5 and 7 of *Il canto sospeso* lend themselves to a demonstration of how Nono assimilated Webern's 'secrets' and took 'motivic ambiguity' a step further for an equally condensed synthesis of expression and form.

## Movement no. 5

Example 2.4 notates the five series of movement no. 5 in exactly the same fashion as Nono notated the four forms of the series of Webern's *Chamber Symphony* op. 21 for Gravesano in 1956. Like Nono, I have highlighted the tritones. As in the case of the row of Webern's op. 21, the tritone links the mirror-symmetric halves of Nono's all-interval series (O) and is also consistently positioned at the centre of the mirror-symmetric 'four-tone motifs' of the four additional rows Nono devised for this particular movement (A, B, C and D). The interrelation between the four additional rows has been discussed both by Bailey and by Motz: the central four-tone motif becomes the beginning motif of each subsequent row. Despite this motif-overlap, there is, however, also an overall process of widening intervals. Disregarding the linking intervals between the motifs, the tritone mirrors major and minor seconds in series A. In series B it also mirrors major thirds. In series C, the mirrored intervals are fourths and minor seconds, and series D then also includes minor thirds. While delighting in Webernian symmetries on the micro-structural level, Nono therefore also moves

**Example 2.4** *Il canto sospeso* no. 5, series.

away from the extreme intervallic reduction which allowed Webern to condense four row forms into two (as Nono explains for both the *Symphony* op. 21 and the *Variations* op. 30). Only the all-interval row has mirror-symmetric hexachords. The symmetric four-tone motifs, however, are cast into four additional rows with a larger, macroscopic process in mind.

The large-scale structure of the movement supports this claim. As in movement no. 3, Nono works with three compositional layers.[125] Each layer makes use of the same duration-factor series but is assigned a different duration value (in movement no. 3, all three layers share the same duration value but are assigned different duration-factor series). The audible result is thus very different. While no. 3 progresses in uniform semiquaver division, the rhythmic fuzziness of the combination of sextuplet, quintuplet and semiquaver divisions provides the much more transparent chamber setting of no. 5 with a certain textural haziness.

Movement no. 5 is limited to three duration factors only: two short factors (1 and 2) and one medium factor (7). In view of the mirror-symmetric pitch patterns, these factors are arranged in four palindromic series, derived from each other by means of permutation (every second number):

| | | |
|---|---|---|
| (a) | 1 2 7 1 7 2 | 2 7 1 7 2 1 |
| (b) | 2 1 2 7 7 1 | 1 7 7 2 1 2 |
| (c) | 1 7 1 7 2 2 | 2 2 7 1 7 1 |
| (d) | 7 7 2 2 1 1 | 1 1 2 2 7 7 |

The mirror-symmetric structure of these four duration-factor series essentially corresponds to the hexachord division of the all-interval series. In other words, when applied to the additional series A–D, only the central four-tone motif of each row will be mirror-symmetric in terms of both pitch and duration. In this sense, the duration series also functions to integrate the larger units of twelve.

Each duration-factor series adds up to 40. Multiplication by the duration values results in three units of different lengths: 10 crotchets for the semiquaver layer, 8 crotchets for the quintuplet layer and 6.4 crotchets for the sextuplet layer. The three continuous voices are layered symmetrically, with the longest layer (4) beginning and ending the movement and staggered entry and exit of the other two (5 and 6). In terms of form, no. 5

[125] On the similarities between movements nos. 3 and 5 also see Bailey, 'Work in Progress', 303; Motz, *Konstruktion und Ausdruck*, 79/88.

is thus much closer to the concluding prolation canons of nos. 2 and 9 than the tripartite assimilation of layers in no. 3.

The central quintuplet layer stands out in that it is assigned to the solo tenor and two tuned percussion instruments only (vibraphone and marimba). In terms of presence of sound, this layer is clearly one of extreme contrast. The solo tenor leads with melodic lines of up to seven continuous pitches. With most of the instruments in all three layers playing single pitches only (occasionally linking two), the solo voice naturally stands out as the integrating melodic force. The two percussion instruments, however, are among the least resonant of the accompanying instruments and thus at the very bottom of the scale of the presence of sound, especially since they mostly render the two short durations. Of the forty medium durations in this layer, they play eleven only. These do stand out, however, because they are rendered tremolo and always placed in a higher register than that of the tenor. To Motz they are thus reminiscent of the utopian 'freedom bells' in movement no. 4.[126]

In concordance with the textual divisions, the central vocal layer makes use of the pitch and duration series as follows:

| | | | |
|---|---|---|---|
| Pitch | A B C D | D(R) C(R) B(R) A(R) | O(R) O |
| Dur. | a b c d | a d c b | a b |
| Text: | *se il cielo fosse carta e tutti i mari del mondo inchiostro* | *non potrei descrivervi le mie sofferenze e tutto ciò che vedo intorno a me* | *Dico addio a tutti e piango* |
| | if the sky were paper and all the seas of the world were ink | I could not describe my suffering and all that I see around me | I say goodbye to all of you and weep |

The layer begins with the four additional series and their retrogrades. The symmetric macroscopic process of widening and contracting intervals is then repeated in condensed form with the all-interval series. Notating the vocal layer in isolation, as Motz has done,[127] demonstrates the freedom of the pitch selection for this integrating vocal line which hardly ever highlights the mirror-symmetric features of the four-tone motifs. In fact, it seems that Nono here deliberately works against this characteristic feature of the base material. The axis-interval of the tritone is mostly hidden in the much quieter percussion parts (10×), or split between percussion and voice (9×). Even when the tritone appears in the voice alone (8×), it hardly ever

[126] Motz, *Konstruktion und Ausdruck*, 91.
[127] Motz, *Konstruktion und Ausdruck*, 89–90.

occurs in the shape of a totally symmetric four-tone motif (with one exception: ['scri-] ver-vi le mie', bar 302, duration factors 1 1 1 1).

The enveloping two instrumental layers, on the other hand, exploit the motivic mirror symmetries to the full, most obviously so at the beginning and end of the movement, when the semiquaver layer is heard in isolation. The series disposition of the two outer layers is the following:

| | | | | | | | | | | |
|---|---|---|---|---|---|---|---|---|---|---|
| (4) | O(R) | O | A | B | C | D | D(R) | C(R) | B(R) | A(R) |
| | d | c | c | d | a | b | c | b | a | d |

| | | | | | | | | | | |
|---|---|---|---|---|---|---|---|---|---|---|
| (6) | O(RI) | O(I) | A(I) | B(I) | C(I) | D(I) | D(RI) | C(RI) | B(RI) | A(RI) |
| | d | c | c | d | a | b | (8) 2+↓------ | | (6) 3+↑ | |
| | | | | | | | c | b | a | d |

The instrumental layers both reverse and invert the pitch process of the vocal layer. They begin with the all-interval series and then run through the additional rows and their retrogrades, whereby the sextuplet layer inverts the pitches of the semiquaver layer (with alterations towards the end). Both layers make use of the same duration-factor series (a true prolation canon, therefore).

The first and last series are assigned the duration-factor series with the most gravitational pull towards its centre: 7722 1111 2277 (d). The mirror-symmetric motifs are beautifully carved out by means of instrumentation. Both times the outer motifs are rendered by the strings and the central semiquaver movement is heard on the harps. The extremely slow speed adds to the suspense of these gradually contracting and expanding lines. As soon as the layers overlap, however, the symmetries are much harder to perceive, even though they are still emphasised by means of instrumentation. The harps, for example, are consistently assigned the shortest duration values and are therefore always at the heart of duration series d. The other chain of regular values (duration series c: 1717 2222 7171) is also marked, but less perceptible. In the semiquaver layer it is consistently played on an up-bow by the strings. In the sextuplet layer, it is rendered by four different wind instruments. Owing to the rhythmic phasing and the canonic overlap, however, the overall impression is one of many 'dots of colour'.[128]

Within this delicate 'impressionist' texture, both instrumentation and dynamics are used to shape a much more perceptible, large-scale process.

[128] Motz, *Konstruktion und Ausdruck*, 79.

Dynamics range from *ppp* to *f* and Nono works with simple dynamics throughout. In the instrumental layers, each series is assigned a set of three dynamics (*ppp–p–mp*, *p–mp–mf*, *mp–mf–f*). Up to the fifth series (C/CI) the dynamics thereby gradually increase from *ppp* to *f*. The process is then reversed and the dynamics gradually decrease back to *ppp*. In each layer, the instrumental choices, too, are governed by this overall dynamic process. The semiquaver layer begins with the warm solo strings and harp. The more colourful palette of wind instruments (from the soft darkness of the bass clarinet to the strident brightness of oboe and trumpet) then gradually drives out the solo strings, although these gain the upper hand again as the process is reversed. The sextuplet layer 'inverts' the semiquaver layer in that the wind instruments (here also including flute and horn) begin and the solo strings are gradually added. However, as the strings take over, they are also increasingly 'effaced' in terms of their presence of sound. All short values (2) are here played pizzicato and thus assimilated with the sound of the harps. With this differentiated process, Nono creates an arch form reminiscent of no. 4, the climax of which poetically underlines the tenor's words 'non potrei descrivervi le mie sofferenze' (I could not describe my suffering).

## Movement no. 7

*Il canto sospeso* reaches its lyrical apotheosis with movement no. 7 and here, too, the condensed vocal lines form part of an extremely transparent serial structure. The palette of instrumental colours is even more reduced than in no. 5. Of the wind instruments, only two flutes remain. However, after the use of the full string section in no. 6 (double basses in no. 6a, all others in no. 6b), the strings remain a collective force for their final appearance. With harp, celesta, vibraphone, marimba, glockenspiel and xylophone, the spectrum of delicate, bell-like sonorities is also extended for this most lyrical of movements. High string harmonics, flutter-tonguing on flutes and tremolo on percussion, and the extremely limited range of dynamics (*ppp*, *p*, *mf*), add to the tender, poetic atmosphere.

The integration of the human voice, too, is almost instrumental. As Lachenmann argues, 'the human voice is treated here as *one* colour among others and the serial threads touch on the human voice in their progression of colour as they touch on every other instrument'.[129] This quasi-instrumental function of the voice is underlined by the frequent use of

[129] Lachenmann, lecture at the Volkshochschule Ulm (1964), 253.

'bocca chiusa', 'bocca quasi chiusa' and 'bocca quasi aperta'. The supporting female voices of the chorus sing without text throughout and, as Lachenmann observes, words are discretely added by the soloist:

> [T]he solo soprano finally smuggles the first and second words 'Addio mamma' into the vowel texture and Nono does not dare to dissect this greeting [. . .] The mute expression of absolute pitch momentarily crystallises into two words of the human language – soon after, however, this linearity breaks down again into the open pointillist constellation and the human voice becomes mute colour once again, until, for a second time, words lift out of the music with the repeat of this address. And finally, we arrive at the only sentence of this text: 'Your daughter Lyubka is going into the moist earth' – and the last vowel of the text, the 'a' of 'terra', is already colour again.[130]

To Lachenmann this movement is further a prime example for overcoming the relics of tonality. 'The use of the tempered scale alone' has a 'tonal effect', he states in 'Zur Analyse neuer Musik', and the choices of pure pitch, traditional playing techniques, a crescendo, a sforzato, a linear development, a tremolo, a cymbal beat, an ostinato figure, even rests, are all understood as 'expressive clichés' of tonal thought, which had to be overcome by giving these elements a new structural basis and function. With the hope of arriving at new 'pure material', the radical, integral extension of the serial principle was to blast through the traditional modes of expression which Webern had still compressed into each individual pitch. In Lachenmann's eyes, Nono is one of the few post-war composers who successfully advanced in this direction. 'If, in Webern, the old expression is transformed into structure', he boldly concludes elsewhere, 'structure becomes new expression in Nono.'[131] To Lachenmann, expressive serial structures such as this one encourage non-linear, structural perception. As the serial threads are projected into the acoustic space with ever-changing sets of parameters, each of these individually crafted moments 'changes the experience of the whole and adds to it without establishing a causal–linear relationship with its immediate context'. Because such music requires an auditive awareness 'in all directions', tonal, i.e. linear, listening gives way to 'dispersed structural perception'.[132]

It cannot be argued, however, that this music is entirely without line. Lachenmann himself remarks that 'the serial threads sometimes prevail longer on 2, 3, 4 pitches' in the voices, 'before they wander from instrument to instrument again'. The strings, too, are briefly strung into lines to

[130] *Ibid.*, 253. [131] Lachenmann, 'Nono, Webern, Mozart, Boulez' (1979), 273.
[132] Lachenmann, 'Zur Analyse neuer Musik' (1971/93), 26.

'voice' the movement's single sentence. Once again, a highly systematic pitch reservoir is set up, from which expressive lines can be drawn by means of free choice. In this case, too, Nono decides to deviate from the all-interval series. The organisation of pitch for movement no. 7 was particularly troublesome, and, at one stage, Nono even considered a set of non-dodecaphonic rows.[133] The twelve dodecaphonic series Nono eventually chose are shown in Example 2.5.

In concordance with Motz, who has discussed the series' interrelationship in detail, the twelve rows are labelled A–M.[134] Motz suggests singing them at a slow speed to grasp their unique melodic potential as well as their many 'quasi-tonal figurations': trichords, scale segments and other quasi-tonal progressions. With the exception of the mirror-symmetric row D, Motz rightly concludes, these series are generally much closer to Schoenberg and Berg than they are to Webern.[135] 'One must not forget', however, Nono later told Restagno, 'that Webern's whole chorality is based on canons.'[136] It is in this structural sense that movement no. 7 is also distinctly Webernian. Canon is indeed at the heart of its 'chorality', but, with one continuous layer only (that of the solo soprano), the canonic structure is much more flexible here than in no. 5. Adding density to the solo soprano layer at key points within the overall form, polyphony is clearly employed as a means of intensification and effectively draws solo song into the collective.

The solo soprano layer runs through the twelve series and their respective series of duration in original form and this progression essentially determines the form of the movement as a whole. As in the preceding movement no. 6, Nono makes use of a spectrum of six duration factors (1 2 3 5 8 12). The solo voice is assigned fewer than half of the pitches of this layer (69 of 144), mostly those of longer duration (factors 8, 12 and 5).[137] Despite the almost equal pitch distribution, Nono thus clearly defines a vocal foreground and an instrumental background here. Both the prevalence of the long durations and the privilege of singing uninterrupted lines of up to eight pitches give the solo voice a strong, lyrical profile. The longest line of the solo soprano emerges from the instrumental dots of

133 'The Song Unsung', 125–27/149.

134 For the derivation of row A see 'The Song Unsung', 127. The derivation of all subsequent rows is shown in Motz, *Konstruktion und Ausdruck*, 111–16.

135 Motz, *Konstruktion und Ausdruck*, 115.

136 Nono, 'Un'autobiografia', *Scritti*, II, 491.

137 On form and durations see 'The Song Unsung', 130. In the solo soprano layer, duration factor 8 is sung seventeen times, factor 12 and factor 5 fourteen times, factor 3 nine times, factor 2 eight times and factor 1 four times.

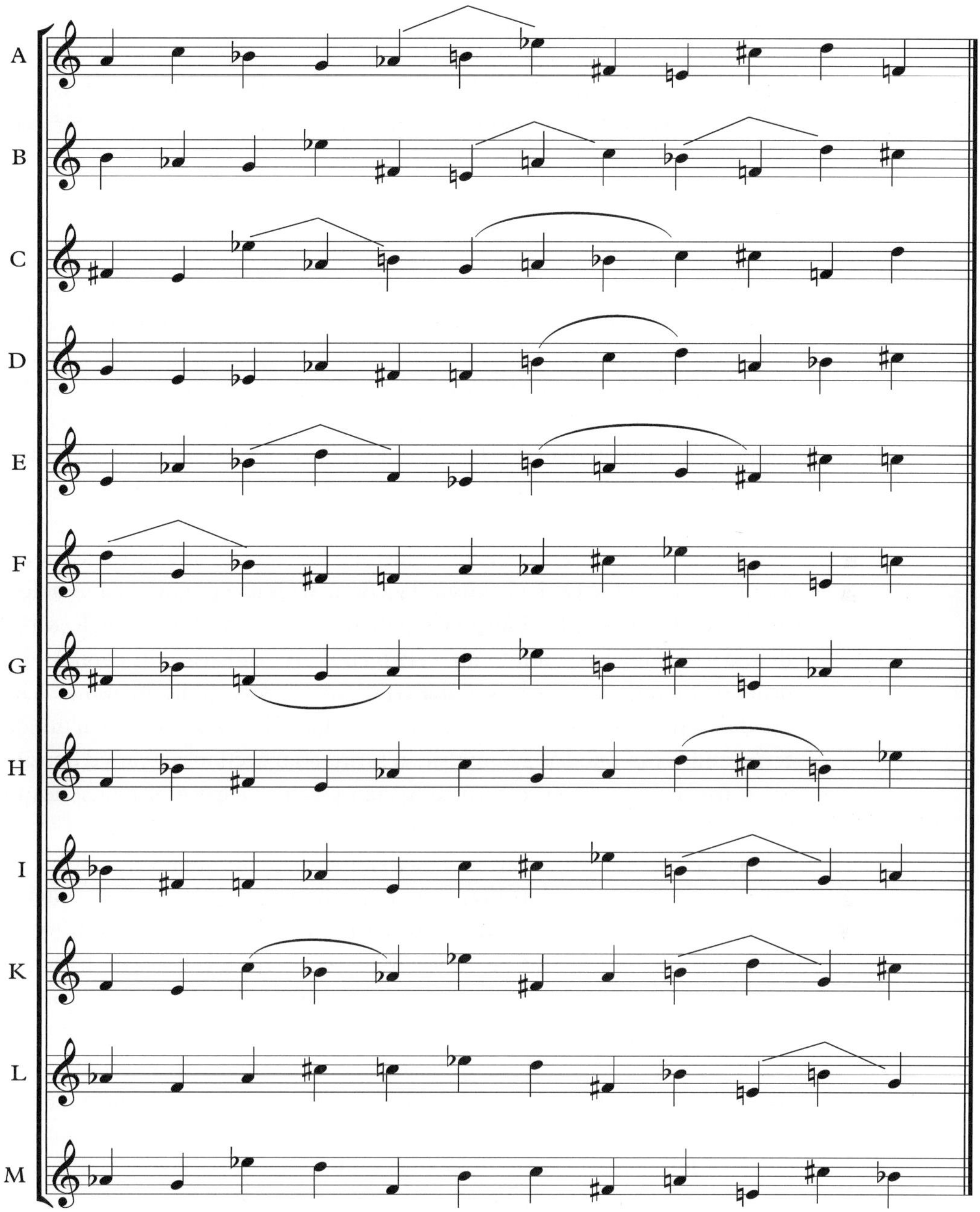


**Example 2.5** *Il canto sospeso* no. 7, series.

Table 2.5 *Series distribution in movement no. 7*

| | I | II | III | IV | V | VI | VII | VIII | IX | X | XI | XII |
|---|---|---|---|---|---|---|---|---|---|---|---|---|
| **SS** | A | B | **C** | **D** | **E** | **F** | G | **H** | **I** | **K** | **L** | M |
| **S** | | LR | | IR | GR | | | ER | CR | AR | | |
| **A** | | MR | KR | | HR | | FR | DR | BR | | | |

colour fairly early on, setting the word 'mam-ma' (bars 434–37; series D, pitches 3–10). Generally, however, the solo soprano links three to four pitches only.

A much greater sense of line is achieved by means of the canonic series additions, which provide the solo soprano lines with collective vocal support of varying density. The two additional layers are assigned to the female voices of the chorus (S/A) and run through the twelve series back to front in retrograde. Their overlap strictly coincides with the series division in the solo soprano layer. Table 2.5 details the density and series combination of each of the twelve sections (sections with text are marked in bold).

The first half of the movement begins and ends with a single serial thread and branches out into three, two and three threads at its core. At the heart of these first six series is the repeated address 'addio mamma'. The second half harbours the sentence 'La tua figlia Liubka se ne va nell'umida terra' and is not quite as symmetric in form. Four sections of varied density open this half, and the solo voice is then given the space of two series to bow out.

Example 2.6(a) shows the first 'polyphonic' section (bars 420–26). The three series are notated as they appear in the score with separate systems for instruments and voices. Each voice sings five pitches only and three of the sung pitches appear in more than one part (B, E♭ and F♯). All common pitches are placed in the same register but differ in terms of colour and dynamics. With partial overlap, E♭ and F♯ are rendered by all three voices. In terms of duration, too, Nono makes sure to establish a common ground. Not only are the voices assigned the longer values ($5 \times 12$, $4 \times 8$, $4 \times 5$, $1 \times 3$), but also together the short linear formations of three to four pitches form an almost continuous line – the lyrical thread that pervades and sustains this movement as a whole. Rather than creating the impression of true polyphony, the voices merge and supplement each other. The solo voice is thereby organically drawn into the vocal collective to uncover the system's common ground.

The last tripartite section (bars 463–69) is another good example of this quest for unity. The three series are shown in Example 2.6(b). Again

(a)

(b)

**Example 2.6** (a) *Il canto sospeso* no. 7, reduction of section II, mm 420–26. (b) Reduction of section IX, mm 463–69.

the voices are assigned fewer than half of the pitches, and again there is considerable pitch overlap. F♯, G♯ and B♭ occur in two of the vocal parts, C and E in all three. However, not all of these common pitches are placed in the same register. The pitch C, for example, is now clearly used to mark the extremes of the vocal range: with the middle C in the choral voices Nono provides extra depth for the soprano's expressive leap to *ppp* $c^3$. At the centre of this two-octave span, the shared pitch E is jointly rendered in middle register while B♭ and F♯ both relate back to the opening vocal constellation (B♭ is now sung two octaves higher, F♯ in the same register). For even tighter vocal unity, the melodic progression G♯–E in the solo soprano part is later heard in the choral voices, simultaneously and again providing maximum vocal depth. While this section is clearly led by the soloist, who here renders the words 'se ne va', the choral voices provide the soaring melodic arch with extra depth and unity.

The section is also remarkable because duration-factor series I happens to fall together with the identical retrograde of series C. Although all duration series have their retrograde equivalent, this is the only time they coincide. Uniquely, the solo soprano layer thus moves in rhythmic unison with the choral soprano layer. In addition, the quasi-tonal features of this particular series combination are further highlighted with minor adjustments to the alto part and the use of particularly homogeneous instrumental colours. The concluding sixth (G–E) in the voices, for example, is extended to pure e-minor by the flute, and answered with the 'supertonic' (F♯–A) in the violins. Why else would Nono curtail the duration of the B in the flute from 12 to 8, if not to cherish this relic of tonality?

'The obvious potential for canonic imitation', Kathryn Bailey remarks in regard to movement no. 5, 'is not exploited.'[138] Here, as in movement no. 7, canonic imitation is simply not the aim. Instead, the polyphonic networks are set up and exploited for maximum lyrical expression. 'I have never composed in a pointillist fashion', Nono later emphasised:

> For me composing was never the mere realisation of pre-existing structures. Elements of improvisation were always involved; I kept my options open to the last moment. [. . .] Critics and interpreters had just got nicely used to pointillist composition, and so they saw my treatment of the text as simply another element in the isolation of acoustic events. [. . .] But in fact I was after something quite different. I wanted a horizontal melodic construction

[138] Bailey, 'Work in Progress', 300.

encompassing all registers; floating from sound to sound, from syllable to syllable: a line which sometimes consists of a succession of individual tones or pitches, and sometimes thickens into chords.[139]

The central part of *Il canto sospeso* focuses predominantly on such 'horizontal melodic construction'. In no. 5 the free-floating line of the solo tenor is beautifully supported by lines that establish themselves between instruments of a similar presence of sound. The solo voice is an emancipated part of the canonic network here and, in terms of both pace and density, the texture is much more close-knit than it is later in no. 7. Lines are then momentarily condensed into blocks for the dramatic confrontation in no. 6a, after which the chorus and strings begin to spin the drawn-out farewell which continues and ascends to hitherto unknown heights in no. 7, the longest, slowest and most transparent of movements with which Nono truly memorialises the fate of Lyubka as one of many. High soprano lines of similar emotional impact would continue to draw the individual into the collective with ever greater compositional freedom in many of Nono's later works.

## Nono and Varèse: Movement no. 8

In Nono's own words, the last instrumental movement of *Il canto sospeso* is 'a laceration of thought, music, and feeling which I feel is very close to Varèse'.[140] Nono first met Varèse in Darmstadt in 1950: he attended his composition seminar and was also present at the European premiere of *Ionisation* (1936).[141] Scherchen had programmed the work just after *A Survivor from Warsaw*, and it made such an impact that it was immediately repeated. Perhaps Nono was even among those who had performed in the work's 'unofficial' European premiere the night before. The instrumental parts had not arrived in time and, as Diether de la Motte recalls, a group of students resolved to write them out from the score overnight:

Did we finish at midnight or 2:00 am? I don't remember, but it was 'very late'. Then someone lit on the idea of putting on a performance as a reward. Did anyone conduct? I can't remember that, either. But we gave it a rousing European premiere with hands and feet, voices for the sustained sounds,

[139] Nono, 'Gespräch mit Hansjörg Pauli' (1969), trans. in Flamm, 'Preface', score, ix.
[140] Nono, 'Un'autobiografia', *Scritti*, II, 512.
[141] On Varèse in Darmstadt see Brinkmann, 'Varèse in Darmstadt'; Borio, 'Varèse und die Utopie der musikalischen Moderne' and '"A Strange Phenomenon"'.

> pencils and waste-paper basket drums. [. . .] The next morning the parts arrived from the publisher after all, and Scherchen didn't need our consignment.[142]

Another of Varèse's Darmstadt students, Dieter Schnebel, describes the effect of *Ionisation* as both a 'prehistoric' and a 'modern catastrophic' assault on the listener. And Nono, too, later commented on the shock effect of Varèse.[143] Yet surprisingly little is known of the actual content of Varèse's composition class. Varèse himself outlined the course in a letter to Steinecke:

> My criticisms and suggestions will be given each student according to his particular temperament and tendencies, for I do not believe in moulds or arbitrary rules. By way of illustration I shall refer to important modern devices and systems, as well as to old works, not neglecting the great neglected primitives. As you say that the young German composers who come to Darmstadt are particularly interested in new technics, I shall give considerable time to explaining my concept of organized sound [. . .], and discussing the technical means of permitting us to come to terms with our world of today. As you see, I want to work in living matter. I am not very much in favour of general forums, discussions producing words and wind and not conducive to positive results. Discussions in class grow naturally out of the problems presented by the students' own works and my criticisms.[144]

Nono's *Variazioni canoniche* were among the works Varèse analysed in class, and Nono was clearly impressed: 'Instead of giving me his opinion, he confronted me with problems. He made me understand the problems of this score by showing me what I had done, sometimes unknowingly.'[145] The long autobiographical conversation with Restagno, which records so many of Nono's Darmstadt reminiscences, was conducted late in life, however, while Nono was residing in Berlin (1987).[146] By then, the music of Varèse was of renewed significance to Nono, and it may even be argued that the 1985 reconstruction of his *Variazioni canoniche* (the score

[142] de la Motte, 'Varèse, *Ionisation*: Europäische Erstaufführung', trans. Zimmermann, in Meyer and Zimmermann (eds.), *Edgard Varèse*, 394.

[143] Schnebel, 'Der körperliche Klang', 6; Nono, 'Intervista di Philippe Albèra' (1987), *Scritti*, II, 419.

[144] Varèse, letter to Steinecke (16 May 1950), in Brinkmann, 'Varèse in Darmstadt', 87–88.

[145] Nono, 'Un'autobiografia', *Scritti*, II, 495.

[146] Nono received grants from the DAAD and the Wissenschaftskolleg to work in West Berlin (1986–88). Although he had agreed to teach at the Hochschule der Künste, he soon resigned due to an insurmountable 'syndrome of traditionalism, fossilisation, disorganisation and inefficiency'; Nono, open letter to the director Ulrich Roloff-Momin (1 June 1988), in Stenzl, *Luigi Nono*, 122.

of which had been lost after the first performance) was a consequence of Nono's renewed interest in Varèse in the mid 1980s.[147] The scores of *Arcana* and *Ecuatorial* accompanied Nono on his trip to Greenland in August 1986, and *Déserts* is dated Khaborusk (*sic.*, Khabarovsk), 18–19 November 1987.[148] Of Greenland, Nono told Restagno the following:

> For ten days we navigated between enormous icebergs, in front of the gigantic glacier that extends from the North Pole, which is the mother of all of the icebergs. The nights were almost as bright as day and when the few passengers went to bed I finally found myself alone in silence with the sea and its colours, below the Pole Star. This particular sea was neither frozen nor dark, but in continuous transformation between indescribable colours filtered through the clouds and icebergs. [. . .] Another unforgettable thing: the sounds, the most violent explosions one hears when icebergs separate from, break off, glaciers. It may have been pure chance, but I had brought the score of *Arcana* by Varèse with me, to study it once again, and I thus happened to hear this score in the midst of the violence of nature.[149]

Even back in the 1950s, however, the influence of Varèse cannot be reduced to the emancipation of percussion and use of non-European elements alone. Stenzl rightly regards the piano resonance in the last twenty-one bars of *Polifonica – Monodia – Ritmica* (1951) as an 'hommage' to *Ionisation.*[150] And also the Brazilian folk song *Yemanjá* may have been used with Varèse's regard for the 'great neglected primitives' in mind.[151] By the time Nono was working on *Il canto sospeso, Déserts* had received its scandalous Paris premiere under Scherchen (2 December 1954) and two subsequent performances with Maderna in Hamburg (8 December 1954) and Stockholm (13 December 1954). In Stockholm, Maderna even reconfigured the interpolations of 'organized sound' according to his own compositional practices, as the NWDR had erroneously sent two copies of the same tape.[152] Of both performances Maderna wrote with great enthusiasm to Nono.[153] *Déserts* would also have been

[147] Michael Gielen conducted the second performance of the work in Freiburg (12 July 1985); see Stenzl, *Luigi Nono*, 19; and Iddon, *New Music at Darmstadt*, 40. Gielen later also recorded the work live in Strasbourg (Astrée E 8741, 1990).

[148] The score of *Arcana* is not at the ALN. *Ecuatorial* is dated 'Ilussat 8–86'; *Déserts* is annotated.

[149] Nono, 'Un'autobiografia', 521. [150] Stenzl, *Luigi Nono*, 21–22.

[151] See Iddon, *New Music at Darmstadt*, 43–44.

[152] See Borio, 'Contacts with the Postwar Avant-Garde', 366–67.

[153] Maderna, letters to Nono, 12 and 20 December 1954 (ALN Maderna/B 54–12–12 m, Maderna/B 54–12–20 m). Maderna edited the work for Scherchen's Ars Viva; see Borio, 'Contacts with the Postwar Avant-Garde', 368.

known to Nono through Scherchen and Xenakis in Gravesano. Thus, when Nono later spoke of the fundamental 'lessons learned from Varèse' for the eighth movement of *Il canto sospeso*,[154] he was most probably referring to Varèse's compositional practice in general: 'problems' which, as Borio argues, manifest and articulate themselves much more distinctly in *Déserts*, the work Nono later regarded as an 'authentic masterpiece'.[155]

'When new instruments will allow me to write music as I conceive it', Varèse dared to dream as early as 1936,

> the movement of sound-masses, of shifting planes, will be clearly perceived in my work, taking the place of the linear counterpoint. When these sound-masses collide, the phenomena of penetration or repulsion will seem to occur. Certain transmutations taking place on certain planes will seem to be projected onto other planes, moving at different speeds and at different angles. There will no longer be the old conception of melody or interplay of melodies. The entire work will be a melodic totality. The entire work will flow as a river flows. [. . .] Today with the technical means that exist and are easily adaptable, the differentiation of the various masses and different planes [. . .] could be made discernible to the listener by means of certain acoustical arrangements. Moreover, such an acoustical arrangement would permit the delineation of what I call 'zones of intensities'. These zones would be differentiated by various timbres or colors and different loudnesses. [. . .] The role of color or timbre would be completely changed from being incidental, anecdotal, sensual or picturesque; it would become an agent of delineation, like the different colors on a map separating different areas, and an integral part of form. These zones would be felt as isolated, and the hitherto unobtainable non-blending (or at least the sensation of non-blending) would become possible.[156]

To Varèse, form was, furthermore, a '*resultant* – the result of a process'.[157] In the present context, it is evident that the form of *Il canto sospeso* as a whole, not just that of movement no. 8, can be understood in these Varèsian terms, especially as regards the use of orchestration and timbre. In other words, movement no. 8, in which the instrumental palette is radically reduced to wind and timpani, is itself part of the overall process for which instrumentation serves as a powerful 'agent of delineation'. On the surface, the scoring for 3 flutes, 2 clarinets, bass clarinet, 6 horns (à 2),

[154] Nono, 'Un'autobiografia', *Scritti*, II, 496.

[155] Nono, 'Un'autobiografia', *Scritti*, II, 516.

[156] Varèse, 'New Instruments and New Music' (1936), in Schwartz and Childs (eds.), *Contemporary Composers on Contemporary Music*, 197.

[157] Varèse, 'Rhythm, Form and Content' (1959), 203.

5 trumpets, 4 trombones and 2 timpani, as also the recurrent use of tone repetition, is further audibly reminiscent of Varèse's *Déserts*. More importantly, also in view of Nono's later fascination with the 'phenomenon of crystallisation', it is the understanding of form as process, the idea of transmutating 'sound-masses' on shifting planes within an organic melodic totality which, to me, is the core element of Varèse's aesthetic in Nono's work.

The contrast between movements nos. 7 and 8 could not be greater, yet the collision of these contrasting 'zones of intensities' is also a totally organic conclusion, a harsh but necessary resolution, as it were, of the symbolically charged contrast between the 'military' wind and percussion and the 'human' string and vocal sound. If the purely instrumental first movement sets the scene for this underlying dichotomy, the last instrumental movement takes the possibility of 'non-blending' to the extreme. The third and last part of *Il canto sospeso* is thus distinctly polarised: the forces which dramatically collided at the centre of the work (no. 6a) are now heard in almost complete isolation. The only common ground of movements nos. 8 and 9, it seems, is the use of the timpani. These two movements, however, are further bound by a similar concern with the density of sound and its structural possibilities.

If the strident brass sonorities and tone repetitions in no. 8 are indeed a deliberate allusion to Varèse, the serial safety net once again ensures the elimination of all remnants of the incantation and melodic-cell formation which are also such characteristic features in the music of Varèse. Again, the all-interval series is not transposed, and runs through thirty-six times. Various strategies of pitch displacement apply, among them the system of preceding rests also used in no. 1.[158] Durations are most finely graded (with the factors 1 to 12 ordered 1 12 2 11 3 10 4 9 5 8 6 7), and Nono makes use of four duration values: quaver divided into 3, 4, 5 and 7.

Insofar as the movement's form is concerned, Nono also works with divisions of four. The relatively homogeneous group of instruments is split into four distinct groups, marked A to D in the sketches:

| | |
|---|---|
| A | 3 trumpets |
| B | 2 trumpets, 1 trombone |
| C | 3 trombones |
| D | 6 horns (à 2) |

158 See 'The Song Unsung', 109–10.

(trumpets may be replaced by flutes, trombones by clarinets and bass clarinet; timpani are added independently of group divisions)

These groups, however, are not assigned a specific duration value. Their allocation changes from section to section. Durations therefore do not evolve in continuous layers. Instead, Nono works with a system that regulates the density of each duration level. This density (or number of parts per duration level), just like the movement's large-scale structure, is derived from the following simple sums:

| | | | | | | | | | | | |
|---|---|---|---|---|---|---|---|---|---|---|---|
| | | | 3 | | | | 2 | | | | 1 |
| | | 3 | 3 | | | 2 | 2 | | | 1 | 1 |
| | 3 | 3 | 3 | | 2 | 2 | 2 | | 1 | 1 | 1 |
| 3 | 3 | 3 | 3 | 2 | 2 | 2 | 2 | 1 | 1 | 1 | 1 |
| 3 | 6 | 9 | 12 | 2 | 4 | 6 | 8 | 1 | 2 | 3 | 4 |

While the numerical columns indicate the number of parts for each level of duration, their sum total determines the number of bars for each of the movement's twelve sections. The columns are reordered to form a balanced three-part structure. Each column is then allocated a different combination of instrumental groups and duration levels. Dynamics, too, are allocated at this early stage. The dynamic series is split into simple and compound dynamics, and sketches reveal three distinct categories:

| | |
|---|---|
| I | *ppp, p, mp, mf, f, fff* |
| II | *ppp–fff, fff–ppp, p–f, f–p, mp–mf, mf–mp* |
| III | Tutto! |

The combination of all parameters results in the three-part structure shown in Figure 2.1.

Number of bars per section (sum totals of the density factors):

| 4 | 2 | 6 | 3 | ‖ 9 | 2 | 8 | 3 | ‖ 4 | 1 | 6 | 12 |
|---|---|---|---|---|---|---|---|---|---|---|---|
| **Density**, *duration value*, instrumental group: | | | | | | | | | | | |
| **1** *4* D | | | | | | **2** *5* C | | | | | **3** *7* D |
| **1** *5* C | | | **1** *5* C | **3** *3* A | | **2** *4* B | | | | **2** *4* B | **3** *3* A |
| **1** *3* B | | **3** *5* B | **1** *3* B | **3** *5* B | **1** *3* B | **2** *7* A | | **2** *7* A | | **2** *7* A | **3** *5* B |
| **1** *7* A | **2** *3* D | **3** *4* C | **1** *7* A | **3** *4* C | **1** *7* A | **2** *3* D | **3** *4* C | **2** *3* D | **1** *7* A | **2** *3* D | **3** *4* C |
| Dynamics, tone repetition (*): | | | | | | | | | | | |
| I* | II | III* | I | III* | I* | II | III | II | I | II | III[*] |
| *fff* | *mp* | *mf* | *f* | *fff* | *mp* | *f* | *mp* | *mf* | *ppp* | *mf* | Tutto |
| *f* | *p* | *mp* | *mf* | *f* | *p* | *mf* | *p* | *mp* | | *mp* | |
| *mf* | | *p* | *mp* | *mf* | *ppp* | *mp* | *ppp* | *p* | | *p* | |
| | | *ppp* | *p* | *mp* | | *p* | | | | *ppp* | |
| | | | | *p* | | | | | | | |

**Figure 2.1** *Il canto sospeso*, preliminary structure for movement no. 8.

**Example 2.7** *Il canto sospeso* no. 8, point of maximum density notated in groups, mm 531–32.

The finished movement adheres to this initial plan with astonishing accuracy. Only the last two sections (initially consisting of 6 and 12 bars) are merged into one of 14 bars, beginning with the density of 4 × 3 (bar 531). This point of maximum density is shown in Example 2.7. Reordering the score according to instrumental group and duration level shows that Nono here strictly adheres to the above guidelines for this density. Clear, too, is the method of pitch displacement, with preceding rests consistently multiplied by factors of 1, 2 and 3 throughout the movement. Coupled with duration value 7, the horns (group D) are the first to enter. Displaced by one triplet rest, group A follows with duration level 3. Groups B and C are displaced accordingly: group B by 2 quintuplet rests, group C by 3 septuplet rests. The displacement of entries within the groups is further governed by factors of 1 and 2 (see Example 2.7). The pitches of the all-interval series are here assigned the original duration-factor series 1 12 2 11 3 10 4 9 5 8 6 7. Generally, the use of tone repetition and the finely graded combination of duration factors convey an urgent sense of disquiet, while the overall shape of the movement is delineated in waves of mutating densities on constantly 'shifting planes'. At the densest points of intersection, the underlying sound symbolism of the work is taken to such an extreme that it is indeed adequate to speak of a 'laceration of thought' as Nono does with reference to Varèse. That is not to say, however, that this least 'melodic' of movements is not also designed to flow 'like a river flows'.

The Varèsian dream of a 'melodic totality' is taken further still in the concluding movement, no. 9, where concern with density is given a much more 'human' guise and the timpani is drawn from relatively conventional contexts into a role of its own. As Nono himself would later remark in connection with *Diario polacco '58*, this is where his concept of melody as 'simultaneity within a differentiated spectrum of unified rhythmic values' took root.[159] In view of attaining ever 'new levels of spirituality, sentiment and consciousness, of understanding and explanation' within and not 'outside history', this concept would occupy him up to *Diario polacco '58* and beyond.

[159] Nono, '*Composizione per orchestra n. 2 – Diario polacco '58* ', *Texte*, 125; *Scritti*, I, 436.

# 3 Towards spatial composition

*Composizione per orchestra n. 2: Diario polacco '58* (1959) is the first of Nono's works to require a spatial distribution of sound sources. Like Stockhausen's *Gruppen* (1955–57), it is a serial group composition, though of a different kind.[1] Consequently, the spatial set-up is completely different. Whereas Stockhausen makes use of three orchestral groups and three conductors to space out and thus clarify the overlapping time layers, Nono regards the spatial dimension as an additional tool to differentiate and move the orchestral sound from within – a precursor of the 'suono mobile' of his late work. The orchestra is divided into four identical groups and each group is assigned a specific position on stage.[2] While each group is conceived as an autonomous unit, the subdivision into strings, woodwind, brass and percussion is also considered in the spatial constellation. Brass and percussion are furthest apart, positioned in an outer semicircle, while woodwind and strings intersect at the centre of the stage. Nono initially also planned to include electronic music, transmitted through four loudspeakers at the sides and rear of the auditorium. In this original spatial scenario, the audience would have found itself fully encircled by live and electronic sound sources.[3] Another year was to pass, however, before

1 Stockhausen's *Gruppen* (1955–57) for three orchestras was premiered under Stockhausen, Maderna and Boulez (Cologne, 24 March 1958). Excerpts of the premiere recording were played in Stockhausen's seminar 'Musik im Raum' (Darmstadt, 4 September 1958). For a detailed analysis see Misch, 'On the Serial Shaping of Stockhausen's *Gruppen*' and *Zur Kompositionstechnik Karlheinz Stockhausens. Gruppen* (published 1963) is among eighteen Stockhausen scores at the ALN, three of which are annotated, namely *Kontra-Punkte* (1953), *Piano Pieces I–IV* and *Zeitmaße* (1957).

2 Each group is made up of ten strings, four woodwind, four brass and four percussionists with a large range of instruments including four whips. The spatial distribution is detailed in the study score AV 66 (Mainz: Ars Viva, 1959). Further see Schaller, *Klang und Zahl*; and Navacchia, 'La concezione drammaturgica'.

3 The work was initially commissioned for Donaueschingen, but an argument with Strobel prompted Nono to pull out. The Hessischer Rundfunk stepped in and the premiere was agreed for Darmstadt, 2 September 1959. By February 1959 Nono still envisaged a 'Concerto for flute (Gazzelloni), tapes and orchestra'; Steinecke, letter to Nono, 15 February 1959 (Steinecke/W 59–02–15 m, ALN). The inclusion of electronic music had to be abandoned, however, because Nono was not granted permission to work at the Studio di Fonologia in Milan at this time. Although it was begun for solo flute and orchestra, the work soon came to be conceived for orchestra alone. The finished score is

the composer was finally able to produce his first electronic composition, *Omaggio a Emilio Vedova*, at the Studio di Fonologia in Milan (October 1960).[4] With the help of Maderna and the chief technician Marino Zuccheri, spatial transmission was then first realised for *Intolleranza 1960*: recorded on four-channel tape, all of the choral passages were transmitted through five sets of loudspeakers distributed on either side of the stage, at the sides and at the rear of the auditorium at La Fenice.[5]

Nono's first attempts to work with electronic means, however, go right back to 1953, the year Stockhausen completed his electronic *Studie I*. 'This is the first composition which makes me happy and which is entirely clear', Stockhausen wrote to Nono at the time.[6] Nono replied almost immediately that he, too, had already contacted Eimert regarding the possibility of working in Cologne. 'You and I would finally have the opportunity to study and work together', Nono answered, 'and I think that would be very beneficial for both of us.'[7] Although Nono visited Cologne that autumn, the joint studio experience never happened.[8] Two years later, while Stockhausen was working on *Gesang der Jünglinge*, Nono again mentions plans for an electronic composition in a letter to Steinecke (1955),[9] now speaking of the 'necessity to work with pure sounds (sine tones)' and the concept of a 'new type of song' for 'Liebesgesänge' ('Love Songs') for two singers and sine tones. No trace remains of this project, but Schaller did find sketches for an autonomous electronic composition in one of the sketchbooks for *Il canto sospeso*.[10]

dated 15.7.59; Schaller, *Klang und Zahl*, 31–32. A tape was added by Nono in 1965. On this version see Nanni, 'Bruch des ästhetischen Spiels'; and Bassanese, 'Sulla versione 1965'. Stockhausen's *Gruppen*, too, was initially to incorporate electronic music; see Decroupet, 'Gravitationsfeld Gruppen'.

4 See De Benedictis, 'Omaggio a Emilio Vedova'; and Novati and Dack (eds.), *The Studio di Fonologia*.

5 On spatial concepts in *Intolleranza* see Santini, 'Multiplicity – Fragmentation – Simultaneity', 77–82.

6 'Dieses ist die erste Komposition, die mich glücklich macht und die ganz klar ist.' Stockhausen, letter to Nono, 23 August 1953 (Stockhausen/K 53–08–23 m, ALN).

7 '[. . .] für mich wäre wichtig so endlich Du und ich die Möglichkeit zusammen lernen und arbeiten hätten. und ich glaube, das sehr fruchtbar für uns beide. [. . .]' Nono, letter to Stockhausen, 12 September 1953 (Stockhausen Foundation Kürten; copy at ALN Stockhausen/K 53–09–12 d). Nono also wrote to Maderna of planning to work in Cologne; see De Benedictis, 'Omaggio a Emilio Vedova', 42, n. 3.

8 Having visited the studio, a further letter to Maderna makes clear that Nono no longer wanted to collaborate with Eimert and Stockhausen; Nono, letter to Maderna, 5 November 1953 (PSS, with thanks to De Benedictis).

9 Nono, letter to Steinecke, 15 January 1955, cited in Schaller, *Klang und Zahl*, 167.

10 Schaller, *Klang und Zahl*, 167.

Two weeks before the premiere of *Gesang der Jünglinge* (30 May 1956), Stockhausen strongly urged Nono to attend:

> [. . .] If at all possible: please come to Cologne for this performance. The reason is: I composed the piece for 5 groups of loudspeakers distributed around the audience in the auditorium. Luckily we have the special machine that is needed to play the 5 synchronised, independently produced tapes. In addition, the firm Telefunken will equip the broadcasting hall of the radio station with a special loudspeaker system (5 × 3) just for these days. In the next few years, nobody in the world will thus have the opportunity to listen to this piece again as it should really sound . . . Once the independent tapes are copied together, the composed *movement* is entirely lost (you have to imagine that the sounds really fly through space, turn, oscillate from side to side etc. and that the loudspeaker distribution – whether 2 or 3 or 4 or 5 are in action, whether the sound is composed to come from the front or the back, whether a section moves clockwise or anti-clockwise etc. – this distribution makes the form clear in the process of listening). Five tapes copied onto one would be equivalent to a photo of a merry-go-round (who gains an inkling of what a merry-go-round is really like when looking at a silly photo!)[11]

Nono did attend the premiere and later confessed that 'You were able to do something with *Der Gesang* of which I've been dreaming for some time. Maybe you don't need to know this, but I wanted to tell you.'[12] Another letter to Stockhausen reveals, however, that Nono's spatial concepts also had other roots:

11 Stockhausen, letter to Nono, May 1956 (Stockhausen/K 56–05–01/02 m, ALN). '[. . .] Wenn es eben geht: bitte komme doch zu dieser Aufführung nach Köln. Das hat den Grund: Das Stück habe ich für 5 Lautsprechergruppen komponiert, die rings um die Hörer herum im Saal verteilt sind. So braucht man also zum Abspielen der 5 synchronen verschieden produzierten Tonbänder eine Spezialmaschine, die wir glücklicherweise haben. Außerdem wird nur für die Tage der Aufführung von der Firma Telefunken der Sendesaal im Funkhaus mit einer speziellen Lautsprecheranlage (5 × 3) ausgerüstet. In den nächsten Jahren wird kein Mensch auf der Welt also wieder die Möglichkeit haben, sich dieses Stück anhören zu können, wie es wirklich klingt . . . Wenn man die getrennten Tonbänder zusammen kopiert, geht die ganze hinein komponierte *Bewegung* verloren (Du mußt Dir vorstellen, daß die Klänge richtig durch den Raum fliegen, sich drehen, hin und herpendeln etc. und daß die Lautsprecherverteilung – ob 2 oder 3 oder 4 oder 5 in Aktion sind, ob ein Klang hinten oder vorne, eine Partie mit Rechtsdrehung oder Linksdrehung etc. komponiert ist – daß diese Verteilung also erst die Form beim Hören klar macht. Eine Kopie der 5 Bänder auf ein Tonband wäre also ein photographiertes Karussel (wer ahnt beim Anblick des dusseligen Photos noch etwas von dem, was ein Karussel wirklich ist!)'

12 Nono, letter to Stockhausen, 8 September 1956 (Stockhausen Foundation Kürten, copy at ALN Stockhausen/K 56–09–08 d). That Nono attended the premiere is clear from a letter to Steinecke, 9 May 1956.

> Do you remember in Darmstadt, after one of Rosbaud's rehearsals of the *Variations for Orchestra* by A[rnold] S[choenberg], you said that so much couldn't be heard which was unnecessary in the music. Just because of the way concerts are realised today, one hears only half of the music perhaps. Because music is given no musical space whatsoever.
>
> If you think, for example of the double chorus [. . .] here in St Mark's, in the time of Monteverdi: they performed masses and other works with 1 to 6 choruses, positioned in different locations of the church, already at that time there was no single sound source. Later and up to the present there has been a single source in concerts (and the same is true for the theatre). Even the type of composition was different (two or more antiphonal choirs), one was supposed to think of different sound sources, but you know this [. . .]
>
> . . . composition with many sound sources is already in front of me, as is the theatre with independent visual–acoustic sources: for some time this has been my goal. But where has such a theatre been built??? it has remained a project, which could be realised; you know, that of Gropius. Today, though, even more should be possible; a totally new sense and function of theatre![13]

Both the extension of 'musical space' and the autonomous use of the visual and acoustic dimensions are later discussed at great length in Nono's texts on *Intolleranza*.[14] This letter already makes clear, however, that the wish to create new spatial conditions for greater listening awareness (which was to find its most visionary realisation three decades later in *Prometeo*) was motivated, in part, by Nono's ongoing interest in Schoenberg in addition to the most advanced technological possibilities in contemporary theatre and music theatre.

*Die glückliche Hand* (1909–13) was of particular interest to Nono because of its independent use of the visual and acoustic dimensions:

> In this 'drama' sung and mimed action alternate and also develop simultaneously, not one as illustration of the other, but each independently characterising diverse situations.
>
> Thus one begins to violate the scheme: I hear what I see and I see what I hear, extending the use of the visual–acoustic dimension.
>
> The chorus, an ambivalent element, has a double function on stage: sonorous and purely visual, in terms of colour and form. In this last function, it is no longer the accompanying chorus awaiting its turn to sing, but

[13] Nono, letter to Stockhausen, 7 May 1956 (Stockhausen Foundation Kürten, copy at ALN Stockhausen/K 56-05-07 d).

[14] Nono, 'Appunti per un teatro musicale attuale' (1961), *Scritti*, I, 86–95; 'Alcune precisazioni su Intolleranza 1960' (1962), *Scritti*, I, 100–117; 'Possibilità e necessità di un nuovo teatro musicale' (1962), *Scritti*, I, 118–32. Also see Santini, 'Multiplicity – Fragmentation – Simultaneity', 78–80.

> integrated into the stage setting and transformed in form, colour and light according to the autonomous and symbolic use of these elements, specified precisely in the score.[15]

In regard to Schoenberg's exploration of space, Nono further mentions *Die Jakobsleiter*:

> Already in the unfinished oratorio *Die Jakobsleiter* [. . .] Schoenberg thinks of employing several sound sources in the auditorium.
>
> In a remark on the final idea of the oratorio he states, still in 1921: 'The soloists and the chorus begin on stage and are then joined, little by little, ever more, by the distant choruses in the distant orchestras such that at the end the music floods into the auditorium from all sides.' (By distant choruses and orchestras – *Fernchöre* and *Fernorchester* – Schoenberg means choruses and orchestral groups distant from the stage and linked by means of microphones to groups of loudspeakers situated at various points around the auditorium).[16]

The most influential of Schoenberg's dramatic works, however, to which Nono turned time and time again, was *Moses und Aron*.[17] Nono first encountered this monumental torso of modern music theatre in 1951, when Scherchen conducted the first concert performance of 'The Dance Around the Golden Calf' in Darmstadt. Schoenberg was too ill to be present, but may still have received Scherchen's exuberant account of the performance:

> The world premiere of the 'Dance Around the Golden Calf' was the greatest triumph I ever experienced with a work of such novelty for the listener.
>
> Furthermore, it was an orientation to many and shattering to all who were fortunate enough to be present because they recognized your unconditional compositional message, the absolute certainty of your artistic construction and the purity of your artistic spirit.
>
> I am happy that I was allowed to erect this, your monument [. . .]

[15] Nono, 'Possibilità e necessità di un nuovo teatro musicale', *Scritti*, I, 124. The correspondence with Stockhausen reveals that Nono attended the 1955 Cologne production of *Die glückliche Hand* under Otto Ackermann. Scherchen recorded the work with Kieth Engen (bass) and the Bavarian Radio Symphony Orchestra in January 1959 (Orfeo C274921B), in one of the most dramatic and exciting interpretations to this day.

[16] *Ibid.*, 124–125. Nuria Schoenberg-Nono remembers that Nono requested the manuscripts of *Die Jakobsleiter* in the late 1950s in order to study Schoenberg's spatial concept; see Schaller, *Klang und Zahl*, 204, note 29.

[17] *Moses und Aron* was later of particular interest in regard to *Prometeo*; see Rizzardi, 'Nono e la "presenza storica" di Schönberg', 244–49.

> The performance was sold out [. . .] already the first performance was a triumph for you – when, after half an hour break, the second performance was over (only about 1/10 of the audience had left the auditorium), the cheering was boundless: I had to come out about 20 times and later on the streets people still gathered in groups, deeply moved [. . .]
>
> Without exception, ALL reviews I have seen so far basically expressed the same idea: that this was THE musical event![18]

Whilst in Darmstadt for the premiere of his *Polifonica – Monodia – Ritmica*,[19] Nono not only attended this event but also, according to Scherchen, was moved to tears when the performance was broadcast a few days later:

> poor Nono cried [. . .] when it became clear to him that he had become much too preoccupied with the most abstract of speculation [. . .] in this respect Schoenberg's work had a cleansing and immensely powerful meaning: the young (and mediocre) have felt that what is important is neither technique nor 'originality', but the complete and mutual correspondence of spirit = matter.[20]

Nono then helped to prepare the performance material for Hans Rosbaud's first concert performance of *Moses und Aron* in Hamburg (12 March 1954). On this occasion, Nono met his future wife, Nuria Schoenberg, whom he married a year later. The first staged production of *Moses und Aron* at the Stadttheater Zürich (1957) was again conducted by Rosbaud. Two years later, just after the premiere of Nono's *Diario polacco '58*, Scherchen conducted the second staged production of *Moses und Aron* at the Städtische Oper Berlin.[21] Of this acclaimed production, the conductor later gave the following account:

> I had the honour of producing *Moses und Aron* together with Gustav R. Sellner, [. . .] one of the most intelligent people working in theatre today, to whom I suggested a well-thought-out plan. If you look at the score of *Moses*

[18] Scherchen, letter to Schoenberg, 6 July 1951, in Schmidt (ed.), *Arnold Schönberg: Sämtliche Werke*, III:8/2b, 32–33. The premiere took place on 2 July 1951 with soloists, chorus and orchestra of the Landestheater Darmstadt; recording on *50 Jahre Neue Musik in Darmstadt* (col legno, 1996), IV.

[19] *Polifonica – Monodia – Ritmica* (1950/51) was premiered under Scherchen (10 July 1951); recording on *50 Jahre Neue Musik in Darmstadt* (col legno, 1996), I.

[20] Scherchen, letter to Pia Andronescu, 11 July 1951, in Spangemacher, 'Schönberg as Role Model', 32.

[21] Gustav Rudolf Sellner produced the work with stage designs by Michel Raffaelli. On the Zurich (1957) and Berlin (1959) productions see Wörner, *Schoenberg's 'Moses and Aaron'*, 104–5.

> *und Aron* it makes you despair [. . .] for how should one perform a choral drama, so that people will listen to it? Nobody understands the chorus! When 20 tenors sing the same thing, no one will be able to understand anything [. . .] The 1st Act takes three quarters of an hour – how can one produce this choral drama so that tension increases right up to the end of the 1st Act?
> I made the following suggestion, which Sellner immediately accepted: in the first scene, which takes place in unreality – the Burning Bush, one of the great visions of antiquity – to realise the Burning Bush with electronic music, so that the music, the spoken word, emerges from behind, from the background of the stage, and the other music – that which goes on in the mind – is heard from the sides, so that music really begins to be around us in space. Also the chorus was spared at first. And then came the second scene, the ghetto. From then on it is really one continuous intensification. [. . .] At the beginning, where the chorus is divided into twelve parts, I suggested the use of soloists (if this is sung by several singers, the result is a mess). He [Sellner] immediately took up this idea and placed the soloists on pedestals in the ghetto, from which they could speak and narrate what was happening, while the chorus was still spared. The next part was built with just one part of the chorus. The whole chorus joined in only at the grand final chorus, when the masses arrive, and thus the act steadily grew in intensity.[22]

The idea of spacing out the music of the Burning Bush with electronic means goes back, of course, to Schoenberg's indication that the six speaking voices representing the 'voice from the Burning Bush' could be separated from each other off-stage 'using telephones which will lead through loudspeakers into the hall where the voices will then coalesce'.[23] Scherchen was indeed well equipped to realise this Schoenbergian vision. In 1954 he had founded his very own studio for electro-acoustic research in Gravesano, to which he regularly invited physicists, sound engineers and musicians to study and develop radio transmission technology. The studio opened with a conference on 'Music and Electronics', the proceedings of which were edited by Meyer-Eppler.[24] Together with Xenakis, Nono regularly contributed to such events, as also to Scherchen's journal, the *Gravesaner Blätter*.[25] Nono later recalled one specific innovation:

22 Scherchen, 'Dramaturgie und Regie der Oper', 203–204.

23 Schoenberg, *Moses und Aron*, Schmidt (ed.), *Sämtliche Werke*, III:A 8/1, 2.

24 Meyer-Eppler (ed.), *Gravesano: Musik, Raumgestaltung, Elektroakustik* (1955) with contributions by Maurice Martenot, Oskar Sala, Pierre Schaeffer, Meyer-Eppler and others.

25 Nono, 'Zur Entwicklung der Serientechnik', *Gravesaner Blätter*, II:4 (May, 1956), 14–18; *Texte*, 16–20; 'Die neue Kompositionstechnik', *Gravesaner Blätter*, II:6 (December, 1956), 19–20; *Texte*, 146. Xenakis published nine articles and three shorter texts in the *Gravesaner Blätter* (1955–66).

> In Gravesano Scherchen had invented a revolving loudspeaker, a loudspeaker made of many loudspeakers: a kind of prism that projected the sounds while rotating in various ways. This invention was underestimated at the time, but was actually full of great potential because it overcame the principle of the fixed sound source, producing superimpositions and reverberations that added up in layers one over the other. For a certain period I thus studied in Milan and Gravesano.[26]

Innovative spatial transmission technology was also on offer at the 1958 World Exposition in Brussels, which Nono attended. In the spectacular Philip's Pavilion, designed by Le Corbusier and Xenakis, Varèse's *Poème électronique* was transmitted through about 400 tiny loudspeakers placed along twelve 'sound routes' that cycled through the architectural space. These loudspeakers governed the high notes, while the low notes were broadcast through twenty-five large woofers attached to the base of the walls. This was the fulfilment of Varèse's long-held prophecy that 'Music will eventually engulf and surround you.' One visitor remarked that 'Here, one no longer hears the sounds, one finds oneself in the heart of the sound source. One does not listen to sound, one lives it.' The composer Earle Brown, who attended the show, recalled in an interview that 'It was spectacular, because you'd hear a sound, and it would go all the way around [. . .] and you could almost trace it in space, almost follow it with your eyes.'[27]

Nono later remarked that Varèse 'had always lamented the inadequacy of the electronic instruments' and thus regarded *Poème électronique* as an example of how 'his intuitive and creative imagination [. . .] was chastened by the limits of the technological instruments at his disposal'.[28] In terms of sound transmission, however, the work was nevertheless remarkable for its time. On entering and leaving the pavilion, Nono would also have heard Xenakis's short electronic 'Interlude sonore' (later named *Concret PH*), transmitted through the same sound system. The effect of this atmospheric essay on the sound of burning charcoal was described

[26] Nono, 'Un'autobiografia', *Scritti*, II, 515. Völker describes the device as a 'spherical speaker (150 kg) with more than twenty single systems irradiating the sound equally while two hemispheres rotate separately with 10 speakers each. [. . .] Weisse had installed four of these heavy spheres underneath the ceiling in the Frankfurt concert hall already in 1954, yet without rotating parts. The intention was to irradiate diffuse sound into the hall.' Völker, 'Acoustical and electro-acoustic sound fields', 248.

[27] Mattis, 'From Bebop to Poo-wip', 310. On *Poème électronique*, including Xenakis's diagram of the sound routes, also see Soriano, *Arquitectura y Música*, 46–51.

[28] Nono, 'Un'autobiografia', *Scritti*, II, 516. Also see Borio, '"A Strange Phenomenon"'.

by Xenakis himself as 'lines of sound moving in complex paths from point to point in space, like needles darting from everywhere'.[29]

Of far greater technological and aesthetic interest to Nono at the Brussels World Fair, however, were the avant-garde production techniques of Josef Svoboda, the director of the Laterna Magika in Prague, and his producer Alfréd Radok.[30] Both were later invited to produce *Intolleranza 1960* in Venice (1961), though only Svoboda was granted permission by the Czechoslovakian authorities while Radok was replaced by Václav Kašlík.[31] Svoboda also produced *Intolleranza* a second time in Boston (1965).[32] Back in 1958, Nono was inspired by a so-called 'Polyekran' ('multi-screen') performance and a Laterna Magika performance with live acting. The Polyekran performance 'projected images on a series of strategically positioned screens' in order to arrive at 'a polyphonic composition of multiple images and high-fidelity sound'.[33] The spatial dimension was emphasised in that sound was transmitted through 'a cluster of loudspeakers arranged to create the illusion that the entire space resounded'.[34] Equally refined projection techniques were coupled with live music, action and dance for the Laterna Magika show:

> Laterna Magika was devised for the Brussels Fair of 1958, where it enjoyed a spectacular success. It consisted of three film and two slide projectors, synchronously controlled, plus a device that enabled deflection of one projection beam to any desired spot, including a moving screen. In a stage space measuring approximately 50′ × 24′ × 20′ were arranged eight types of

[29] As cited in Rowell, *Thinking about Music*, 241. On *Concret PH* further see Valle, Tazelaar and Lombardo, 'In a Concrete Space'.

[30] Nono had already met Svoboda and Radok in Prague earlier that year; Nono, 'Josef Svoboda' (1968), *Scritti*, I, 246.

[31] Despite asking Togliatti for support, Nono did not manage to procure Radok. For Nono's letter to Togliatti (30 January 1961) see Trudu (ed.), *Luigi Nono: Carteggi concernenti politica, cultura, e Partito Comunista Italiano*, 9–11; and De Benedictis, Mastinu (eds.), *Intolleranza 1960*, 89–90; the latter also includes the reply Nono received from the Czechoslovakian Ministry of Culture (15 January 1961).

[32] While there were problems with the 1961 production in Venice and much of the visual material was eventually provided by Emilio Vedova, Svoboda later named the Boston production as a particularly successful example of 'how new technologies, new expressive resources emerge'; Svoboda, *The Secret of Theatrical Space*, 104–106. Nono is more critical, stating that Svoboda was only able to realise 'half of what he had invented and prepared'; Nono, 'Josef Svoboda', *Scritti*, I, 247; and 'Lettera da Los Angeles' (1965), *Scritti*, I, 177–81. On the Boston production further see Wilcox, 'Political Allegory or Multimedia Extravaganza?' and Vincis, ' "To Nono: a No" '.

[33] Svoboda, *The Secret of Theatrical Space*, 10; also see Burian, *The Scenography of Josef Svoboda*, 81.

[34] Svoboda, *The Secret of Theatrical Space*, 105.

> mobile screens with special, highly directional reflecting surfaces; they could rise, fall, move to the side, rotate, appear and disappear in precise rhythm with the actors. The stage itself was provided with a moving belt to accommodate the need for the virtually instantaneous live action in response to the film. One of the screens, moreover, was equipped with a diaphragmatic framing shutter curtain that could alter both the size and shape of the screen. And the total presentation was enhanced by multi-speaker stereophonic sound.[35]

Nono's later contribution to Denis Bablet's *La scena e l'immagine. Saggio su Josef Svoboda* makes clear that the composer was particularly impressed by Svoboda's expressive use of technology, which was 'not purely experimental or "avant-garde"' but strove to portray the idea of a work faithfully with advanced technological means. Rather than dwelling on the two productions of *Intolleranza* (both of which, to Nono, were far from ideal), the composer homes in on the breadth of Svoboda's knowledge and understanding of theatre and thus reveals some of his own concerns:

> His experiences, his studies and his research influenced me and helped me in my own studies from Monteverdi to the Japanese *kabuki* and *nō*, from Meyerhold to Flanagan's Federal Theatre Project, from Mussorgsky to synagogue ritual, from Piscator to the theatre of Bali, from the production techniques of the early nineteenth century to the Bolshevik theatre of the masses, from *Fidelio* and *Il trovatore* to Weill and Schoenberg.
>
> Studies and analysis of history, in order to surpass it.
>
> And in order to surpass the Eurocentric limitations of European theatrical culture (be it even the great Italian tradition).[36]

As also Santini argues, Nono's spatial concepts were from the very outset intrinsically linked to the dramatic arts, evolved with his concept of the 'azione scenica' and eventually culminated in the dramatic use of space in *Prometeo* (of which much will be said in the latter part of this book). It is all the more remarkable, therefore, that *Diario polacco '58* puts spatial composition into practice on autonomous musical grounds. But even this daringly fragmentary orchestral 'diary' is not entirely removed from dramatic thought. As Nono himself explains,

> The spatial concept of music, as I imagine it, refers to the principle of the Venetian School around 1500, particularly as it manifests itself in the music of Andrea and Giovanni Gabrieli. It differs from the Venetians, however, in the fundamentally different concepts of composition and sound. This ping-pong concept, whereby music moves from right to left and from left to right like a ping-pong ball, and everything dissolves into effect, is alien to my music.

[35] Burian, *The Scenography of Josef Svoboda*, 85.

[36] Nono, 'Josef Svoboda', *Scritti*, I, 246.

> I compose the sound spatially by making use of different, spaced-out sound sources. This concept will also serve as a foundation for the realisation of a new music theatre which I am planning.[37]

Arnold Schoenberg, too, is named as a pioneering figure:

> Ingeniously begun by Arnold Schoenberg, the concept of serial composition (instead of the tonal order, the function of which has now been exhausted), has undergone a consistent historical development and gradually expanded from the determination of melodic-thematic interval relationships to the determination of all parameters of the musical language. With it, a new compositional mentality evolved according to which each formal musical element is seen in relationship to every other element. There are no schemes, dogmas, recipes, but each moment represents a unique, immutable, necessary possibility that presented itself for realisation at this specific moment.[38]

## 'The presence of history' in *Diario polacco '58* (1959)

Roughly a year after the premiere of *Composizione per orchestra n. 2: Diario polacco '58* (1959) and Nono's outspoken lecture 'Geschichte und Gegenwart in der Musik heute' in which he warned of all too light-hearted, if not irresponsible, use of chance procedures, the journal *Melos* conducted a survey entitled 'The Avant-garde – Genuine or Fabricated?'. Stockhausen responded with a photomontage entitled 'The managers of the avant-garde face the people's tribunal'. The upper half of the image shows representatives of the musical avant-garde. 'Those who have been to Darmstadt,' the young Lachenmann responded soon thereafter, 'will know them all':

> Stockhausen, the spokesman at the front, holds up the sign with the words 'genuine or fabricated?'. Next to and behind him are Boulez, Maderna, Berio, Kagel, Brown, Pousseur, etc. – all dressed in dark clothes. To the left of the group, dressed in contrasting white, is the prosecutor, appropriately posed. The lower part of the picture shows the people's tribunal itself, with Heinrich Strobel etc. That prosecutor, however, is – Luigi Nono. [. . .] And for those who know how to read it, the title of this photomontage was 'The dissident faces the tribunal of the avant-garde'.[39]

37 Nono, 'Diario polacco '58' (1959), *Texte*, 124.

38 Nono, 'Diario polacco '58', *Texte*, 125.

39 Lachenmann, '[Luigi Nono]', lecture at the Hochschule für Musik, Stuttgart (26 October 1960), in De Benedictis and Mosch (eds.), *Alla ricerca di luce e chiarezza*, 219–20, including a reproduction of Stockhausen's photomontage, 220; henceforth referred to as 'Stuttgart lecture'.

In the course of his response, Lachenmann, who had just completed his studies with Nono in Venice and also assisted with the German formulation of Nono's Darmstadt lectures (1959/60), offers unique insight into the conflict that caused Nono's dissociation from Darmstadt and West German cultural life in general. The following year, Lachenmann himself would begin to doubt Nono's political orientation, while working on the piano reduction of *Intolleranza 1960* and in regard to the sensitive issue of the Berlin Wall.[40] At the time of his Stuttgart lecture, however, Lachenmann still fully backed his teacher and defended him with an outright onslaught on the 'regressive' traits in the music of Boulez and Stockhausen. 'Up to now', Lachenmann here boldly proclaimed, 'I have not yet seen or heard a work by Boulez in which the fascination of his music surpasses the attraction of the material itself in the totally banal sense of an aesthetic sensation.'[41] The music of Boulez is further viciously reprimanded for its 'objective lack of content' and total 'indifference towards its time'.[42] Lachenmann bases this extremely harsh critique solely on the all-too-schematic first book of *Structures* (1952) and *Le Marteau sans maître* (1953–55), two scores which Nono owned and annotated.[43] 'The delight with which the snob hears the vibraphone and marimba sounds of Boulez's *Marteau sans maître* today', Lachenmann argues in much stronger terms than Nono the year before,

> is no different from the delight experienced around the turn of the century when listening to some kind of oriental music. It is the delight of incomprehension in the face of a lack of content.[44]

Stockhausen fares little better, though the 'spokesman' with 'Führeranspruch' (claim to leadership, not without Nazi connotations) is also grudgingly recognised for his groundbreaking theoretical achievements:

[40] See Nonnenmann, *Der Gang durch die Klippen*, 184, 204–17; and De Benedictis and Mosch (eds.), *Alla ricerca di luce e chiarezza*, 84–90, 173–77.

[41] Lachenmann, 'Stuttgart lecture', 224. [42] *Ibid.*, 224.

[43] Of Boulez's scores in Nono's possession, the *Sonatine* (1953), the first book of *Structures*, *Le Marteau sans maître* and two of the *Improvisations sur Mallarmé* are annotated. *Structures* is briefly discussed in Nono, 'Zur Entwicklung der Serientechnik' (1956). Maderna wrote to Nono of his experience with Boulez's *Polyphonie X*: 'The Scarlatti Orchestra worked with an incredible musicianship and self-sacrifice . . . I believe the result will be the best and I regret to say that the broadcast will be most interesting. I regret this because the human principle of *Polyphonie* is completely wrong'; Maderna, letter to Nono, May/June 1953 (Maderna/B 53–05/06?-?? m, ALN).

[44] Lachenmann, 'Stuttgart lecture', 224.

> Nobody will deny Stockhausen admiration for being the first and only one to tackle, think through and solve many of the really decisive tasks of our time. [. . .] To me, however, composing does not end with the solution of theoretical compositional problems, especially when they are of such generally binding character as is credited to those Stockhausen exposes at regular intervals to his congregation. Because of very specific, concrete elements which Stockhausen's musical temperament seemingly does not want to do without, I believe that the development of his music is already cast into chains and hindered from arriving at new forms, let alone means of expression.[45]

To back up this claim, Lachenmann refers to a climactic passage for brass, piano and percussion in *Gruppen*. As shown by Misch, this particular passage does not comply with the serial organisation of the work but is part of the freely composed, cadenza-like insertions.[46] To Misch, this climax is nevertheless the 'zenith of structural writing' that annuls all criteria of traditional Western music.[47] Lachenmann, however, sees it in a very different light:

> the piano [. . .] creates a link to a section performed on percussion, a gigantic percussion solo as it were, the similarity of which to compelling improvisations of jazz musicians such as Max Roach or Jo Jones is almost embarrassing in terms of its instrumentation. The percussion sound and the numerous brass signals gradually amount to a further mass, a climax as it were. The listener is faced with a mass of gestures, of uncoordinated movements, which eventually peter out at a fitting moment in time.[48]

If Nono did indeed accuse Stockhausen of writing 'fascist mass structures' after his 1959 Darmstadt lecture, as Misch and Bandur claim,[49] Lachenmann comes close to grasping the root cause of this politically charged outburst. Of all the serial composers only Nono is believed to have overcome relics of tonality, such as the 'melodic-cell formation' Stockhausen and Boulez still adhered to. Nono's particular compositional rigour is grasped and understood as historically necessary precisely because it is not merely the product of elegant musical theory or the spirit of 'l'art pour l'art' but the means to address fundamental sociological and political

[45] *Ibid.*, 225.

[46] 'With a twinkle in his eye' Stockhausen revealed to Misch that this last tutti had initially been shorter. A few more bars had been added because he thought the 'noise' should last a little longer; Misch, *Gruppen*, 202–18.

[47] *Ibid.*, 218.

[48] Lachenmann, 'Stuttgart lecture', 225–26.

[49] Misch and Bandur (eds.), *Karlheinz Stockhausen bei den Internationalen Ferienkursen*, 210.

concerns. Not the serial technique per se, but content, communication and the function of the artist in society are thus at the very heart of this dispute. And an artist like Nono who continued to address issues such as the holocaust, Lachenmann quite rightly concludes, was not to be diverted from his path by feeble accusations of stagnation:

> That he [Nono] was continuously and unwaveringly concerned with compositional problems which others merely dabbled in for fun or turned into much more entertaining and thus all the more sensational problems, that of course was a *faux pas* for modernists (and reactionaries alike). For those who judge such things seriously, however, it is testament to an absolutely pure character and an artistic spirit aware of his task and the path ahead.[50]

'Darmstadt: again – of course – many are angry!!!!!!! A good sign.' Nono wrote to Lachenmann just after the courses in 1960, but then also observes in a much more serious vein:

> read in *Beiträge* III what Stock[hausen] writes on music and graphics:
> today they are preoccupied with how to notate something because it is easier.
> now, the result of what they notate and write is so conventional and banal that it in no way justifies their mythomania.
> the case of Pousseur is typical: his *repons pour 7 musiciens*: no necessity to communicate, to speak with music in the music, and then the most stupid little games to cover up the vacuity.
> clothing apparently full of chok-wirckung [*sic.*, shock-effect] – but empty, with neither character nor communication. why fear or be scared of speaking???? of communicating????? of stating and taking a position today?????[51]

The aesthetic debate surrounding and arising from the ultimately unavoidable clash between Nono and Stockhausen has been well documented and contextualised, most recently by Iddon.[52] Much theoretical depth, underlain by the philosophy and sociology of Adorno, Horkheimer and Luhmann, is provided by Mário Vieira de Carvalho.[53] My aim here is to take a detailed look at what Nono intended and managed to communicate 'with music' in his *Diario polacco '58*, the work which largely

[50] Lachenmann, 'Stuttgart lecture', 232.

[51] Nono, letter to Lachenmann, 23 July 1960 (Lachenmann/H 60–07–23 d, PSS), in De Benedictis and Mosch (eds.), *Alla ricerca di luce e chiarezza*, 54–55.

[52] Iddon, *New Music at Darmstadt*. Also see Decroupet, 'Aleatorik und Indetermination'.

[53] Vieira de Carvalho, *A tragédia da escuta*.

conditioned his demand for greater responsibility and historical awareness in music at that time.

By 1958, a number of key works on the holocaust had been published in Italy.[54] Fascist oppression and genocide gained renewed political significance in the context of Algeria, where Nazi atrocities seemed to repeat themselves all too quickly: widespread practice of torture, executions without trial, rape, the destruction of whole villages and thousands of deaths in detention camps.[55] Worse, these atrocities were now being committed by the French, who had only recently celebrated their liberation from Nazi occupation. As Nono later told Pauli,

> Many of us recognised the situation of the Resistenza in Algeria, transposed to the present, under altered geographical and historical circumstances, as for me, I realised that the struggle against fascism and oppression was not just a memory, but that it continued in the Third World, and had now shifted to have Algeria as its centre.[56]

Two unrealised music theatre projects document Nono's continued preoccupation with Nazi crimes: the project on Anne Frank which he discussed with Giuseppe Ungaretti in 1957–58 and the preliminary 'Torture' project with texts by Henri Alleg and other members of the Algerian resistance, some of which were later used for *Intolleranza*. Of the Anne Frank project, Nono first wrote to Steinecke, in July 1957,

> I am now thinking about the Anne Frank Diary. One should rework the whole thing, not in the way it is now being put on stage; almost everything as choral commentary – chorus as a symbol of Anne Frank; on stage only the essential. The chorus would be written entirely new. Again I spoke to Ungaretti in Rome: he said it could be a piece as clear-cut as a [drama by] Aeschylus, as strong, as complex, as classical.[57]

[54] Anne Frank's *Diary* and *The Human Race* by Robert Antelme were published in Italy in 1954, as was the Italian edition of *The Scourge of the Swastika* by Lord Russell of Liverpool (Nono owned the second edition of 1960). Of great impact, too, was Alain Resnais's film *Nuit et Brouillard* (1955) with music by Hanns Eisler. Primo Levi's *Se questo è un uomo* made its breakthrough in a new edition of 1958 (Nono owned this Einaudi edition, not the first edition of 1947). Another widely read publication (also in Nono's library) was Höss, *Comandante ad Auschwitz* (1960).

[55] The massacre and burning of Rivet on 10 May 1956, for example, was compared to Oradour. The French town was burnt and its population massacred by the Germans on 10 June 1944; see Simone de Beauvoir, *Force of Circumstance*, 338.

[56] Nono, 'Gespräch mit Hansjörg Pauli' (1969), *Texte*, 201; *Scritti*, II, 25; trans. in Durazzi, 'Luigi Nono's *Canti di vita e d'amore*', 454.

[57] Nono, letter to Steinecke, 6 July 1957 (Steinecke/W 57–07–06 d, Internationales Musikinstitut Darmstadt): 'jetzt ueberlege ich das Anne Frank-tagebuch: man sollte das

While this project was in the planning stages with Ungaretti, Nono also wrote to Alfred Andersch, asking him to collaborate on a music theatre project for 1958. 'My idea: as a theme: Intolerance. Possibly with 3 or 4 episodes, in which intolerance is demonstrated to the maximum', or '3 episodes of intolerance' juxtaposed with three of 'love' and 'understanding'. As a source for these ideas Nono mentions the silent film *Intolerance* (1916) by D. W. Griffith.[58] Preliminary notes for *Intolleranza* in a notebook entitled *Per il teatro* then combine the names of Anne Frank, Alleg and Fučík. Nono had obviously discarded the idea of an independent work on Anne Frank and was now contemplating the topic in connection with the practice of torture in Algeria. In another letter to Andersch, Nono also alludes to the danger of sentimentality that comes with a topic such as Anne Frank: 'what I now fear the most, and exactly this is happening, is the restoration! and always this poor emotion-feeling-disease!'[59] Simone de Beauvoir expressed a related opinion:

> Every evening, a sentimental audience wept over the past misfortunes of little Anne Frank; but all the children in agony, dying, going mad at that moment in a supposedly French country was something they preferred to ignore. If you had attempted to stir up pity for them, you would have been accused of lowering the nation's morale.[60]

Notably, the work with which Nono then first dared to address the holocaust is the purely instrumental *Diario polacco '58*, in which the 'drama' does not rely on any form of text but takes place solely in music and space. Moreover, the memory of the holocaust is given contemporary relevance in that it is placed in the context of post-Stalinist Poland.

If the brutally suppressed insurrection in Hungary in 1956 had caused major disillusionment and prompted many intellectuals like Maderna and

ganze bearbeiten, nicht wie auf Buehne jetzt geht; fast alles mit Choere-Commentar und Choere als Simbol von der Anne Frank; auf Buehne nur das Essentail; die Choere sollten ganz neu geschrieben werden. war wieder in Rom mit Ungaretti gesprochen: er sagt: es koennte ein Stuck klar wie ein eschilos werden, so stark, so komplex, so classik.' The mentioned stage version is by Goodrich and Hackett; Nono owned the German translation *Das Tagebuch der Anne Frank: Ein Schauspiel* (1958). The project is further discussed in correspondence with Ungaretti (ALN).

58 Nono, letter to Andersch, 25 September 1957 (Andersch/A 57–09–25 d, Deutsches Literaturarchiv Marbach), in De Benedictis, 'Dramaturgical and Compositional Genesis of Luigi Nono's *Intolleranza 1960* ', 104.

59 Nono, letter to Andersch, 19 November 1957 (Deutsches Literaturarchiv Marbach, copy at ALN Andersch/A 57–11–19 d): 'was am meisten ich fürchte jetzt, und genau jetzt passiert, ist die Restauration! und immer die arme Emotion-Gefuehl-Krankheit!'

60 Beauvoir, *Force of Circumstance*, 384.

Calvino to leave the PCI, the situation in Poland seemed much more promising. Following the Polish October in 1956 and in the course of Władysław Gomułka's thaw, Poland was slowly opening up to the West, without abandoning communism or its economic ties with the Soviet Union. In terms of politics and music, Nono's first journey to Poland thus turned out to be an exhilarating experience. Being able to attend the 1958 Warsaw Autumn, Nono wrote to several of his socialist friends, had been his 'most wonderful experience as a human-being–musician' to date.[61] To Karl Amadeus Hartmann, Nono enthuses about 'the great feeling of hope!!!!!!!!!!!!!!!', a musical situation based on human understanding – 'no clique, no snobbery' – and the exuberant reception of works of the Second Viennese School: 'An audience of 2,000 people enthusiastic about Schoenberg and Webern: *A Survivor from Warsaw* repeated and requested for a third time, the same for the *Psalm* as well as the *Five Movements for String Quartet* and *Five Pieces for Orchestra* by Webern.'[62]

But Nono also took the opportunity to visit the Warsaw Ghetto and Oświęcim (Auschwitz). He did so with a firm focus on the Polish resistance. The book *Ricorda cosa ti ha fatto Amalek* by the Polish Jew Albert Nirenstein is heavily marked, and the title presumably inspired Nono's own title, *Ricorda cosa ti hanno fatto in Auschwitz* (1966). Nirenstein's history of the Polish Jewish resistance was published in Italy in 1958 and may have accompanied Nono to Poland. A large part of the book is dedicated to the resistance in the Warsaw Ghetto. The final two chapters contain accounts of resistance in other urban centres and the concentration camps, including the *Sonderkommando* revolt at Auschwitz. Nono marked and annotated passages such as the manifesto of The Jewish Combatant Organisation, addressed to the citizens of Warsaw:

> Poles! Citizens! Soldiers of Liberty! [. . .] With your own eyes you see how the ghetto has been completely transformed into the fortress it will remain. [. . .] We shall all die in this struggle, but we will never surrender [. . .] It is a struggle for our liberty and yours! For your human dignity and ours![63]

A much more sinister passage, also marked by Nono, describes the so-called 'bath' in the Sobibór camp (extermination by means of gas). The description concludes with the words: 'Everything was perfectly organised, according

[61] Nono, letter to Hartmann, 21 October 1958, in Wagner (ed.), *Karl Amadeus Hartmann und die Musica Viva*, 211; almost identical wording is found in a letter to Paul Dessau.

[62] Nono, letter to Hartmann, 21 October 1958, in Wagner (ed.), *Karl Amadeus Hartmann und die Musica Viva*, 211.

[63] Nirenstein, *Ricorda cosa ti ha fatto Amalek*, 168 (ALN); *A Tower from the Enemy*, 109.

to the latest advances in German technology'.[64] This shocking account by the Russian Jew Alexander Pechersky (who led and survived the Sobibór revolt) also contains the image of the German oppressor with a whip in hand. The crack of four whips is later among the most violent sounds in *Diario polacco '58.*

Ultimately, however, no book can prepare for or capture the reality of such places as the Warsaw Ghetto and Auschwitz. Together with a delegation from the Frankfurt Auschwitz trial (defence, prosecution and the accused), Peter Weiss later also made the journey to Auschwitz. Having followed the trial, and being in the process of writing *Die Ermittlung*, Weiss arrived at Auschwitz extremely well informed. And yet, Weiss recollects in his powerful report *Meine Ortschaft* (*My Place*), all knowledge seemed to crumble when confronted with the reality of the now barren surroundings:

> Here are the kitchens on the main square, and in front of them a wooden sentry-box, with a high pointed roof and a weather-vane, with gaily painted stone dovetailing, as if built from a castle construction kit. It is the *Rapportführer* 's [Report Leader, low-ranking SS officer] hut, from which the roll call was supervised. I once knew of these roll calls, of these hours of standing in the rain and snow. Now I know only this empty, loamy square at the centre of which three posts supporting an iron rail are rammed into the ground. I know also how they stood here under the rail on stools, and how the stools were then knocked away from underneath them, and how the men with the *Totenkopfmützen* [death's-head caps] would hang onto their legs, in order to break their necks. Hearing and reading about it, I had seen it in front of me. Now I do not see it any more.[65]

The desolation and frustration felt on visiting Auschwitz, Weiss concludes, essentially results from the realisation that it is impossible to experience and fully understand what happened here:

> A living man has come and what happened here hides itself from him. The living man who comes here, from another world, has nothing but his knowledge of figures, written reports, statements by witnesses, which are a part of his life; it lies heavily upon him, but he can only grasp what he experiences himself [. . .] Now he is only standing in a vanished world. Here there is nothing more for him to do. For a while everything is utterly still. Then he knows that it has not ended yet.[66]

[64] *Ibid.*, 307; trans. amended.
[65] Weiss, *My Place*, in Middleton, *German Writing Today*, 23–24; trans. amended.
[66] *Ibid.*, 28; trans. amended.

'Nazi violence – and the natural life that continues, nevertheless', Nono wrote in early sketches for *Diario polacco '58*, and also 'remember journey towards Birkenau – then suddenly Oświęcim'.[67] Like Weiss, it seems, Nono was particularly struck by the discrepancy between the lost world of Auschwitz and life that continues – *Trotz alledem!* Nono's journey on the whole was marked by the constant clash of experiences at opposite ends of the emotional scale: the exhilarating music festival and the Warsaw Ghetto, the beauty of Kraków and the Tatra Mountains, and the pilgrimage to Auschwitz. In his programme note for *Diario polacco '58*, Nono would later write that 'one of the characteristics of this encounter' was 'the fast succession, often simultaneity, of different personal and natural situations which made an indelible impression on me during these days'. He goes on to add that 'this is also a fundamental characteristic of this music of mine'.[68]

Much has been said by Schaller and Nanni on the complex genesis of *Diario polacco '58*.[69] According to Nono himself, the piece derives from three key experiences: consternation and dismay on visiting the Warsaw Ghetto and Auschwitz, admiration and amazement at the beauty of some of the places visited, and enthusiasm for the determination of the Polish people to live and fight for free human existence: 'their violent resistance to Nazism, the glorious insurrection in Warsaw in 1944 and, after the cyclone of Nazi barbarism, the material, economic, social and cultural formation of a new Poland based on new core structures'.[70] As Nono himself explains, these three states of mind – consternation, amazement and enthusiasm – gave rise to three different 'modes of being' in music.[71] In the sketches these 'modes of being' are marked A, B and C and each mode or type of

[67] 'Violenza nazista – e la vita naturale che continua, malgrado'; 'ricorda viaggio verso –/ poi Oświęcim improvviso/ Birkenau', in Nanni, *Auschwitz: Adorno und Nono*, 190.

[68] Nono, '*Composizione per orchestra n. 2 – Diario polacco '58* ' (1959), *Scritti*, I, 433.

[69] The most detailed analysis is found in Schaller, *Klang und Zahl* (1997). Schaller provides a complete list of substitution tables with which it is possible to comprehend most of the serial generation of the music without further recourse to the sketches. Schaller's book and personal assistance was indispensable to my own analysis. Nanni's analysis in *Auschwitz: Adorno und Nono* (2004) is less concerned with the serial organisation than with the 'meaning' of perceptible structural units and their interpretation in terms of Adorno's philosophy. Both Schaller's and Nanni's analyses are not entirely satisfactory. Schaller does not explain the serial generation step by step and concludes with an unfortunate analogy to sonata form, which, in my view, is incompatible with the underlying structural idea of this piece. Nanni takes only the larger formal units into account and thus misses vital aspects of the serial organisation. The terminology of my own analysis concurs with that of Schaller.

[70] Nono, '*Composizione per orchestra n. 2 – Diario polacco '58* ', *Scritti*, I, 433.

[71] *Ibid.*, 435.

sound is differentiated by means of its serial generation. However, what in theory sounds very simple – three states of mind translated into three types of sound – is far more complex in practice, so much so that it is impossible to tell for sure which experience is represented by which type of sound. The overriding idea, it seems, is to create a sense of the fast succession, near simultaneity, of the fluctuating experiences, going from one extreme to the other, clashing but also merging into a single impression. As Nono specifies in his text, 'the rapid succession, often simultaneity, of the different situations I experienced corresponds to the speed with which the different "diary-like" gestures succeed each other: rapid and sudden changes where the unexpected always arrives and surprises in its variety'.[72] He later told Pauli that he 'did not want to create a diary in the sense of Schubert, Schumann or Janáček, but to juxtapose fragments, like jottings of impressions and intuitions which, in a diary, are often captured in a single sentence or exclamation'.[73]

*Diario polacco '58* is a difficult, perhaps even not entirely successful, work, precisely for this reason. It is very fragmented, marked by constant fluidity and change, and offers few structural markers to the listener. At times the succession of events is so rapid that they can hardly be grasped (fragments of one or two bars): one reason, perhaps, why Nono resorted to slower speeds and inserted general pauses of various lengths in the revised version with tape of 1965. The piece is extremely interesting in regard to later music by Nono, however, precisely because of its fragmented form, its use of compositional layers and how the memory of Auschwitz is highlighted and distinguished from the layer of ordinary human experience through musical means that deliberately defy the underlying serial system.

In terms of both subject matter and musical fabric *Diario polacco '58* harks back to *Il canto sospeso*, where the most violent sonorities are rendered by wind, brass and timpani, and instrumental violence is often effectively enhanced by means of flutter-tonguing and tone repetition. With similar instrumental techniques and a much extended brass and percussion section, Nono would attain far higher degrees of violence in *Diario polacco '58*. Yet, even in 1965, the eighth movement of *Il canto sospeso* continued to serve as a point of reference for *Die Ermittlung*.[74] As

[72] *Ibid.*, 435.

[73] Nono, Conversation with Pauli (1969), in Stenzl, 'Luigi Nono und Cesare Pavese', *Texte*, 427.

[74] Sketch 28.1/05v contains the annotation: 'CANTO SOSPESO No. 8 ottoni'. Owing to the electronic transformation, it is difficult to ascertain whether material from this movement was actually used. The material from *Diario polacco '58* is more recognisable.

discussed in Chapter 2, movement no. 8 of *Il canto sospeso* is one of the first examples of the structural use of density in Nono's oeuvre. Similar, but more complex, procedures are at work in *Diario polacco '58*. In addition to the four orchestral groups on stage, the orchestra also divides into three instrumental sections (brass, wind and strings) and three corresponding percussion sections (metal, wood and felt). Factors 3 and 4 of the all-comprising number 12 also pervade most other aspects. First of all, the work is conceived in four parts (I: bars 1–107, II: bars 108–240, III: bars 240–82, IV: bars 282–306; see Table 3.1).[75] The three types of sound or 'modes of being' evolve within these four parts. Each type is distinguished by the nature of its pitch groups (within which the order of pitch is free). As will be explained in more detail, type A combines chords and linear pitch progressions, type B is the only type of sound in which a single pitch may be rendered by two or more instruments, resulting in a spatial mobility that anticipates the 'suono mobile' of Nono's late works, while type C is restricted to linear pitch groups (although they, too, may be layered). A fourth type of sound (D) results from the combination of types A and B. All types of sound occur in four densities (indicating the maximum overlap of pitch groups).

Nono further devises four types of sound projection: coordinated pitches (rhythmic unison) from all four orchestral groups ('1111'), coordinated pitches from either side ('1122'), coordinated pitches from the two inner groups only ('1223'), and uncoordinated pitches from all four groups ('1234').[76] The choice of projection is determined serially and changes with every pitch. The type of projection thus hardly adds to the clarity of the sound. Instead, it, too, supports the impression of constant fluctuation, inner mobility, flexibility and fluidity.

On the more microscopic level of pitch generation, the duration factors (numbers 1 to 12) are divided into three groups of four: predominantly short values ('breve'), predominantly long values ('lungo') and the remaining medium values ('medio'). As shown in Table 3.2, Nono further allows the addition of double duration values in the second half.

Throughout the work, these three sets of duration factors are consistently applied to four duration values: crotchet divided by 4, 5, 6 and 7 (semiquavers, quintuplets, sextuplets and septuplets). Their conjunction is not fixed, but treated as variable. In other words, the determination of the

[75] When Nono returned to the work in 1965, he marked Parts III and IV as Parts C and C′, suggesting a three-part rather than a four-part division.

[76] ALN 19.08/01 lists the four types of projection in numerical representation. The sketch is reproduced and discussed in Schaller, *Klang und Zahl*, 212–13.

Table 3.1 Diario polacco '58 – *formal overview*

| Part I (bars 1–107) | Part II (bars 108–240) | Part III (bars 240–82) | Part IV (bars 282–306) |
|---|---|---|---|
| **BI** (1–6) | **CIII** (108–36) | **CI** (240–43) | **DIV (A + B)** (282–85) |
| F♯, *R1–R2* | G, *R7–R4* | D, *R12* | F, F♯, E, G, *R12–R9* |
| Br. | Str. Ww. Perc.// | Str. Br. Timp. | Str. Ww. Br. |
| **Type B** | Br. Ww. Perc. | | |
| | **Echoes** | | |
| **CIV** (6–16) | **DI (A + B)** (136–46) | **AII** (243–49) | **C** (285–93) |
| F♯, *R2–R12* | A♭, *R8–R11* | E♭, *R1–R2* | F, F♯, E, G, *R11–R8* |
| Str. Ww. Br. Perc. | Str. Ww. Br. Timp. | Br. Ww. Timp. | Str. Ww. Perc. |
| | **Blocks** | | |
| **CI** (16–19) | **CII** (147–66) | **BIV** (249–74) | **A + B + C** (294–95) |
| F♯, *R3* | A, *R9–R4* | E, *R2–R8* | F, *R10* |
| Str. | Br. Str. (+ Ww. Perc.) | Str. Ww. Br. Perc. | Ww. Br. |
| **Type C** | **Echoes** | **Violent outburst** | |
| **BIII** (19–38) | **DIII** (166–71) | **AII cont.** (275–81) | **C cont.** (295–98) |
| F♯, *R4–R11* | B♭, *R10–R12* | E♭, *R3–R4* | G, E♭, *R8–R7* |
| Str. Br. Perc. | Str. Ww. Br. Perc. | Ww. Str. | Perc. Ww. Br. |
| | **Blocks** | | |
| **AI** (38–42) | **BII** (171–75) | **CI cont.** (282) | **A + B cont.** (298–301) |
| F♯, *R5* | B, *R11–R12* | D, *R1* | E♭, A♭, D, *R8–R6* |
| Ww. (flutes) | Br. // Str. Ww. | Str. Ww. Br. | Str// Ww. Br. |
| **Type A** | | | |
| **CIII** (42–53) | **AIII** (176–81) | | **A + B cont.** (302–304) |
| F♯, *R6–R1* | C, *R12–R1* | | C♯, B♭ (A?), C, *R5–R3* |
| Br. Ww. Str. (db, vcl) | Br. Ww. Str. | | Str. Ww. |
| **AIV** (53–107) | **CI** (181–85) | | **A + B cont.** (304–306) |
| F♯, *R7–R6* | C♯, *R1–R2* | | B♭, B, F, F♯, |
| Str, Ww. Br. Perc. | Str. | | Str. Ww. Br. Perc. |
| **Blocks** | | | **Climax of violence** |

**DIII cont.** (185–91)
B♭, *R1–R3*
Str. Ww. Br.
**Block** (189)
**AIII cont.** (191–213)
C, *R2–R10*
Ww. Str.// Full orch.
**Blocks** (whips)
**CI cont.** (213–19)
C♯, *R2–R4*
Str. Ww.
**Echoes**
**AIII cont.** (219–26)
C, *R11–R12*
Str. Ww.
**BII cont.** (226–30)
B, *R12–R1*
Str. Ww. Br. + Timp.
**DIII cont.** (230–40)
B♭, *R3–R5*
Str. Ww. Br. (+ Perc.)
**Blocks**

Table 3.2 *Duration-factor distribution in* Diario polacco '58

| Type | Parts I and II | Parts III and IV |
|---|---|---|
| 'breve' | 1, 3, 5, 11 | + 2, 6, 10, 22 |
| 'lungo' | 2, 8, 10, 12 | + 4, 12, 20, 24 |
| 'medio' | 4, 6, 7, 9 | + 8, 12, 14, 18 |

Table 3.3 *Allocation of duration factors to types of sound*

| Type of sound | Part I | Part II | Part III | Part IV |
|---|---|---|---|---|
| A | 1, 3, 5, 11 | 2, 8, 10, 12 | 4, 6, 7, 9 (×2) | 1, 3, 5, 11 (×2) |
| B | 2, 8, 10, 12 | 4, 6, 7, 9 | 1, 3, 5, 11 (×2) | 2, 8, 10, 12 (×2) |
| C | 4, 6, 7, 9 | 1, 3, 5, 11 | 2, 8, 10, 12 (×2) | 4, 6, 7, 9 (×2) |

actual length of the pitches (which has a great deal of effect on the nature of a sound or texture) is not used to distinguish the different types of sound. Instead, the allocation of duration factors rotates from part to part. As shown in Table 3.3, each type of sound is thus composed with each set of duration factors at least once, and in Part IV the allocation of duration factors returns to that in Part I (obscured by the additional use of doubled factors).

The pitch material again derives from the all-interval series. The prime series is that on F♯ (the familiar series on C in retrograde).[77] For the first time since 1955, Nono also introduces transposition. The series remains un-transposed throughout the whole of Part I, until and including the long section AIV, which, in the sketches alone, is entitled 'Oświęcim'. Thereafter, it is transposed with each new section, ascending chromatically from F♯ (G, A♭, A, B♭, C, C♯ in Part II; D, E♭, E in Part III). In the last part the process of transposition accelerates even more and the transposition changes with each row of the underlying magic square. With this accelerating process of transposition, Nono clearly moves on from his preferred means of unification: the relentlessly recurring prime series.

77 According to Nanni, *Diario polacco '58* is based on the all-interval series on C; *Auschwitz: Adorno und Nono*, 194. This view is possible because of the retrograde relationship between the series on C and F♯. My own analysis concurs with Schaller and therefore regards the series on F♯ as the prime series.

| | | | | | | | | | | | |
|---|---|---|---|---|---|---|---|---|---|---|---|
| 1 | 12 | 2 | 11 | 3 | 10 | 4 | 9 | 5 | 8 | 6 | 7 |
| 6 | 9 | 1 | 10 | 5 | 8 | 2 | 11 | 4 | 7 | 3 | 12 |
| 3 | 11 | 6 | 8 | 4 | 7 | 1 | 10 | 2 | 12 | 5 | 9 |
| 5 | 10 | 3 | 7 | 2 | 12 | 6 | 8 | 1 | 9 | 4 | 11 |
| 4 | 8 | 5 | 12 | 1 | 9 | 3 | 7 | 6 | 11 | 2 | 10 |
| 2 | 7 | 4 | 9 | 6 | 11 | 5 | 12 | 3 | 10 | 1 | 8 |
| 8 | 1 | 10 | 3 | 12 | 5 | 11 | 6 | 9 | 4 | 7 | 2 |
| 10 | 2 | 11 | 6 | 7 | 3 | 9 | 1 | 12 | 5 | 8 | 4 |
| 11 | 4 | 9 | 1 | 8 | 6 | 12 | 2 | 7 | 3 | 10 | 5 |
| 9 | 5 | 12 | 2 | 10 | 1 | 7 | 4 | 8 | 6 | 11 | 3 |
| 12 | 3 | 7 | 4 | 11 | 2 | 8 | 5 | 10 | 1 | 9 | 6 |
| 7 | 6 | 8 | 5 | 9 | 4 | 10 | 3 | 11 | 2 | 12 | 1 |
| *R1* | *R2* | *R3* | *R4* | *R5* | *R6* | *R7* | *R8* | *R9* | *R10* | *R11* | *R12* |

**Figure 3.1** *Composizione per orchestra n. 2 – Diario polacco '58* – magic square.

The magic square which governs the pitch generation in *Diario polacco '58* is shown in Figure 3.1. The same square was previously used for *Cori di Didone* (1958). The first horizontal set of numbers is the number equivalent of the all-interval series, moving from the largest to the smallest interval. Lines 2 to 5 derive from this first line by means of the permutation 11 8 1 6 9 10 3 4 7 12 5 2. The following lines 7 to 12 are retrogrades of lines 6 to 1. Nono does not use the horizontal sets of this square, but consistently reads the vertical columns from left to right and from bottom to top (hence my labelling at the bottom of the square).[78] These vertical sets are clearly grouped into two groups of six (numbers 1–6 and 7–12), which undergo internal permutation and change position with each new column (above and below the dividing line). Not that any of these numbers appear in the music itself. Unlike the squares for *Il canto sospeso*, which generate concrete pitch structures and provide actual duration-factor series, this square serves as a purely abstract substitution guide and thus allows Nono to move on from the determination of individual pitches to group composition. The following examples of the generation of the three types of sound will clarify the advanced serial system.

[78] As in Schaller, *Klang und Zahl*, 131.

**Example 3.1** *Diario polacco '58*, opening section B1, mm 1–6.

The piece begins with section BI (bars 1–6), the simplest example of sound type B, which Nono himself called 'vibrazioni' (vibrations). The short section, shown in Example 3.1, is rendered by brass alone and cut off by a single strike on a steel plate.[79] Only rarely are the types of sound presented in such clarity, as a distinct phrase rendered by a single orchestral section. The special status of the brass is thus clear from the outset. Throughout Part I, type B is assigned the duration factors 2, 8, 10, and 12. In addition, Nono adds two further factors to each section *ad libitum*.

[79] In the 1965 version this first section is further distinguished by the insertion of a general pause.

[Vibrations]

*R1 + R2 (1):*

| | 7 | 12 | 9 | 11 | 10 | 8 | 2 | 4 | 5 | 3 | 6 | 1 | 6 |
|---|---|---|---|---|---|---|---|---|---|---|---|---|---|
| DF | 8 | 8 | 12 | 10 | 2 | 6 | 8 | 3 | 10 | 2 | 2 | 2 | 2 |
| DV | 2 | 1 | 1 | 4 | 4 | 4 | 3 | 3 | 2 | 2 | 3 | 1 | 3 |
| G | **2** | 1 | **3** | 3 | 1 | **2** | 3 | **1** | **2** | 2 | **3** | 1 | 3 |
| | F♯ | G | F | A♭ | E | A | E♭ | B♭ | D | B | C♯ | C | F♯ |
| G1 | 8 (6) | 8 (7) | 12 (7) | 5 (5) | 1 (6) | 1 (7) | 5 (6) | 2 (5) | 7 (6) | 2(6) | 1 (6) | 2 (7) | 1(6) |
| G2 | 8 (6) | 8 (7) | 12 (7) | 2 (7) | 2 (4) | 2 (6) | 8 (5) | 1 (7) | 7 (6) | 2(6) | 1 (7) | 2 (7) | 1(7) |
| G3 | 4 (7) | 8 (7) | 12 (7) | 4 (4) | 1 (7) | 3 (5) | 8 (5) | 1 (7) | 5 (7) | 1 (7) | 1 (7) | 2 (7) | 1(7) |
| G4 | 4 (7) | 8 (7) | 12 (7) | 3 (6) | 1 (5) | 6 (4) | 3 (6) | 2 (6) | 5 (7) | 1 (7) | 2 (5) | 2 (7) | 2(5) |
| | tb.1 | hrn1/2tb.1 | | hrn1/2trp.1 | | hrn1/2tb.1 | | trp.1 | hrn1/2tb.1 | | tb.1 | hrn | trp.1 |
| | tb.2 | hrn3/4tb.2 | | hrn3/4trp.2 | | hrn2/3tb.2 | | trp.2 | hrn3/4tb.2 | | tb.2 | hrn | trp.2 |
| | tb.3 | hrn5/6tb.3 | | hrn5/6trp.3 | | hrn5/6tb.3 | | trp.3 | hrn5/6tb.3 | | tb.3 | hrn | trp.3 |
| | tb.4 | hrn7/8tb.4 | | hrn7/8trp.4 | | hrn7/8tb.4 | | trp.4 | hrn7/8tb.4 | | tb.4 | hrn | trp.4 |
| | *p–mf* | *f–p* | *p–f* | *p–mf* | *f* | *fff* | *f–p* | *f–fff* | *p–mf* | *mf–p* | *f* | *fff* | *f* |
| | *mf–f* | | | *f* | *mf–f* | *f* | *p–fff* | *fff* | *f–p* | *mf* | *fff* | | *fff* |
| | | | | *f–p* | *mf* | *mf–f* | *f–fff* | *f* | | | *f-fff* | | *fff–f* |
| | | | | | | *f–p* | | | | | | | |

Group Characteristics:
Virtually simultaneous entries of pitches
Group dynamics:

| | | | | | |
|---|---|---|---|---|---|
| *p–f* | *p–f* | *f–p* | *f–fff* | *p–f–p* | *f–fff–f* |
| *f–p* | *f–p* | *p–fff* | | | |

| Movement/projection of sound | | | Group entries Positive | Preceding rests Negative |
|---|---|---|---|---|
| Group 1: | | | | 8 (7) |
| 7: | F♯ | G1/G2–G3/G4 | 8 (6) | |
| 12: | G | G1/G2/G3/G4 | | |
| Group 2: | | | | 10 (6) |
| 9: | F | G1/G2/G3/G4 | 10 (4) | |
| 11: | A♭ | G3–G1–G4–G2 | | |
| 10: | E | G2–G4–G1–G3 | | |
| Group 3: | | | | 8 (5) |
| 8: | A | G4–G3–G2–G1 | 8 (5) | |
| 2: | E♭ | G2/G3–G1–G4 | | |
| Group 4: | | | | 3 (5) |
| 4: | B♭ | G1–G4–G2/G3 | 3 (5) | |
| Group 5: | | | | 10 (5) |
| 5: | D | G1/G2–G3/G4 | 10 (6) | |
| 3: | B | G1/G2–G3/G4 | | |
| Group 6: | | | | 2 (5) |
| 6: | C♯ | G4–G1–G2/G3 | 2 (5) | |
| 1: | C | G1–G2–G3–G4 | | |
| 6: | F♯ | G4–G1–G2/G3 | | |

Groups have approximately the same length as the rests that precede them.

**Figure 3.2** *Composizione per orchestra n. 2 – Diario polacco '58*, generation of section BI (bars 1–6).

Table 3.4 *Substitution chart for section BI (bars 1–6)*

| | 1 | 2 | 3 | 4 | 5 | 6 | 7 | 8 | 9 | 10 | 11 | 12 |
|---|---|---|---|---|---|---|---|---|---|---|---|---|
| DF | 2 | 8 | 2 | 3 | 10 | 2 | 8 | 6 | 12 | 2 | 10 | 8 |
| DV | 1 | 3 | 2 | 3 | 2 | 3 | 2 | 4 | 1 | 4 | 4 | 1 |
| G | 1 | 3 | 2 | 1 | 2 | 3 | 2 | 2 | 3 | 1 | 3 | 1 |

In this opening section, the added factors are 3 and 6. Only these six factors are used for the substitution chart shown in Table 3.4.

DF indicates the duration factor, DV the number of duration values per 'vibration' and G the number of pitches per group. The process of substitution begins with row *R1* and the first digit of *R2* of the underlying number square (Figure 3.1). Each number of these columns of the square is substituted with the indications it is assigned in the substitution chart shown in Table 3.4. The result of this substitution and its conjunction with the pitches of the all-interval series on F♯ is shown in the generation table at the top of Figure 3.2. When read in conjunction with Example 3.1, it becomes clear how the 'vibrations' of this opening section, BI, are generated.

The section is rendered by one trumpet, two horns and one trombone in each orchestral group and comprises six groups of one to three pitches. The number of pitches per group is indicated by the bold numbers in the third line of the generating table (Figure 3.2).[80] The first group contains the first two pitches of the prime series: F♯ and G. The second line indicates the number of duration values to be used. For the pitch F♯ this number is 2; for G it is 1. For the rendition of the F♯ Nono thus makes use of septuplets (7) and sextuplets (6); septuplets are used for the pitch G.[81] The duration factor 8 happens to be the same for these two pitches. Thus F♯ has the overall duration of 8 sextuplets, and this duration is rendered in full by the trombones in Groups G1 and G2. The trombones in Groups G3 and G4 join slightly later with a duration of 4 septuplets, but end simultaneously with the trombones in G1 and G2. It is this inner differentiation and spatialisation of a single pitch that Nono calls 'vibrazione'. Almost

[80] The remaining numbers are of no consequence. Only the first number of a group constellation is valid. The term 'group' is ambiguous insofar as it may refer to a compositional unit of pitch or the orchestral groups. I will therefore consistently refer to compositional groups in lower-case letters while using capital G for the orchestral groups.

[81] The distribution of duration values always begins with the fastest value: 1 = 7, 2 = 7 + 6, 3 = 7 + 6 + 5 and 4 = 7 + 6 + 5 + 4.

simultaneously with the F♯, the G is added in rhythmic unison by all eight horns with the single duration of 8 septuplets. Dynamics are different for each pitch, ranging between *p* and *f*. Trombones crescendo on F♯ while the horns diminuendo on G. This adds to the inner flexibility of the spatialised sound event. However, there are no more than two dynamic tendencies per group. The idea is to give each group a clear dynamic shape that progresses logically within the larger unit of the section (see 'Group Characteristics' in Figure 3.2).

All other pitch groups of this section are generated in the same way. Particularly interesting is the generation of pitches with four different internal durations. The first one of these is the A♭ in the second group. Nono assigns this pitch to the horns. The horns of G3 begin with a duration of 4 semiquavers. G1 follows with a duration of 5 quintuplets, G4 with 3 sextuplets and G2 with 2 septuplets. Together the durations add up to the prescribed total of approximately 10 semiquavers. In this case the vibration happens not simultaneously (as with the opening F♯) but in linear form. Simultaneity is achieved with the other two pitches of the group, F and E. One of these has a long duration of 12 septuplets (unison), the other is a short spatialised accentuation of a total duration of 2 semiquavers. As a general rule in this section, the pitches of each group begin almost simultaneously (Nono delights in the fuzziness of near simultaneity), but endings are staggered and may differ considerably as in this second group. Another group of two pitches follows, then an extremely short and loud intervention on a single pitch by the trombones, followed by two further groups, ending with short, loud and dissonant vibrations on the pitches C♯, C and F♯. Each group is preceded by a silence of approximately the same duration. Long groups follow long silences, short and energetic interventions enter with minimal separation. This creates a kind of speech rhythm that logically ties together the individual sound events. The overall shape of the section is determined by means of register and dynamics. With the exception of the first group, sound generally vibrates in middle register. The shortest values, however, consistently stand out in the octave above as strident trumpet accents.

Types A and C are generated in similar fashion, though spatialisation here always includes several pitches and thus happens within groups or between groups, but never on a single pitch as in type B. Type A features note-chains and chords of up to four pitches. Its constitution is thus not too dissimilar from that of type B. From Part II onwards the two types are also combined to form a further type D (A + B). The most basic example of sound type A is section AI for four flutes (bars 38–42). The generation of this section is similar to that of section BI and is summarised in Figure 3.3.

[Chords/Aggregates]

DF: 3, 5, 11, +6

Substitution chart:

| | 1 | 2 | 3 | 4 | 5 | 6 | 7 | 8 | 9 | 10 | 11 | 12 |
|---|---|---|---|---|---|---|---|---|---|---|---|---|
| DF | 3 | 6 | 11 | 3 | 6 | 6 | 11 | 5 | 5 | 3 | 3 | 5 |
| G | 4 | | 1 | | | | | | 1 | | 4 | 2 |

*R5*

| | 9 | 11 | 10 | 8 | 7 | 12 | 6 | 1 | 2 | 4 | 5 | 3 |
|---|---|---|---|---|---|---|---|---|---|---|---|---|
| DF | 5 | 3 | 3 | 5 | 11 | 5 | 6 | 3 | 6 | 3 | 6 | 11 |
| G | **1** | **4** | | | | **2** | | **4** | | | | **1** |
| | F♯ | G | F | A♭ | E | A | E♭ | B♭ | D | B | C♯ | C |
| fl.1 | 5 (7) | | | 5 (6) | | | 6 (7) | | 6 (5) | | | 11 (7) |
| fl.2 | 5 (7) | 3 (4) | | | | | 6 (7) | | | | 6 (7) | 11 (7) |
| fl.3 | 5 (7) | | 3 (5) | | | 5 (6) | | 3 (4) | | | | 11 (7) |
| fl.4 | 5 (7) | | | | 11 (7) | 5 (6) | | | | 3 (6) | | 11 (7) |
| | +flutt. | | | | | +flutt. | +flutt. | | | | | +flutt. |
| | *p* | *ppp* | | | | *p* | | *mf* | | | | *ppp* |

| Group | Rotation of sound | Positive | Negative (rests) |
|---|---|---|---|
| 1 | | | 6 (7) |
| F♯ | G1/G2/G3/G4 | 5 (7) | |
| | | | 5 (7), *ca.* 3 (5) |
| 2 | | | |
| F–A♭–G–E | G3–G1–G2–G4 | 3 (5) + 9 (5) | |
| | | | 6 (7) |
| 3 | | | |
| E♭–A | G1/G2–G3/G4 | 6 (7) | |
| | | | 3 (6) |
| 4 | | | |
| B–B♭/C♯–D | G4–G3–G2–G1 | 3 (5) + 6 (5) | |
| | | | 11 (7) |
| 5 | | | |
| C | G1/G2/G3/G4 | 11 (7) | |

**Figure 3.3** *Composizione per orchestra n. 2 – Diario polacco '58*, generation of section AI (bars 38–42).

The section comprises five groups of one, two and four pitches, arranged in mirror-symmetric order. Again the groups are separated by silences corresponding to the duration of the following sound event. Dynamics remain constant for each group of pitches. The groups themselves are thus much more unified than those in section BI. Dynamic contrast, too, is kept to a minimum (*ppp*, *p*, *mf* ) and the general effect is one of utmost homogeneity, although the combination of normal sound production

[Interlocking lines]

DF: 4, 6, 7, 9, +11, +12

Substitution table:

| | 1 | 2 | 3 | 4 | 5 | 6 | 7 | 8 | 9 | 10 | 11 | 12 |
|---|---|---|---|---|---|---|---|---|---|---|---|---|
| DF | 7 | 7 | 7 | 7 | 9 | 9 | 9 | 4 | 4 | 6 | 11 | 12 |
| G | 1 | 2 | 3 | 4 | 1 | 2 | 3 | 1 | 2 | 3 | 4 | 4 |

*R3*

| | 8 | 7 | 12 | 9 | 11 | 10 | 4 | 5 | 3 | 6 | 1 | 2 |
|---|---|---|---|---|---|---|---|---|---|---|---|---|
| DF | 4 | 9 | 12 | 4 | 11 | 6 | 7 | 9 | 7 | 9 | 7 | 7 |
| G | **1** | **3** | 4 | 2 | **4** | 3 | 4 | 1 | **3** | 2 | 1 | **2** |
| | F♯ | G | F | A♭ | E | A | E♭ | B♭ | D | B | C♯ | C |
| G1 | 4 (4) | | | 4 (7) | | | 7 (6) | | | | 7 (7) | |
| G2 | | | | | | 6 (5) | | | 7 (5) | | | |
| G3 | | 9 (5) | | | | | | | | 9 (6) | | 7 (7) |
| G4 | | | 12 (6) | | 11 (4) | | | 9 (7) | | | | |
| | vln | vln | vln | vln | vla | vln | vla | vla | vla | vln | vla | vla |
| | *p* | *ppp* | *ppp* | *mf* | *p* | *mf* | *ppp* | *ppp* | *mf* | *ppp* | *ppp* | *p* |

| Group | Rotation of sound | Positive | Negative |
|---|---|---|---|
| 1 F♯ | G2 | **4 (4)** | **4 (4)** |
| 2 G–F–A♭ | G3–G4–G1 | **9 (5)** + 12 (6) + 4 (7) | **9 (5)** |
| 3 E–A–E♭–B♭ | G4–G2–G1–G4 | **11 (4)** + 6 (5) + 7 (6) + 9 (7) | **11 (4)** |
| 4 D–B–C♯ | G2–G3–G1 | 7 (5) + 9 (6) + 7 (7) | 3 (5) |
| 5 C | G3 | 7 (7) | |

**Figure 3.4** *Composizione per orchestra n. 2 – Diario polacco '58*, generation of section CI (bars 16–18).

and flutter-tonguing in the lower flute register also conveys a distinct sense of disquiet.

Type C is distinct from both A and B in that it is primarily conceived as a network of overlapping lines. The most basic example of this type of sound is section CI (bars 16–19), scored for violins and viola in middle and high register. Again quiet dynamics predominate (the dynamic range is identical to that of section A1: *ppp*, *p*, *mf* ). The section is generated as shown in Figure 3.4. *R3* of the number square is used to generate five groups of one, three and four pitches, again in mirror-symmetric order. All pitches are linked, resulting in lines (groups) of one to four pitches. The section begins with a single high F♯ in G2, followed by a silence of the same duration (4 semiquavers). The three pitches G, F and A♭ form the next group and meander through Groups G3, G4 and G1. The third group of four pitches (E, A, E♭ and B♭) enters almost simultaneously with the second pitch of the second group (F) and takes yet another path through the orchestral Groups (G4, G2, G1 and G4). The following fourth group (D, B and C♯) enters almost simultaneously with the second pitch of the preceding group (A), and moves through G2, G3 and G1. The last group, a single C in the violas (G3), enters on the second pitch of group 3. All lines are internally spatialised, i.e. each line moves through as many orchestral Groups as there are pitches. Thus the distribution of pitches per Group is even: each orchestral Group is allocated three of twelve pitches. The result is a mobile network of interlocking lines with an agglomeration of pitches at the centre of the section. Its textural transparency, quiet dynamics, choice of register and more or less homogeneous duration factors ($2 \times 4$, $1 \times 6$, $3 \times 9$, $4 \times 7 + 1 \times 11$ and $1 \times 12$) exemplify the ethereal calm with which Nono sought to resolve the expressive tension of denser textures such as that of the preceding section CIV for full orchestra (bars 7–16).

The most basic examples of the three types of sound are all found within the first forty-two bars of the work. Moreover, they are each rendered by a single instrumental section: BI by the brass, CI by the high strings and AI by the flutes. Clear exposition of each type of sound, however, was hardly one of Nono's primary concerns. In contrast to the striking opening statement by the brass, sections AI and CI are already much less distinct. Both emerge from or lead into denser textures and are therefore necessarily perceived in context, as part of the general flow. In comparison with all other sections in Part I, these prototypes are also extremely short: brief glimpses of purity within a network of complex relationships and juxtapositions of varying density. The central idea of the work, after all, was to express the turmoil of conflicting sensations in a fleeting and fragmentary, diary-like, form. If, as both Stenzl and Nanni have argued, there is sound symbolism at work in this piece (like the recurring desolate sound of the four flutes, the extremely expressive long floating lines soaring up to the highest registers in the violins, flutes and clarinets, or the increasingly violent percussion and brass interventions), it comes to the fore only momentarily, as brief focal points within the general process of constant change and transformation.[82]

With the aim of expanding the scope and expressive potential, each type of sound occurs in four densities. The maximum density of a section is indicated by the Roman numerals I, II, III and IV. These numbers refer to the maximum number of overlapping groups, but also (with some exceptions) to the number of instrumental sections employed. How density and instrumental combinations vary can be seen in the formal outline of *Diario polacco '58* (Table 3.1). In Part II sections may also be cut off to be continued at a later stage, not always with the same instrumental combinations. Sections BIV (bars 249–74) and AII (bars 275–81) towards the end of Part III are good examples of the mutating densities and instrumental combinations. Section BIV contains one of the climactic outbursts of utmost violence which Nono imagined in association with Auschwitz in the early sketches for this piece. The *fff* cracking of the four whips in bar 268 is among the most graphic allusions to violent oppression and torture in Nono's catalogue of sounds. Untuned percussion is here coupled with pitched instruments: the whips with the trumpets (C♯), the tom-tom and tambourine with flutes (F♯) and oboes (D), the timpani with the double basses (F). A concentration of short duration values and the use of tone repetitions in wind and brass effectively maximise the number of *fff* attacks. The ambitus is tight: dense chromaticism in the central register adds to the immense impact of this emphatic bolt of terror.

Two substitution charts and seven rows of the number square (*R2–R8*) are used to generate a total of twenty-four bars of music. The entire section is based on the series on E and can be divided into three subsections: BIVa (bars 249–54, *R2–R3*), BIVb (bars 255–67, *R4–R5*) and BIVc (bars 267–74, *R5–R8*). Despite belonging to the same type of sound, the three subsections are audibly distinct. The final climax determines the type of density (IV) and orchestration (full orchestra: strings, woodwind, brass, percussion). BIVa is the subsection with the highest group density. Twelve groups are here juxtaposed in such a way that density culminates at its centre. Dynamics range from *p* to *ff* and underline the increase and decrease in density (*mf–ff–p*). Additional devices such as tone repetition, flutter-tonguing in the horns, tremolo on timpani and string pizzicato add to the extremely heterogeneous sound-world. The texture fades out on metal percussion (felt sticks on cymbals and steel plates) and is followed by the extremely quiet and transparent subsection BIVb, in which groups do not

[82] On sound symbolism in *Diario polacco '58* see Stenzl, 'Luigi Nono und Cesare Pavese', 427–28; and Nanni, *Auschwitz: Adorno und Nono*, 212–22.

overlap but progress linearly. Moving from middle to high to low register, Nono creates a linear arch of eerie calm. Prolonged by the use of double duration factors, it is indeed as if the music comes to a halt. The use of soft cymbals, high flutes and violins is again a symbolically charged moment of 'canto sospeso'.

All the more dramatic is the following outburst of violence. BIVc is split into two: an initial bolt of violence and a longer passage to absorb the force of the blow. It is in this subsection that Nono begins to use a second substitution table, which allows the aggressive accumulation of short duration values. The final passage, however, again makes use of double factors and thus reverts to durations of medium length. The prescribed group divisions are here completely ignored. Instead, Nono couples pitches of similar duration. Just like earlier in subsection BIVb, which peaks on a prominent high major third (A♭–C) in flutes and violins, Nono again does not shy away from remnants of tonality.[83] The dyad D–F (vla/vln, bars 270–71) with added A♭ and B (cl/ob 3) is resolved with the dyad G–E (fl/hrn, bars 271–72). E, F and G are added for a further 'vibration', re-articulating the sustained pitches of the preceding series in the same middle register with different instrumental colour. The quasi-tonal progression is framed by almost identical, stridently dissonant groups of pitches in the horns and trumpets: C–C♯–F♯ (bar 270) and C♯–D–F♯ (bar 272). The durations of all the unwanted pitches of the serial generation process are simply assigned to untuned metal percussion (wooden sticks), leading seamlessly into section AII.

Nono's reaction to the previous thrust of violence is typical: the music gradually fades out as it ascends to great heights. Sound type A is here rendered by the strings and soft woodwind (flutes and clarinets), and the density of the texture is determined by a constant overlap of two groups. Using the series on E♭, Nono generates five groups for each row of the underlying square (*R3–R4*) and these overlap with strict adherence to group order. The order of pitches within groups, however, is free. Also the use of single and double duration factors is handled with great flexibility. Underlined by a two-fold *rallentando*, the interwoven groups of pitches are increasingly drawn out to double length as they ascend.

[83] Much weight is given to such quasi-tonal progressions in Nanni, *Auschwitz: Adorno und Nono*. Generally, consonant intervals result from the free order of pitches within groups. Nono makes use of this compositional freedom according to each specific context, thus proving that interval-conscious composition is indeed possible within rigorous serial limits. BIVc is an exception in that the group divisions dictated by the substitution table are disregarded.

Sections BIV and AII demonstrate the flexibility with which Nono uses the predetermined serial system. In terms of group formation, density and the spatial movement of sound, all three types of sound are constantly varied. The advancing process of transposition goes hand in hand with increasing fragmentation: larger sections are split apart, divided into two or more subsections and intertwined with similar fragments of other sections. With the introduction of durations of double length in Part III, sounds and textures gradually become more sustained and drawn out, as do the silences. Going back to the level of content, it could be said that the memories of Poland in 1958 increasingly overlap, merge and become much harder to distinguish as they begin to peter out and dissolve. To counteract this immense fluidity and the gradual process of disintegration, Nono introduces two solidifiers with which he effectively defies the serial system: blocks of sound and echo formations.

Block sonorities are first introduced in AIV (bars 53–107), the section which, in the manuscript score of 1959 and also in that of the later version with tape of 1965, carried the working title 'Oświęcim' (Auschwitz).[84] Nono wisely omitted this title from the printed score, for it could have implied the intention of representing Auschwitz musically. The section concludes Part I and is by far the longest and most coherent section of the entire piece (fifty-four bars). It evolves in two parts. The first (bars 53–74) is a wave of sound that picks up on elements that have already been exposed. A dense texture for full orchestra grows from exceedingly quiet percussion sounds (metal/wood). At the height of its intensity it is dominated by loud tremolo and tone repetition in strings and percussion, and particularly effective loud flutter-tonguing and tone repetition in brass and wind. The segment's arch form recalls movement no. 4 of *Il canto sospeso*, and Nono may well have thought of a comparable state of agony.

Much more terrifying, however, is the second part (bars 74–107). It is here that Nono first makes use of block sonorities that do not comply with the serial system. Extra notes are added to form dense and narrow blocks of three to six pitches. Chromatic relationships prevail. Many are straight chromatic clusters, and all pitch constellations have the narrowest possible ambitus. The dense interlocking blocks are all crammed into the middle register. They are also marked by a much tighter, unified sound projection, addressing the audience in a much more direct way than the serially generated textures. The overall effect of these block sonorities is one of impermeable confinement leaving hardly any space to breathe. In three

84 ALN 19.11.01/10. See Schaller, *Klang und Zahl*, 138, n. 27, and Nanni, *Auschwitz: Adorno und Nono*, 215.

consecutive phases, always beginning with untuned percussion sounds, this block composition gradually moves from *ppp* to *fff*, ending with a violent gesture of tone repetition in brass and strings and a last roar of trilling woodwind. Orchestral violence is not yet as explicit here as in the outbursts towards the end of the piece. The effect, however, is all the more arresting. The impermeable density of the instrumental texture, its narrow range, the unified sound production and projection, the directed and extremely clear-cut musical shape all work to create a sensation of growing anguish and trepidation. The tension is resolved with an exceedingly quiet afterthought in the horns and, after another, fainter, thrust of violence, the flutes. Accompanied by the otherworldly sound of metal percussion, the flutes finally ascend to a higher register, a tentative attempt at escape from the strict boundaries of the preceding passage.

The sensation which Nono creates with this central section of *Diario polacco '58* is comparable, perhaps, to that of entering the Holocaust Tower in the Jewish Museum in Berlin. Influenced in part by Walter Benjamin's *One-Way Street*, Daniel Liebeskind's museum design is structured around 'two lines of thinking, organization and relationship. One is a straight line, but broken into many fragments, the other is a tortuous line, but continuing indefinitely.'[85] The Holocaust Tower is part of the underground system of intersecting straight lines, positioned at the end of the Axis of the Holocaust. Visitors enter through a large, heavy iron door and find themselves in a bare, narrow space enclosed by four towering raw concrete walls, which rise to the full height of the three-storey building in the shape of an irregular tetrahedron. In the most elongated corner light falls in through a single slit high above the ground. The narrow angle of this corner functions as a kind of focal point from which the view is directed to the only source of light above. The architectural void, the damp cold air, the symbolically charged ray of light and subdued city noise compel one to silent reflection. Nobody dares speak in this environment in which 'abandonment, doubt, fate, and helplessness all manifest themselves architecturally'.[86]

'For a while everything is utterly still. Then he knows that it has not ended yet.' The most powerful holocaust memorials, it seems, are those which evoke silent reflection of this kind: reflection informed by and channelled into historical awareness. Nono's piece, it becomes exceedingly clear, is not primarily about individual experience, but rather constitutes an essay in remembrance. Just like Liebeskind's Holocaust Museum,

[85] Braun, 'The Architectural Language of Daniel Liebeskind', 178. [86] *Ibid.*, 179.

Nono's orchestral work is essentially structured around two lines of thought, one straight but fragmented, the other tortuous but continuous. Nazi violence, that which defies human experience, is represented by the straight line of thought: outbursts of orchestral violence, increasingly spaced out, but progressively gaining in force. This line of thought encompasses the non-serial device of the sound blocks which stand out in their much more direct and unified sound projection. The second, tortuous line of thought is that of continuous transformation and development and it, too, contains a non-serial device: very still echo formations. Such echo formations occur just in Part II and only in structures of sound type C. Here, too, the method of projection is distinct. An entire serial texture is rendered by a single orchestral group while selected pitches of its texture are echoed in another. These echo formations are placed either in the two outer or in the two inner orchestral groups. Nono thereby creates two distinct spatial effects: a channelled projection of sound from the centre of the stage or a void in the centre and sound from the outer groups. The extreme calm and stillness of these musical echoes and their distinct spatial effect emphasise the reflective function of this tortuous line of thought – the layer of human experience – which becomes more and more complex but also progressively more drawn out towards the end of the piece.

'Violent orchestra in outbursts! VIOLENTISSIMO! dramatic/ and "canto sospeso"' one reads in an early sketch when Nono was still planning to write a work with four distinct programmatic episodes.[87] The fundamental split implied in this sketch for the Auschwitz episode was to have impressive and utterly convincing structural consequences for the entire work: a spiral form from which the violent elements associated with the memory of Auschwitz and the Warsaw Ghetto emerge with increasing force while the layer of individual experience becomes ever more tortuous and eventually begins to dissolve. There could indeed be no other conclusion to this work than a final dramatic outburst, a forceful reminder not to forget.

With memory and remembrance at the heart of its discourse, *Diario polacco '58* is truly a memorial piece, much more conclusively so than *Il canto sospeso*. This does not mean, however, that it is any less committed. And precisely this commitment is also at the heart of Nono's lecture *Geschichte und Gegenwart in der Musik heute* and, even more overtly so, in *Text – Musik – Gesang* (1960) in which he refers back to Schoenberg's *Survivor from Warsaw* as the great model of Sartrean commitment in music and the 'musical aesthetic manifesto of our epoch'. The reflection on the

[87] 'Violenta orchestra a scatti!/ VIOLENTISSIMO! drammatico/ e «canto sospeso»', as cited in Nanni, *Auschwitz: Adorno und Nono*, 190.

importance of Sartre's *Qu'est-ce que la littérature?* ends with words that are just as applicable to Nono's own anti-fascist music:

> And if anyone rejects Schoenberg's *docere et movere*, and in particular *A Survivor from Warsaw*, the words of the nineteen-year-old student Giacomo Ulivi, in his last letter written before being executed by the fascists in Modena in 1944, are addressed also to him: 'Do not say that you don't want to know any more about it. Remember that everything occurred because you didn't want to know any more about it.'[88]

If Nono chose to remember this particular work in these terms at Darmstadt in 1960, he did so with the intention of leaving a stark warning. That this warning was not received favourably at the time is only partly due to the contemporary fascination with chance procedures as a way out of the serial straightjacket. The West German political climate was such that the publisher Schott was actively trying to dissuade Nono from using text by Brecht for *Intolleranza 1960.* Ditching his publisher and leaving Darmstadt for good, Nono was obviously no longer prepared to tolerate such attitudes and constraints. After the premiere of *Diario polacco '58*, he would only return to the West German platform with a new work on the subject of a political bombshell: *Die Ermittlung* (1965) by Peter Weiss, based on the Frankfurt Auschwitz trial.

[88] Nono, 'Testo – musica – canto' (1960), *Scritti*, I, 65. Ulivi's letter is cited from Malvezzi and Pirelli (eds.), *Lettere di condannati a morte della Resistenza europea*, 539. In his text *Orator*, advocating the development of new forms of expression, Cicero stressed the need to prove one's thesis (*docere*) and to move the audience emotionally (*movere*).

# 4 Music to *Die Ermittlung* by Peter Weiss (1965)

The Frankfurt Auschwitz trial (1963–65) was the first major prosecution of Nazi war criminals in West Germany since the Nuremberg trials (1945–46), and much had changed since then. Until 1948 the Allies pursued a far more thorough policy of purging in Germany than was ever the case in Italy. By the end of 1945 more than 200,000 party officials and SS members had been arrested. Of the 5,000 perpetrators tried in the French, British and American zones, 800 were sentenced to death, and approximately a third of the death sentences were carried out.[1] Another consequence of the Allies' politics of purging was the immediate and unconditional mass dismissal of civil servants: more than 100,000 were dismissed in the American sector alone.[2] However, the Allies insisted on the completion of the process of denazification by 1948, and, with the foundation of the Federal Republic of Germany under Konrad Adenauer in 1949, all denazification policies were abolished. The first amnesty law came into force in December 1949, whereupon about 800,000 civil servants were immediately reintegrated into West German society. Well concealed by the Nazi-infested judicial system, about 10,000 Nazis who had committed serious crimes profited from the amnesty, including some who had participated in the Kristallnacht pogroms of November 1938. Another amnesty law was enacted in 1951, and further relaxation of restrictions followed every federal election between 1953 and 1960. Even former members of the Gestapo were allowed to return to public service, and former Waffen SS officers began to demand state jobs and pensions. Reconciliation (Wiedergutmachung), Frei poignantly argues, came to mean reconciliation for the victims of the Allies' politics of purging, rather than for those of the Nazi regime.[3]

Public opinion shifted in the mid fifties when it became apparent that major Nazi officials had been able to make their way back into positions of high rank, even in government. Theodor Oberländer, for example, a Nazi expert on the East, was appointed Minister for Refugees under Adenauer. Another extremely high-profile case was that of Hans Globke, the head of

[1] Frei, 'Coping with the Burdens of the Past'.

[2] In Italy civil servants were dismissed only after completion of the legal process; see Woller, *Ausgebliebene Säuberung*, 161.

[3] Frei, 'Coping with the Burdens of the Past', 32.

Adenauer's chancellery, who, it emerged, had written a legal commentary approving the Nuremberg Race Laws of 1935. As late as 1968 the Federal President, Heinrich Lübke, and the Chancellor Kurt Georg Kiesinger, were former members of the Nazi party. In many cases, such as that of Globke, the Nazi past of high-ranking officials was exposed by the East Germans. The intention here, of course, was to demonstrate the evils of Western capitalist society. Entire 'brown books' were published to this end (including English translations), revealing the Nazi careers of government officials, civil servants, judges and business managers alike.[4] Also initiated by East Germany was the leaflet campaign 'Hitler's Murderous Judges in Adenauer's Service'. The East German state's ideology was founded on anti-fascist values, and its own record in this respect was indeed a clean slate compared with that of the West. What remained unmentioned, of course, was the fact that East Germany's strict policy of purging had eradicated not only former Nazis but also the more liberal socialists.[5]

Similar divisions manifested themselves in literature and the arts. Fučík's prison notebook is but one revealing example: published in East Berlin in 1948, it had to await publication in the West until 1976. Anti-fascist themes defined East German literature from the outset, not only with authors such as Brecht and Anna Seghers, but also for those of the younger generation, for example Franz Fühmann and Heiner Müller. The Nazi past was addressed considerably later in the West. Classics like Andersch's *Sansibar oder der letzte Grund* (1957), Grass's *Blechtrommel* [*The Tin Drum* (1959)] and Böll's *Billard um halb Zehn* [*Billiards at Half-past Nine* (1959)] were all published in the late fifties as the 'politics of restoration' began to be recognised more fully. Two important films to engage with the Nazi-infested economic and judiciary systems were Kurt Hoffmann's *Wir Wunderkinder* (1958) and Wolfgang Staudte's *Rosen für den Staatsanwalt* (1959).[6] A marked politicisation of Germany's Nazi past was further brought about by the Eichmann trial in Jerusalem (1961). In the aftermath of this highly publicised event, the first to be broadcast on TV worldwide, a series of West German documentary dramas propelled the debate further into the public domain: Hochhuth's *Der Stellvertreter* [*The Representative* (1963)], for example, with its sensational charge that the Roman Catholic

[4] See, for example, National Front of the GDR (ed.), *Brown Book: War and Nazi Criminals in West Germany* (Dresden, 1965).

[5] See Welsch, '"Antifaschistisch-demokratische Umwälzung"'.

[6] Both films were produced in the West. Staudte's other classic of anti-fascist cinema, *Die Mörder sind unter uns* [*The Murderers Are Among Us* (1946)], was the first ever DEFA production (East Berlin).

Church and its 'representative' Pope Pius XII had done little to prevent the extermination of the Jews, but also Kipphardt's *Joel Brand* (1965) based on Brand's testimony at the Eichmann trial, exposing lucrative deals between Eichmann and those attempting to save the lives of Jews.

With *Die Ermittlung* Peter Weiss, too, made use of the court-room scenario with its aura of judicial authority, to publicly name and shame the major German industrial corporations IG Farben, Krupp and Siemens, and the Deutsche Gesellschaft für Schädlingsbekämpfung (producers of the gas Zyklon B), for having profited from the holocaust.[7] The drama's fundamental charge against capitalist society lies at the heart of Canto 4 'The Possibility of Survival', in which Weiss is thought to have given himself a voice as Witness 3:

> We must drop the lofty view
> that the camp world
> is incomprehensible to us
> We all knew the society
> that produced a government
> capable of creating such camps
> The order that prevailed there
> was an order whose basic nature
> we were familiar with
> For that very reason
> we were able to find our way about
> in its logical and ultimate consequence
> where the exploiter
> could expand his authority
> to a degree never known before
> and the exploited
> was forced to yield up.
> the fertilizing dust
> of his bones[8]

[7] In Canto 1: The Platform the former station master, now holding 'a high executive position in the management of the German Railways', is asked to identify the industries at Auschwitz and names IG Farben, Krupp and Siemens; Weiss, *The Investigation*, 120–21; *Die Ermittlung*, 13. Managers of IG Farben were tried by an American tribunal in Nuremberg (1947–48). Ten of twenty-four were acquitted; all of the others had been absolved by 1951. Five took on leading positions in Germany's chemical industry. IG Farben was liquidated in 1952 and twelve new companies were founded. Compensation to Jewish victims was agreed in 1957, after which shares for 'IG Farben in Liquidation' rose by 10%. See Steinbacher, *Auschwitz: Geschichte und Nachgeschichte*, 112–13.

[8] Weiss, *Investigation*, 191; *Ermittlung*, 85–86.

While completing the play, Weiss further publicly announced his commitment to socialism at a writers' congress in East Germany and thereby sparked a hot political debate. As shown by Christoph Weiß in his two volumes on *Die Ermittlung* and its reception in East and West, this debate was to dominate the reception of the work well before it was even produced.[9] Nono, too, was fully aware of this politically charged situation and comments in his programme note that 'above all with *Die Ermittlung*, Peter Weiss unequivocally affirms his choice in today's world. This is one reason why his work is so fundamentally new to German literature. The opportunity to work with him is not only manifestly obvious, logical and consistent for me, I am also truly happy for it.'[10]

Nono himself actively supported workers in northern Italy at the time, and unions of workers in metallurgy plants in particular. Several statements of workers from the Italsider plant in Genova are set in *La fabbrica illuminata* (1964), including the provocative 'fabbrica come lager' (factory as camp). In a letter to the participating workers Nono refers back to this particular statement in the context of the Vietnam War:

> today Vietnam too is present in every one of our factories.
> the heroic struggle of the partisans and of the Vietnamese National Liberation Front [Việt Cộng] is also the struggle in each of our factories, where the power of capital is opposed and contested.
> and like Vietnam, each one of our factories (including Italsider, the 'illuminated' example of workers' oppression) indicates and prepares for the true communist nature of the finally liberated man.[11]

Nono wrote this letter to the workers of Italsider less than a month after the premiere of *Die Ermittlung* on 19 October 1965, and it is against the background of this active engagement in the Italian workers' struggle that one has to understand the composer's equally passionate programme note on the music for *Die Ermittlung*. Nono begins with two fundamental questions: 'how and why music for *Die Ermittlung*? and above all: why still today – 1965 – Auschwitz?'[12] Why has it taken twenty years for you to come to terms with Auschwitz, Nono here seems to ask his West German

[9] Weiß, *Auschwitz in der geteilten Welt*.

[10] Nono, 'Musica per "Die Ermittlung" di Peter Weiss', *Scritti*, I, 450; original German in the programme for Piscator's production, Goertz (ed.), *Die Ermittlung von Peter Weiss*, 8–9; trans. in *Luigi Nono: Complete Works for Solo Tape*, CD booklet, 47–48 (amended); henceforth referred to as 'Music to *The Investigation*'.

[11] Nono, 'Lettera di Luigi Nono agli operai dell'Italsider di Genova-Cornigliano' (21 November 1965), *Scritti*, I, 186–87.

[12] Nono, 'Music to *The Investigation*', 47.

contemporaries, and goes on to attack the trial itself: 'why do trials such as the Frankfurt trial only take place twenty years after the end of the war? and why such mild and shameful verdicts?'[13] In a letter to Piscator, Nono goes even further: 'The accused and the judges: they are all the same! the country that allows this: a poor country!!!!!!!!!'[14] Had it been up to Nono, *Die Ermittlung* would have been produced as an outright political onslaught:

> Piscator: show them who *the true Piscator* is, still today [. . .]
> 'die ermittlung' can only be an explosion.
> and not an 'objective' demonstration.
> otherwise one would agree with the Frankfurt conclusion!!!!!
> and I can't go along with that!
> surely you can't either! and surely Weiss can't either!!!!!!
> the brown book remains of importance! even more so, the idea of projecting 'anonymous' texts along with the music.[15]

Piscator reacted to this passionate demand with great reservation. With Weiss's public declaration of socialist convictions, the production was already turning into a 'slanging match' between East and West before it had even been seen. In response to Nono, Piscator thus emphasises the need for political neutrality and reminds the composer that the main purpose of the drama is to confront the people with the facts about Auschwitz and to try 'to "change" their way of thinking, their attitude, their actions – even if the chances are slim'.[16] In his own programme note, the West German press is reprimanded for accusing Weiss of exploiting the theme of Auschwitz for the purposes of anti-Western propaganda. Capitalist oppression and exploitation, Piscator argues, is just one aspect of the drama and a comparatively minor one. The drama as a whole is a distilled 'concentrate' of the findings of the Frankfurt Auschwitz trial and deals exclusively with 'the facts' of Auschwitz. 'It could well be', Piscator concludes, 'that these facts speak against us, against the way we come to terms with them; they certainly speak against the kind of public opinion which at all costs seeks to brand the facts as manipulated propaganda.'[17] For this reason Piscator ultimately refrained from projecting extracts of brown

[13] Nono, 'Music to *The Investigation*', 47.

[14] Nono, letter to Piscator, 20 August 1965, original German (carbon copy by Nono, Piscator/E 65–08–20 d, ALN), Italian in De Benedictis and Schomerus, 'La lotta "con le armi dell'arte" (II)', 181–82.

[15] *Ibid.*, 181–82.

[16] Piscator, letter to Nono, 24 August 1965 (Piscator/E 65–08–24 m, ALN); *ibid.*, 182–83.

[17] Piscator, 'Anmerkungen zu einem grossen Thema' (October 1965), 322.

books or any other texts and images, a possibility which had obviously been discussed and was usually at the heart of Piscator's political theatre.[18]

The music was, therefore, all the more important. The purpose of this music, it had been agreed from the outset, was to represent the six million dead – those who could no longer speak out: as Nono states in his programme note, 'music functioning exclusively as a means of representing that which the text and action cannot: the 6 million murdered in the concentration camps, with an autonomous musical concept'.[19] In 'Musica e teatro' (1966) he explains this further: 'choruses [. . .] which alternate with the "canti" of the text, but developing on their own time scale in a manner distinct from that which is occurring on stage'.[20] It was also decided that this music between the scenes should be extremely brief: 'Music of maximum 1′/ minimum 5″–10″' Nono wrote in one of his earliest sketches.[21] This severe time limit is generally adhered to: the shortest of the thirty-five fragments for *Die Ermittlung* lasts a mere 8″, the longest 1′47″, and the average duration is about 30 seconds. In fact, Nono was here asked to compose what he had already done for *Diario polacco '58*: a series of interrelated fragments. On measuring the individual sections of the orchestral work in real time, one is left with an astonishingly similar picture: thirty-two sections with durations ranging between about 5″–10″ and 1′. The average duration is perhaps even slightly shorter, about 20″, though the 'Oświęcim' episode stands out in this respect, having an exceptionally long duration of 2′22″. Another very important analogy between *Diario polacco '58* and the music to *Die Ermittlung* is the progressive increase in violence. In Weiss's drama this idea provides the single most important structural guideline. Employing the structure of Dante's *Divina commedia* as his model, Weiss progressively moves towards the final solution in eleven Cantos (thirty-three scenes, three per Canto).[22] The play begins with the arrival at the camp (Canto 1: The Platform), followed by reports on the

[18] On plans to project documentary images see Nanni, *Auschwitz: Adorno und Nono*, 306–307. Nono later expressed a preference for the production by Hanns Anselm Petern in Rostock (East Germany), for which his music was also used. Petern is praised for taking on the charge against the German industry and for his use of amplification and collective speech. Nono, 'Musica e teatro' (1966), *Scritti*, I, 212–13.

[19] Nono, 'Music to *The Investigation*', 47.

[20] 'cori [. . .] che si alternasseri al "canti" del testo, con un proprio tempo di sviluppo rispetto a quello scenico' Nono, 'Musica e teatro', *Scritti*, I, 213.

[21] ALN 28.01/03v.

[22] *Die Ermittlung* was originally conceived as the 'Paradiso' part of a trilogy based on Dante's *Divina commedia*. The project was mentioned in *The Times* (19 August 1964) on the occasion of Peter Brook's production of Weiss's *Marat/Sade*; see Weiß, *Auschwitz in der geteilten Welt*, I, 57. Weiß discusses the Dante project and also published the incomplete *Inferno*.

inhumane living conditions (Canto 2: The Camp), the torture of political prisoners (Canto 3: The Swing), medical experiments on women and death by hanging for those attempting escape (Canto 4: The Possibility of Survival). The central two Cantos then focus on individuals, a direct confrontation of victim and oppressor: Lili Tofler (Canto 5), secretary of the Political Department, tortured and shot for having written a letter of support to one of the political prisoners whose identity she is not prepared to reveal, and SS Corporal Stark (Canto 6), a young and zealous Nazi, responsible for countless shootings and killing by gas, attempting to excuse his actions by citing the indoctrination he experienced throughout his education and the pressures to obey. Singled out between intervals, these two Cantos were at the centre of Piscator's production and also central to Nono's music. The process of increasing violence then continues: shootings at close range, including that of a child (Canto 7: The Black Wall), death by injection, including of a group of 119 children (Canto 8: Phenol), death by starvation and the first killing by gas of Soviet prisoners of war (Canto 9: The Bunker Block), the perfection of this technique (Canto 10: Zyklon B) and, finally, a detailed description of mass murder and mass cremation in furnaces working at full capacity (Canto 11: The Fire Ovens). These 'facts' are laid bare in all their brutality, but the trial ends without a verdict. The last word is given to one of the accused with 'loud approbation' from all the defendants:

> Today
> when our nation has worked its way up
> to a leading position in the world
> we ought to concern ourselves
> with other things
> These recriminations
> should have fallen
> under the Statute of Limitation
> a long time ago.[23]

When Piscator asked Nono for music to this hard-hitting documentary drama he immediately approached him with a concrete musical idea: 'I thought of a chorus, such that the music would be for voices alone; in effect, the voices of the six million dead.'[24] Without yet having read the text, Nono initially replies as follows:

> Of course, you are right: only a chorus – only song.
> this could be: just chorus, at times, or just a solo voice;

[23] Weiss, *Investigation*, 296; *Ermittlung*, 198–99.

[24] Piscator, letter to Nono, 7 May 1965 (Piscator/E 65–05–07 m, ALN), trans. in Kontarsky, 'Stage Music for *Die Ermittlung*', 45.

> this could be: a live chorus which is also recorded on tape and transmitted into the auditorium through several loudspeakers (right – left – front – back – above etc.)
> tape offers several possibilities: with a small chorus (about twenty people suffice) one could have a chorus of 200–1,000 people, sung, live, and transformed (so that the expression is also varied) and transmitted through many loudspeakers in the auditorium.[25]

Having read the text, however, Nono decided that the music to this drama could not be restricted to vocal sonorities alone. Once again, Nono chose to work with three different types of sound: vocal, instrumental and electronic. All three layers would include new material as well as material from previous pieces of which recordings were available. These materials were first analysed by Matthias Kontarsky in his comparative study of Nono's and Paul Dessau's music to *Die Ermittlung*.[26] Nanni later added valuable details on the use of previous material.[27] However, neither Kontarsky nor Nanni had access to Nono's annotated typescript of the play. I thus argue for a slightly different reconstruction of the distribution of the music. The position of each fragment in the drama (as I understand it) is detailed in Table 4.1, together with particularly relevant passages from the text. All timings refer to the commercially available RAI recording.[28]

After *Omaggio a Emilio Vedova* (1960), the recording of the choral material for *Intolleranza 1960* (1961) and *La fabbrica illuminata* (1964), Nono's music for *Die Ermittlung* was no longer the work of a novice in electronic music. Considerable experience had been gained at the Studio di Fonologia in Milan with the production of the four-channel tape for *La fabbrica illuminata*. As mentioned in Chapter 1, this tape merges a wide range of industrial noise with electronically produced synthetic sound and confronts this sound-world of 'mechanical reproduction' with an equally wide range of vocal material: snippets of workers' statements (also recorded at Italsider), recordings with the Coro Polifonico di Milano (spoken and sung) and recordings with Carla Henius, who sang the live solo part at the Venice premiere in 1964.[29] To the dimensions of electronic

[25] Nono, letter to Piscator, 10 May 1965 (carbon copy by Nono, Piscator/E 65–05–10 d, ALN), Italian in De Benedictis and Schomerus, 'La lotta "con le armi dell'arte" (II)', 179.

[26] Kontarsky, *Trauma Auschwitz*, 52–59/100–108.

[27] Nanni, *Auschwitz: Adorno und Nono*, 280–89, 319–29. On Nono's music to *Die Ermittlung* further see Spangemacher, *Dialektischer Kontrapunkt*.

[28] *Luigi Nono: Complete Works for Solo Tape* (Ricordi, STR 57001, 2006) On the recordings Nono derived for radio broadcast from the original multiple-track tapes see Novati, 'The Tapes of the Archivio di Fonologia', 3.

[29] See Jozefowicz, *Das alltägliche Drama*, 61–89; and Henius, *Carla Carissima*.

Table 4.1 *Nono's music in Piscator's production of* Die Ermittlung *by Peter Weiss (1965), my reconstruction*

| No./ Scene | Time | Length | ***Motifs***, *typescript annotations*, text |
|---|---|---|---|
| **1** | 0.00 | 1′40″ | ***Canto dei morti*** [*Ricorda* I (0.00–0.56)] |
| | | | **Canto 1: The Platform** |
| **I.1** | | | 'I saw smoke [. . .] I thought/ those must be the bakeries' |
| **2** | 1.40 | 53″ | ***Canto dei morti*** + ***fischio gas*** [*Ricorda* I (0.56–2.00)] |
| **I.2** | | | [*The* DEFENDANTS *laugh*] |
| | | | '***silenzio*** senza musica' |
| **I.3** | | | 'Each one of them still believed/ he could survive' |
| **3** | 2.35 | 33″ | ***Coro*** + ***cattiva educazione*** [*Ricorda* I (2.00–2.28)] |
| | | | **Canto 2: The Camp** |
| **II.1** | | | Pregnant woman drowned |
| **4** | 3.14 | 18″ | ***Donne e bambini*** + ***gas*** + ***voci e c. Educazione*** [*Ricorda* I (2.32–2.44)] |
| **II.2** | | | Prisoner choked to death with walking stick |
| **5** | 3.36 | 16″ | [*Ricorda* I (2.28–2.32)] |
| **II.3** | | | Witness: denies shooting prisoners who attempted escape |
| **6** | 3.59 | 1′04″ | ***Fischi*** [*Ricorda* I (3.21–4.15)] |
| | | | **Canto 3: The Swing** |
| **III.1** | | | Boger's 'talking machine' in the 'Political Division' |
| **7** | 5.08 | 13″ | '*molto violento*' |
| **III.2** | | | Boger justifies 'pole-hanging' |
| **8** | 5.26 | 12″ | |
| **III.3** | | | Torture of political prisoners on 'the swing' |
| **9** | 5.42 | 43″ | '*lunga con vari elementi acustici* ' ***fischi*** [*Ricorda* I (2.50–3.21)] |
| | | | **Canto 4: The Possibility of Survival** |
| **IV.1** | | | Defendants deny responsibility |
| **10** | 6.31 | 18″ | '*la forza di distruzione*' '*un grido*' |
| **IV.2** | | | Critique of capitalist society |
| **11** | 6.54 | 21″ | '*con sospiri donne*', ***fischi*** [*Ricorda* I (4.54–5.28)] |
| **IV.3** | | | Medical 'experiments' on women |
| **12** | 7.18 | 41″ | '*passa da respiro a canto Lili* ' [*Ricorda* I (4.15–4.54)] |
| | | | **INTERVAL I** |
| **13** | 8.04 | 42″ | ***Canto dei morti*** [*Ricorda* II (5.32–6.07)] |
| | | | **Canto 5: The End of Lili Tofler** |
| **14** | 8.52 | 31″ | During **V.1** |
| **15** | 9.28 | 18″ | During **V.1** |
| **16** | 9.50 | 32″ | '*Fabbrica 3′40″*' |
| **V.2** | | | Capitalist exploitation of prisoners |
| **17** | 10.28 | 20″ | |

Table 4.1 (*cont.*)

| No./ Scene | Time | Length | ***Motifs***, *typescript annotations*, text |
|---|---|---|---|
| **18** | 10.52 | 41″ | ***Canto dei morti*** [*Ricorda* II (7.06–7.46)] |
| | | | Statement of Witness 9 up to end of **V.3** |
| | | | **Canto 6: SS Corporal Stark** |
| **1 R?** | | 15″ | '*Canto dei morti* motivo a'/opening statement accusing Stark of shooting a mother and her two children |
| **19** | 11.39 | 10″ | '*continua rumori – SS!*'/Stark's statement on his duties (**VI.1**) |
| **20** | 11.54 | 30″ | *Interlude* between **VI.1** and **VI.2** |
| **VI.2** | | | 'Such wholesale accusations are completely meaningless' |
| | | | [*The* DEFENDANTS *laugh, nodding in agreement*] |
| | | | '*senza musica*' '*subito avanti*' '*silenzio – buio*' |
| **VI.3** | | | Killing by gas: '*senza musica*' |
| **20 R?** | | 20″ | '*inizio fischio +*' '*educazione*'/Stark blames his education |
| | | | [*Assenting laughter from the* DEFENDANTS] |
| | | | '*silenzio – Pause intervallo*' '*risata – e muti – lasciarli pensare*' |
| | | | **INTERVAL II** |
| **21** | 12.29 | 1′47″ | *Prelude* (highest density) [*Ricorda* III (8.40–. . .)] |
| | | | **Canto 7: The Black Wall** |
| **VII.1** | | | Shootings at the Black Wall |
| **22** | 14.22 | 19″ | ***Schwarze Wand*** [*Ricorda* II (8.27–8.37)] |
| **VII.2** | | | Shooting of a child (end substantially cut by Piscator) |
| **23** | 14.45 | 18″ | [*Ricorda* II (7.46–7.54)] |
| **VII.3** | | | Shooting of a family; courtyard full of corpses |
| **24** | 15.06 | 34″ | |
| | | | **Canto 8: Phenol** |
| **VIII.1** | | | 'That's preposterous [. . .] That wouldn't have left anybody but the band' [*The* DEFENDANTS *laugh*] |
| | | | '*riso senza musica*' |
| **VIII.2** | | | Statement of the leading doctor at the camp |
| **25** | 15.47 | 26″ | '*centro come grido ira protesta*' |
| **VIII.3** | | | Killing of 119 children by injection of phenol |
| **26** | 16.17 | 30″ | |
| | | | **Canto 9: The Bunker Block** |
| **IX.1** | | | Death by starvation in standing cells |
| **27** | 16.54 | 19″ | |
| **IX.2** | | | Death by suffocation in 'hunger cells' |
| **28** | 17.16 | 26″ | |
| **IX.3** | | | First killing by means of gas |
| **29** | 17.46 | 34″ | |

Table 4.1 (*cont.*)

| No./ Scene | Time | Length | ***Motifs***, *typescript annotations*, text |
|---|---|---|---|
| | | | **Canto 10: Zyklon B** |
| **X.1** | | | Handling and effect of Zyklon B |
| **30** | 18.26 | 33″ | |
| **X.2** | | | Profits from the manufacture of gas |
| **31** | 19.03 | 14″ | |
| **X.3** | | | Transport of gas to the gas chambers |
| **32** | 19.22 | 51″ | [*Ricorda* III (10.12–10.32)] |
| | | | **Canto 11: The Fire Ovens** |
| **XI.1** | | | 'I heard a humming from down there/ as if a lot of people were underground' |
| **33** | 20.21 | 10″ | |
| **XI.2** | | | Mass killing by gas, cremation |
| **34** | 20.33 | 8″ | |
| **XI.3** | | | 'These recriminations/ should have fallen/ under the Statute of Limitations/ a long time ago' |
| **35** | 20.45 | 1′18″ | ***Canto dei morti*** |

and vocal sound, Nono would add instrumental sound for *Die Ermittlung*, where the 'human' dimension was again of primary concern.

New vocal material for *Die Ermittlung* was recorded with the children's chorus of the Piccolo Teatro di Milano, and Nono also decided to make use of hitherto unused material, which had been recorded with the Polish soprano Stefania Woytowicz in Rome (1959), possibly for *Diario polacco '58*.[30] A common characteristic of these vocal strata is the almost exclusive use of phonemes. With the children's voices in particular, Nono experimented with degrees of colour and brightness on different vowel sounds and their possible mutation.[31] The children were also asked to articulate the word 'Mam-ma', and this word is one of the few intelligible building blocks in the finished work. Text is of course also at the heart of the choral material which Nono chose to reuse for this work. By means of electronic sound transformation, however, Nono makes sure that these excerpts are never understood as renditions of text, but instead are perceived as musical texture alone. The words of the passages that can and have been identified are nevertheless not completely at odds within their new context. On several occasions, for example, Nono quotes from the verses 'il grido, sola, del mio

[30] See Kontarsky, *Trauma Auschwitz*, 56.

[31] On the use of vowel sounds see Nanni, *Auschwitz: Adorno und Nono*, 284–86.

cuore' (the scream, alone, from my heart) from the second movement of *Cori di Didone*, a passage repeatedly referred to as 'grido' (scream) in the sketches. In its original mythological context this desperate cry of passion is also a scream of utter despair in the face of imminent death – Dido's suicide. In this sense, it is also totally appropriate in the context of *Die Ermittlung*.[32] Another poetic image from *Cori di Didone* made its way into Canto 1: The Platform (fragment 3, CD 2:35, leading into I:3). 'Aveva speranza per tutti/ non chiara la morte' (There was hope for everyone/ death was not evident), Nono comments in his typescript, and the chosen 'sound image' from *Cori di Didone* does indeed provide such a tentative glimpse of hope:

> [A bufera s'è aperto, al buio, un porto
> Che dissero sicuro]
> Fu golfo constellato
> E pareva immutabile il suo cielo;
> [Ma ora, com'é mutato!]
>
> [In the storm there opened, in the darkness, a harbour
> Which they said was safe]
> A gulf, full of stars,
> And its heaven seemed immutable;
> [But now, how it has changed!][33]

Similarly, a quotation from *Ha venido* in fragment 5 (CD 3:36), setting the words 'madre despertar' (bars 108–13), is not out of place in a play that repeatedly uses the fate of innocent women and children to underline the merciless brutality of Nazi oppression.[34] In purely compositional terms

[32] The image of screaming is used extremely sparingly by Weiss, usually in connection with torture. Nono heavily underlined the word in Stark's statement on killing by gas (*Ermittlung*, 119; *Investigation*, 222). One prominent quotation first identified by Nanni is the bass entry on 'gri' (*Cori di Didone*, bar 69) in fragment 32 (CD 19:22) which introduces Canto 11: The Fire Ovens.

[33] Ungaretti, *La terra promessa* as set in the fourth movement of *Cori di Didone*, in *Luigi Nono: Choral Works*, SWR Vokalensemble Stuttgart, dir. Huber (Hänssler Classic, 2001), CD booklet, 8/16. Verses three and four (*Cori di Didone*, bars 143–52) are quoted in the third fragment of *Die Ermittlung*. Fragment 3 was in second place at first, but later exchanged with fragment 2. Nanni uses this fact to underline the autonomous nature of Nono's music. Autonomy has its limits, however. This particular quotation from *Cori di Didone* was clearly meant as a commentary on the arrival at the camp and could not have been transferred to any other Canto. The two fragments were probably exchanged to achieve a more organic overall form. Sketches show that Nono first envisaged an a–b–a form for this Canto, but the final a–a′–b format fits much better into the overall development.

[34] Canto 2 contains the harrowing image of a pregnant woman being drowned.

this choral material also provides a textural dimension of greater force, depth and density, and adds a further register: the low range of the 'uomini' (men) (tenor/bass). While the solo soprano and the children's voices primarily feature in linear polyphony, the material for mixed chorus allows much denser textures and a wider ambitus. With occasional shorter, louder and more articulated utterances, the chorus also functions as a powerful element of disruption (the male voices in particular). With some electronic modification, the high degree of differentiation of this vocal material is explored to the full in the eerie lament, the so-called 'Canto dei morti' (Song of the Dead), which opens and closes the play.

The ratio of sustained sounds and elements of violent disruption is turned into its opposite in the layer of instrumental material which predominantly consists of loud and disruptive brass and percussion sounds from *Diario polacco '58*, *Cori di Didone*, *Il canto sospeso* no. 8, even earlier works such as the first *Epitaffio per Federico García Lorca* (1951–52) and perhaps the second of the *Due espressioni* (1953). If the vocal layer is inspired by 'motifs' such as 'grido', 'mamma/madre' and the 'song of the dead', the corresponding motifs of the instrumental layer are 'percussione Stark' and 'educazione cattiva' – the 'bad education' that led Nazi officials to commit atrocities 'unknowingly'. In Nono's sketches the term 'percussione Stark' consistently refers to hard-hitting percussion sounds, while 'educazione cattiva' may refer to the dimension of added electronic sound and the way in which the violent interventions by brass and percussion are transformed electronically.

Typically, percussion is cast into four distinct categories: 'pelle/ legno/ metalle/ con ottoni' (skin/ wood/ metal/ with brass).[35] Again Nono considers the nature of the sound as well as its previous connotation. Most of the percussion sounds stem from *Diario polacco '58*. The recurring motif for Stark ('legno/pelle'), for example, is taken from section BIII (bars 35–36).[36] The extremely violent sound of the 'lastre' (metal plates), too, stems from *Diario polacco '58*. This sound is used to great effect in fragment 22 (CD 14:22) for Canto 7: The Black Wall. An equally menacing metallic sound, an intense crescendo on cymbals, is taken from *Cori di Didone*, where it occurs repeatedly in movements IV and V. The origins of the sounds on felt percussion (sustained drum rolls) are harder to distinguish. It may be that Nono used the beginning of the second of the *Due espressioni* (1953), a section he had already reused in *Intolleranza*

35 ALN 28.01/06r.

36 This was first identified by Nanni. Nono used a live recording of *Diario polacco '58* with the Orchestra Sinfonica di Roma della RAI conducted by Maderna (Venice, 1 October 1959). The recording was kindly made available to me by Nanni.

to accompany 'projections of racial fanaticism', including the infamous slogan 'Arbeit macht frei' crowning the gate to Auschwitz.[37] One remarkable exception, in terms of content, is the quotation from the percussion finale of *La Guerra*, the second movement of Nono's first Lorca Epitaph. This quotation, which is based on the rhythm of *Bandiera rossa*, is clearly meant to represent the resistance, not the Nazi oppressors. 'B. rossa' duly appears in fragment 9 (CD 5:42), the prelude to Canto 4: The Possibility of Survival, which gives voice to the resistance at Auschwitz.[38]

Divisions between victims and oppressors are thus not quite as clear-cut as one might think. Another dimension that adds to this all-important ambiguity is provided by the newly recorded instrumental material: long sustained pitches on clarinet (primarily in the low register, with some multiphonics in the middle register) and a single strike on a resonant low gong. Like the slow-moving vocal lament with which it is often coupled, the 'breathing' clarinet sound is essentially imbued with a 'human' quality that is absent from the disruptive violence of brass and percussion.[39] Together with the fateful blow on the gong, the sustained clarinet pitches clearly belong to a category of drone-like sounds that also includes an electronic drone. Although essentially non-violent in nature, these instrumental and electronic drones are among the most sinister sounds of the piece, and one cannot but feel that they are meant to represent total dehumanisation and death. The drama itself draws the connection between drone and death. In Canto XI the driver of the van transporting the gas Zyklon B is asked to describe what was heard on lifting the hatches of the gas chambers, to which he replies 'I heard a drone from down there/ as if a lot of people were underground'.[40] In the manuscript Nono marks this passage with a circle (the sign used to indicate music), and at the end of the Canto the gong is named as one of the elements to be used. And indeed the music leading into Canto XI:1 (fragment 32, CD 19:22), one of the densest and most violent fragments, breaks off with a final blow on the gong that eerily reverberates into silence. This gestural and highly dramatic use of the gong is certain to create a feeling of anguish and trepidation,

[37] The quotation of the second *Espressione* in *Intolleranza 1960*, II:3 (bars 294–313) was pointed out to me by De Benedictis.

[38] 'B. rossa' and 'Lorca' are mentioned on sketch ALN 28.01/06r and so is 'Didone', giving vital clues to the origins of the percussion sounds.

[39] Nono recorded these sonorities with the clarinettist William O. Smith, who also took part in the experimental music theatre piece *A floresta é jovem e cheja de vida* (1966). On Nono's collaboration with Smith (1963–66) see Jozefowitz, *Das alltägliche Drama*, 139–47. Nono worked with Smith at the Studio di Fonologia in August 1965.

[40] *Investigation*, 279 (trans. amended); *Ermittlung*, 181.

especially when transmitted in complete darkness and from loudspeakers below the floor, as was done in Piscator's production.[41]

Equally disconcerting is the use of the highest register: quiet but piercingly high whistling electronic frequencies that one might associate with buzzing insects, especially when used in glissandos. 'We knew exactly how Stark would behave when he came from a killing', a witness reports at the beginning of Canto VI:2. 'Everything in the room had to be in order and absolutely clean and we had to chase the flies out [. . .] If he spotted a fly he would go into a rage.'[42] In the preceding scene Stark had just been asked to testify on the extermination of prisoners at the small crematorium. 'Death by gas', Nono writes in between these two scenes, and, next to the powerful image of the unwanted flies, he first makes use of the term 'fischi' (hissing or whistling sounds) – a term which is then consistently linked to the 'motivo gas'. 'Motivo gas' may primarily refer to the actual deed of killing by gas (the hissing sound of gas streaming through open valves), but it is clearly also inspired by the tense anxiety following the execution of such horrendous orders. The buzzing high electronic frequencies with which Nono realises this idea are certainly supposed to create a similar kind of anxiety in those who look on. The disconcerting sonority is perhaps at its most effective when it creeps in on the high vocal lines (soprano and children's chorus) to gradually consume the vocal sound, i.e. to transform the vocal polyphony into purely electronic sound as is immediately the case in fragment 2 (CD 1:40). Another fragment which leaves no doubt about the connection 'fischi' – 'motivo gas' is the transition between Canto 9: The Bunker Block and Canto 10: Zyklon B (fragment 29, CD 17.46). Like the fourth movement of *Il canto sospeso*, this is a simple wave of sound, beginning from silence, gradually intensifying and then receding back into silence. As the high whistling sounds grow in strength (possibly enhanced by a quotation from *La fabbrica illuminata* at 3:40), two other elements are briefly blended in: the drone and the children whose voices are almost immediately sucked back into the dominant electronic sonority. 'Now I'm relieved/ Now that we have

41 Nono describes the conditions in 'Musica e teatro', *Scritti*, I, 213: 'loudspeakers everywhere' and 'a true feast for the use of the entire acoustic space [. . .] Each movement is decided a) for purely musical reasons b) in relation to what happens on stage c) in relation to the audience which is placed not in front but at the centre of everything.' For a reconstruction of the spatial movement of the music and the use of lighting see Kontarsky, *Trauma Auschwitz*, 82–95.

42 *Investigation*, 215, *Ermittlung*, 111. A swarm of flies also hovers over mutilated bodies in the yard of Experimental Block Ten, *Ermittlung*, 138. In this apocalyptic context the image takes after Sartre's *Les Mouches*.

this gas/ we'll be spared all those bloodbaths', the Commandant comments just before the audience is confronted with this music.[43]

The choice of a purely electronic sonority for this 'motivo gas' is clearly related to the technological aspect of the holocaust and, with it, the much debated charge against capitalist society. 'The most recent advances in German technology' are further poignantly alluded to by means of standard elements of synthesised sound, which Nono had already used for *Omaggio a Emilio Vedova*. In the music to *Die Ermittlung* these are first introduced in conjunction with the soprano's drawn out lament in Canto 5: The End of Lili Tofler. Within this most lyrical part of the work (fragments 14–18, CD 8:52–11:39) synthesised elements from *Omaggio a Vedova* are present only in fragment 16 (CD 9:50), following the detailed account of IG Farben's exploitation of slave labour from the camp.[44] Nono's most powerful charge against the disgraceful role of Krupp, Siemens, IG Farben and the Deutsche Gesellschaft für Schädlingsbekämpfung, however, is the industrial scraping noise and loud bang of an iron gate slammed shut, by far the most violent material of the piece, which stems from *La fabbrica illuminata*.[45]

Another key motif of the play is the 'approving laughter of the defendants' with which Weiss occasionally concludes his scenes. The feeble testimony of SS Corporal Stark, 'Your Honour/ Our thinking was taken away from us/ Others did it for us', ends with such laughter.[46] So does the testimony of sanitary officer Klehr, accused of killing at least 16,000 prisoners by means of injecting phenol straight into the heart (VIII.1). Klehr's arrogant denial of this charge is typical: 'I'm supposed to have executed sixteen thousand people/ when there were only sixteen thousand in the whole camp/ That wouldn't have left anybody but the band.'[47] Approving laughter dramatically emphasises the defendants' shocking unwillingness to take on any responsibility for the crimes committed. Annotations to the manuscript show that Nono was very impressed by

[43] *Investigation*, 170; *Ermittlung*, 168.

[44] For this scene (V:2) Nono initially jotted down 'Fabbrica 3′40″', indicating a precise moment in *La fabbrica illuminata*. At 3:40 one hears quiet high frequencies not dissimilar to the 'fischi' of the 'motivo gas'. The passage was later not used for fragment 16 but possibly for the opening sound in fragment 29, CD 17:46. Merged with the children's voices, the synthesised sounds from *Omaggio a Emilio Vedova* resurface once more in Canto IX (fragment 28, CD 17:16).

[45] *La fabbrica illuminata*, 5:10. A less violent strike on metal is also quoted, *Fabbrica illuminata*, 4:15. Both quotations were first identified by Nanni, *Auschwitz: Adorno und Nono*, 305.

[46] *Investigation*, 223 (trans. amended); *Ermittlung*, 120.

[47] *Investigation*, 245; *Ermittlung*, 144. This passage is annotated by Nono: '*riso/ senza musica/* subito avanti' (*laughter/ without music/* move on immediately).

this dramatic device. Laughter is always heavily marked and was at first considered a possible element for the music itself. 'Il riso/ un elemento violento della musica' (Laughter/ a violent element of the music), Nono notes in his typescript after Canto I.2 (the first scene to end with such laughter), and 'fare un risate' (make laughter) at the beginning of Canto IV. Nono's material is never one-dimensional, however, and laughter was to be complemented with another vocal element: highly stylised gestures of human suffering – sighs, gasps, gagging noises, sobbing, even screaming – which were probably recorded with the actress Elena Vicini.[48] A fragment of music was initially composed with this material for Canto IV, but later deemed inappropriate.[49] Human suffering, Nono wisely decided, would have to be expressed on a much more abstract level, with 'composed', even already-processed material such as the 'scream' from *Cori di Didone*. The much admired element of laughter was thus left to speak for itself. The scenes ending in laughter are never followed by music, even just before the interval. On Stark's final testimony Nono comments 'SILENZIO – PAUSE intervallo/ risate – e muti – lasciarli pensare' (SILENCE – PAUSE interval/ laughter – and silence – let them think).

From a purely compositional point of view, Nono thus establishes three types of sound, the individual components of which all refer to recurring key concepts of the play. All three types of sound comprise a wide range of register, a number of quiet sustained sounds and various elements of violent disruption, as well as quotations from previous works. Each type in itself allows a high degree of contrast and transition from the individual to the collective. The possibilities of a dialectical approach are of course much enhanced on combining all three categories, but Nono also deliberately exploits the structural similarities between the types of sound, striving to eliminate the boundaries. A fast tremolo on cymbals is exceedingly difficult to distinguish from a buzzing electronic sound from *La fabbrica illuminata*, for example. Equally challenging is the distinction between a low electronic drone and an electronically modified clarinet sound, or a real and an electronically produced gong sound. Even the vocal material is eerily transformed into electronic sound. The ambiguity achieved by means of electronic sound transformation is perhaps the single most important characteristic of this piece. While maintaining a high degree of sound symbolism, the distinction between victim and oppressor is thus

[48] Sketches mention the name Elena.

[49] On the discarded passage see Nanni, *Auschwitz: Adorno und Nono*, 308–312. The sound of a whistling railway engine ('the signal that a new shipment had arrived') was also discarded. For Canto XI:1 Nono initially noted 'Locomotiva motivo continuo in sala' (ALN 28.01/03).

also powerfully undermined. The music becomes truly disconcerting precisely because the boundaries between the human voice, man-made instrumental sound and electronically produced sound are deliberately blurred. With this uncomfortable and most thought-provoking ambiguity of sound, Nono essentially underlines the play's fundamental charge: 'We all knew [and are still part of] the society that produced a government capable of creating such camps.'

Inspired by Weiss's drama, Nono was able to produce the kind of material he had perhaps already dreamt of at the time of writing *Diario polacco '58*. It is at this point in time that the history of the two works becomes truly intertwined. Not only does Nono extract material from *Diario polacco '58* for use in the music to *Die Ermittlung*, but also he reuses this material for a new version of *Diario polacco '58* itself, now (as originally envisaged) with an additional one-channel tape.[50] As has been shown by Nanni, Nono uses the tape primarily to transfer passages of the work back onto themselves with minimal delay (one of the first applications of the phasing technique with live orchestral sound in Nono's oeuvre).[51] At the end of the work, however, as the straight line of violent oppression comes to its climactic close, Nono also decides to quote from *Die Ermittlung*. Fragment 21 (CD, 12:29), the densest fragment of all, which combines all elements in a single 'tour de force' and thus sums up the entire piece in condensed form, is inserted with the crack of the four whips at bar 268. The interweaving genesis of the two works does not end here, however, but would culminate in the independent electronic piece *Ricorda cosa ti hanno fatto in Auschwitz*.[52]

## *Ricorda cosa ti hanno fatto in Auschwitz* (1966)

An independent electronic composition based on the materials from *Die Ermittlung* was planned from the outset and was even publicly announced by Nono: 'I will use parts of this music – always on tape – for an

[50] On the second version of *Diario polacco '58* see Nanni, *Auschwitz: Adorno und Nono*, 250–276; and Bassanese, 'Sulla versione 1965'. The revised version was premiered under Andrzej Markowski (Warsaw Autumn, 1965).

[51] A letter to Markowski reveals that the electronically modified orchestral material on the tape was to provide an additional spatial dimension; Nono, undated letter to Markowski, in Nanni, *Auschwitz: Adorno und Nono*, 250.

[52] The most detailed analysis of *Ricorda cosa ti hanno fatto in Auschwitz* is found in Nanni, *Auschwitz: Adorno und Nono*, 312–64, including an extremely useful audio score, 318–29. Further see Kontarsky, *Trauma Auschwitz*, 126–49; Spangemacher, *Dialektischer Kontrapunkt*; and Gramann, *Die Ästhetisierung des Schreckens*. My own comments focus on the structural similarities to *Diario polacco '58*.

autonomous work "Music to *Die Ermittlung* by Peter Weiss".'[53] For this autonomous piece Nono was of course no longer bound to the structure of the play and was able to select and combine his 'motifs' much more freely. Moreover, the aphoristic snapshots could now be worked into a coherent musical discourse. Even in terms of scale, this discourse is not dissimilar to that of *Diario polacco '58*.[54] Another common denominator is the use of three types of sound. These types are now much more distinct in character, however, and Nono works with degrees of presence (foreground/middle/background) rather than simple juxtaposition. Another decisive difference is the predominance of the vocal sound. In structural terms, this extremely fluid yet also most unified layer is *Ricorda*'s very own tortuous line of thought. Throughout the three parts of the work – Part I: Canto del lager (0′00″–5′32″), Part II: Canto della fine di Lili Tofler (5′32″–8′40″), and Part III: Canto della possibilità di sopravvivere (8′40″–11′15″)[55] – this vocal thread constantly mutates in register, ambitus, density and dynamics, and is only ever completely eradicated by the motif of death (low drone/gong) which concludes each of the three parts. Again the tortuous line of thought effectively intersects with a straight line of thought, the function of which is to represent the 'macchina repressiva' (machinery of repression).[56] All of the elements are exposed in Part I. Nono here makes use of long and essentially recognisable quotations from the music for *Die Ermittlung*, but immediately devises a different order.[57] As in the music for the play, Nono begins with the Canti dei morti (0′00″–0′56″).[58] The first oppressive element to be added is the 'motivo gas' (0′56″–2′00″). The vocal texture is then more forcefully enveloped by instrumental interventions (percussion/brass, 2′00″–2′50″). This is followed by another wave of sound, in

[53] Nono, programme book to *Die Ermittlung*, 9: 'von Teilen dieser Musik werde ich – immer auf tonband – ein autonomes werk "musik zu der *Ermittlung* von Peter Weiss" herstellen'.

[54] With a total duration of 11′15″, *Ricorda* is only slightly shorter than the first version of *Diario polacco '58* (12′29″ on the recording of the premiere, *Musik in Deutschland 1950–2000: Rundfunk als Mäzen*, BMG-RCA, 2000).

[55] This three-part division concurs with Nanni's audio score. The titles from Weiss's play were used by Nono in a programme note for a concert in Rome (28 February 1970); Nono, '*Ricorda cosa ti hanno fatto in Auschwitz*' (17b), *Scritti*, I, 453.

[56] Nono employed this term for oppressive forces of any political denomination. The Marxist term 'Unterdrückungsmaschinerie' is used by Engels in his preface to the 1891 edition of Marx, *The Civil War in France*, which features in *Al gran sole carico d'amore*.

[57] On Nono's use of the music to *Die Ermittlung* in *Ricorda* see Kontarsky, *Trauma Auschwitz*, 145–46.

[58] Timings refer to the CD *Luigi Nono: Complete Works for Solo Tape*.

which the vocal line is eventually blocked out by loud 'industrial' white noise. The use of this virtually impermeable electronic block sonority – the ultimate negation of musically defined sound – is strikingly similar in effect to that of the chromatic blocks in the 'Oświęcim' episode of *Diario polacco '58*. Block sonorities of this kind had already been taken a step further in *Canti di vita e d'amore* (1962), where a tightly knit microtonal texture in the middle register stands for the ultimate threat of nuclear destruction.[59] A very similar texture was later associated with the 'machinery of repression' in *Al gran sole carico d'amore* (1972–74). Equally impermeable blocks of white noise take on similar function in *Ricorda*. The texture of the piece is then dramatically reduced: a lyrical afterthought not unlike that of horns and flutes in the Auschwitz episode of *Diario polacco '58* resonates over and into the long and desolate low drone which concludes this first Canto del Lager. The soprano then opens the Canto della fine di Lili Tofler (Part II) with unadorned solo song. This brings to mind both the lyricism with which Nono pays tribute to the Algerian resistance fighter Djamila Boupacha at the centre of *Canti di vita e d'amore* and the extremely still and reflective echo passages at the beginning of the second part of *Diario polacco '58*. The solo soprano material had already been used to similar effect in Canto V of the play (fragments 14–18, CD 8:52–11:38). In this new Canto della fine di Lili Tofler, however, the lyrical soprano is merely a starting point, and begins to weave in and out of a growing collective of voices, ending with chorus and children's chorus. In the process, the original music to *Die Ermittlung* becomes increasingly fragmented, dissected beyond recognition and intertwined in manifold new ways. Although some elements, like the material from fragment 21 (CD 12.29) at the beginning of Part III (8:40), are easily recognised, it is evident that Nono now moves away from the structure of the music as it was conceived for the stage. The effect and unity of the individual fragment had been paramount for the music to *Die Ermittlung*, where the combination of the various motifs was largely determined by related imagery in the text. The same motifs and the symbolic meanings they had acquired in conjunction with Weiss's text are reused for *Ricorda*, but with an independent musical

[59] The full spectrum of pitch (24 quartertones) is here rendered by woodwind, brass and strings in a single octave in middle register. The dense and seemingly impermeable orchestral texture is heard towards the end of the first of three parts. Printed above is the final section of Anders' 'On the bridge of Hiroshima': 'As long as it takes to ban the danger which killed 200,000 when it first struck, this robot [a man mutilated by the bomb] will stand on this bridge and sing his song. He will stand on all other bridges that lead into our common future as an eyesore and a messenger'. Also see Durazzi, 'Luigi Nono's *Canti di vita e d'amore*'.

discourse in mind. It is as if the validity of this symbolically charged material were thus being tested. Does this kind of material lend itself to autonomous discourse even without the support of the related text? The experiment, to my mind, was closely modelled on the structure of *Diario polacco '58*. The exposition of basic materials from the original music to *Die Ermittlung* (Part I) concludes with a seemingly inescapable compression of sound. This sets off a process of increasing fragmentation and dissolution whereby the two contrasting lines of thought are gradually drawn out. With pronounced lyricism, the tortuous vocal line continues to undergo constant change, meandering between solo song, linear polyphony and the full choral collective. Interventions by the 'machinery of repression' are increasingly spaced out, but progressively gain in force and electronic alienation. Including the climax of orchestral violence from *Diario polacco '58* (bars 268–73) as well as material from the dense fragment 21 which Nono decided to insert into the second version of *Diario polacco '58*, this line of thought is now essentially directed towards a final allusion to capitalist exploitation: the industrial 'gong' from *La fabbrica illuminata* (4′15″), after which the piece fades out on a last desolate low drone.

A long, tortuous thread has been spun from Calvino's *Impiccagione di un giudice* to this concluding 'motif of death' in *Ricorda cosa ti hanno fatto in Auschwitz*, the last of Nono's strictly anti-fascist works. Compositional technique and intention may have taken many different turns during these two eventful decades, but it is obvious that intense reflection on the European anti-fascist resistance and the holocaust fundamentally shaped Nono's compositional idiom, resulting in structural ideas, material choices and a certain vocabulary of sounds that would continue to be of great relevance in the changing political and musical contexts. One fundamental aesthetic principle of this multi-dimensional music, which delights in allusion and ambiguity of meaning and thus lends itself to reflection, was put to us by Nono himself in his programme note for *Die Ermittlung*:

> Not music motivated by rebellion–protest.
>
> Only musical awareness and understanding of yesterday and today for a tomorrow that is finally free.[60]

[60] Nono, 'Music to *The Investigation*', 47.

# PART II

# Music as Memory

# 5 Towards other shores

After intense preoccupation with the holocaust, *A floresta é jovem e cheja de vida* [*The Forest Is Young and Full of Life* (1965–66)], for soprano, three actors, clarinet, metal plates and two four-channel tapes, is much less a memorial work than a political manifesto. Together with Giovanni Pirelli, the editor of the *Lettere*, who had since engaged with the African liberation movements and opened the Centro Frantz Fanon in Milan, Nono compiled a disparate collage of text that commemorates the violent upheavals of African decolonisation with text by Fanon, Lumumba and an Angolan freedom fighter. The work further includes statements by Fidel Castro (Cuba), Pedro Duno (FALN, Venezuela) and Nguyễn Văn Trỗi (South Vietnam) and from the Italian and American protest movements.[1] The electronic music incorporates an American student appeal to end the Vietnam War[2] as well as the shockingly inhumane article 'Escalation as a Strategy' by the military strategist and consultant to the US Department of Defence (1966–68), Herman Kahn.[3] The latter was at the heart of Nono's recording sessions with The Living Theatre in May 1966, among short extracts of the company's previous productions, such as the 'Reading of the Dollar Note' from *The Brig* (after Kenneth Brown, 1963) and the opening of *Frankenstein* (after Mary Shelley, 1965), as well as entirely non-verbal evocations of the 'Jungle'.[4] Key anti-war texts such as the *Lettere dal Vietnam* (later reused for *Al gran sole carico d'amore*) were recorded in similarly experimental fashion with actors of the Teatro Piccolo di Milano. Nono recorded further material with the clarinettist William O. Smith and the soprano Liliana Poli. Live interventions were subsequently worked out in close collaboration with the participating performers who uniquely, and ephemerally, contributed to this hard-hitting protest piece.[5] The first

1 For all texts see Jozefowicz, *Das alltägliche Drama*, 92–96. The correct Portuguese spelling of the title should be *A floresta é jovem e cheia de vida*.

2 'L'America è in guerra' (appeal of the Vietnam Day Committee, Berkeley University, California, 16 October 1965), trans. in the magazine of the Federazione Giovanile Comunista Italiana, *La città futura*, 14 (November 1965).

3 Kahn, 'Escalation as a Strategy', *Fortune* (April 1965) and *On Escalation*.

4 See Jozefowicz, *Das alltägliche Drama*, 139/150–53; transcripts of conversations with members of The Living Theatre, 253–71.

5 See Jozefowicz, *Das alltägliche Drama*, 90–168.

performance took place at La Fenice (7 September 1966), produced and lit by Virginio Puecher from the Teatro Piccolo. Against Pirelli's wishes, Nono dedicated *A floresta* to the National Liberation Front of Vietnam, a gesture which only added to the hostility Nono's work was increasingly met with in the USA, and also closer to home.[6]

Despite its pronounced topicality and thus historicity, *A floresta* is one of the key works in Nono's oeuvre, anticipating many of the elements and methods of his much more universally cherished work of the 1980s. As Stenzl observes,

> Those who listen out for the sound transformations in this work will soon realise that the texts here function as signals which set off processes of sound transformation. These seamless transformations define this key work of the sixties as much as its harsh cuts. [. . .] in embryonic form *A floresta* is fundamentally already a *Prometeo*. The agitation, however, which defines the 'Escalation' part, and the violence with which the contradictions here clash, meant that *A floresta* was at first perceived primarily as a political–musical manifesto of its time, as one among many demonstrations against the Vietnam War.[7]

The shocking violence of this anti-war 'dramma in musica' certainly had a profound effect also on the ex-partisan Italo Calvino. About two weeks after the premiere, the writer responded with a truly remarkable letter:

> What I would like to say to you does not concern the structure of your work which I perceived in its full strength and quality: blocks of absolute, total, black noise, juxtaposed with blocks of luminous music, dramatically human [. . .]
>
> The following reflections [. . .] arose from the representation of war, bombings, etc. in *Floresta*. And I wondered: is it right to represent bombardments with noise? Wouldn't it make more sense to focus on the silence that comes with the exploding bombs? At a closer examination, the prevailing element during an air raid is silence: when the alarm goes off the population strains its ears trying to detect the sound of the approaching planes, their descent over the city, the whistling of the bombs, trying to locate the explosions; and nothing compares to the silence which follows an air raid. I imagine that aboard a bomber plane, also, the background noise of the engines and the distant falling of the bombs create an atmosphere of paradoxical silence. Above all, in a bombardment there is no element of force:

[6] On Nono's difficulties with the American authorities on the occasion of the 1965 production of *Intolleranza* in Boston see Sallis, 'Problems and Issues Surrounding the Early North American Reception of the Music of Luigi Nono', 139–64.

[7] Stenzl, *Luigi Nono*, 74.

an air raid is made of weakness and fear: the pilots who drop the bombs are terrified, more so than their victims; bombing is an act of weakness, the bombs fall lazily, riding on the force of gravity. If we acknowledged that a bombardment is an act of strength, we would only be playing the bombers' game.

Now, I wouldn't want these thoughts I just articulated to be confused with the pretence of all celebratory arts (including 'socialist realism'), to depict war not in all its horror, but as something heroic and unrepulsive; I completely agree with you on this, on your intention and ability to describe war as an atrocity. I am only suggesting we look at war in its essence, anti-naturalistically and anti-romantically, and *A Floresta* led me to reflect on the acoustic essence of the war, which is crucial.

Also in partisan battles – and in all battles, I think – the key element for every fighter is hearing, in the sense of trying to pinpoint and distinguish the shots as well as any other sound within the general racket, in trying to interpret the sudden silences at the heart of the fight, so as to figure out what is going on, how the battle is unfolding, how comrades and enemies are changing their positions, in order not to end up being cut off from one's comrades etc. Partisan life as a whole depends on a heightened sense of hearing, a scrupulous awareness of noises and silences, especially at night and in ambushes and sweeps. I think I perceived such acoustic wealth precisely in the section of your composition where the forest emerges, though of course I don't mean these things in the sense of an illustration; I am speaking of musical images in a broader sense. [. . .]

While European culture used to be confronted with a depiction of the universality of suffering and struggle in a world of explicit tragedy, in works of art ranging from *Guernica* and *Conversazione in Sicilia* to *A Survivor from Warsaw*, today we are faced with a different picture: the tragic reality of the world is being concealed in large parts of the world, where everybody is somehow under the obligation to conceal it (even China, which has to minimise the tragedy of a total war). But how to articulate this? How to turn this into a worldview, a stylistic process? I can't say: if only I knew!

Perhaps your 'c'è stato chi ha tradito' ['there were traitors'] might be enlarged upon in the following way: parallel to the escalation of the bombs there is an escalation of the particularity of individual interests and those of single nations, the pull towards seeing only the 'particular' and the impossibility for anyone of embodying the universal. [. . .][8]

[8] Calvino, letter to Nono, 25 September 1966 (Calvino/I 66–09–25 m, ALN), in Calvino, *Lettere*, 934–37; with many thanks to Giovanna Calvino for checking and improving the translations of her father's letters. Stenzl quite rightly remarks that 'c'è stato chi ha tradito' can also be read as 'the state that betrayed', foreshadowing the biting critique of the state in *Guai ai gelidi mostri* (1983); Stenzl, *Luigi Nono*, 74.

In view of Nono's later fascination with the fertile ground between sound and silence, Calvino's letter of 1966 seems almost visionary. Stenzl remembers that Nono repeatedly left the auditorium during one of his lectures in the late eighties whenever excerpts of his works of the sixties and early seventies were played because he himself now experienced them as 'far too loud'.[9] Specifically in regard to *A floresta*, Nono further told Albèra in 1987 that

> I have been asked many times to do it again, but I said no, because it would be necessary to choose the voices anew, work for at least a month, discover new possibilities . . . and I prefer to write another work. Evidently this kind of attitude totally fails to meet the needs of the market! In any case, there remains a recording and that is sufficient, even if it conveys only 10% of the reality.[10]

On no account does this mean, however, that Nono later renounced any of his earlier work. The composer himself made this blatantly clear in a letter to Pestalozza, with whom relations turned increasingly frosty as Nono dared to write not only a solo piano piece for Maurizio Pollini, but even a string quartet, the epitome of bourgeois music, which would indeed have been unthinkable in Nono's oeuvre up to 1975:[11]

> I don't aim to liberate myself from the shadows of the past.
> I don't repudiate my work, thought and acts of the past.
> I have neither need nor motive to liberate myself from them.
> I am just seeking to broaden and deepen my thought in my work, in my life.
> I am also seeking to understand various dismemberments that have taken place within me (lacerations of various types leading to other discoveries of diverse quality and with various consequences) [. . .]
> I am simply discovering other possibilities [. . .]
> What I am studying literally upsets me because it opens me up to other thoughts, it doesn't just make me question myself but makes me surpass the limits of the preceding thoughts and sentiments (why repudiate them if I come from there, why refute them if they are continuing in other ways in me????) and at times in the joy of such *intra-listening* [*intraascolto*] I find myself alone.[12]

[9] The lecture took place in Villeneuve-lès-Avignon in 1989.

[10] Nono, 'Intervista di Philippe Albèra', *Scritti*, II, 424.

[11] In 1975 Nono still spoke of the need to 'eliminate' instruments such as the violin and the piano. Instruments, he insisted, should relate to the living environment, like the metal plates which take on a prominent role also in *Al gran sole*; see Jozefowicz, *Das alltägliche Drama*, 156 (n. 235).

[12] Nono, letter to Pestalozza, September/October 1981 (copy by Nono, Pestalozza/L 81–09–20 m R, ALN), in Trudu (ed.), *Nono: Carteggi*, 244.

Nono's reaction to Pestalozza's reproach of an 'incomprehensible' turn towards 'Nietzschean matters'[13] is all the more explicit because the musicologist did not hesitate to voice such criticism in print. Pestalozza's article on the 'new' Nono 'after the *Quartet*', which opens the 1981 *Musik-Konzepte* volume on Nono, pessimistically concludes that, 'all too seductively, the *Quartet* also forecasts the path of integration, which it still resists'.[14] And the brief 'Post scriptum' continues as follows:

> In view of the violent power of the mass media – including academic criticism and journals – the figure of the great misunderstood, unrecognised genius and the image of the manipulation he suffers are outdated and themselves part of these machineries of power. They are part of a game, lubricate the clockwork. [. . .] In materialist terms there would indeed be room to deny one's complicity, that is to say: room for music that does not succumb to *beauty*. The latter has to remain decisively secondary – though no less necessary – to the element of disquiet (not to make use of the ambiguous term of contradiction): otherwise aesthetics would triumph once again.[15]

'Come on Luigi, don't block off Cacciari on Nietzsche', Nono counters in his typically shorthand reply, 'because that would be limiting Cacciari's knowledge itself.'[16] With Cacciari, Nono had obviously moved on from the Marxist materialism Pestalozza still firmly adhered to in 1981. And with *Prometeo* (1975–85) in particular, Nono would ultimately demonstrate that, perhaps now more than ever before, beauty was put at the service of disquiet in order to win the game against the machinery of power and to break out of an all too rigid materialism, which had lost its appeal not only to Walter Benjamin.

The following discussion of the string quartet *Fragmente – Stille, an Diotima* (1979–80) and *Prometeo* (1985) aims to examine and illuminate Nono's late aesthetics from within. Much in the way Cacciari understood the 'unpolitical' as a dimension that arises from the political to overcome and supersede it, Nono's late thought is shown to grow out of previous concerns in order to go beyond them. Nono's late endeavour to 'embody the universal', it will thereby become exceedingly clear, is by no means less political than anything else he ever wrote.

[13] Pestalozza, letter to Nono, 20 September 1981 (Pestalozza/L 81–09–20 m, ALN), *ibid.*, 242.

[14] Pestalozza, 'Ausgangspunkt Nono', 9. [15] *Ibid.*, 10.

[16] Nono, letter to Pestalozza, September 1981 (Pestalozza/L 81–09–20 m R, ALN), in Trudu (ed.), *Nono: Carteggi*, 245.

# 6 *Fragmente – Stille, an Diotima* (1979–80)

> . . . want continually to change my situation, believe I foresee my salvation in the change . . .
>
> Franz Kafka, *Tagebücher 1914–1923* (1 III 1915)[1]

The string quartet *Fragmente – Stille, an Diotima* is one of the seminal chamber works with which Nono began his 'epic' journey towards *Prometeo* (1984/85) and first employs the 'scala enigmatica' from Verdi's *Ave Maria* (1898) from which much of his later music is derived. Another crucial concept was put to the test in . . . . . *sofferte onde serene* . . . (1975–77) and *Con Luigi Dallapiccola* (1979), the two other groundbreaking works of the period: undulating layers of sound which seamlessly weave in and out of each other within a range of related speeds that variously repel and assimilate each other. Each of these layers or 'waves' of sound – Nono himself spoke of 'onde' (waves) – is itself kept in a constant state of flux and evolution, which, at times, makes the distinction of the individual layers exceedingly difficult. As in much of Nono's earlier music, the blurring of boundaries is fully intentional and a challenge to engage with the '. . . geheimere Welt . . .' (world of greater secrets) of his late compositional thought.

'Pensiero musicale' (musical thought) is a term Nono repeatedly turned to at this time; so, too, at the beginning of his discussion of *Fragmente – Stille, an Diotima* on the occasion of the work's unofficial premiere on 1 June 1980:

> I have to say immediately that, for me, composing music is not just a technical matter, not just craftsmanship, it is about thought. This was expressed so beautifully in a booklet by Schoenberg, I believe: Schoenberg taught us to think, not to compose. Renaissance treatises, Zarlino, Zacconi, Artusi, up to Padre Martini, also always discussed different ways of thinking musically. [. . .] And after *Al gran sole*, that was a time of much reflection for me . . . in terms of language, musical language . . . I was very irritated, I say this openly [. . .] especially in Italy, because *Al gran sole* was either accepted or rejected depending on the ideological perspective. This, to me, is very

1 '. . . will meinen Zustand immerfort verändern, glaube zu ahnen, daß in der Veränderung meine Rettung liegt . . .' Kafka, *Tagebücher 1914–1923*, 79; *The Diaries of Franz Kafka*, 116; *Diari 1910–1923*, ALN, underlined by Nono.

superficial; a fideistic or dogmatic kind of attitude, because it has a title: some are for it, all are against it, without testing what there is musically. This is also a deficiency of music critics, especially those on the left. They should rather demonstrate the possibility of really penetrating the surface, analysing what happens in the music![2]

I here wish to offer a reading of *Fragmente – Stille, an Diotima* which, I hope, comes close to what Nono expected of his critics and is concerned primarily with 'what happens in the music'. Without much speculation on the possible reasons for Nono's so-called 'Wende' (turning-point), I would simply like to propose a path into this composition that sheds light on the use of the scala enigmatica and also clarifies the hitherto equally enigmatic music–text relationship.[3] My analysis is based on Nono's sketches in particular, but also the wealth of literary sources that influenced and shaped the work. I believe that Nono's engagement with these literary sources (not just Hölderlin) had musical consequences that are best brought out by means of re-association. This association is subjective, of course, but often these related texts capture the emotional essence of this music better than any analytical observation ever would, which is why they are integral to my analysis.

*Fragmente – Stille, an Diotima* was commissioned by the city of Bonn for its thirtieth Beethovenfest, and Beethoven is recalled by means of the two performance instructions 'mit innigster Empfindung' (with innermost feeling) and 'sotto voce' which Nono borrows from the slow movement of Beethoven's quartet op. 132, *Heiliger Dankgesang eines Genesenen an die Gottheit, in der lydischen Tonart.*[4] This serene example of Beethoven's late compositional thought served as a model also in a broader sense: 'much more important to me was Beethoven's idea of using a special kind of

[2] 'Wie Hölderlin komponierte', Nono in conversation with the LaSalle Quartet (Bonn, 1 June 1980; official premiere 2 June), in Kirchert, *Wahrnehmung und Fragmentierung*, 203–218 (original WDR recording included on CD); edited cut in Wagner (ed.), *Nono: Dokumente Materialien*, 156–67. For Walter Levin's account of the collaboration see Spruytenburg, *The LaSalle Quartet*, 257–69.

[3] The literature on *Fragmente – Stille, an Diotima* is exceptionally large. The most serious study to date is Spree, *'Fragmente – Stille, an Diotima'*. Other book publications are Linden, *Luigi Nonos Weg zum Streichquartett*; Allwardt, *Die Stimme der Diotima*; and Kirchert, *Wahrnehmung und Fragmentierung*. Another groundbreaking study of this period, though not specifically on the quartet, is Paulo de Assis, *Luigi Nonos Wende*. The work is discussed with reference to Blanchot in Metzer, *Musical Modernism*. Articles will be cited as pertains to my argument.

[4] Beethoven, String Quartet op. 132, 'Sacred Song of Thanksgiving to the Deity from a Convalescent, in the Lydian Mode'. In the early stages, Nono briefly considered *Mit innigster Empfindung* as a possible title (ALN 44.04.01/03rsx).

material, the Lydian mode, for his thanksgiving. And I, too, have used a special material, the scala enigmatica by Verdi, in order to thank various people in various ways'.[5] As is already well documented, two of the people for whom Nono chose this 'special material' were Hermann Scherchen and Bruno Maderna.[6] The scala enigmatica from Verdi's *Ave Maria* is clearly linked to Scherchen, who discussed the work at his conducting course in Venice in 1948.[7] The name 'Scherchen' appears in a preliminary sketch next to reflections on the scala enigmatica on C.[8] The same sketch also reveals the association of Maderna with *Malor me bat* (or *Malheur me bat, Misfortune Assails Me*), a chanson ascribed to Ockeghem in Petrucci's *Harmonice Musices Odhecaton A* (1504), which Maderna and his students arranged for performance, also in the late 1940s.[9] Under the heading 'OKEGHEM (ODHECATON A 1504)' Nono notates the beginning of *Malor me bat* on E with 'Bruno 1948' encircled in the margin. 'Verdi–Scherchen–Ave Maria' is later tied to 'Ockeghem–Bruno–Ave Maria'.[10] 'Mi: *malor me bat*' follows in clear separation. In essence this already encapsulates the final form of the quartet: two parts with material based on the scala enigmatica from which the archaic melody *Malor me bat* eventually rises with unprecedented clarity as a kind of final focal point: a Benjaminian 'tiger's leap into the past' as it were.[11] This momentary glimpse of a bygone

[5] Nono, in conversation with Kropfinger, '... kein Anfang – kein Ende ...', 168; *Scritti*, II, 455.

[6] The link to Maderna was first drawn by Döpke in 'Fragmente – Stille, an Diotima', 18–20; On the link to Scherchen see Frobenius, 'Luigi Nonos Streichquartett', 188.

[7] For Nono's 1948 transcription of Verdi's *Ave Maria* see Pellegrini, 'Musica o diritto?', 22. Scherchen later described the scala enigmatica as a synthesis of the major, minor, whole-tone and chromatic scales; Scherchen, 'I quattri pezzi sacri' (1951), in Frobenius, 'Luigi Nonos Streichquartett', 188. For the conference Music in Italy in the 1950s (Venice, April 1978), Nono reminded himself 'Scherchen 48/ corso internazionale: Ave Maria – Verdi/ Bach – Arte Fuga/ Mahler/ Schönberg'; Nono, *Appunti*, M05.141/01 (ALN).

[8] ALN 44.04.01/01rdx

[9] See Noller, 'La storia e la crisi della stampa musicale'. Noller observes, and Stenzl confirmed this, that the published manuscript score of this 'Odhecaton Suite' (Ars Viva, now Schott) is in Nono's handwriting. The fact that *Malor me bat* is rendered on viola in *Fragmente – Stille, an Diotima* is generally understood as a direct reference to Maderna's 1948 setting of this song for three violas. Sketches show, however, that Nono initially assigned the tune to the cello.

[10] The two 'Ave Maria' units are linked to different speeds. In his score of Verdi's *Ave Maria*, Nono marks the cantus-firmus-like scala enigmatica segments in red and the much-faster-moving harmonisations in black. Verdi's speed indication ♩ = 84 is marked 'Matto! 60/66 anche meno 46' (Crazy! 60/66 even slower 46).

[11] According to Vieira de Carvalho, *Fragmente – Stille, an Diotima* is the first of Nono's works to 'consciously refer to Benjamin's philosophy of history'; Vieira de Carvalho, 'Idiom, Trauerspiel, Dialektik des Hörens', 193. Though references to Benjamin are to be

era is soon absorbed again into the fragmentary stream of fleeting gestures, unstable textures, suspended sound and silence from which it emerged and is organically integrated into Nono's avant-garde idiom.

A similar final point of focus is also found in *Con Luigi Dallapiccola* for six percussionists and live electronics (ring modulation and amplification). In this preceding work, Nono explores the resonant spaces of the 'fratello' motif of Dallapiccola's *Il prigioniero* (F–E–C♯) and its transposition by a tritone (B–B♭–G) in fixed instrumental registers and chord placements spanning seven octaves. A seemingly endless variety of gestural and textural combinations is derived from overlapping sets of duration values within this fixed realm of pitch and instrumentation. Only towards the end of the piece are the interlocking waves of different types of resonance channelled into a single rhythmic line, to which Nono notes with great humour: 'non Vivaldi'.[12] Yet here, too, this moment of exceptional clarity is soon engulfed again by the more textural sonorities of the combined sound waves, led by the 'Ur-schrei' of the 'leone' (lion's roar) into the concluding otherworldly resonances of low tubular bells and ring-modulated steel plates.

The most important figure behind the 'special material' of this atmospheric percussion piece is, of course, Luigi Dallapiccola. In this case, too, Nono refers back to Scherchen, whose introduction to Dallapiccola's 'musical thought' had inspired him to compose his own *Liriche greche* (1948–49).[13] The second of these early songs, *Ai dioscuri* for mixed chorus, piano and percussion, already contains a hidden reference to the 'fratello' motif from *Il prigioniero*: three groups of four pitches (adding up to a ten-tone row) are each allocated one of the motif's three pitches.[14] A particular interest in series-segmentation is further evident in Nono's annotations to *Congedo di Girolamo Savonarola*, the last of Dallapiccola's *Canti di prigionia* (1938–41). As Nono himself remarked at the time, this song 'is based on two series and one citation (the Gregorian *Dies irae*)'.[15] The first series

found only in the sketches for *Prometeo*, Vieira de Carvalho rightly regards Nono's practice of citation as truly Benjaminian; see Vieira de Carvalho, 'Towards Dialectic Listening' and '*No hay caminos*?'.

12 ALN 43.07.01/11sx,13r.sx.

13 Nono, 'Con Luigi Dallapiccola', *Scritti*, I, 483. For a brief analysis of the first of Nono's *Due liriche greche* (1948–49), *La stella mattutina*, see Borio, 'L'influenza di Dallapiccola', 366–69.

14 This was presented by Impett in 'Accelerated learning: Nono's years of study 1942–1950'. On Scherchen's practice of working with small pitch sets also see de Assis, *Luigi Nonos Wende*, 150–54.

15 Nono, 'Luigi Dallapiccola e i *Sex Carmina Alcæi*', *Scritti*, I, 3.

is split into three four-note segments, and each segment undergoes its own development. Nono marks the segments A, B and C, and his annotations focus primarily on how segment A is coupled with the *Dies irae* in always-changing constellations.

Both the 'fratello' motif and *Congedo di Girolamo Savonarola* would resurface in Nono's musical thought no less than three decades later. *Con Luigi Dallapiccola* cites the 'fratello' motif in its original form (F–E–C♯). The instrumentation, Nono himself remarked, is modelled on *Congedo di Girolamo Savonarola.*[16] Moreover, B–B♭–G, the only other transposition of the 'fratello' motif in *Con Luigi Dallapiccola*, is precisely the transposition Dallapiccola chose for the motif's reappearance in *Canti di liberazione* (1955). Dallapiccola himself spoke of the 'authentic sweetness' the motif attains in the latter work by means of 'rigorous dodecaphonic treatment'.[17] With similar compositional rigour, Nono makes use of these two 'authentic' transpositions to venture ever deeper, *with* Luigi Dallapiccola, into the 'immense space and infinite worlds' of his own 'pensiero musicale'.[18]

Dallapiccola, however, is not the only 'brother' Nono turns to. Moving into the 'fourth dimension' of live-electronic sound projection, he undoubtedly also had Varèse in mind.[19] The use of the lion's roar, ring-modulated steel plates and the resonance of suspended cymbals is too similar to the lion's roar and the sirens in *Ionisation* (1929–31) not to be understood as an allusion to this groundbreaking percussion piece, the European premiere of which Nono heard on his first visit to Darmstadt in 1950.[20] Nono later visited Varèse in New York and discovered the composer's passion for Afro-Cuban music. In Havana, Nono then came across the correspondence between Varèse and the Cuban composer Amadeo Roldán, revealing the influence of Roldán's percussion pieces on *Ionisation.*[21] For *Con Luigi Dallapiccola*, however, a more abstract

[16] Nono, 'Un'autobiografia', *Scritti*, II, 544. *Con Luigi Dallapiccola* shares timpani, tubular bells, cymbals, triangle and bass drum with *Congedo di Girolamo Savonarola*. The additional choice of lion's roar, wood blocks, temple blocks, sapo cubana and sleigh bells is closer to Varèse.

[17] Dallapiccola, 'Notes for an Analysis', 16.

[18] Nono, 'Con Luigi Dallapiccola', *Scritti*, I, 483–84. Nono here speaks of a 'conflicting simultaneity of signals and thoughts' in the *Canti di liberazione*, which may have influenced his concept of simultaneous 'onde'.

[19] Varèse, 'The Liberation of Sound', 197; underlined by Nono in Varèse, *Écrits*, ALN.

[20] On Nono's earlier allusion to *Ionisation* see Chapter 2, n. 150.

[21] In conversation with Garavaglia, Nono mentions a piece entitled *Cinque Toque* of 1929; Nono, 'Intervista di Renato Garavaglia' (1979–80), 240. However, the list of works by the Cuban composer Amadeo Roldán y Gardes (1900–39) contains no work of this title and

compositional concept was again of primary interest. 'The lesson learned from Varèse', Nono told Garavaglia at the time,

> urged me to search for a number of things other than those achieved by him. This has less to do with the challenge of the effect of sound or the search for melody on percussion, the use of instrumental timbre or the search for a compositional logic. Instead it is a study on the simultaneity of waves, sound bands in which every now and then a counterpoint happens, not between lines, but when an interaction between waves that rise and others which recede is established.[22]

This concept of interacting waves is absolutely fundamental also to *Fragmente – Stille, an Diotima*. The aim of the following analysis is to show how Nono generates three waves of sound from the 'scala enigmatica', how these independent layers relate, and how the text is essentially chosen to match and reflect this musical wave structure. The underlying system of duration, Nono himself explained in conversation with the LaSalle Quartet, remains the same as in *Con Luigi Dallapiccola*. In a sense, the dialogue with his early mentors is thus simply continued with other forces. In order to refine (or even re-define) his compositional method, Nono continues to look back 'mit innigster Empfindung' to his formative years in the late 1940s and early 1950s, taking old premises as new starting points. All this happens with an acute sense of loss and mourning as, one by one, mentors, friends and family had passed away, some of them very recently.[23]

Uncertainty and isolation are certainly at the core of the Kafka diaries, Nono's original choice of text for the quartet.[24] Among the diary entries Nono highlighted are 'The terrible uncertainty of my inner existence'[25] and 'I am more uncertain than I ever was, I feel only the power of life. And I am

it is most likely that Nono meant to refer to Roldán's *Rítmicas V* and *VI* (1930) for Cuban percussion instruments, which are known to have influenced Varèse's *Ionisation*.

22 Nono, 'Intervista di Renato Garavaglia' (1979–80), *Scritti*, II, 240–41.

23 Maderna and Malipiero both died in 1973, Dallapiccola in 1975. Nono was also mourning the loss of his parents, who died within three months of each other (in 1975 and 1976). Dessau died in 1979.

24 As shown by de Assis, Nono had already engaged with Kafka in the context of ..... *sofferte onde serene* ... (1976); de Assis, *Luigi Nonos Wende*, 174–80; also see Kirchert, *Wahrnehmung und Fragmentierung*, 192–94. The choice of Kafka may refer back to Maderna's *Studi per "Il processo" di F. Kafka* (1950). In the context of *Prometeo*, it is more likely, however, that Nono discussed Kafka with Cacciari, who mentions the *Diaries* in his *L'Angelo necessario* (1986); *The Necessary Angel*, 24–25/108, note 21.

25 'Die schreckliche Unsicherheit meiner inneren Existenz' (3 May 1913), Kafka, *Tagebücher 1912–1914*, 176; *The Diaries of Franz Kafka 1910–1913*, 283.

senselessly empty.'[26] Uncertainty is linked to a distinct sense of disquiet – 'Unruhe': 'A feeling of disquiet again. From what did it arise? From certain thoughts which are quickly forgotten but leave disquiet unforgettably behind'[27] and also 'heart disquiet'.[28] Nono further consistently underlines Kafka's many entries on insomnia. But there is also 'Ruhe' and 'Stille', precisely the kind of quiet which gives rise to disquiet: 'A little calmer. How needed it was. No sooner is it a little calmer with me, it is almost too calm. As though I have the true feeling of myself only when I am unbearably unhappy.'[29] Solitude, however, is seen as a necessity for artistic focus: 'Being alone has a power over me that never fails. My interior dissolves . . . and is ready to release what lies deeper.'[30] Nono also underlines 'The firmness, however, which the most insignificant writing brings about in me is beyond doubt and wonderful. The comprehensive view I had of everything on my walk yesterday!'[31] Dreaming also falls into this realm of artistic creativity. Nono was particularly taken by Kafka's entry of 29 October 1911 in which three totally unrelated fictional episodes are brought together in a dream sequence. Each of the episodes is introduced by a short preamble that defines it as a dream: 'I dreamed today', 'in addition I dreamed' and 'then I dreamed'.[32] The same three preambles are found in Nono's sketches (marked A, B and C), and it may well be that the idea of working in three layers goes back to this free alliance of dream sequences.[33]

[26] 'Ich bin unsicherer als ich jemals war, nur die Gewalt des Lebens fühle ich. Und sinnlos leer bin ich.' (19 November 1913), Kafka, *Tagebücher 1912–1914*, 203; *Diaries 1910–1913*, 309.

[27] 'Wieder kam Unruhe. Woher? Aus bestimmten Gedanken, die schnell vergessen werden, aber die Unruhe unvergesslich hinterlassen' (23 January 1922), Kafka, *Tagebücher 1914–1923*, 206; *The Diaries of Franz Kafka 1914–1923*, 208 (trans. amended).

[28] 'Herzunruhe' (22 January 1922), Kafka, *Tagebücher 1914–1923*, 207; *Diaries 1914–1923*, 209 (trans. amended).

[29] 'Ein wenig stiller. Wie notwendig war es. Kaum ist es ein wenig stiller, ist es fast zu still. Als bekäme ich das wahre Gefühl meiner Selbst nur wenn ich unerträglich unglücklich bin.' (20 January 1922), Kafka, *Tagebücher 1914–1923*, 202; *Diaries 1914–1923*, 205.

[30] 'Das Alleinsein hat eine Kraft über mich, die nie versagt. Mein Inneres löst sich . . . und ist bereit Tieferes hervorzulassen.' (26 December 1910), Kafka, *Tagebücher 1909–1912*, 110; *Diaries 1910–1913*, 39. This fragment was of particular importance to Nono, as he reminds himself on the inner cover of his edition: 'p. 22 intimo/ lasciare via libera a qualcosa più profondo'.

[31] 'Die Festigkeit, aber, die das geringste Schreiben mir verursacht, ist zweifellos und wunderbar. Der Blick, mit dem ich gestern auf dem Spaziergang alles überblickte!' (27 November 1913), Kafka, *Tagebücher 1912–1914*, 209; *Diaries 1910–1913*, 314.

[32] 'Ich träumte heute', 'außerdem träumte ich' and 'dann träumte ich', Kafka, *Tagebücher 1909–1912*, 160–62; *Diaries 1910–1913*, 119–20.

[33] ALN 44.04.01/01vdx.

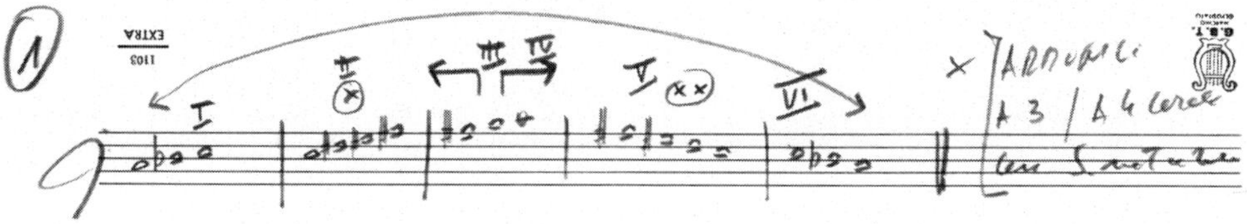

**Example 6.1** Scala enigmatica on C, ALN 44.04.01/03rsx.

Kafka is also specifically linked to the use of harmonics ('Kafka = armonici')[34] and dreaming is tied to the inspirational walk: 'come passeggiate su Okeghem = Kafka = sognai + armonici naturali'.[35]

Tables of natural harmonics make up much of the lists of materials and possible articulations Nono compiled in preliminary sessions with the LaSalle Quartet. They were conceived as a link between the scala enigmatica material and *Malor me bat*. Example 6.1 shows the scala enigmatica on C as notated on the sketch that links 'Okeghem' and Kafka.[36] Already at this early stage the scale is divided into characteristic sets of intervals, the first three of which would later serve as bases for the generation of the three layers. At this stage Nono was obviously still considering the descending second half of the scale with its characteristic F (instead of F♯ in the ascending first half). The two arrows above the scale suggest a mirror structure in two parts, while Roman numbers indicate the three scale segments to be used for the generation of each of the parts (I–III, IV–VI). For the two variants of the central four-note segment (II and V) Nono further notes 'armonici – a 3/ a 4 corde – con s.[uoni] naturali'. This links the scala enigmatica material to the 'passeggiate su Okeghem' for which Nono also intended to use natural harmonics. For this reason, I believe, all available open strings (from which natural harmonics are derived) are given particular attention. Example 6.2 shows Nono's chart of the twelve scala enigmatica transpositions as notated on a sketch that was later reused for *Prometeo*.[37] All open-string pitches on violin, viola and cello are here boxed (C, G, D, A, E). Nono further marks the number of open-string pitches per scale (ascending and descending) in either margin.[38] Although he later does not work with transpositions of the scale as such, open strings

[34] ALN 44.04.01/02. [35] ALN 44.04.01/03rsx. [36] ALN 44.04.01/03rsx.

[37] The sketch is reproduced on the inner book covers of Cacciari (ed.), *Luigi Nono: Verso Prometeo* (1984) and Nono, Cacciari (eds.), *Luigi Nono: Festival d'automne à Paris 1987*.

[38] This sketch is no longer with the materials for *Fragmente – Stille, an Diotima*. Another sketch entitled 'Tabella Arm. Nat.' shows all of the open-string pitches derived from the

**Example 6.2** List of scala enigmatica transpositions.

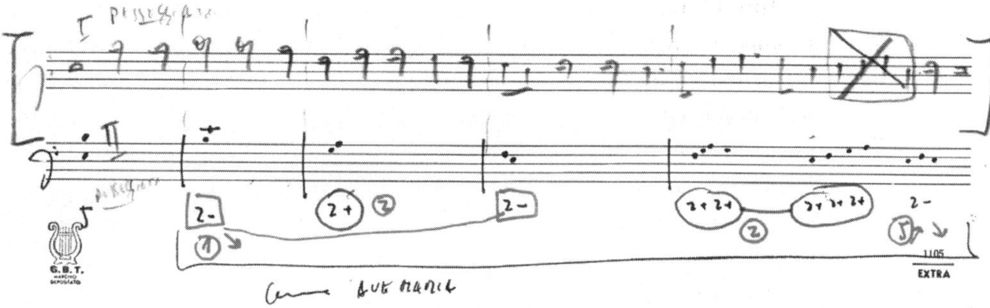


**Example 6.3** *Malor me bat*, ALN 44.04.04/01rdx.

become one of the elements that may be added *ad libitum* to the basic interval sets derived from the scala enigmatica. The other element to be handled with such freedom is the tritone. In the last of his scala enigmatica transpositions (on B) Nono points out the many occurrences of the tritone. In the ascending scale the tritone divides the octave in half (B–F–B) and also appears as the framing interval of the central whole-tone segment (E♭–A). The descending scale no longer features the octave dividing F, but instead adds a further tritone between pitches 2 and 5 (B♭–E).

Perfect fifth and tritone are also inherent features of the chanson *Malor me bat* in the Phrygian mode on E. As can be seen in Example 6.3, the tune begins with a fifth on E, but the open quality of this interval is later diffused by the prominent use of the Phrygian F.[39] Of the six diatonic pitches in use, four are available on open strings (E, A, G, C). *Malor me bat* thus particularly lends itself to the derivation of natural harmonics and probably inspired the idea of being able to 'walk freely' between one type of material and the other. Nono's own comparative analysis, however, focuses on the semitone and whole-tone progressions, precisely the sets of intervals with which tritone and open strings are later combined (Example 6.3).

In preliminary sessions with the LaSalle Quartet, Nono further determined the ambitus of each instrument and, as previously with the percussionists of La Scala, explored a great variety of timbres, articulations and sound qualities.[40] Among the many possibilities of sound production

scala enigmatica transpositions in isolation, maintaining the same order and manner of notation (ALN 44.04.04/02rsx).

39 Also see Frobenius, 'Luigi Nonos Streichquartett', 189.

40 Levin dates the sessions back to early September 1979 and recalls that Nono 'still hadn't written any music, just a few possibilities on staff paper, which we were supposed to try out. [. . .] he wanted to work with us, experimenting with sounds, and combinations of

Nono jotted down *arco normale*, *arco col legno*, *col crine*, *gettato*, *balzato*, *battuto*, *martellato*, *flautato*, *flautato* on harmonics (with a reference to Schoenberg), *spazzolando*, *tremolo* and *pizzicato*. Also explored were the different areas of the bow (point, middle, frog) and its point of contact with the string: on the fingerboard (*tasto*), normal position (*normale*), near the bridge (*ponte*) and behind the bridge (*dietro il ponte*). Different speeds of trills, tremolo and vibrato were also tested.[41] Under the entire list of possibilities Nono writes and underlines in red: 'sempre mit innigster Empfindung!!!'[42] Much thought was also given to density and ambitus (combinations of one to four instruments in low, medium and high registers).

Having thus prepared his canvas and a highly differentiated palette of timbres or 'sound qualities', Nono goes on to define some of the work's fundamental concepts.[43] It is in these notes that he first mentions a theme of love, though not yet with reference to Friedrich Hölderlin and Susette Gontard, the 'Diotima' behind much of the poetry that would later pervade the music. Instead, Nono names the Russian poet Vladimir Mayakovsky and his lover Lili Brik, whose problematic relationship (and Mayakovsky's suicide) had already been of concern in the context of ..... *sofferte onde serene* ... (1975–76).[44] These notes are reproduced and translated in Figure 6.1. Extreme fragmentation, it becomes clear, is to encapsulate the 'Zerrissenheit' (rupturedness) of modern man – be it Mayakovsky, Kafka, Musil or Benjamin – modern man tormented by passion, anger, exasperation and a utopian yearning for a better future. Already at this stage, Nono had a very clear idea of how this image of inner torment was to become music. The next sheet of notes is

sounds. And when something corresponded to what he had in mind, he wrote it down. Over and over again he wanted to hear what it sounded like when we produced strange sounds with the instruments or distorted intonations or dissonances.' Spruytenburg, *The LaSalle Quartet*, 266.

41 Nono was no novice in regard to extended string techniques. Similar sessions had already been conducted with Rudolf Kolisch for *Varianti* (1957); see Kolisch, 'Nonos Varianti'; Zenck, '"La di Ella inaudita finezza"'.

42 ALN 44.04.03/03 43 ALN 44.04.03/11–13.

44 Nono first planned a piano piece entitled *Notturni – Albe* (1974–75) with a theme of love relating to Mayakovsky and Lili Brik (the wife of the literary critic Ossip Brik). The plan was brought to an abrupt halt with the death of Nono's parents and bereavement also in Pollini's family; see Stenzl, *Texte*, 443; *Luigi Nono*, 92; and de Assis, *Luigi Nonos Wende*, 156–63. After Lili Brik's death, *l'Unità* announced 'Un quartetto di Luigi Nono dedicato a Lili Brik e Maiakovski' (10 August 1978); see Ramazzotti, *Luigi Nono*, 190. 'Perhaps, also, another reminder of Lili Brik and Vladimir Maiakovsky', Nono further states in his preface to *Fragmente – Stille, an Diotima* (score).

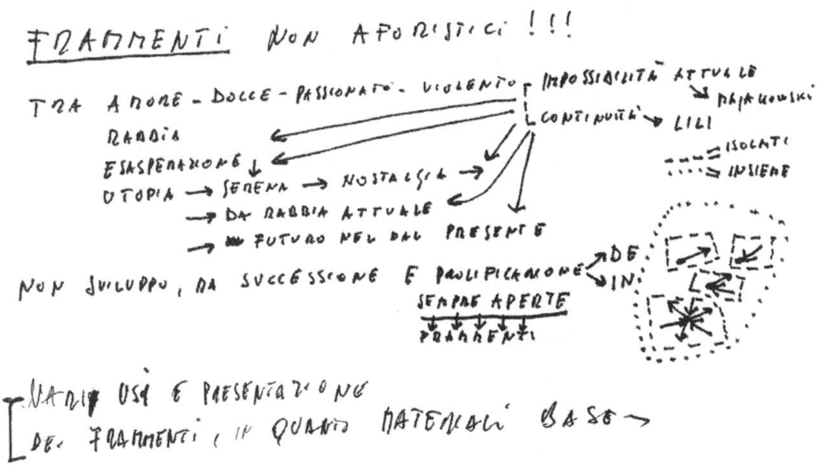

NON-APHORISTIC FRAGMENTS!!!

BETWEEN LOVE – SWEET – PASSIONATE – VIOLENT – CURRENT IMPOSSIBILITY

ANGER → MAYAKOVSKY

EXASPERATION CONTINUITY → LILI

UTOPIA → SERENE → NOSTALGIA --- = ISOLATED

→ OUT OF CURRENT ANGER .... = TOGETHER

→ FUTURE IN FROM THE PRESENT

NOT DEVELOPMENT, BUT SUCCESSION AND PROLIFERATION → OF

→ IN

ALWAYS OPEN

FRAGMENTS

VARIOUS USES AND PRESENTATIONS

OF THE FRAGMENTS, AS OF THE BASIC MATERIALS

**Figure 6.1** *Fragmente – Stille, an Diotima*, lower section of sketch 44.04.03/12.

reproduced in Figure 6.2.[45] Singled out with arrows, crosses and exclamation marks are the two key concepts 'continua le .... Onde ....' (continue the .... Waves ....) and 'sempre !interrotti!' (always interrupted). Detailed, too, are the types of sound to be employed: percussive sounds, sustained sounds, motif-like fragments ('frammenti motivi') and fields of

[45] ALN 44.04.03/13.

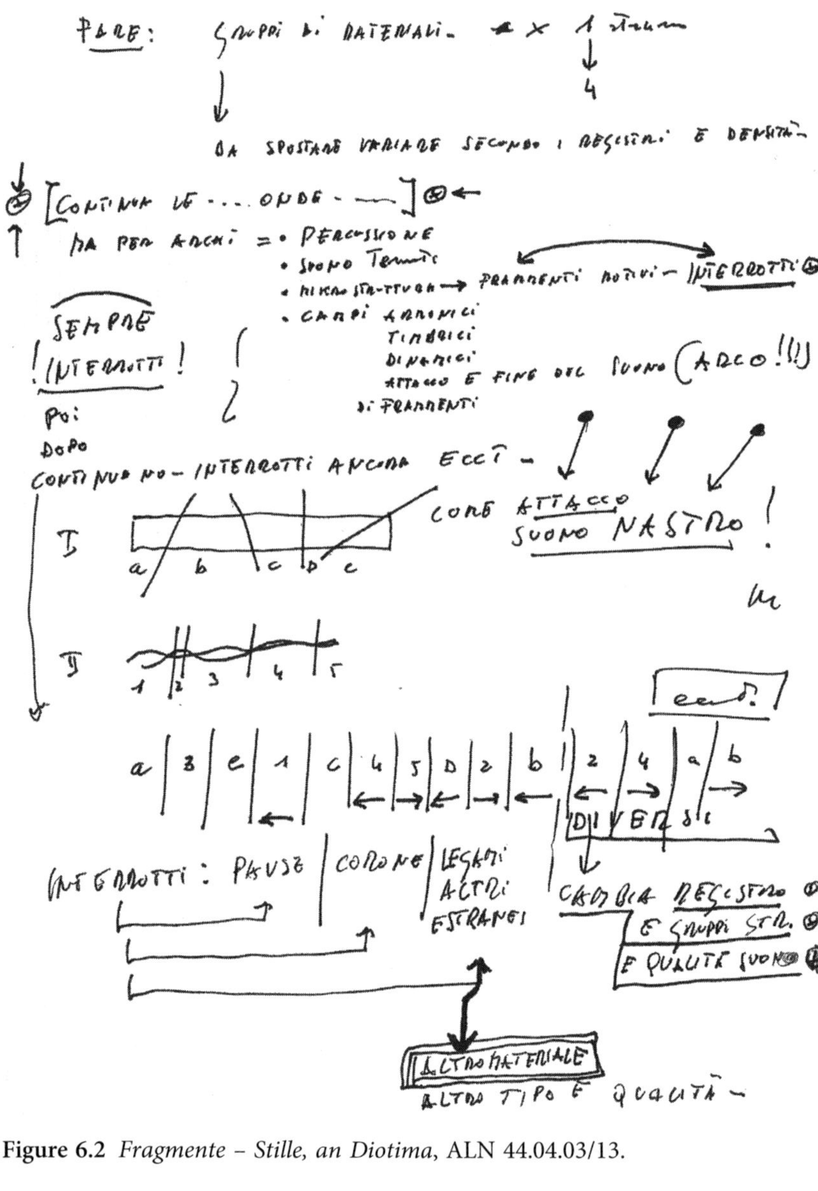


**Figure 6.2** *Fragmente – Stille, an Diotima*, ALN 44.04.03/13.

sound ('campi'), for which harmonics, timbres, dynamics and articulation are specified as means of differentiation. Interruption and stagnation, it becomes clear at the bottom of the sketch, were to be achieved by means of rests and fermatas as well as 'foreign' material, regarding which Nono specifies only that it should be of a different type and quality.

In addition, two drawings summarise the basic structural idea in graphic form: a rectangular block is dissected into five irregular sections (a b c d e), and two overlapping undulating lines slowly assimilate each other. These lines, too, are cut into five irregular sections (1 2 3 4 5). The labelled block segments and line segments are then juxtaposed in irregular fashion, and Nono also begins to map out the order and retrograde movement of related fragments for a second part in which the registers, instrumental combinations and sound quality are to be fundamentally altered. In terms of form, this preliminary scheme already represents a very accurate picture of what would be accomplished in the finished work.

Exactly when Nono decided to work with text by Hölderlin is not entirely clear. Klaus Zehelein from the Frankfurt Opera introduced Nono to the Frankfurt Hölderlin Edition by Dietrich E. Sattler in 1978.[46] Nono was immediately fascinated with this new critical edition and later told Restagno that

> For years I have read and studied Hölderlin in the new and remarkable *Frankfurter Ausgabe*, an edition that reproduces the original manuscripts by anastatic methods. Here one can follow Hölderlin's thought process: onto an initial line others are superimposed, written out in differently coloured inks, even using Greek or other thoughts in French. Over one word you thus find another two, three, four, five, like a process of elaboration which advances by means of accumulation of various types of material, various types of thought, various possibilities of drawing together extremely uncommon and unrelated words. At times Hölderlin works with a selection of these materials, at other times not: the thought process remains open without reaching a conclusion. For me this second hypothesis is fundamental. The *Frankfurter Ausgabe* is therefore completely different from the many philological editions which intend to show the sketches and variants as a process destined to arrive at a single solution. This principle of an openness towards a multiplicity of meanings and possibilities is fundamental.[47]

In Hölderlin's poetry, it seems to me, Nono found an ideal fund for what he had in mind, in terms of both topic and sound world, but also, and perhaps even primarily so, in terms of the compositional process. The name Diotima (with its additional meanings in Plato and Musil)

[46] See Stenzl, *Luigi Nono*, 92. Nono was in Frankfurt for the first German production of *Al gran sole carico d'amore* (1978). On Sattler's edition also see my article 'Quiet Revolutions'. Nono owned selected volumes of this Frankfurt edition (still incomplete at the time), but chose the texts from his bilingual Mandruzzato edition, *Diotima e Hölderlin* (1979). Nono's choice of text is further documented on three sketches in the possession of Hans-Jürgen Nagel, published in Mauser, '*An Diotima* . . .: Dichtung als Partitur'. Hölderlin had already been mentioned in sketches for *Con Luigi Dallapiccola* (1979) (ALN 43.01/02) and would feature prominently in *Prometeo*.

[47] Nono, 'Un'autobiografia', *Scritti*, II, 546–47.

presented itself as a rich abstraction of the artist's muse and as such encapsulated the infinite variations of sound and meaning that fascinated Nono in Hölderlin's poetry and which Nono strove to explore in his music. Though he was inspired by Kafka and Hölderlin, it must not be forgotten that Nono essentially thought musically, in categories of sound and sound quality, and the infinite possibilities of their inflection. Among reflections on pitch and duration for Part I, four fragments from the poem *Diotima* (1796) show that Nono did indeed begin to write this music with Hölderlin in mind.[48] However, text is never set to music in the conventional sense. Most of the music was in fact composed without any reference to text at all, and the final choice of text took place only at the very end of the compositional process. Yet text was omnipresent throughout this process in that each of the compositional layers is intrinsically linked to an underlying poetic idea that undergoes as many transformations in Nono's music as it does in the poetry which was eventually assigned to it. The result is an intricate, multi-layered web of interrelations, which I shall now endeavour to disentangle by means of a more detailed analysis of the finished score.

The most basic structural feature of *Fragmente – Stille, an Diotima* is its division into two parts. This division is hardly evident from the score, but Nono was so certain of it that, as soon as Part I was finished (at 26 bar 1), he sent it to the LaSalle Quartet for rehearsals to begin.[49] Contrary to what is implied by the numbers in the score (26 + 26 = 52), the second part is longer and not in perfect symmetry with the first. The numbers in the score have, in fact, caused much confusion in terms of analysis. They are merely rehearsal numbers and first appear in the first complete manuscript score, where they simply number the pages (amounting to 69 instead of the final 52). Because of the lack of bar numbers, I will use these rehearsal numbers to indicate a position in the score, but they have no structural significance and should on no account be understood as 'fragment' numbers. Much more important, in structural terms, are the double bars, but even within these larger units the fragmentation often goes much further, with changes between layers occurring in infinitely

[48] '– Zephirstöne/ – von dem toten Porte/ – kalt und bleich/ – in meiner Nacht', ALN 44.05/ 02dx; *Diotima* (1796), in Hölderlin, *Gesammelte Werke*, II: 'Lieder und Hymnen', 275–99. For reasons of accessibility I refer to the *Frankfurter Hölderlin Ausgabe*, henceforth abbreviated as FHA. In his bilingual edition Nono underlined these later discarded fragments in red; other fragments (some later included in the score) are underlined in green. Nono dates the poem 'Luglio 1796 mandata a Schiller/ 1797 in Musenalmanach'.

[49] According to Levin, Part I arrived in December 1979; Kirchert, *Wahrnehmung und Fragmentierung*, 210.

smaller units. How fast these changes can occur is evident from the very first appearance of what I will call the *Diotima* layer. This layer is consistently generated from the central whole-tone segment of the ascending scala enigmatica and corresponds to Nono's drawing of the rectangular block. The principal motif for the *Diotima* layer in Part I first appears after [5] under the poetic heading '... seliges Angesicht ...' (blessed countenance).[50] The text here simply refers to what is written underneath: the sextuplet ending on open D in the violins (vln 2 behind the bridge), an atmospheric tremor produced by means of a very quiet aperiodic tremolo at the tip of the bow near the bridge at the moderate speed of ♩ = 72. The same type of sound then resurfaces with increasing urgency (♩ = 112) in sections [8] and [9], and again at [10] under the related text '... die seligen Augen ...' (the blessed eyes).[51] From these two references to different poems it is already clear that Nono chose his texts thematically and did not give 'particular attention' to any one poem (as has been argued by Allwardt).[52] Instead, he responds to central poetic ideas in Hölderlin's oeuvre, in this case the memory of Diotima. From a fund of poetic references Nono chose and allocated texts that best match the musical content and development of his own compositional layers. The chosen texts, in turn, help to distinguish these layers. When two fragments as similar as '... seliges Angesicht ...' and '... die seligen Augen ...' head the same characteristic type of sound, this musical material is shown to be associated with the underlying poetic idea of Diotima. Furthermore, this *Diotima* layer is introduced in such a distinct way that it can be perceived as an independent type of sound. The dynamics and articulation of the characteristic tremolo sonority remain unchanged so far (*pp, alla punta aperiodico sul ponte*). Fixed, too, are the register and pitch reservoir. Throughout Part I this layer derives from the central whole-tone segment of the scala enigmatica on B (E♭–F–G–A). This span is filled out chromatically to form the pitch reservoir E♭–E–F–F♯–G–G♯–A. The register is that above middle C ($E\flat^4$–$A^4$), a comfortable first position on the D-string of violin and viola. For more body of sound Nono then adds the open strings G and D *ad libitum* (with open

[50] Hölderlin, *Wohl geh' ich täglich ...* (1800), FHA, V, 751–54 (754/v. 8). Nono informed his players about the origin of the text and sent them a copy of the Mandruzzato edition together with a letter detailing all the references (Levin/W 80–03–27 d, copy by Nono; ALN 44.32/08). On Levin's ambivalent reaction see Spruytenburg, *LaSalle Quartet*, 164–66.

[51] Hölderlin, *Hyperions Schicksalslied* (1798), FHA, V, 399–401 (401/v. 13).

[52] Allwardt, *Die Stimme der Diotima*, 77.

A already included in the pitch reservoir).[53] Resonant open strings thus mark the boundaries of this central block sonority, the parameters of which essentially remain the same throughout Part I.[54]

What, however, happens after [11], under the heading '... ins tiefste Herz ...' (deep into the heart),[55] where this tremolo sonority first manifests itself in isolation? Accelerating to its fastest speed (♩ = 132), the quiet tremor becomes ever more agitated and repeatedly breaks out of the prescribed pitch reservoir into higher octaves.[56] Open strings now also include the E on violins, but are generally less prevalent as they make way for the addition of tritones, resulting in gradual expansion into the chromatic total (E♭–A + A–E♭). Sound waves of fluctuating instrumental combinations oscillate irregularly between speeds ♩ = 36, 72, 112 and 132 and gradually increase in dissonance, density and dynamic contrast (*ppp–ff* ). This build up of nervous agitation is eventually cut off by a silence (7″–9″) just before [14], followed by a *ppp* echo without tremolo and another silence (5″–7″). Only then do we return to the original confines of this sonority: the pitch span E♭–A, open strings, *ppp*, tremolo, *aperiodico tasto.*

By means of the simple device of added tritones, Nono here breaks his own rules almost as soon as they are set up and assimilates the prime characteristics of another layer with which this tremolo sound was first coupled at [8], '... wenn aus der Tiefe ...' (when out of the depth).[57] This heading clearly refers to the viola and cello parts (moving at the parallel speeds ♩ = 36 and ♩ = 72). From the opening leap on cello it is clear that this layer is of the meandering kind and strides through the registers in all possible directions. Its characteristic use of the tritone is again a result of the chromatic extension of the basic pitch cell. The layer is generated from the chromatic third segment of the scala enigmatica, which Nono regarded as a fund of '2– 7+ 9–'. For Part I Nono selects the segment

[53] On ALN 44.07/01 the quintuplets are notated linearly within this pitch span, to which Nono then simply adds 'Con sol/re = corde vuote' (With G/D = open strings).

[54] Examples of this type of sound are also found under '... wenn aus der Ferne ...' at [16] and '... hoffend und duldend ...' at [25].

[55] Hölderlin, *Diotima*, FHA, II, 292, v. 77.

[56] Levin complains that ♩ = 132 is too fast for the tremolo quintuplets: 'technically not realisable in this tempo. (At least for us!!)'. To this Nono notes 'Berg = ♩ =140', but also 'possibile senza tremolo alla punta?' (Levin/W 80–01–05 m, ALN). Towards the end of the passage at [14] a few of the quintuplets are indeed notated without tremolo.

[57] Hölderlin, *Der Frühling* (1843), FHA, IX, 207–210 (210/v. 1). Section [8] was initially conceived as the opening of the work; sections [1] to [7] were added later on in the compositional process.

**Example 6.4** Pitch generation of the layer of *Tiefe*, ALN 44.09/02rdx.

C♯–D–E♭ (from the scala on E♭).[58] As shown in Example 6.4, the segment is extended to a full chromatic scale and split into two hexachords.[59] Nono moves through the pitches of these chromatic hexachords in steps of 7+ and 9–, covering all registers in all possible directions. The two hexachords are further overlapped, and this procedure results in the undulating sets of chromatically interlocked tritones that make up much of this layer. In the final work Nono also uses linking intervals other than the semitone (the segment's framing interval of a major second, for example). Mostly, however, this layer consists of interwoven chains of tritones linked by a semitone, major-seventh or minor-ninth relationship. Its meandering motion further closely resembles Nono's drawing of the undulating lines.

If the central *Diotima* layer with its characteristic block sonority is consistently linked to the poetic idea of Diotima, the text associated with this meandering tritone layer muses on sources of artistic inspiration. A key term here is *Tiefe*, with its array of literal and figurative meanings: depth, lowness, intensity, profundity, all of which apply to modes of

58 ALN 44.05/01sx details the pitches used to generate the three layers in Part I: 'A: fa♯–sol–sib | B: mib–fa–sol–la | C: do♯–re–mib'. In other words, Nono uses the scala enigmatica transpositions on F♯ (segment 1, layer A), B (segment 2, layer B) and E♭ (segment 3, layer C).

59 ALN 44.09/02rdx.

human feeling and expression. The fragment '. . . wenn aus der Tiefe . . .' (assimilated into the *Diotima* layer with '. . . ins tiefste Herz . . .') certainly implies a search for innermost feeling and depth of expression and, to my mind, is inherently related to an entry Nono highlighted in his Kafka diaries: 'Mein Inneres löst sich . . . und ist bereit Tieferes hervorzulassen' (My interior dissolves . . . and is ready to release what lies deeper).[60] With 'Libero "sogni" (F.K.)' Nono reminds himself of Kafka in sketches for this initial opening fragment (now at [8]), and the performance instruction 'tutto un po' libero' for the independent cello part may well be a relic of this idea.[61]

The concept of *Tiefe* resurfaces once more at [21] with '. . . tief in deine Wogen . . .' (deep into your surge).[62] The undulating tritone layer is now associated with the sea, and this poetic image is then consolidated at [23] '. . . im heimatlichen Meere . . .' (in the native sea).[63] The subtle change in meaning highlights an equally subtle change in articulation. If the beginning of this layer was consistently marked *flautato* (*ponte-tasto*, *tasto-ponte*), the sound now becomes distinctly more raw and naturalistic with the instruction *legno-crini* (*tratto/battuto*). Also in terms of duration values, this layer is about to get wilder: to the quaver and its multiples (the layer's basic duration value so far), Nono now also adds triplets at [21] and quintuplets at [23]. A further assimilation to the *Diotima* layer happens in terms of speed (♩ = 66/112). On reading the poems from which Nono chose this sea imagery (later of great importance also in *Prometeo*), it becomes clear that this natural depth, too, is rich in metaphorical meaning: to delve 'deep into the waves', in Hölderlin, is to give in to surges of enthusiasm, and 'the native sea' is home to a 'fresh tide of life'.

A further Kafka diary entry comes to mind in this context: the inspirational walk on which experience of nature gives rise to exceptional artistic insight and clarity of thought. After all, this increasingly choppy 'sea' of tritones flows out of the two bars '. . . wenn in einem Blick . . .' '. . . und Laut . . .' (when with one glance . . . and sound) at [19].[64] Concisely shaped and with the exceptional use of *arco normale* (*ponte-normale-ponte*), this, it seems, is 'the comprehensive view I had of everything on my walk yesterday!'[65] With dynamic direction (*pp–f*, *p–ff*) and increasingly

[60] Kafka, *Tagebücher 1909–1912*, 110; *Diaries 1910–1913*, 39.

[61] ALN 44.06.03/01vsx. 'Libero "sogni" (F.K.)' is found among tritone passages for viola and cello.

[62] Hölderlin, *Diotima*, FHA, II, 293, v. 123.

[63] Hölderlin, *Der Jüngling an die klugen Ratgeber* (1796–97), FHA, II, 253–73 (272/v. 8).

[64] Hölderlin, *Diotima*, FHA, II, 292, v. 82.

[65] Kafka, *Diaries 1910–1913*, 314; see n. 31.

dramatic speed, these two bars perhaps come closest to representing what Nono initially referred to as 'motif-like fragments' ('frammenti motivi'). In a letter to the LaSalle Quartet, Nono would later characterise his Hölderlin fragments as 'BOLTS of sensations, of surprises of every kind [i.e. Nature–Mankind–Thought–Interiority (Kafka) + (Musil)]'.[66] Especially the second bar of 19, the speed of which greatly surpasses all other speed indications in the quartet, comes close to representing such bolts of lightning musically. Its extremely fast directional force, exceptional presence of sound and mono-rhythmic contour is utterly surprising and capable of cutting through any other texture. In their characteristic brevity both 'Blick' and 'Laut' are highly recognisable dramatic gestures. Unchanged in pitch, rhythm, dynamics and basic articulation, they later recur, first at the end of Part I (25 bars 6 and 8), and then again in Part II (40 bar 6; 42 bar 4), now increasingly spaced out, reversed in order and with texts relating to the subject matter their layer is to attain in this part.

Before going on to Part II, there is yet another layer to be unravelled in Part I. This layer comprises the fragments '. . . wenn in reicher Stille . . .' (when in rich silence)[67] after 18 and at 20, '. . . in stiller ewiger Klarheit . . .' (in still eternal clarity)[68] at 22 and '. . . ruht . . .' (rests)[69] at 24. In Part I, this third layer is consistently generated from the first segment of the scala enigmatica on F♯ (F♯–G–B♭).[70] Like the central whole-tone segment for the *Diotima* layer, this segment, too, is regarded as an interval span rather than a set of intervals. Again this span is filled out, now right down to the level of quarter-tones.[71] 'CON CAMBI DI REGISTRO per ¼ in ottava/ FINO USO ARMONICI' Nono wrote in one of his preliminary sketches.[72] Quarter-tone division and use of harmonics are thus initially linked to the idea of placing this layer in the highest

[66] 'BLITZE von Gefühlen von Überraschungen jeder Natur [also Natur–Mensch–Denken–Interiorität (Kafka) + (Musil)].' Nono, letter to LaSalle Quartet, 27 March 1980 (Levin/W 80–03–27 d; ALN 44.32/08).

[67] Hölderlin, *Diotima*, FHA, II, 292, v. 81.

[68] Hölderlin, *Hyperions Schicksalslied*, FHA, V, 401, v. 14–15.

[69] Hölderlin, *Der Jüngling an die klugen Ratgeber*, FHA, II, 272, v. 8.

[70] ALN 44.05/01sx. This scale segment is strikingly similar to Dallapiccola's 'fratello' motif and here, too, Nono uses the tritone-related transpositions F♯–G–B♭ (Part I) and C–C♯–E (Part II). These are Dallapiccola's thirds '. . . when out of the depth . . .'.

[71] Nono first used quarter-tones in *Canti di vita e d'amore* (1962) to create impermeably dense orchestral textures. In the quartet, Nono himself explained, quarter-tones are primarily employed to avoid octaves; 'Wie Hölderlin komponierte', in Kirchert, *Wahrnehmung und Fragmentierung*, 214.

[72] ALN 44.05/02: 'WITH CHANGES IN REGISTER ¼ tones in the octave/ UP TO THE USE OF HARMONICS'.

possible register. Nono was obviously thinking of 'campi armonici' (fields of harmonics) here, ethereal textures in hitherto unknown heights, shimmering islands of calm for which he uses the slowest of speeds (♩ = 30) and the duration model 'B calmo' from *Con Luigi Dallapiccola* with its variety of longer durations.[73] This most textural of layers is clearly associated with the poetic idea of *Stille* (silence/calm). Before this layer of *Stille* is introduced in full, however, it potently announces itself by means of sustained natural harmonics. Long open-string harmonics are present from the very outset, on D and G (before and behind the bridge) in the violins at [8]. With the added text '. . . mit deinem Strahle . . .' (with your radiance)[74] after [14] they begin to attain a poetic significance of their own. After the dramatic build up of '. . . ins tiefste Herz . . .', Nono not only returns to the original confines of the *Diotima* layer but also obviously feels the need to develop an element of inner calm. 'Mirage' is the term the composer himself coins for the re-emerging harmonics in this section.[75] The viola, Nono explains to his players, leads the 'first mirage' on G ([14] bar 2). The second mirage follows on G♯ in vla and vln II ([14] bar 3), and the third is the long 'G harmonic + I. vno' ([14] bars 4–5) that extends into the seemingly 'ENDLOS!?' (endless) violin harmonics on G and D ([15]), joined by E♭ and A in the cello ([15] bars 2–3).

In terms of pitch, these 'mirages' are beautifully ambiguous. The prominent G and G♯ may already point towards the segment F♯–B♭ from which the emerging layer of *Stille* is to be generated. They are, however, just as integral to the segment E♭–A of the *Diotima* layer, the span of which is emphasised by the harmonics on cello. G is of course also an open-string pitch, and G♯ can also be seen as a tritone addition to open D. The opening pitch progression F–G–C♯ on viola, too, is reminiscent of the undulating tritone layer, as is the *flautato* (*tasto/al ponte/legno + crine*) articulation. The only truly defining characteristic of these mirages is the newly introduced Beethovenian performance instruction 'sottovoce' (consistently written as one word in Nono's sketches and the score), which

[73] In *Con Luigi Dallapiccola* Nono works with two systems of duration, 'A veloce' and 'B calmo'. Duration values are the same, but the length of the actual durations is determined by different sets of duration factors, which are probably generated by means of a number square (ALN 43.03.01/01). Durations for the *Stille* layer in Part I of *Fragmente – Stille* comply with the 'B calmo' model. This connection was first made by Erika Schaller, who catalogued the sketches.

[74] Hölderlin, *Diotima*, FHA, II, 291, v. 43.

[75] Nono, first of two letters to the LaSalle Quartet (undated reply to Levin's letter of 5 January 1980), ALN 44.32/04v. The term 'mirage' may stem from Baudelaire's poem *Le vin des amants* from *Les fleurs du mal*, which is later quoted in *Prometeo*.

Nono paraphrases as 'fast in sich selbst' (almost within oneself), giving it a sense of turning inward, from outward projection to inner reflection.[76] As this contemplative streak takes precedence, the *Diotima* layer gradually recedes into the distance: '. . . wenn aus der Ferne . . .' (when from afar)[77] is marked *pppp* for the first time, and '. . . aus dem Aether . . .' (out of the ether)[78] emerges only a fleeting memory of the nervous agitation at '. . . ins tiefste Herz . . .'. Meanwhile the harmonics climb ever higher from G to A, to F♯ and C, and the last 'mirage' is sustained in radiant heights by the first violin whose *pppp* D harmonic is carried over into the first true appearance of the *Stille* layer, '. . . wenn in reicher Stille . . .' after [18].

The generation of this layer can be traced back to a sketch where Nono notes the quarter-tone division of the segment F♯–G–B♭, in addition to that of the other two scale segments.[79] In the finished work, the high harmonics consistently stem from this first scala enigmatica segment (F♯–B♭) and only the pitches from this segment include quarter-tones. Vln II, vla and cello all begin on G and venture outward, ending on F¾↑ (vla), G♯ (vln II), A (vcl), B♭ (vln I). Occasionally, however, this extremely close-knit quarter-tone texture is broken up by shorter lower pitches: Nono intersperses the pitches B, C♯, E♭ and F, and these additional pitches stem from the chromatic span B♭–F♯ (without further quarter-tone division). Once again the two spans complement each other and add up to the chromatic total. In the final '. . . ruht . . .', however, Nono dispenses with the lower pitches altogether and the layer comes to 'rest' on the original scala enigmatica pitches F♯–G–B♭.

If pitch progression is deliberately kept to a minimum in this *Stille* layer, the 'richness' of these glistening quarter-tone textures is fully achieved on the level of articulation. Nono here truly realises his ideal of a 'suono mobile'. The wide range of duration values (2, 3, 4, 5, 6, 7, 8) opens up infinite combinatorial possibilities, and Nono makes sure that patterns of articulation and of tone repetition are always varied and never fall together.[80] In addition, the basic *pppp tasto* sound is to be broken up by a free and aperiodic *arco gettato verso il ponte* ([18] and [22]) or *saltato al ponte* ([20]). *Tasto* becomes *flautato* at [22] and Nono gradually reduces the

[76] ALN 44.32/04v. [77] Hölderlin, *Wenn aus der Ferne*, FHA, IX, 37–63 (62/v. 1).

[78] Hölderlin, *Der Jüngling an die klugen Ratgeber*, FHA, II, 272, v. 20.

[79] ALN 44.13.01/01sx. For each segment the quarter-tone intervals are counted, semitones marked, and the original scala enigmatica pitches are highlighted. In the margin Nono also notes all intervals other than 2– and ¼.

[80] The *Stille* layer encompasses the full range of duration values (2 3 4 5 6 7 8; 6 comes into use only in Part II) and can thus be regarded as the fund from which the values of all other layers are extracted.

tone repetition. The layer thus also comes to 'rest' on the level of articulation with sustained *ppp flautato* harmonics.

'... ruht ...' is not the very last appearance of this layer in Part I, however. It, too, is knotted into '... hoffend und duldend ...' (hoping and suffering), the section in which all three layers are finally recombined. The fragment begins and ends with the *Diotima* layer, which also resurfaces very briefly in [25] (bar 5). Much more prominent is the undulating layer of *Tiefe*, with its allusion to '... tief in deine Wogen ...' (bar 2), a short dip into 'the native sea' (bar 5, beginning) and the already-discussed quotations of 'Blick' and 'Laut' (bars 6 and 8). But Nono also introduces a new gesture, which ends on loud repeated tritones (bars 3–4). Such tritones are already present in the opening '... wenn aus der Tiefe ...', though this was not a feature Nono chose to develop significantly in Part I. The new gesture in '... hoffend und duldend ...' suddenly catapults these repeated tritones into the open, and Nono thus sows seeds for new developments. Forebodings of Part II are also inherent in the return to the ambiguous world of 'mirages' with *flautato sottovoce* (bar 7). The slow speed, the articulation and the 'endless' G♯–A–B♭ on vla and cello (bar 9) all indicate that the layer of *Stille* has been drawn into the depths of the layer of *Tiefe* and is about to take on a very different guise.

If Part I is indeed the 'Verdi–Scherchen–Ave Maria' part envisaged in the early stages, Scherchen's teachings must have been of a much more orderly kind than Maderna's. The second part 'Okeghem–Bruno–Ave Maria' is about to become infinitely more adventurous. Nono here not only continues the principles set out in Part I, but branches out into related layers, continuing the three layers on two levels. In order to understand what happens in Part II, it makes sense to summarise the large-scale developments so far. Table 6.1 details the parameter settings for each of the three layers in Part I. All three layers are combined in the beginning and concluding sections '... wenn aus der Tiefe ...' at [8] and '... hoffend und duldend ...' at [25]. These sections are important nodal points in the structure of the work. The central 'block' of Part I is the *Diotima* layer. Firmly grounded in the middle register and its characteristic tremolo sonority, it moves in quintuplets throughout and is assigned three of the faster speeds. These characteristic fluctuations in speed (a hallmark of Nono's later idiom) are used to create the impression of an oscillating wave of sound. Upon emerging from the depths of the *Tiefe* layer, this wave climaxes quickly, then gradually recedes. As the image of *Diotima* recedes, there emerges the contemplative layer of *Stille*, the slowest layer of all, with the greatest variety of duration values.

Table 6.1 *Layer specifications for Part I (beginning – [26], bar.1)*

| Layer | Number | Pitch | DV | Articulation | Speed |
|---|---|---|---|---|---|
| *Stille* | 18 | **Segment 1** | 2, 3, 4, 5, | tasto/ | ♩ = 30 |
| (high) | 20 | scala on F♯ | 7, 8 | flautato + | |
| | 22 | F♯–G–B♭ | | gettato/ | |
| | 24 | filled out (¼) | | saltato al ponte | |
| | mirages: | | | *mirages*: | |
| | 14–18/25 | | | flautato sottovoce | |
| *Diotima* | 5, b.2 | **Segment 2** | 5 | tremolo alla punta | ♩ = 72, 112, |
| (centre) | 8–10 | scala on B | | aperiodico | 132 |
| | 11–15 | E♭–F–G–A | | (tasto/ponte) | |
| | 16 | filled out (2–) | | | |
| | 17–18 | *ad libitum*: | | | |
| | 25, | open strings | | | |
| | 1 and 5 | tritones | | | |
| *Tiefe* | 8–11 | **Segment 3** | 2 | flautato | ♩ = |
| (undulating) | 14–15 | scala on E♭ | + 3 and 5 | (ponte/tasto) | 36/72 |
| | 19 | C♯–D–E♭ | | normale | 60/240 |
| | 21 | (chromatic | | (ponte, normale, | 66/112 |
| | 23 | extension) | | tasto) | |
| | 25, 2–8 | *ad libitum*: | | legno + crini | |
| | | tritones | | (tratto/ battuto) | |

Ascending to great heights, it lingers in shimmering quietude and gradually moves towards complete standstill. Correspondingly, the 'mirages' associated with this layer get ever longer, progressing from the duration of a minim with a normal fermata (after [14]) to the second 'ENDLOS!?' in '... hoffend und duldend ...' (*ca.* 18″–21″).[81]

In contrast to the *Diotima* and *Stille* layers, which both peak and recede, the layer of *Tiefe* – that of artistic creativity – is much more fragmented and twisted. This layer with the greatest contrast of speeds is virtually defined by undulating motion and its characteristic interval of the tritone. Although it, too, eventually comes to rest in the depths of the 'native sea', there is nevertheless a sense of increasing urgency, with a steady advance towards faster duration values. All three layers are then recombined in '... hoffend und duldend ...', the important nodal point between Parts I and II,

[81] The first 'ENDLOS' after [15] is marked *ca.* 15″–17″.

where quietude suddenly turns to disquiet, much in the sense of Kafka's diary entry: 'A little calmer. How needed it was. No sooner is it a little calmer, it is almost too calm.'[82] Here is what Nono told the audience after the work's first performance:

> Walter Levin said at the beginning that this is a calm piece, calm music. When I heard it, it gave me total disquiet . . . Why does one think of this as calm music, why does one hear this as totally calm? I don't believe this is so. I think something that seems really calm gives rise to great disquiet.[83]

Part II is generally marked by a far greater degree of fragmentation than Part I, but this is not the only level on which disquiet – *Unruhe* – presents itself. Disquiet really does emerge from quietude. The layer of *Stille* now radically branches out into its opposite and '. . . ruht . . .' literally becomes '. . . ich sollte ruhn? . . .' (should I rest?).[84] This radical change from *Stille* to *Unruhe* takes place before and after [27] with two groups of repeated chords marked by strong contrast in dynamics and speed (*ppp*/*sff*, ♩ = 46/92).[85] Building on the gestural element of tone repetition in '. . . hoffend und duldend . . .', these chords effectively mark the entry of the layer of *Unruhe*, which, like the *Stille* layer in Part I, is also consistently derived from the first segment of the scala enigmatica. Sketches reveal that new branches of all three layers are now derived solely from the scala enigmatica on C.[86] For Part II the scale is divided into the same segments and the following pitch sets are added: C–C♯–E ('Base 1'), E–F♯–G♯–B♭ ('Base 2') and B♭–B–C ('Base 3'). Various chords and register placements are devised for all three segments (layers) and again open strings and tritones are added *ad libitum*. For the first set Nono further notes the segment transpositions C–C♯–E and C♯–D–F as well as the adjoining quarter-tone transpositions. Quarter-tones thus become an integral part of the pitch structure and are no longer confined to the high register only. The aforementioned chords at [27] exemplify this novel use of quarter-tones: the *ppp* quavers combine C–C♯–E with the segment's upper

82 Kafka, *Diaries 1914–1923*, 205; *Tagebücher 1914–1923*, 202.

83 'Walter Levin hat am Anfang gesagt, ist eine ruhige Stück, ruhige Musik. Als ich habe gehört, das hat mir vollkommen Unruhe gegeben . . . Warum man denkt, das ist eine ruhige Musik, das man hört ganz ruhig? Ich glaube nicht das, ich glaube von etwas, die ganz ruhig scheint, bringt eine große Unruhe heraus.' Nono, in 'Wie Hölderlin komponierte', 211.

84 Hölderlin, *Der Jüngling an die klugen Ratgeber*, FHA, II, 272, v. 1.

85 The preceding '. . . heraus in Luft und Licht . . .' belongs to the layer of *Luft* and was added later on in the compositional process.

86 ALN 44.16/01–04. Nono's term 'base unica' refers to the common transposition on C.

quarter-tone transposition in the middle register. The following *sff* chords are placed in the same register but add an octave(!) on D. These Ds are part of the next higher transposition, C♯–D–F, which is added in full to the following fragment '... denn nie ...' (because never).[87] The chords are now spaced out in register, duration values 3 and 5 are added, dynamic contrasts are developed (*p*<*fff*, *pp*, *mf* >*al niente*), and Nono also fleetingly alludes to the tremolo *al ponte* sonority of the *Diotima* layer in Part I, all at the speed ♩ = 72. This brief, but dramatic introduction to the layer of *Unruhe* is elongated, suspended in time, by two extremely long fermatas (*ca.* 12″–15″ and 15″–20″).

With '... wie so anders ...' (how so different)[88] at [28] Nono then returns to the parameters of the original *Stille* layer, giving it an almost unrecognisable, indeed totally 'different' guise. Anticipated by the fallen 'ENDLOS!?' in 'hoffend und duldend', the original pitch set of this layer (F♯–B♭) is now placed at the opposite end of the registral scale and combined with open strings (D–G). The speed and dynamic are carried over from Part I (♩ = 30, *pppp*), but, with *non vibrato tasto* articulation and the occasional sharp *sf al ponte*, 'stille Klarheit' now turns decidedly icy. This frosty texture concludes with a further dramatic gesture of *Unruhe*: the last dyad on the cello (F♯–G) is carried over and combined with yet another quarter-tone transposition of segment 1 (D♯–E–G) to be played *flautato al ponte* and *vibrando molto*. The following '... in leiser Lust ...' (with quiet pleasure)[89] at [30] is again a very different, much more textural manifestation of *Unruhe*. That this may be 'Herzunruhe' (Kafka) is implied by the now much more pronounced use of the tremolo *alla punta aperiodico* from the *Diotima* layer in Part I. The transpositions Nono uses for this muted but dynamically active texture are the original C–C♯–E and its upper quarter-tone transposition. The friction between adjoining quarter-tone transpositions intensifies in '... ich sollte ruhn? ...'[90] at [31] (C♯–D–F plus upper and lower quarter-tone transposition). The contrast between the repeated chords at [27] is now effectively transferred to the textural dimension. Nowhere, perhaps, is *Unruhe* as apparent as it is in these waves of maximum dynamic contrast (*pppp*/*ffff*). These extreme fluctuations lead nowhere; they do not manage to break out of the strict confines of pitch and register. Kafka's diary entry of 30 August 1914 comes to mind:

[87] Hölderlin, *Lebenslauf* (1801), FHA, V, 471–78 (478/v. 9).

[88] Hölderlin, *Diotima*, FHA, II, 290, v. 9. [89] Hölderlin, *Diotima*, FHA, II, 290, v. 29.

[90] Hölderlin, *Der Jüngling an die klugen Ratgeber*, FHA, II, 272, v. 1.

> I feel too strongly the limits of my abilities, narrow limits, doubtless, unless I am completely gripped by emotion. And I believe that even in the grip of emotion I am swept along within these narrow limits, which, however, I then no longer feel because I am swept along. Nevertheless, within these limits there is room to live, and for this reason I shall probably exploit them to a despicable degree.[91]

As if to capture different states of 'Ergriffensein' (being gripped by emotion), Nono demands various degrees of vibrato in this fragment ('*non vibrato–vibrato–molto–poco–non vibrato*') to be applied according to each player's judgement. The constrained pitch field eventually disperses with irregular *spiccato–sautillé* articulation and *ad libitum* rests at [32], '. . . ins Weite verfliegend . . .' (dispersing into the distance).[92] We then return to the icy remnants of the *Stille* layer (F♯–B♭ plus open strings), now entitled '. . . einsam . . . fremd sie, die Athenerin . . .' (lonely . . . estranged, she, the Athenian).[93] The *legno + poco crine* and *legno battuto* articulations, already known from the depths of the native sea, are now used to break up the sound. The instruction '*legno + poco crine*', Nono explains in the score, means that the music is to be played 'in such a way that the sound cannot be continuous'. Another element of alienation is the eerie metallic sound of open strings behind the bridge.

Into this bleak vision of the estranged muse bursts '. . . staunend . . .' (wondering),[94] a permutated quotation of '. . . tief in deine Wogen . . .', but with a much greater presence of sound in terms of both articulation and dynamics (*arco normale*, *f*, *sfff*, *p*). The element of surprise and the unusual presence of sound are close in spirit also to 'Blick' and 'Laut' (all three from the original layer of *Tiefe*). The choice of text here seems particularly apt as regards the use of *arco normale*:

> Staunend seh ich dich an, Stimmen und süßen Sang,
> Wie aus voriger Zeit, hör ich und Saitenspiel,
> Und die Lilie duftet
> Golden über dem Bach uns auf.

[91] 'Ich fühle allzusehr die Grenzen meiner Fähigkeit, die, wenn ich nicht vollständig ergriffen bin, zweifellos nur eng gezogen sind. Und ich glaube selbst im Ergriffensein nur in diese engen Grenzen gezogen zu werden, die ich dann allerdings nicht fühle, da ich gezogen werde. Trotzdem ist in diesen Grenzen Raum zum Leben und dafür werde ich sie wohl bis zur Verächtlichkeit ausnützen.' Kafka, *Tagebücher 1914–1923*, 37; *Diaries 1914–1923*, 91 (trans. amended); highlighted with three arrows by Nono.

[92] Hölderlin, *An einen Baum*, Mandruzzato edition, 198.

[93] Hölderlin, *An ihren Genius* (1798), FHA, VI, 103–104 (104/v. 4).

[94] Hölderlin, *Der Abschied* (1798), FHA, V, 481–93 (493/v. 33).

Wondering I look at you, voices and lovely song
As from distant times, music of strings, I hear
And the lily unfolds her
Fragrance, golden above the brook.[95]

The underlined 'Wie aus voriger Zeit' (as from distant times) also features in Nono's sketches, but was later discarded. 'Tormenti' (torments), Nono writes next to this verse,[96] and one wonders whether the following series of manifestations of *Unruhe* is indeed stirred up by the many lost voices (and not only those of his mentors) that inspired Nono throughout his composing career: '. . . eine Welt . . . jeder von Euch . . .' (A) '. . . wie gern würd ich . . .' (B) '. . . unter euch wohnen . . .' (C) '. . . ihr, Herrlichen!' (D) [a world . . . each one of you (A), how I would love (B), to live amongst you (C), you, magnificent! (D)].[97] Fluctuating between speeds of ♩ = 30, 66 and 92, the layer of *Unruhe* again manifests itself with a mixture of tone repetition and sustained chords. What is new is the introduction of hard pizzicato, and dynamic contrast is driven to the extreme, climaxing in '. . . wie gern würd ich . . .' with *fff* <+*possibile* on the concluding tremolo C–C♯–E ('Herzunruhe'?). The fragments now also extend into the lower octave, and again there is a sense of prolongation: '. . . ihr, Herrlichen!' is given exactly the same duration as '. . . ins Weite verfliegend . . .', but at half the speed.

'. . . das weisst aber du nicht, . . .' (but that you cannot know) we are told in interpolated fragments of a very different kind (at [34], [36], [38], [43] and [45]). With this text from *Wenn aus der Ferne* Nono returns to *Diotima*. The poem is unique in Hölderlin's oeuvre in that it gives Diotima a voice. But this voice, too, is a voice from the past. Imagined by Hyperion, who outlived Diotima, it is heard from afar, across the divide between present and past, life and death, a voice that leaves him (and us) with a distinct sense of possibility:

Du seiest so allein in der schönen Welt,
Behauptest du mir immer, Geliebter! das
Weißt aber du nicht,

That you're so alone in this beautiful world,
You always claimed, my Love! but that
You cannot know,[98]

[95] Hölderlin, *Der Abschied*, FHA, V, 493, v. 33–36, Nono's underlining; *The Farewell*, in Hölderlin, *Poems & Fragments*, trans. Hamburger, 150.

[96] ALN 44.18/01dx. [97] Hölderlin, *Die Eichbäume* (1796), FHA, III, 39–53 (53).

[98] Hölderlin, *Wenn aus der Ferne*, FHA, IX, 63, v. 49–51. *If from the Distance*, in Hölderlin, *Poems & Fragments*, 654–57 (657).

This open and ambiguous '... das weisst aber du nicht, ...' (the only text that is consistently reassigned to its related music) heads Nono's very own 'Dankgesang' with Beethoven's performance instructions 'sottovoce' and 'mit innigster Empfindung'. The first '... das weisst aber du nicht, ...' at 34 is indeed a continuation of the *Diotima* layer, for which Nono now uses the whole-tone segment from the scala enigmatica on C (E–F♯–G♯–B♭) and its adjoining field of quarter-tone transpositions. In all five fragments the dynamic remains constant (*pp–al niente*) and so does the speed (♩ = 60). Surrounded by the highly varied dynamic contrasts and fluctuations in speed of the new branch of *Unruhe*, this 'Dankgesang' manifests itself in polished crystals of sound. And each time Nono presents us with different crystallisations of pitch. At 34 the basic set E–F♯–G♯–B♭ emerges from its upper quarter-tone transposition in high register and its transposition by a semitone (F–G–A–B) in middle register. The duration value 5 is the same as in Part I, but the compositional units are now no longer marked by fast inner motion. It is as if the former *Diotima* 'motif' has been distilled into something much purer – distilled memories that are perhaps infinitely more mysterious in this new guise.

Table 6.2 details the pitch development within the five '... das weisst aber du nicht, ...' fragments. The table makes clear that, once again, principles are abandoned almost as soon as they are set up. On two occasions Nono deliberately breaks out of the layer's strict parametric constraints with a gesture of tone repetition that clearly assimilates the layer of *Unruhe* in terms of dynamic, duration and speed. The conjunction has its consequences for the layer of *Unruhe* itself as it continues at 39 with '... dem Raum ...' (to space) (E) and '... in freiem Bunde ...' (in free alliance) (F).[99] What happens here is beautifully captured by the added text. Within the constraints of the layer of *Unruhe* Nono makes 'space' for a 'free alliance' between 'base 1' (*Unruhe*) and 'base 2' (*Diotima*). This move in turn gives rise to an entirely new layer, which Nono himself referred to repeatedly in the sketches with the word *Luft* (air). This new layer, too, is based on a combination of 'base 1' and 'base 2'. Its undulating quaver motion, however, is much more closely related to the layer of *Tiefe*. That Nono thought of this layer in close conjunction with that of *Tiefe* is evident from a sketch where the text 'Wenn aus der Tiefe' is circled and complemented by 'Wenn neu das Licht' (when new the light).[100] With the keyword *Luft* in mind, Nono later chose a different but equally uplifting fragment for the opening of Part II: '... heraus in Luft und Licht ...'

[99] Hölderlin, *Die Eichbäume*, FHA, III, 53, v. 10/13; 'den Raum' is changed to 'dem Raum'.
[100] ALN 44.18/01dx. *Der Frühling*, FHA, IX, 173–74 (174/v. 1).

Table 6.2 *Pitch development in '... das weisst aber du nicht, ...'*

| No. | Register | Pitch | DV |
|---|---|---|---|
| 34 | High/middle | E–F♯–G♯–B♭ ¼↑ and F–G–A–B | 5 |
| | Middle | E–F♯–G♯–B♭ | |
| 36 | Middle | E–F♯–G♯–B♭ and ¼↑ | 5 |
| | High/middle | F–G–A–B and ¼↑ | |
| | Spaced out | F–G–A–B and ¼↑ | |
| 37 | | Tone repetition (assimilating *Unruhe*) | 4 |
| bar.2 | Spaced out | E–G♭–G♯–B♭ and ¼↓ | (accel. to ♩ = 92) |
| 38 | Spaced out | D♯–F–G–A and ¼↑ | 5 |
| | Spaced out | D♯–F–G–A and ¼↑ | |
| 43 | Middle | E–F♯–G♯–B♭ and ¼↓ | 3 |
| | High/middle | E♭–F–G–A and ¼↑ | |
| | Spaced out | E♭–F–G–A and E–F♯–G♯–B♭ ¼↑ | (♩ = 92) |
| | | Tone repetition (assimilating *Unruhe*) | |
| | Middle/low | E♭–F–G–A and E–G♭–A♭ ¼↑ | |
| | Spaced out | E–G♭–A♭ ¼↑ and E–F♯–G♯–B♭ | |
| 45 | Max. ambitus | E♭–F–G–A and ¼↑ [*sic.*] | 3 |
| | Middle | E–F♯–G♯–B♭ and ¼↑ | |
| | Spaced out | E–F♯–G♯–B♭ ¼↑ and F–G–[A]–B | |
| | Middle | E–F♯–G♯–B♭ and ¼↑ | |
| | Max. ambitus | E♭–F–G–A and ¼↑ [*sic.*] | |

(out into air and light).[101] *Luft* does not come out of *Tiefe* in the way *Unruhe* emerges from *Stille*, however. Instead of using the same segment of the scala enigmatica, Nono exchanges it for the other two. In fact, elements of all three layers are merged: pitch derives from segments 1 and 2 of the scala enigmatica on C (in alternation), duration values and the type of motion relate to the *Tiefe* layer of Part I, and the speed, dynamics and articulation are essentially the same as in *Diotima*'s '... das weisst aber du nicht, ...'. Precisely because *Luft* merges all three layers into one, '... verschwende ...' (I), '... die Seele ...' (II), '... an die Lüfte ...' (III) [waste (I) your soul (II) to the skies (III)][102] then seems to grow entirely organically out of '... in freiem Bunde ...', the 'free alliance' of the *Diotima* and *Unruhe* layers after 39.

*Luft* also brings about a return to the original *Tiefe* and *Stille* layers. '... leiser ...' (quieter) (α) is indeed a quieter (and slower) version of the

101 Hölderlin, *Diotima*, FHA, II, 290, v. 6.

102 Hölderlin, *Emilie vor ihrem Brauttag* (1799), FHA, III, 117–45 (121/v. 17–18).

repeated tritones in '. . . hoffend und duldend . . .', while '. . . Mai . . .' (May) (β) and '. . . säuselte . . .' (rustled) (γ) quote the original 'Blick' and 'Laut' in reverse order.[103] All three gestures are taken from the original *Tiefe* layer and, now in conjunction with *Luft*, emphasise the theme of spring awakening. In the midst of this spirit of revitalisation there is, however, also an element of doubt, another prolonged 'ENDLOS!?' entitled '. . . umsonst!' (in vain!). This is one of the moments where knowledge of the textual context is extremely enlightening because it seems to mirror the composer's fundamental concerns:

> Umsonst! mich hält die dürre Zeit vergebens,
> Und mein Jahrhundert ist mir Züchtigung;
> Ich sehne mich ins grüne Feld des Lebens
> Und in den Himmel der Begeisterung;
>
> In vain! Barren time holds me fruitlessly,
> and my century to me is castigation;
> I am ardent for the green pastures of life
> and the heaven of enthusiasm.[104]

With this 'Umsonst!', the last and longest of the 'mirages', Nono effectively anticipates the deathly *Stille* of '. . . Schatten stummes Reich . . .' (mute kingdom of shadows) at [41],[105] which he tellingly marked 'senza vibrato! freddo' in the first continuous score of Part II.[106] From this icy stillness (*legno sul ponte*) a tentative 'glance' at *Diotima* briefly gives rise to *Unruhe*. But then, before *Diotima*'s voice fades out completely and also the motif of her memory recedes into the far distance at [46], '. . . wenn in die Ferne . . .' (when into the distance),[107] the layer of *Stille* suddenly takes another decisive turn: '. . . wohl . . . andere Pfade . . .' (other paths perhaps).[108] This new process (which will eventually bring the work to its conclusion) encompasses the four fragments '. . . wohl . . . andere Pfade, . . .' (1), '. . . dem Täglichen gehör ich nicht . . .' (to the commonplace I do not belong) (2),[109] '. . . wo hinauf die Freude flieht . . .' (into the heights to which joy escapes) (3)[110] and

103 Hölderlin, *Diotima*, FHA, II, 290, v. 30–31.
104 Hölderlin, *Der Jüngling an die klugen Ratgeber*, FHA, II, 273, v. 41, trans. Harry Gilonis (with many thanks).
105 Hölderlin, *Diotima*, FHA, II, 291, v. 40.
106 ALN 44.23/01–21.
107 Hölderlin, *Die Aussicht* (1843), FHA, IX, 223–24 (224/v. 2).
108 Hölderlin, *Wohl geh' ich täglich . . .*, FHA, V, 754, v. 1.
109 Hölderlin, *Emilie an Klara*, FHA, III, 127, v. 168–70.
110 Hölderlin, *Diotima*, FHA, II, 291, v. 58.

'. . . an . . . Neckars friedlichschönen Ufern . . . eine stille Freude mir . . . wieder . . .' (on Neckar's peaceful banks quiet joy comes back to me) (4).[111] Much in the manner of the 'mirages', this last guise of *Stille* is at first ambiguous. In '. . . wohl . . . andere Pfade' at 44, the violins are first assigned an open-string pitch each (A/G), which they play in different registers, including a range of natural harmonics. The viola and cello, in turn, are assigned a tritone (vla: E–B♭, vcl: C–F♯). The registers vary and selected pitches appear as harmonics. Both instrumental groups thus render pitches that could in principle be regarded solely as *ad libitum* additions. Together, however, they form the core fragment F♯–G–(A)–B♭ of the original *Stille* layer (with tritones added to the framing pitches). The articulation and dynamics are not yet clearly linked to *Stille*, being more similar to those of the original layer of *Tiefe*. The most ambiguous of all articulations is the *flautato* with its links to the *Tiefe* layer, the 'mirages' and the later fragments of *Stille* in Part I.

One of the main characteristics of the original *Stille* layer is, of course, the use of harmonics in high register. Harmonics are now reintroduced, but move much more freely through the registers. In keeping with his original idea 'come passeggiate su Okeghem = Kafka = sognai + armonici naturali', Nono here begins to set the harmonic field for the truly dreamlike appearance of *Malor me bat*. The process continues in '. . . dem Täglichen gehör ich nicht . . .' at 47 from which *Malor me bat* eventually emerges. Once again Nono gradually broadens the pitch spectrum and this process of diffusion is supported by the reintroduction of the aperiodic *arco balzato*. The pitches A and G in the violins are now heard either as high harmonics or as 'impure' octaves modified by quarter-tone additions to the higher pitch (¼↑). The tritones in viola and cello (C–F♯, E–B♭), too, are transposed a quarter-tone up. Particularly the tritone of the cello is thus given a leading function. Notated as F♭–B♭ (¼↑), its quarter-tone friction finally resolves into the opening fifth E–B of *Malor me bat*, which, not by coincidence, is accompanied by open strings A and G in the violins and yet another tritone (D–G♯) on the cello.

The process of quarter-tone transposition continues after the viola's 'versione libera' of *Malor me bat* – or '. . . wenn ich trauernd versank, . . . das zweifelnde Haupt . . .' (when grief depresses me, . . . the head full of doubt).[112] The tritone F–B in '. . . wo hinauf die Freude flieht . . .' (again assigned to the viola) is precisely the tritone inherent in the Phrygian tune on E. However, it is also the upper quarter-tone transposition of the

111 Hölderlin, *Emilie an Klara*, FHA, III, 132, v. 284.

112 Hölderlin, *Ihre Genesung* (1798), FHA, V, 507–512 (511/v. 14).

tritone with which the cello led into *Malor me bat*. Via the connecting link of *ad libitum* tritones, Nono thus seamlessly moves back into the surrounding scala enigmatica material. Also the second tritone (on cello) is now transposed a quarter-tone up to C♯–G. The two violins, in turn, contribute to the general ascending motion ('. . . wo hinauf die Freude flieht . . .') with further upper quarter-tone deviations from B♭, A, G♯ and G in their 'impure' octaves. This leads to a brief recapitulation of the layer of *Luft* in '. . . zum Aether hinauf . . .' (up into the ether)[113] at 50 to which also the long fermata (*ca.* 15″–17″) at the end of '. . . im Grunde des Meers . . .' (at the bottom of the sea)[114] belongs. The layers of *Luft* and *Tiefe* are here combined to form one last organic undulation. In '. . . zum Aether hinauf . . .' only the viola ascends. All other parts lead down to 'the bottom of the sea', the final abyss of the layer of *Tiefe* where tritones alternate with minor ninths in waves of maximum dynamic contrast (*pppp–sfff* ). This joint wave of *Luft* and *Tiefe* is eventually also enveloped by *Stille*. The 'impure' octaves in the violins now correspond to the preceding minor ninths of '. . . im Grunde des Meers . . .' and so do the tritones. In terms of dynamics, articulation and pitch, Nono gradually seems to return to the field of '. . . wohl . . . andere Pfade . . .' with its core segment F♯–G–(A)–B♭. B♭ is omitted, however, and replaced by the pitch that first initiated the layer of *Stille* in Part I: a long D harmonic, now at the other end of the registral scale on the cello. In its openness this ending clearly foreshadows that of *Prometeo*. Three of the final pitches are natural harmonics derived from the open strings G–D–A and, in terms of the combination of strictly systematic and free elements in this piece, represent a final expression of absolute liberty. One by one the fleeting harmonics are thinned out and only the D harmonic on the cello remains. Like Diotima's '. . . das weisst aber du nicht, . . .', it, too, gradually fades *al niente*.

'The ability to conceive of everything there might be just as well, and to attach no more importance to what is than to what is not' is how Musil defines the 'sense of possibility' in *Der Mann ohne Eigenschaften* (*The Man Without Qualities*).[115] Nono was fascinated by Musil's 'sense of

113 Hölderlin, *Götter wandelten einst . . .* (1799), FHA, VI, 127–33 (132/v. 16).

114 Hölderlin, *Hyperion*, Hyperion to Diotima, FHA, XI, 729. The origin of this text was first identified by Linden in *Luigi Nonos Weg zum Streichquartett*. The section reads as follows: 'Speech is a great superfluity. The best is ever for itself, and rests in its own depth like the pearl at the bottom of the sea.' Hölderlin, *Hyperion and Selected Poems*, 98.

115 Musil, *The Man Without Qualities*, I, 11. The passage stems from Chapter 4: 'If there is a sense of reality, there must also be a sense of possibility'.

possibility' and quotes this definition in one of his letters to the LaSalle Quartet.[116] Fragmentation, he here explains, allows the simultaneous development of different ideas. But what constitutes an idea? According to Musil,

> [. . .] ideas can never maintain themselves in the state in which they are most powerful; they're like the kind of substance that, exposed to the air, instantly changes into some other, more lasting, but corrupted form [. . .] Idea is what you are: an idea in a particular state. You are touched by the breath of something, and it's like a note suddenly emerging from the humming of strings, in front of you there is something like a mirage; out of the confusion of your soul an endless parade is taking shape, with all the world's beauty looking on from the roadside. All this can be the effect of a single idea. But after a while it comes to resemble all your previous ideas, it takes its place among them, becomes part of your outlook and your character, your principles or your moods; in the act of taking shape it has lost its wings and its mystery.[117]

Musil here beautifully captures the fleeting and ephemeral nature of ideas that is also at the heart of *Fragmente – Stille, an Diotima*. Nono develops not one idea, but three ideas simultaneously. They are not always easy to distinguish, because each idea undergoes a flux of states, and changes from one state to another can occur in a flash. Each idea takes its course in the form of a 'wave' with its own amplitude and range of speeds. The three interlocking waves are 'most powerful' in Part I, where each of them emerges and peaks with a distinct set of pitches, duration values, characteristic articulations and speeds. Yet, as Musil observed, 'ideas can never maintain themselves in the state in which they are most powerful'. As the ideas gradually lose their power, they set off other, even conflicting, ideas. *Stille* gives rise to *Unruhe*; *Luft* complements *Tiefe*. The piece thus branches out into related strains of thought, each of which it explores in combination with the other three. With an increasing degree of fragmentation, the boundaries become more and more blurred; ideas begin to overlap and assimilate each other.

Table 6.3 summarises the main features of all of the layers and their related branches in Part II. In comparison with Table 6.1 (the equivalent summary for Part I) there is indeed a high degree of assimilation here. If the layers were clearly distinguished in terms of register, type

[116] Nono, letter to LaSalle Quartet (Levin/W 80–03–27 d; ALN 44.32/03v). Musil's 'sense of possibility' was from then on repeatedly referred to by Nono, e.g. in 'Das atmende Klarsein' (1981), *Scritti*, I, 487; 'Solidarnosc elettronica' (1982), *Scritti*, II, 273; 'L'erreure comme nécessité' (1983), *Écrits*, 257, *Scritti*, I, 522; 'Un'autobiographia', *Scritti*, II, 490.

[117] Musil, *The Man Without Qualities*, I, 384.

of motion, articulation and range of speeds in Part I, these distinctions are abandoned in Part II, where all of the layers take on a much more textural guise, undulating through the registers. Articulations overlap and the speeds increasingly assimilate each other, gradually winding down to ♩ = 30/44. The three ideas thus begin to 'resemble' each other and become part of a general 'outlook'. This does not mean, however, that they lose their 'wings' and their 'mystery'. As Nono branches out into ever richer combinations, the sound-world becomes increasingly diffuse, delighting in more subtle differences. With added transpositions of each of the pitch segments (including quarter-tone transposition), this diffusion is also greatly supported on the level of pitch. In all aspects Nono fans out from the initially distinct strains of thought to create a true 'sea' of sounds and colours from which the archaic tune *Malor me bat* finally rises like the distant contour of a ship or shipwreck in Turner's late seascapes.[118]

From Nono's own discussion of *Fragmente – Stille, an Diotima* it is clear that he himself regarded this 'versione libera' of *Malor me bat* as a fragment which, although distinct in every respect, is totally integrated and integral to the work's overall structure:

> [. . .] this type of fragment is something completely different from aphorism [. . .] [They] do not end in themselves, are not subsequently levelled out by means of a synthetic moment; but reveal special moments of potential, of life, which can also be developed in a conflicting manner. To me, dialectical movement is impossible here, only a growth of various different possibilities, potential forces, or weak moments, which together provide a great multiplicity of thought, of life, of existence, much more so than when geared towards a dialectical moment, a synthesis, a goal, with which one levels them out. These contradictions are much more important to me [. . .] because there is this necessity of the wanderer: Benjamin, Nietzsche. With the wanderer – there is no fixed moment, but one always searches for something. Sometimes this is expressible – Wittgenstein – but sometimes one can't say anything at all, it is *ineffabile* [inexpressible] [. . .] Why not also in music? According to this type of thought of *mémoire*, there are only caesuras, only moments that appear, return illuminated, *retour à*, but not a *retour* to how it was, *retour* in the way Ockeghem also returns here. There is a moment at the end, a quotation that isn't a quotation as it is used today – in the manner of a collage. This song is not by Ockeghem, but a folksong of the

[118] Nono briefly discussed Turner's late work with Restagno: 'You are right, these really are vortices of light, but not vortices in which one feels caught up [. . .] These are silent vortices from which sound springs forth with an unheard-of and inaudible violence.' Nono, 'Un'autobiografia', *Scritti*, II, 522.

Table 6.3 *Layer specifications for Part II (26, bar 2 to end)*

| Layer | Number | Pitch | DV | Articulation | Speed |
|---|---|---|---|---|---|
| *Unruhe*<br>(tone<br>repetition) | 26, b.7<br>27<br>29, b.3<br>30–32<br>33, b.4<br>35, 37, 39 | **Segment 1**<br>scala on C<br>C–C♯–E<br>+ ¼ trsp. ↑ | 2, 4, 5, 6, 8 | normale<br>tremolo<br>flautato<br>sordina<br>spiccato<br>aperiodico | ♩ =<br>46/92<br>52<br>60<br>44/88<br>66/30/92 |
| *Stille*<br>(low) | 28<br>32, b.4<br>41 | **Segment 1**<br>scala on F♯<br>F♯–G–B♭<br>filled out (¼)<br>*ad libitum*<br>open strings | 2, 3, 4, 5, 7,<br>8 | non vibrato<br>legno + poco crine<br>battuto<br>legno sul ponte | ♩ =<br>30, 46, 30 |
| *Stille*<br>(undulating) | 44<br>47<br>49<br>51–52 | **Segment 1**<br>scala on F♯<br>F♯–G–A–B♭<br>+ ¼ transp. ↑<br>*ad libitum*<br>tritones<br>open strings | 2, 3, 4, 5, 6,<br>8 | harmonics<br>normale<br>battuto<br>flautato<br>balzato aperiodico | ♩ =<br>44, 72,<br>72/30<br>30/44 |
| *Diotima II*<br>(undulating) | 34<br>36<br>37, b.2<br>38<br>39, b.2–5 | **Segment 2**<br>scala on C<br>E–F♯–G♯–B♭<br>+ ¼ trsp ↑↓ | 5, 3<br>(4/8) | normale<br>sottovoce<br>mit innigster<br>Empfindung | ♩ =<br>60 (92) |
| *Diotima I*<br>(centre) | 46 | **Segment 2**<br>scala on B<br>E♭–F–G–A<br>filled out (2–)<br>*ad libitum*:<br>open strings | 5 | tremolo alla<br>punta aperiodico | ♩ = 132 |
| *Luft*<br>(undulating) | 26, b.2<br>39, b.6<br>40, b.2<br>40,<br>b.4–5<br>50 | **Segments 1 and 2**<br>alternating<br>scala on C<br>C–C♯–E/<br>**E**–F♯–G♯–B♭ | 2 | normale<br>sottovoce | ♩ = 60 |

Table 6.3 (*cont.*)

| Layer | Number | Pitch | DV | Articulation | Speed |
|---|---|---|---|---|---|
| *Tiefe I* (undulating) | 33, b.3<br>40<br>40, b.5<br>42, b.3–4<br>50, b.3 | **Segment 3** scala on E♭ C♯–D–E♭ (chromatic extension) *ad libitum*: tritones | 2, 3, 5 | normale sottovoce | ♩ = 112/66 60/120 (♩) 92/60/44/ 30 |

> time: *Malheur me bat – Misfortune Assails Me.* This was one of the many songs used as a tenor by the Netherlands School. And also Ockeghem used it for a mass: there is a mass called *Malheur me bat.* And this song appears not as a quotation, not as collage, but is visited anew [...] One visits something from the old times but in this moment lets it come to life and vibrate in a new way.[119]

In truly Benjaminian fashion, *Malor me bat*, Nono's final 'comprehensive view' into the distant past, can be seen to replace the synthetic moment the piece deliberately lacks: '... when from the depth ...' of written music history *Malor me bat* finally appears in Nono's 'versione libera', it emerges from the surrounding scala enigmatica material like an 'Angelus novus' in the Benjaminian sense. With its gaze turned towards the past, this 'angel of history', too, would 'like to stay, awaken the dead, and make whole what has been smashed' but is irresistibly propelled into the future by a storm that 'keeps piling wreckage upon wreckage'.[120] The angel's visitation is not without consequence, however. It powerfully heightens our awareness of what there is, what there is not and what there might be.

In this sense, both Musil's 'sense of possibility' and Benjamin's concept of 'Stillsetzung' (arrest of happening) are also at the very heart of the differentiated web of fermatas which, like that of the Hölderlin texts, was

119 Nono, 'Wie Hölderlin komponierte', 207–208. *Malor me bat*, ascribed to Ockeghem in Petrucci's *Odhecaton A*, is now generally attributed to Johannes Martini or (with greater probability) to the Franco-Flemish composer Malcourt (or Malcort). Josquin des Prez, Jacob Obrecht, Agricola and Andreas Sylvanus each composed a Mass on *Malor me bat*. No mass by Ockeghem makes use of this chanson. A copy of Spark, *Cantus Firmus in Mass and Motet*, 264, is among the sketches and shows that Nono knew of the Mass by Obrecht.

120 Benjamin, 'Theses on the Concept of History' (1940), Thesis IX, in Löwy, *Fire Alarm*, 60–62. In Cacciari's 'versione libera', Benjamin's theses later form part of *Prometeo*.

added fairly late in the compositional process. 'Each fermata', Nono writes in his preface to the score, 'should always be felt differently, with free fancy

| | |
|---|---|
| – di spazi sognanti | – of dreaming spaces |
| – di estasi improvvise | – of sudden ecstasies |
| – di pensieri indicibile | – of unutterable thoughts |
| – die respiri tranquilli | – of tranquil breaths |
| e | and |
| di silenzi da «cantare» «intemporali». | of silences 'intemporally' 'sung'. |

Kafka, Musil and Hölderlin all resonate in this poetic description of the work's real-time *Stille* and one begins to wonder which silence is more 'real': *Stille* or the composed idea of *Stille*? The 'silent vortices' with which Nono continuously halts the flow of his ever more fragmented structure certainly add another level of secrecy to the '... geheimere Welt ...' (world of greater secrets)[121] of this highly differentiated composition.

The piece is indeed most 'secretive' at the outset, where nothing has been established and 'ideas' have yet to be born. The pronounced ambiguity of this extremely sparse and porous opening monody ([1]–[7]) is at its most extreme in the allusive '... allein ...' (alone)[122] at [3]: three solitary pitches with nothing else to hold onto but the careful differentiation of articulation and dynamics. The tritone is a 'free' element and the pitches F and A♭ fall within the range of the *Diotima* layer that is yet to be established. With emphasis on the *ad libitum* additions (tritones and open strings), the pitch fields of Part I are tentatively sounded out. Some intervals, such as the opening C♯–E from the *Tiefe* layer and A–E♭ from the *Diotima* layer, occur over and over again, in ever changing guises, contexts and combinations. Very briefly, at [7], Nono also anticipates the central whole-tone segment of the scala enigmatica on C, which is to become the voice of *Diotima* in Part II. Gestures and types of motion, too, begin to crystallise, but, with the exception, perhaps, of the tremor under '... seliges Angesicht ...', none of the emerging ideas is yet clearly defined. What is clear from the outset, however, is that this piece, which so often moves on the brink of silence but also breaks out into fragments of incredible musical force and energy, endeavours to expand boundaries and penetrate ever deeper into the 'immense space and infinite worlds' of musical thought.

[121] Hölderlin, *Götter wandelten einst ...*, FHA, VI, 133, v. 12.

[122] Hölderlin, *An Diotima* (1797), FHA, VI, 87–93 (92/v. 2).

'All such writing is an assault on the frontiers', Nono underlined in Kafka's diaries, and 'if Zionism had not intervened, it might easily have developed into a new secret doctrine, a Kabbalah.'[123] With Kafka and Hölderlin, Scherchen and Maderna, Verdi and 'Okeghem', and many others, it seems, Nono embarked on his very own quest for such a 'secret doctrine'. This quest would occupy him for years to come and lead him ever deeper into the intellectual and spiritual spheres of Jewish thought which, with much more prominent recourse to the philosophy of Walter Benjamin, are at the very heart of *Prometeo*.

[123] Kafka, *Tagebücher 1914–23*, 199; *Diaries 1914–1923*, 202–203.

# 7 *Prometeo. Tragedia dell'ascolto* (1975–85)

*Aujourd hui l'espace est splendide!*
*Sans mors, sans éperons, sans bride,*
*Partons à cheval sur le vin*
*Pour un ciel féerique et divin!*

*Comme deux anges que torture*
*Une implacable calenture*
*Dans le bleu cristal du matin*
*Suivons le mirage lointain!*
Charles Baudelaire, *Le Vin des amants*[1]

Nono's last and most utopian work of music theatre, *Prometeo*, was premiered in Venice in September 1984, almost a decade after the composer had embarked on the project with his friend and librettist, the philosopher Massimo Cacciari, in 1975. During this exceptionally long genesis, all ideas of a possible staging were gradually abandoned.[2] Even the planned projection of colours, based on theories by Goethe, Runge, Itten and Kandinsky, was eventually dropped in rehearsal, and Emilio Vedova was merely put in charge of the lighting.[3] By then, however, Nono

[1] 'Comme deux anges . . . dans le bleu cristal du matin' is quoted in Cacciari's notes for the libretto (ALN 51.07.04/03) and alluded to with the line 'Il cristallo di un MATTINO' in '3 Voci a'.

[2] *Prometeo* was first envisaged as a third *azione scenica*, for which Nono approached Jürgen Flimm (who produced *Al gran sole* in Frankfurt and Amsterdam, 1979). No longer with a full production in mind, Nono later also approached Tadeusz Kantor. In their *Dziennik podróży z Kantorem* (*Diary of Journeys with Kantor*), the actors Wacław and Lesław Janiccy note for 30 September 1983: 'The renowned contemporary composer Nono – a sort of Italian Penderecki – appeared. He proposed that Kantor prepare the stage scenery and direct the movement of the performers in his new opera titled *Prometeo*. It would be staged in Venice in November 1984 and then played for a week at La Scala. Nono furthermore desired that the whole Cricot troupe participate in the realisation of this undertaking.' W. and L. Janiccy, *Dziennik podróży z Kantorem*, 140, trans. Steven Holt (with many thanks). According to Cacciari, Peter Brook was also considered; Cisternino, 'Con Luigi Nono', 25.

[3] The colour scheme is well documented in sketches and interviews. Nono repeatedly refers to Goethe's *Farbenlehre* (1808–1810), Otto Philipp Runge's *Farben-Kugel* (1810), Johannes Itten's *Kunst der Farbe* (1961) and Kandinsky's *Unterricht am Bauhaus* (1982); annotated editions, ALN (though Nono's edition of Goethe's *Farbenlehre* is lost). Nono worked with

was adamant: his *Prometeo* was 'not an opera', but 'a tragedy composed of sound in complicity with a space – two spaces in fact – without the support of any staged or visual elements'.[4]

The outer shell and architectural basis for this complex performance space was the redundant church of San Lorenzo (completed in 1595 under the direction of Simone Sorella). Hans Peter Haller vividly recounts how Nono decided on this location.[5] Together they immersed themselves in the disused church space and tested its acoustics. Shortly thereafter, Nono came across a drawing demonstrating that San Lorenzo had previously been used for music in *cori spezzati*.[6] He was extremely excited, telling Haller 'I heard this space correctly, the tradition proves it. We will do *Prometeo* here.'[7] Nono then approached none other than Renzo Piano to design and manufacture a multi-level, wooden inner shell to fit the unusual church interior.[8] Piano would later describe this '*Prometeo* Musical Space Design' (1983–84) as 'an extraordinary experience, for the space was born with the work and for the work, and was therefore part of the same process of creation'.[9] By the time the architect joined Nono's high-powered team (or, in Piano's own words, the 'band of madmen'),[10] this process was already far advanced. Piano quickly understood that the music was the true protagonist of this interdisciplinary venture and designed a gigantic sound-box in the shape of an ark, which has since become known as the

thirteen colours in twelve shades each. The idea was to move through shades of colour and to use them, like the music, to 'discover the space'; Nono, letter to Piano (6 December 1983), in Cecchetto and Mastinu (eds.), *Nono Vedova. Diario di bordo*, 103. For the projection Vedova designed a series of slides (partly reproduced in *Diario di bordo*, 93–101). On their use also see Cacciari, letter to Nono (4 July 1984); *ibid.*, 104–105.

4 Nono, 'Parte la nave di Prometeo' (1984), *Scritti*, II, 332.

5 Haller, *Das Experimentalstudio*, II, 158.

6 Franzoi and Stefano, *Le chiese di Venezia*, 468–69.

7 Haller, *Das Experimentalstudio*, II, 158.

8 On Piano's design see Piano, '*Prometeo*. Uno spazio per la musica' and *The Logbook*, 86–87; Glancey and Sammartini, 'Piano + Nono'; Garbato and Mastropietro (eds.), *Renzo Piano Building Workshop*, 150–55; Buchanan, *Renzo Piano Building Workshop*, I; Pizzi, *Renzo Piano*, 84–85. On architecture for *Prometeo*, including Arata Isozaki's concert hall for the Akiyoshidai International Art Village (1998), further see Soriano, *Arquitectura y Música*, 113–77.

9 Piano, *Logbook*, 86. The design was commissioned by the Teatro alla Scala. Unlike Piscator and Meyerhold, Nono was thus in the fortunate position of being able to have a performance space designed to his own specifications.

10 Piano, *Logbook*, 86. The team included Nono, Cacciari, Vedova, Abbado and Piano. They were later joined by the sound engineers Alvise Vidolin (Padua) and Hans Peter Haller (Freiburg).

'struttura'.[11] San Lorenzo was thus temporarily transformed into a sixteenth-century boatyard.[12] The curving timber beams of the ark's hull were raised and supported three metres above the uneven marble floor. Two flights of steps led up to the ark's 'deck' or sounding-board, which seated an audience of up to 400 and opened up the view into the high-vaulted ceilings of the split church interior with its two naves facing a massive central altar piece. Extending to the full height of the church walls, the thick timber ribs supported three narrow gangways for the performing musicians. Interconnected by slender steel ladders, these gangways circumnavigated the entire listening space and allowed soloists to move from one position to another. Nono himself imagined such walkways when first approaching Piano:

> Islands = episodes of Prometheus/ Cacciari will inform you and will give you the text/ fragments come from Aeschylus from Hesiod – from Greek poetry to Nietzsche to Hölderlin to Benjamin [. . .] Cacciari has invented a language of his own, using fragments – Everything will be discontinuous/ torn apart/ interpolated/ fragmented/ with recapitulations/ with superimpositions of the individual episodes–islands/ [. . .] from the lateral walkways you will need to invent maps of navigation routes connecting all of the elements: soloists in motion – *sounds reading the space/* creating *a new spatial dramaturgy/* from the slightest amount of space subjected to variation/ to the whole space totally filled with live sound and sound elaborated by means of live electronics [. . .] mobile sounds that read, discover, empty, fill the space[13]

The all-important acoustics for this spatial dramaturgy were fine-tuned with a combination of straight and curved plywood panels. These formed the outer wall of the design, but could be left out in places in order to open out into the resonant church acoustics. The variable panels also allowed the structure to be adapted to other spaces, such as the former Ansaldo plant in Milan, where it was set up once more for the performance of the revised final version of *Prometeo* (1985) the following year. The Ansaldo factory hall was again an extremely large and resonant space, in which Piano's wooden structure served as an adjustable acoustic

[11] 'It is a question of respect for the "central" emotion in an interdisciplinary artistic venture. This does not mean the total absence of architecture, however, [. . .] but an attentive and, as much as possible, balanced interpretation of the relationships one intends to establish between the various disciplines in play.' Piano, '*Prometeo*. Uno spazio per la musica', 133.

[12] To enter the 'struttura' inspired by Renaissance ship building was 'like boarding some sixteenth-century man o'war', Glancey and Sammartini, 'Piano + Nono', 55.

[13] Nono, letter to Piano (Piano/R 83–12–06 d, Nuria Nono), in *Diario di bordo*, 102–103.

enclave. Haller describes the challenging and fascinating effect of this interactive acoustics for San Lorenzo:

> In the afternoon, rehearsal with Ingrid [Ade-Jesemann] and Monika [Bair-Ivenz] (soprano). First result: *piano* and *pianissimo* voices sound relatively dry in the inner space (*struttura*). They can be heard everywhere and are easy to locate. Second result: when the voices get louder, from *mezzoforte* to *fortissimo*, the outer church space with its large reverb begins to resonate as well. Sound movements are nevertheless perceptible in the inner space. It is fascinating – a voice sings in a dry interior and, at the same time, depending on the dynamics, a second resonant space is mixed in, partly from above, partly from below and from the sides, and this results in completely new sound formations.[14]

Already in Milan, however, Nono decided to dispense with the movement of musicians (which had proven too loud in Venice). From then on the movement of sound was controlled by the live electronics alone. This and the expenditure and effort needed to dismantle and reconstruct the 'struttura' meant that Piano's intelligent design with its fascinating acoustic possibilities has never been used since and is now sadly rotting away in a warehouse in Milan.

During Nono's lifetime, *Prometeo* was further performed at the Alte Oper Frankfurt (1987), the Théâtre National de Chaillot (Paris, 1987) and the chamber-music hall of Scharoun's Philharmonie (Berlin, 1988). For these and almost all performances since, the Experimentalstudio Freiburg was and is in charge of the live electronics, first under the direction of Hans Peter Haller, now under André Richard. In regard to performance practice, the Frankfurt performance of 1987 has provided the most important guidelines insofar as Nono's choreography of sound is concerned. It was the first with sufficient documentation to establish a consensus as to how *Prometeo* was set up and choreographed under Nono's direction. Since my own reflections on the spatial choreography of *Prometeo* are primarily based on information very kindly provided to me by Richard, I, too, will use the set-up of the Frankfurt performance as a grid for the illustration of all spatial processes in the final version of the work.[15]

[14] Haller, *Experimentalstudio*, II, 174.

[15] I first had the opportunity to work with André Richard at the International Interpretation Course of Luigi Nono's Works with Live Electronics in Venice (3–7 November 2007), performing 'Hölderlin' and the Finale of *Das atmende Klarsein*. I later visited Richard for detailed explanations of the use of the live electronics (20–22 March 2009). Without this information, the writing of this chapter would have been completely impossible. Much of what follows is based on Richard's vast knowledge and performance practice of Nono's late works, and I am extremely grateful for his help and cooperation.

## Notes on the libretto

According to Cacciari, *Prometeo* had more than one beginning. First of all, it was Nono's 'long-standing love for Aeschylus' that prompted the two intellectuals and fellow political activists to re-read and discuss *Prometheus Bound* in the summer of 1975.[16] At the height of the PCI's electoral success, they turned to the very tragedy which Marx is said to have re-read every year.[17] However, under the shock-waves of Enrico Berlinguer's proposal of the 'historic compromise' with the Christian Democrats and the PCI's ever stronger commitment to Eurocommunism, their reading of the Prometheus myth was to go far beyond the Marxian vision of Prometheus as a revolutionary 'saint and martyr'.[18] Nono had this to say about his wider understanding of the myth:

> Conversations both with Massimo and with Francesco Dal Co have broadened my interpretative horizon regarding the figure of Prometheus and how the Prometheus myth has been understood in various historical epochs, above all insofar as the relationship between the laws and their transgression in order to attain a new formulation thereof is concerned. Prometheus is not understood as a rebel, or liberator, as Schelling or Schiller had it. What interests me is the struggle between the foundation of the principles of life and the continuing dynamic which brings about their supersession, in a continually conflictual relationship. This was developed by means of other texts, both Greek ones (pre-Socratic and after) and a few Latin texts, readings dating from the sixteenth century, Hölderlin (his relation to Achilles and his idea of 'the gods who are dead and the new gods who have

[16] Nono first considered *The Persians*; see 'Ecco il mio Prometeo', *Scritti*, II, 260. Aeschylus is already mentioned in the context of the Anne Frank project with Ungaretti (1958), see Chapter 2.

[17] The PCI gained more than a third of the votes in local elections in 1975 and in the general elections of 1976. Nono was elected to the Central Committee in 1975. Cacciari joined the party in 1976 and served as a parliamentary representative until 1983, when he decided to leave party politics behind. Nono's and Cacciari's paths first crossed in the mid 1960s. At that time, Cacciari was a member of the extra-parliamentary left and one of the first in Italy to study the philosophy of Walter Benjamin. With Cesare de Michelis he founded the journal *Angelus Novus* (1964–66). Nono was firmly attached to 'the categories of "orthodox" Marxism' at the time, and only truly warmed to Cacciari in their discussions of early Lukács around 1970; Biraghi, 'Entretien avec Massimo Cacciari', 147. For English introductions to Cacciari's philosophy see Lombardo, 'The Philosophy of the City', in Cacciari, *Architecture and Nihilism*, ix–lviii; and Carrera, 'On Massimo Cacciari's Disenchanted Activism', in Cacciari, *The Unpolitical*, 1–44. On *Cacciari's collaboration with Nano* further see Nanni, 'Politica come silenzio'; and Impett, 'The tragedy of listening'.

[18] Marx, foreword to the doctoral dissertation *The Difference Between the Democritean and Epicurean Philosophy of Nature* (March 1841), Karl Marx Internet Archive (2000).

> not yet come'), up to Benjamin. Thus it is not Prometheus as such that is at the heart of the work, but the whole discourse that revolves around his figure.[19]

The many source texts which shaped Nono's and Cacciari's interpretation of the Prometheus myth are already well documented by Lydia Jeschke and Irene Comisso.[20] From the very outset, however, the conception of *Prometeo* also involved a second line of thought: a philosophical framework that was initially modelled not on Benjamin's *Theses on the Concept of History* (the later *Maestro del gioco*) but on poetry by Rainer Maria Rilke, his *Duineser Elegien* [*Duino Elegies* (1912–22)] in particular. Hence Cacciari speaks of a further beginning: '*Das atmende Klarsein*, the title of which is inspired by a line of Rilke (veritable "fixed star" of our friendship)'.[21]

Among the materials for *Das atmende Klarsein*, two sheets of notes on the *Duineser Elegien* give insight into this other, philosophical beginning of *Prometeo*.[22] They show that the mythological core was to take on the form of Greek tragedy (with a prologue, several episodes and a final exodus) and fragments of the *Duineser Elegien* were to link and reflect these formal sections of the tragedy. With their potent symbols of transcendence (lovers, young heroes and, above all, the figure of the angel), symbols which fuel Rilke's poetic quest for transcendence in language, the *Elegien* were to provide a philosophical outlook that is very much steeped in Cacciari's own discourse on language and the modernist crisis at the time.[23] The concept for *Prometeo*, Cacciari reflects in these notes on Rilke, was to move 'from the Prologue's original *Flucht* [flight] – NOT towards *Gestein* [rock] (the "solid", unalterable NOMOS [law]), but towards *Fruchtland* [harvest land] (the "dawn" of the Wanderer, the Angel, the annunciation of Mnemosyne, the love of the last beats . . . the MOMENT)':

[19] Nono, 'Intervista di Renato Garavaglia', *Scritti*, II, 245. Like Cacciari and Manfredo Tafuri, Francesco Dal Co taught at the Venice Institute of Architecture.

[20] Jeschke, *Prometeo*; Comisso, 'Luigi Nonos *Prometeo*'.

[21] Biraghi, 'Entretien avec Massimo Cacciari', 150. 'Nach spätem Gewitter, das atmende Klarsein' (after a late storm, the breathing clarity), Rilke, *Duineser Elegien*, Seventh Elegy.

[22] Cacciari, 'da Rilke, *Duineser* ' (ALN 45.01.01/02–03). Cacciari sent Nono the sheets on 19 August 1980. Also see Melkert, «*Far del silenzio cristallo*», 17, and Durazzi, *Musical Poetics and Political Ideology*, 195–204.

[23] I primarily refer to English translations of Cacciari's work: *Posthumous People* [*Dallo Steinhof* (1980)]; *The Necessary Angel* [*L'Angelo necessario* (1986)]; *Architecture and Nihilism*; and *The Unpolitical.*

| | |
|---|---|
| Fänden auch wir ein reines | [If only we too could find a pure |
| MENSCHLICHES | HUMANNESS |
| einen unseren Streifen | our own strip |
| FRUCHTLANDS | OF HARVEST LAND |
| zwischen Strom und Gestein ... | between stream and rock ...][24] |

To Cacciari, this narrow 'strip of harvest land' is not only the territory of Rilke's Angels, but also that of Nietzsche's all-too-human 'Wanderer', the solitary free spirit who seeks 'the philosophy of the morning' and wanders on Earth 'not as a traveller *to* a final destination' ('for such a destination does not exist'), but to 'watch and observe and keep his eyes open to see what is really going on in the world' and who, 'for this reason', does not 'adhere too firmly to any individual thing', but 'takes pleasure in change and transience'.[25]

The idea of the wanderer is further intrinsically tied to Wittgenstein's discourse on language. If, as Wittgenstein proposes in the *Tractatus*, language is strictly confined to the 'Tatsachenraum' (domain of facts and data) but continuously strives to express that which lies beyond this domain, it, too, will have no final destination, but only the capacity of leading 'irgendwohin' (some place). Hence, 'language can lead, but not to the end, to the goal. It can only lead from chance to chance, from event to event.'[26] Against the background of the unutterable, yet forever confined to the utterable, language is understood as continuous struggle, a 'search without end', an 'oscillating' dialogue, as Cacciari notes for *Prometeo*, between the Wanderer and Rilke's

| | |
|---|---|
| Es wäre ein Platz | suppose there's a place |
| den wir nicht wissen ... | we don't know of ... |
| Zeigten die Liebenden | Lovers could show |
| ihre Türme aus Lust | their towers of ecstasy |
| wo Boden nie war ... | where there was never any ground ...[27] |

Motivated by '*Liebe und Abschied* [Love and Parting] – as if they were a SINGLE NAME ...' this utopian dialogue was to become 'just audible, just comprehensible', like an 'impossible echo' manifesting itself on the brink between sound and silence.[28]

24 Cacciari, 'da Rilke, *Duineser* ' (ALN 45.01.01/02), Second Elegy, in Komar, *Transcending Angels*, 57. Cacciari's layout deviates from Rilke's verse structure.

25 Nietzsche, 'The Wanderer', in *Human, All Too Human*, 203.

26 Cacciari, 'The New Domain of Trauerspiel', in *Posthumous People*, 19.

27 Cacciari, 'da Rilke, *Duineser* ' (ALN 45.01.01/02); Rilke, *Duineser Elegien*, Fifth Elegy *Gesammelte Gedichte*, 461; *Duino Elegies*, 56.

28 Cacciari, 'da Rilke, *Duineser* ' (ALN 45.01.01/02); Rilke, *Duineser Elegien*, Second Elegy *Gesammelte Gedichte*, 447; *Duino Elegies*, 33.

Attaining clarity on this near-impossible search for 'our own strip of harvest land' is further fundamentally opposed to the 'ongoing, continuous, dedicated solution to problems' that is generally regarded as the hallmark of progress. Wittgenstein's 'Klarheit', Cacciari argues, lies not in progressive and typically constructive reasoning, but in 'means to render transparent the very foundation of construction, to constantly return to that same thing, constituted by its problem, to render its non-constructive foundation evident'.[29] In this entirely 'gedeutete Welt', 'the world reversed in thought, the world of interpretation', we are only ever momentarily given *das atmende Klarsein*, 'the clarity of the word that preserves, the interior where endless acts, memories and things occur and elapse,' where indeed 'Hiersein ist herrlich' (Being here is magnificent) and

| | |
|---|---|
| eine Stunde war jeder, | where each has always |
| vielleicht nicht ganz eine Stunde, | an hour, perhaps not even, |
| kaum Meβliches | hardly measurable |
| zwischen zwei Weilen | between two whiles |
| Alles. | Everything. |
| Die Adern voll Dasein [...] | Veins filled with existence [...][30] |

Fleeting, but filled to the brim with existence, such *Klarsein* is also 'the Benjaminian moment that shatters the duration'.[31] Only this moment of absolute clarity, Cacciari argues, is capable of turning our gaze (which, like that of Benjamin's Angel, is 'as though reversed' and forever facing the past) into 'das Offene' (the open), 'das Freie' (freedom).[32] And precisely this clarity, too, is at the heart of *Trauerspiel* (tragedy), 'the great form of the critique of constructive and productive rationalism' which, according to Cacciari, 'argues with the semblance of progress' and 'slashes at its claims with pure crystal, until it reveals a dark, remote motif': the metaphysical gap between *logos* and *aletheia* (Greek for 'truth' or 'unconcealment'), 'a gap whose continual reformulation as a problem is a critique of *ratio typisch aufbauend* [typically constructive reason]' and itself 'the basis of *ratio* as *the* problem to which there can never be *the* solution'.[33]

[29] Cacciari, 'A Critique of the Modern', in *Posthumous People*, 30.

[30] Cacciari, *Architecture and Nihilism*, 174 (trans. amended). This passage is also cited in Cacciari's notes for Nono (ALN 45.01.01/02–03); Rilke, *Duineser Elegien*, Seventh Elegy, *Gesammelte Gedichte*, 467.

[31] Cacciari, *Architecture and Nihilism*, 174.

[32] The terms 'das Offene' and 'das Freie' stem from Rilke's Seventh and Eighth Elegies and are also at the heart of Heidegger's discourse on 'man's settlement and dwelling'. See Cacciari, *Architecture and Nihilism*, 173.

[33] Cacciari, 'A Critique of the Modern', 32.

Many of the extracts from Rilke's *Duineser Elegien* that shaped Cacciari's initial concept of *Prometeo* were then merged with fragments from *Die Sonette an Orpheus* [*Sonnets to Orpheus* (1923)] for the text of *Das atmende Klarsein*.[34] Rilke's poetry is not the only source, however. The remaining text (partly in Greek and partly in Italian) stems from a number of Orphic inscriptions found on small gold plates in ancient graves in southern Italy and elsewhere in the ancient Greek world. These gold plates (dating from the fourth century B.C. or earlier) had the purpose of guiding the deceased on their way to the underworld. More or less standard inscriptions warn of a spring by a white cypress on the left of the houses of Hades. This was believed to be the source of the 'waters of Lethe'. Lethe (Greek for 'forgetfulness' or 'concealment') was one of several rivers of Hades, and the 'Plain of Lethe' is described by Plato as a place of 'stifling heat', 'bare of trees and all plants that grow on Earth'.[35] In this desert of oblivion thirsty souls would drink from the river of forgetfulness, wipe out their past existence, and thus enter the torturous cycle of reincarnation. To the right of the houses of Hades, however, was believed to be the lake of Mnemosyne (goddess of memory and mother of the muses). Only 'pure' and just souls would be allowed to drink from this 'water of memory' and thereby break through the cycle of reincarnation. In order to be granted this final favour, the Orphic inscriptions instructed the deceased to address the lake's custodians:

> Say, 'I am a child of Earth and starry Heaven;
> But my race is of heaven alone. This ye know yourselves.
> But I am parched with thirst and I perish. Give me quickly
> The cold water flowing forth from the Lake of Memory
> And of themselves they will give thee to drink of the holy spring,
> And thereafter among the other heroes thou shalt have lordship.[36]

With a text built from similar inscriptions, Cacciari isolates what, to him, is the crucial element in Greek tragedy, DRÂN: a 'singular and irrevocable decision' and 'total responsibility in the face of true *daímon*', 'the moment of decision' that determines the course of the entire tragedy and is also the moment of most intense suffering for its tragic hero at the crossroads. Here is what Cacciari wrote for the Freiburg performance of *Prometeo* in 2003:

[34] On the use of Rilke's *Sonnets to Orpheus* see Durazzi, *Musical Poetics and Political Ideology*, 195–204; and Junker, 'Zum Verhältnis von Text und Musik', 327.

[35] Plato, *The Republic*, 359.

[36] Plate from Petelia (Italy, fourth century B.C.), in Guthrie, *Orpheus and Greek Religion*, 171.

> It is precisely the plot that represents a single, irrevocable decision that is tragic. Antique tragedy called this DRÂN. Our understanding of drama as a series, movement, narrative no longer has anything in common with this meaning of DRÂN. Schopenhauer and Nietzsche, however, understood to what extent antique drama was DRÂN: the tragic theory of the moment of decision, the moment of most intense suffering that the hero cannot escape. Nietzsche's critique of Wagner can only be understood in terms of DRÂN: Wagner betrayed it in the end, to return to the consoling comfort of narrative and figurative drama.[37]

In *Das atmende Klarsein* this decisive moment, *drân*, is no less than that of our human soul at the crossroads between forgetfulness and memory, *lethe* and *a-letheia*, between 'concealment' or 'forgetting of Being' (which Heidegger, above all, identified as a major problem of modern philosophy)[38] and the 'unconcealed', 'true' Being advocated in Rilke's *Duineser Elegien*.

The concept of *drân* is also at the heart of Cacciari's text for the 1984 premiere of *Prometeo*:

> *Prometeo* is a *drân dell'ascolto*. That which encounters itself and enters into conflict with itself, that which 'happens', that which 'becomes', is *sound* alone. Each 'movement' withdraws into the *invisible* of the sound. It seemed to us that the very term *drân* itself imposed this 'conversion' of the traditional structure of 'music theatre' [*dramma musicale*]: if *drân* is decision *setting off from* every single happening–becoming, from every 'physical' figuration, then in its essence it must be envisaged as a drama of sound and of listening to the sound. *Prometeo* dwells in the insurmountable 'and' of this distance in which silence ventures into sound and sound into listening – and listening, anew, always requires the most profound silence in order to be able to seize that particular sound, infinitesimal and unrepeatable, in order not to mistake it for another, in order to de-marcate it [de-ciderlo] from everything else.[39]

*Prometeo*, however, is by no means a mere compilation of fleeting crystallisations of sound. Despite the work's tendency towards the fragmentary, it is also a coherent, large-scale musical structure. Within this structure each moment may be pervaded by the urgency and intensity of the idea of *drân*, but Nono certainly also thought of it as drama. However 'non-narrative' and 'non-figurative' it may be, the overall design of this 'tragedy of

[37] Cacciari, 'Zeit, die bricht, reisst und teilt', 35.

[38] Much of Cacciari's philosophical thought, his Nietzsche reception in particular, is influenced by Heidegger's late philosophy. The importance of Heidegger will become clear in the course of this text.

[39] Cacciari, 'Verso Prometeo', 128.

listening' is fundamentally based on Cacciari's reading of the Prometheus myth and on the text *Il Maestro del gioco* (*The Master of the Game*), the poem which eventually replaced the Rilke texts, with its quotations from Benjamin's *Theses on the Concept of History* together with allusions to many other source texts such as poetry by Charles Baudelaire and Georg Trakl.[40] In order to understand this multi-layered collage of text and the musical structure to which it gave rise, a look at Cacciari's preliminary 'narrative' is extremely helpful.[41]

The starting point in these preliminary notes is not the philosophical framework, but the tragedy. Citing Pindar, Cacciari begins with the fundamental idea (present also in the Orphic inscriptions used for *Das atmende Klarsein*) that man and god share a common descent: 'One is the race of men and the gods. From one mother we both draw our breath.'[42] The common mother, or origin, of god and man is Gaia (Earth). In ancient Greek mythology, Gaia was the primordial goddess, the first god to emerge from the intangible darkness and 'yawning space' of chaos.[43] According to Hesiod's *Theogony* (fragments of which are later used for the Prologue), Gaia 'first gave birth to starry Ouranos [sky]', then 'the tall mountains' and 'the barren sea'.[44] With the creation of the elements (Earth, Air and Water), the scene is set for the extremely violent genealogy of god and man. The lineage of man begins with Prometheus' father, the Titan Iapetos. From the very outset, Prometheus is thus placed at the crossroads: the split between the race of gods and that of men. *Prometheus the Fire-bringer* essentially enables 'man to exist as man'.[45] In possession of fire, man is empowered to work (and Nono here explicitly invokes the

[40] See Cacciari, 'Libretto for *Prometeo*', in Pauler (ed.), 'Libretto & Listening score'. Cacciari's allusions are not always easy to identify. The Italian poet Umberto Saba and the Persian poet Omar Khayyam, for example, are named in the sketches, but I have not been able to establish concrete links to their work.

[41] Cacciari, preliminary notes for *Prometeo* (A and B), ALN 51.02.05/1–31. Part B is published in Jeschke, *Prometeo*, 278–87; Part A is merely summarised, *ibid.*, 22. Also see Comisso, 'Luigi Nonos *Prometeo*'.

[42] Pindar, *Nemean Ode* VI, ALN 51.02.05/01. Cacciari translated all texts for *Prometeo* himself; see Nono, 'Ascoltare le pietre bianche', *Scritti*, II, 301. The idea of a common lineage of god and man is also present in Hesiod's *Works and Days*, 69 (109).

[43] The 'yawning space' of Chaos was believed to be 'the first created thing, an intangible void beneath the Earth, full of darkness'. Howatson and Sheffield, glossary to Plato, *The Symposium*, 74.

[44] Hesiod, *Theogony*, 16 (126–31).

[45] *Prometheus Bound* is the central play of a trilogy by Aeschylus, preceded by *Prometheus the Fire-bringer* (of which only one line exists) and followed by *Prometheus Unbound* (of which a few fragments survive).

working class).[46] But fire also provides man with the power to reveal and 'illuminate'. Thus empowered, man inevitably withdraws from his origin, the 'natural laws' set down by Gaia and Themis (goddess of divine justice). This withdrawal from nature essentially constitutes the human guilt-of-existence for which mankind is forever punished.

In comparison with man on Earth, the race of the gods is much more fortunate. Cacciari's starting point, Pindar's sixth *Nemean Ode*, leaves no doubt that, despite their common origin, there are worlds between these 'unhappy brothers':

> There is one race of men, one of gods; but from one mother [Gaia, Earth] we both draw our breath. Yet the allotment of a wholly different power separates us, for the one race is nothing, whereas the bronze heaven remains a secure abode forever.[47]

The 'allotment of wholly different powers' is blatantly evident also at the beginning of Aeschylus' *Prometheus Bound*. The drama opens with the violent scene of Prometheus being nailed to the rock, his punishment for having stolen the fire from Zeus. Zeus himself, however, is noticeably absent. Secure in his 'heavenly abode', he rules on Earth with Kratos and Bia (Strength and Violence). This 'duo infernale' (as Nono annotates) drags Prometheus onto the scene, duly followed by Zeus' willing executioner Hephaestus, whose task it is to carry out the extreme punishment.[48]

Prometheus, the tragic hero and 'champion of the human race', however, is not entirely powerless. He alone knows of Zeus' fate, and Zeus is well aware of this. So, how and what does Prometheus know? Through Gaia–Themis and her chorus of Oceanides (including Prometheus' mother Clymene), Prometheus knows that the lineage of goddesses who set up their sons against their fathers was to be continued by the 'magnificent' Thetis. Thetis would bear Zeus an immortal son, 'one who will find a flame hotter than lightning-strokes, a crash to overwhelm the thunder' and kill his father.[49] Knowledge of this destiny, the possible fallibility of Zeus, gives Prometheus the power to present mankind with the great utopian hope for

[46] Nono annotates 'classe operaia' twice: in Episode II (Prometheus' monologue on his gifts to man) and Episode IV (Prometheus' prophecy of the fall of Zeus); Aeschylus, *Prometheus Bound*, 33–35/47. Also see Ramazzotti, *Luigi Nono*, 122–23.

[47] Pindar, *Nemean Odes, Isthmian Odes, Fragments*, 59. The libretto alludes to Pindar's sixth Nemean Ode at the end of 'Hölderlin'. God and man are here referred to as 'fratelli infelici' (unhappy brothers).

[48] Nono annotated Aeschylus, *Le tragedie*, ed. Carena (Turin: Einaudi, 1956).

[49] Aeschylus, *Prometheus Bound*, 47. Gaia herself armed Cronos against Ouranos and Rhea armed Zeus against Cronos.

liberation from the violent, 'jealous and subversive' god. 'Prometheus is Angel', Cacciari notes, precisely because he is able to 'announce' this utopia of liberation: the death of Zeus, which, to Cacciari, is the 'great impossible Utopia' in ancient Greek mythology and thought.[50]

Prometheus does indeed announce this utopia. He announces it to Io, the female fellow sufferer, who, persecuted and driven to the brink of insanity by the relentless stings of a gadfly and the ghost of the herdsman Argus, is subjected to precisely 'those same forces', Kratos and Bia, who also torture Prometheus. Io personifies the persecuted and oppressed, and in Nono's annotations to the play is marked 'metafora–simbolo della lotta repressa' (metaphor–symbol of the repressed struggle).[51] The figure of Io is so 'fundamental', Cacciari argues, that Prometheus decides to prophesy and give her hope in disclosing the secret of Zeus' possible fall from sovereignty.

This prophecy, however, is precisely also the reason why Zeus is eventually saved. Because Prometheus does NOT continue to rebel, but decides to prophesy, the god is able to avert his own death and secure his celestial seat. Thetis will not go to Zeus, but to the mortal Peleus, with whom she has a mortal son: Achilles. And it is in Achilles that 'the impossible utopia of the liberation from Zeus' lives on in disguise. 'As only Hölderlin understood', Cacciari argues, Achilles is unique among the Greek heroes. With Achilles man's utopia of liberation ceases to be such. 'FINE UTOPIA' (End of Utopia) Nono would later repeatedly write in his sketches, and 'finita la speranza del "ribelle"' (finished the hope of the 'rebel').[52]

*Drân*, the irrevocable decision that determines this entire tragedy, is Prometheus' decision not to *rebel*, but to *prophesy*, to effect the conciliation between man and god, at the cost of utopia. 'THIS IS THE TRAGEDY', Cacciari writes in his notes, 'not the "rebellion".'[53] Man is thus in possession of fire for his *Works and Days*, yet without utopia. Zeus is able to consolidate his rule, yet without the fire. Both man and god have been forced to accept their limits in the face of Ananke (Necessity). In Aeschylus, Cacciari argues, Prometheus is directly exposed to the 'primordial law' of Ananke, the power of which is far greater than man's '*techne*' (art, craft, technical skill), and than the laws of Zeus. In the face of this primordial force, man is consigned to a *tragic* existence without utopia, his *Works and Days* confined to Necessity. Zeus, who survived only because he

[50] ALN 51.02.05/06–07

[51] Aeschylus, *Prometeo incantenato*, reproduced with Nono's annotations in Ramazzotti, 'Il dubbio, la lotta, la speranza', 149.

[52] ALN 51.03.07/01 [53] ALN 51.02.05/10

obtained the secret of his destiny from man by force, is equally impotent. Idle, he retreats to his secure abode in Heaven, 'not dead but *as if* dead' to man's existence on Earth. Precisely this is the situation Hölderlin laments in *Brod und Wein*, the poem both Heidegger and Cacciari understood as a paradigm of modern times:

> Aber Freund! wir kommen zu spät. Zwar leben die Götter,
> Aber über dem Haupt droben in anderer Welt.
> Endlos wirken sie da und scheinen uns wenig zu achten,
> Ob wir leben, so sehr schonen die Himmlischen uns.
> [. . .] und wozu Dichter in dürftiger Zeit?
>
> Ah, friend! We have come too late. True, the gods are alive,
> But they're over our heads, above, in a different realm.
> Endlessly they are active and seem to care little for us,
> Whether we live or not – so great is celestial concern.
> [. . .] and of what use are poets in miserable times?[54]

Hölderlin's poetic oeuvre, including the *Schicksalslied* (*Song of Destiny*) (parts of which were later set), is distinguished by this 'tragic awareness' of 'the "retreat" of the god'. Furthermore, Cacciari sees this tragic awareness continued in Schoenberg. The text of the second of Schoenberg's *Six Pieces for Male Chorus* op. 35, *Das Gesetz* (*The Law*), makes the following assertion: 'that there is one who rebels, that is a trite banality'. 'Consider, however', Cacciari continues with Schoenberg,

> Daß es ein Gesetz gibt,
> dem die Dinge gehorchen, wie du deinem Herrn,
> das den Dingen so gebietet, wie dir dein Herr.
> [...]
> Dieses solltest du als Wunder erkennen.
>
> That there should be one law
> And all things on Earth obey it,
> As thou dost thy Lord?
> [...]
> Surely that should be the wonder thou knowest.[55]

[54] Hölderlin, *Brod und Wein* (1801), with many thanks to Harry Gilonis for this translation.
[55] Schoenberg, *Six Pieces for Male Chorus* op. 35, no. 2, 'Das Gesetz', trans. D. Millar Craig and Adolph Weiss.

Thus Schoenberg's law, to Cacciari, becomes synonymous with 'the law of Ananke'. Necessity in turn is then also associated with the idea of the unrepresentable god in *Moses und Aron*. 'This god', Cacciari argues,

> is also the death of god – he does not exist.
> And his absence makes space for the manifold forms of man's Techne.
> But these now manifest themselves 'free' of utopia,
> 'free' also of the vicinity of god,
> 'remembered' in Hölderlin –
> they manifest themselves *in dürftiger Zeit*. [...]
> Yes, Hölderlin's *dürftige Zeit* is under the sign of Schoenberg's impossible god –
> since Moses can only live in the desert – in der Wüste –
> In the desert alone he is invincible.
> Only in the *absence* of the desert.
> because god is totally invisible–unrepresentable in the desert:
> totally absent –
> present,
> as law,
> as Spinozian 'nature',
> is Ananke alone.[56]

Ultimately, therefore, the 'authentic tragedy' at the heart of the conciliation between Prometheus and Zeus which is celebrated in *Prometheus Unbound* (the final play in Aeschylus' trilogy) is 'the recognition of the *Grenzen der Menschheit* [*Limits of Humanity*]',[57] the recognition that in search of the illuminating fire, 'a harsh law establishes itself':

> a law which, within *these limits*, transforms
> works
> 'opens other paths' –
> recognises the fallibility of
> one's own language,
> consisting of memories,
> intuitions –
> never 'absolute'
> *never divine*.
> To arrive at this desert –
> where the idea of man
> which man has of himself
> is *invincible*

[56] ALN 51.02.05/16–17.

[57] A reference to Goethe's poem *Grenzen der Menschheit* (*ca.* 1780).

> Prometheus prophesied to Zeus;
> 'sacrificed' himself.
> the conclusion is: *das Lied von der Erde* . . .[58]

Thus ends Cacciari's first and radically new reading of the Prometheus myth. Section B of these preliminary notes is a more detailed recapitulation of section A, yet the additional padding also somewhat dilutes the core argument. However, the law of Ananke is now directly linked to the political. Since this law is of the 'most elevated spirituality – not mysticism, not rebellion' but 'most sublime abstraction', it 'does not "appear"'. But because it '"moulds" the *techne*, the work, the life of man' it is 'necessarily *political*'. In recognition of the political significance of this law, Prometheus returns 'no longer simply a prophet of the death of god – as if the death of god were equivalent to the liberation of man' but as the 'problem of the liberation of man', the problem 'of the relationship between spirituality and politics in the liberation of man', the problem which 'tragically' condemns man to keep searching and 'wandering', with his 'techne' alone 'in dürftiger Zeit' towards humanity's very own domain or 'dwelling', a destination which remains uncertain precisely because it is not defined in its relationship to Zeus (the ruler) and Dike (the law of the rulers, as opposed to the law of Ananke, which is Ekdike, 'outside' and above the law of the rulers).[59]

This intrinsically political tragedy is later combined with *Il Maestro del gioco*, Cacciari's allusive philosophical commentary in twelve stanzas which is primarily based on Benjamin's *Theses on the Concept of History*.[60] The title, *The Master of the Game*, is undoubtedly inspired by Benjamin's first Thesis:

> There was once, we know, an automaton constructed in such a way that it could respond to every move by a chess player with a countermove that would ensure the winning of the game. A puppet wearing Turkish attire and with a hookah in its mouth sat before a chessboard placed on a large table. A system of mirrors created the illusion that this table was transparent on all sides. Actually, a hunchbacked dwarf – a master at chess – sat inside and guided the puppet's hands by means of strings. One can imagine a philosophic counterpart to this apparatus. The puppet, called 'historical materialism', is to win all the time. It can easily be a match for anyone if it enlists the services of theology, which today, as we know, is small and ugly and has to keep out of sight.[61]

[58] ALN 51.02.05/19–20. [59] ALN 51.02.05/30–31.
[60] For drafts of *Il Maestro del gioco* see ALN 51.07.04.
[61] Benjamin, 'Thesis I', in Löwy, *Fire Alarm*, 23.

The automaton's mechanical puppet, Löwy argues in his illuminating analysis of Benjamin's *Theses*, is by no means to be confused with 'true' historical materialism.[62] By 1940 (the year the *Theses* were written and suicide was to become Benjamin's 'one-way street' out of fascism), so-called 'historical materialism' had turned into a stalemate method, a purely 'mechanical materialism' fuelled by the false assumption that 'development of the productive forces, economic progress and the "laws of history" lead necessarily to the last crisis of capitalism and the victory of the proletariat (Communist version) or the reforms that will gradually transform society (Social Democratic version)'.[63] Such a 'manikin' or 'mechanical doll' is clearly not capable of 'winning the game' against the historic enemy, the ruling classes (Benjamin's fascist oppressors at the time) and incapable, too, of winning the struggle against the oppressors' view of history. In order to ensure a win at all times, this soulless puppet requires the help of the hidden 'hunchbacked dwarf', the *Master of the Game*, who, in Benjamin's philosophical counterpart, is 'theology, which today, as we know, is small and ugly and has to keep out of sight'.

With the term 'theology', Benjamin refers to two fundamental concepts that were also of great importance to Cacciari: 'remembrance (*Eingedenken*)' and 'messianic redemption (*Erlösung*)'. Is this 'theological' aspect of Benjamin's materialist concept of history not also the philosophical backbone for the abstract spirituality of Ananke in Cacciari's reading of Prometheus? The concept of an 'abstract spirituality' that is 'necessarily political' seems as firmly 'in the service' of historical materialism as Benjamin's theological dwarf. As Löwy argues,

> Theology for Benjamin is not a goal in itself; its aim is not the ineffable contemplation of eternal verities, nor, even less, reflection of the nature of the divine Being, as might be thought from its etymology: it is in the service of the struggle of the oppressed. More precisely, it must serve to re-establish the explosive, messianic, revolutionary force of historical materialism – reduced to a wretched automaton by its epigones. The historical materialism to which Benjamin subscribes in the following theses is that which results from the vivification, this spiritual activation by theology.[64]

Benjamin, to Löwy, is thus both 'a Marxist *and* a theologian', one who 'enlists the services of theology' to reclaim 'true' historical materialism and who therefore 'liked to compare himself to a Janus figure, one of whose faces was turned towards Moscow and the other towards Jerusalem'.[65]

[62] Löwy, *Fire Alarm*, 25. [63] Löwy, *Fire Alarm*, 25. [64] Löwy, *Fire Alarm*, 27–28.

[65] Löwy, *Fire Alarm*, 20. Löwy distances himself from the 'materialist school' (Brecht), the 'theological school' (Scholem) and the 'contradictory school' (Habermas and

With the question 'Moscow – who are you?' at the centre of Nono's *Quando stanno morendo. Diario polacco n. 2* (1982), it seems that also Nono and Cacciari increasingly turned towards Jerusalem to escape the 'orthodox wolves'.[66] The quality of 'listening', so often associated with the Jewish faith in Nono's texts, becomes of paramount importance precisely during the time of Berlinguer's 'historical compromise', a decisive move away from the belief in the 'utopia' of revolution towards the 'necessity' of Eurocommunism, a move which Nono clearly endorsed, but which was effectively also the beginning of the party's demise.[67] Of Nono's many texts and interviews, it is his tribute to Berlinguer, written shortly after the politician's sudden death in 1984, which contains some of the most revealing insights on the spiritual and political premises of *Prometeo*:

> The long silence now of E[nrico] B[erlinguer].
>
> And his thoughts, often correctly upsetting, which live on in many of us. Thoughts that are finally being acknowledged and contemplated by those who have been deaf and blind until now.
>
> The mortals: 'had eyes, but sight was meaningless;
> Heard sounds, but could not listen'
> (Aeschylus, *Prometheus Bound*, second episode)
>
> [. . .] Disquiet [. . .] His ability to listen, so rare today [. . .] Moments of solitude [. . .]
>
> Risks – conflicts – differentiations – major rethinkings and conflicting innovations. In contemporary, modern life.
>
> Thought and life in technological transformation – technologies – different organisation and function of the working class – and of the party of course.
>
> New necessities.
>
> Attempting and wanting the unheard of, the fantastic, the liberating, *in short*, in non-univocal reality, with a non-univocal vision.
>
> E[nrico] B[erlinguer] reminds us what Wittgenstein wrote in *On Certainty* – Oxford 1969, section 559 [*sic.*]:

Tiedemann), all of which tend to separate the political from the theological and/or show their inherent contradictions.

66 The second movement of *Quando stanno morendo. Diario polacco n. 2*, written in response to the imposition of martial law in Poland by General Jaruzelski (December 1981) and the repression of the Solidarity movement, sets a poem by Velimir Khlebnikov which poses the question 'Moscow, who are you?' and answers 'I know that you are orthodox wolves.' On *Quando stanno morendo* see Ogborn, 'When they are dying, men sing . . .' and Sallis, 'Segmenting the Labyrinth'.

67 On Judaism and listening see, for example, 'Ascoltare le pietre bianche', *Scritti*, II, 294: 'Think of the incredible difference between the Hebrew religion and the Catholic one. A Catholic would say 'I believe', whereas 'I listen' counts for the Jews. These are such different concepts. What I learned in recent times is listening.'

'In philosophy one feels forced to look at a concept in a certain way. What I do is to suggest, or even invent, other ways of looking at it. I suggest possibilities of which you had not previously thought. You thought that there was one possibility, or only two at most. But I made you think of others ... Thus your mental cramp is relieved ...'[68]

## Notes on the musical 'language'

Thoughts develop with language.
Karl Kraus

Time and again Nono refers to this phrase by Kraus in relation to the evolution of his musical thought after 1975.[69] Key to this new 'language' development was the composer's close collaboration with a group of performers who, throughout the 1980s, would join him for prolonged periods of study and experimentation at the Experimentalstudio Freiburg. The first to embark on this long-lasting collaboration was the flautist Roberto Fabbriciani. Nono first met Fabbriciani in 1978 at La Scala after a performance of Camillo Togni's *Blaubart* in which the flautist performed the role of the boy. Soon thereafter Fabbriciani found himself at Nono's house in Venice for a preliminary exchange of ideas and to 'listen' to the sounds and voices of the city's iconic alleyways and courtyards.[70] Fabbriciani vividly recalls these first encounters:

> We spent those Venetian days talking about music, art, philosphy and politics, walking through the calli, along the canals, sometimes taking the boat out for a swim and then ending up in a *trattoria* for some black squid risotto. [...] I would leave the Giudecca carrying the instruments we had not touched all day, yet feeling professionally enriched and stimulated to work towards new horizons.[71]

And, more recently, in *Flauto in scena*:

> Gigi and I were in agreement with the idea that music is a thought in the making, in which exploration, with all the risks this involves, is a necessity.

68 Nono, 'Le sue parole e le sue grandi drammatiche solitudini' (1984), *Scritti*, I, 397–99. The Wittgenstein quotation stems from Malcolm, *Ludwig Wittgenstein*, 50. Nono quotes this passage from Gargani, *Wittgenstein tra Austria e Inghilterra*, 15, but references it incorrectly. See 'Luigi Nono: Für Helmut', in Lachenmann, *Musik als existentielle Erfahrung*, xiii–xv.

69 For example in Nono, 'Ascoltare le pietre bianche', *Scritti*, II, 287.

70 Fabbriciani, *Flauto in scena*, 19. Fabbriciani dates his first visit to November or December 1978. He was twenty-nine at the time.

71 Fabbriciani, 'Walking with Gigi', 8.

> [...] In this way the fantastical ideas of the composer awaken the creativity of the interpreter and invite him to venture with his instrument to the extreme limits of his art. The performer actively participates in the creation of the musical work, improvising on cues given to him by the composer and often also providing 'basic material' – for example new or uncommon timbral possibilities – that is then systematised and reorganised by the composer.[72]

Nono and Fabbriciani worked briefly at the Studio di Fonologia in Milan to record one last tape together with Marino Zuccheri, material from which was later used for the final bass flute section of *Das atmende Klarsein* (1981).[73] The piece as a whole, however, which Nono always regarded as an important breakthrough, was the first to result from Nono's ground-breaking experiences at the Experimentalstudio der Heinrich-Strobel-Stiftung in Freiburg, where he and Fabbriciani arrived, unannounced at first, towards the end of 1980.[74]

In Freiburg Nono was extremely lucky to find the technological facilities and working environment that allowed him to conduct the necessary research and experimentation for the linguistic evolution he had had in mind ever since his encounter with John Chowning at the Center for Computer Research and Musical Acoustics at Stanford University in 1975.[75] Chowning's pioneering research in computer music took on a particular model function for Nono because advanced technology was not simply applied to conventional models of thought, but aimed at the modification and transformation of musical thought as such.[76] With 'new technological possibilities but a mode of thought that had not yet evolved to their level', Nono regarded this kind of research as the only real way forward.[77]

72 Fabbriciani, *Flauto in scena*, 19. On Nono's collaboration with Fabbriciani further see Zattra, 'A colloquio con Roberto Fabbriciani'; Zattra, Burleigh and Sallis, 'Studying Luigi Nono's *A Pierre*'; and Dollinger, *unendlicher Raum – zeitloser Augenblick*.

73 The session took place on 1–2 December 1980; Dollinger, *unendlicher Raum – zeitloser Augenblick*, 34.

74 Fabbriciani tells the story of how he and Nono drove to Freiburg, but were so nervous on arriving at the studio that they first drove into the Black Forest in order to gain courage. The following day Professor Haller welcomed them with open arms and gave them a first tour of the facilities; Fabbriciani, personal communication, Venice, 3 November 2007.

75 Chowning introduced Nono to advanced computer technology that was not available at the Studio di Fonologia in Milan. Nono contemplated a period of study with Chowning, but went to Freiburg instead when he heard that the Experimentalstudio, too, offered the possibility of working with delay. Nono, 'Un'autobiografia', *Scritti*, II, 550.

76 See, for example, Nono, 'Intervista di Renato Garavaglia' (1979–80), *Scritti*, II, 238–39.

77 For this reason, Nono regarded Chowning's research as superior to that at IRCAM. See Nono, 'Anche la dolcezza è rivoluzionaria' (1982), *Scritti*, II, 272.

Likewise, he thrust himself into unbound studio experimentation, attempting to liberate himself from all 'conventional models of thought':

> When I enter the Studio in Freiburg I don't have any idea. I take no stance, be it conceptual, ideological, technical, acoustic or musical. I simply work with the technicians of the Studio, get to know the mechanisms, the procedures, try out some combinations. I start by subjecting a signal, which could be a human voice or an instrument, to various transformations in real time. 'Real time' means that the transformation takes place at the same time as the emission of this sound, by which means that which is extended is the whole of the habitual way of perceiving music, and it is extended in crazy ways [. . .] In short, you do not arrive at a unified whole, but attain a diversified multiplicity. Be it from the point of view of research or in terms of ideation, thought, musical notation and thus musical realisation, this completely opens wide the seven heavens to you.[78]

The instrument Nono worked with most intensively was the sonoscope, the digital successor of the sonograph. The sonoscope was used not for sound transformation, but to analyse the pitch, tempo and intensity of any received sound signal. Nono was fascinated by the precision of this analytical tool because it revealed the most subtle changes of sound and timbre and thus opened doors to entirely new ways of perceiving sound, of listening anew.[79] As Nono explains in 'Verso *Prometeo*', the sonoscope recorded the 'results of minimal lip movement' which would not usually be heard in the concert hall: 'surprising' harmonics and extremely high aeolian sounds, between 11 and 15 kHz, the perception of which is possible only by means of 'modulated amplification'.[80]

The sonoscope was also of immense benefit for microtonal analysis. In 'Verso *Prometeo*' Nono regards microtonality as an extension to chromaticism as it had been taught and practiced since the Renaissance. Zarlino's *Dimostrationi harmoniche* (1571) and Nicola Vicentino's *L'antica musica ridotta alla moderna prattica* (1555) are cited as fundamental models, as are the motets by Vicentino, Gesualdo's 'astonishingly chromatic madrigals' and the 'sublime' chromaticism in the music of very "few notes" by John Ward and John Wilbye.[81] However, Nono also places microtonal inflection in the context of a completely different cultural sphere: Andalusian Gypsy Song, the Rumanian Christmas Carols collected and studied by Béla Bartók and the music and theory of Alois Hába. Above all, however, Nono was fascinated by Jewish song, with its extremely refined

[78] Nono, 'Ascoltare le pietre bianche' (1983), 289.
[79] See Haller, *Experimentalstudio*, II, 141–47.
[80] Nono, 'Verso *Prometeo*' (1984), *Scritti*, I, 385. [81] *Ibid.*, 387.

differentiation of pitch, articulation and timbre. Nono owned all ten volumes of Idelsohn's critical edition of Hebrew song, and was greatly impressed by practices such as the 'attentive use of the lips, the tongue, the teeth, in relation to the phonic Hebrew alphabet, for micro-intervals and microtones'.[82] Nono used the sonoscope precisely in order to perceive, record and experience 'each minimal consequence of what Idelsohn indicates'.[83] In addition, Nono was undoubtably attracted to the spiritual dimension of Jewish chant. As he later told Restagno,

> The great Jewish laments of 1600 and 1700 after the pogroms in Poland and the Ukraine [. . .] were suddenly brought back to me by the great poet Edmond Jabès, in Paris. These laments express not just sorrow but simultaneously also feelings of hope, of gratitude, of remembrance, and this seemingly contradictory multiplicity of feelings is expressed through the infinitesimal oscillations in the vocal part [. . .] I feel that death navigates perhaps between spaces and times that open up in different ways: death for me is not a transformation. A spiritual force transforms itself and becomes something else, wanders into other spaces with other memories, anticipates or brings with it new feelings. Not by chance, my *Epitaffi per García Lorca* were linked to a particular study on dance rhythms. In Granada I found out that, on the anniversary of Lorca's death, the gypsies gather at the place where the poet was shot and dance. And similar testimonies can be found also in the Hassidic tales collected by Martin Buber. All these testimonies concur with Jabès's interpretation: in the infinite multiplicity of vocal inflections there coexist the various moments of lament, hope, love, discouragement, absence, forgetting, needing and awaiting [. . .] And also the difference between traditional Hebrew chant, ritual or not, rendered mobile by micro-intervals, and that of the Christian–Gregorian tradition, with its fixed pitches. That is to say: the profound difference between the culture of 'listening' and that of 'believing'.[84]

His work in Freiburg, Nono repeatedly emphasised, was essentially a process of learning to 'listen' in this sense. In other words, the sophisticated studio technology was primarily employed with the aim of exploring and creating a new 'listening' awareness. As Nono sums up in his typically disjunct style for *Guai ai gelidi mostri*,

> mobile, not static, sound for the monolithic formants –
> micro-intervals with a difference of as little as 1 Hz –

[82] *Ibid.*, 386. Idelsohn, *Hebräisch-orientalischer Melodienschatz.*

[83] *Ibid.*, 386. Nono owned various recordings and also mentions the sonograph analyses of Jewish chant in Walbe, *Der Gesang Israels und seine Quellen.*

[84] Nono, 'Un'autobiografia', *Scritti*, II, 537–38.

various transpositions of an acoustic spectrum, which is no longer a univocal one –
other vibrations, other filters for the diffusion of sound with the compositional use of space that needs to be studied specifically.
differentiation also between the memory-presence of Gregorian chant and the memory-presence of synagogal chant.
differentiation also in the production of sound that is not a given monad but open to other multiplicities, be it the diverse qualities of the human voice or those of instruments, enhanced by live electronics in real time.
ongoing necessity of research, of experimentation with other possibilities, also and above all in the service of the creative imagination, with further difficult consequences for perception, if passively rendered banal and degraded to the 'normality' of 'seeing music': *star sistem* [*sic.*], meta-language.
infinite openness to the surprising, to the unknown, to putting things up for discussion, even with a maximum of uncertainty (certainty in uncertainty), with maximum verzweifelte Unruhe (Ruhe in der verzweifelten Unruhe) [despairing disquiet (quiet within the despairing disquiet)] – the searching infinitely more important than finding.
listening!
knowing how *to listen* to the red and white stones of Venice at sunrise –
knowing how *to listen* to the infinite bow of colours on the Venetian lagoon at sunset –
knowing how *to listen* to the magical undulations of the Black Forest: colours, silences, naturally *live*, of the 7 heavens.
('the great Maghid of Mežiriči, in his youth, liked to get up at dawn to walk on the banks of long rivers and lakes: he learned the art of listening'; from *Hassidic Celebrations* by Elie Wiesel).
Hölderlin and his tower – Gramsci and his cell.[85]

## *Das atmende Klarsein*

The music for *Prometeo*, too, began with *Das atmende Klarsein*. One of the basic materials, the scala enigmatica from Verdi's *Ave Maria*, had of course already been used for *Fragmente – Stille, an Diotima*. The real breakthrough into the harmonic sphere of *Prometeo*, however, came with *Das atmende Klarsein*. Nono himself regarded the piece as one of the 'fundamental steps towards *Prometeo*' and, according to Stenzl, always remained particularly fond of it.[86] Much has already been written on this important milestone by Hella Melkert, Peter Evan Edwards, Bruce Durazzi and

[85] Nono, 'Guai ai gelidi mostri' (1983), *Scritti*, I, 491–92.
[86] Nono, 'Prometeo' (1985), *Scritti*, I, 493; Stenzl, *Luigi Nono*, 98–101.

Christina Dollinger.[87] My overview here is specifically aimed at a better understanding of the harmonic system of *Prometeo*.

Sketches show that *Das atmende Klarsein* was initially planned on a far larger scale. Most probably due to the complexity of the studio technology, the composer soon settled for more realistic, smaller forces: 'Roberto' on bass flute, a small chorus and live electronics.[88] The use of the live electronics, too, is still relatively simple. Each of the twelve singers (three to a part) is equipped with a microphone, the flautist with two. The live sound is recorded, amplified and transformed at times, and transmitted through six sets of loudspeakers positioned in a rectangle around the audience. Over the course of approximately thirty minutes, four extremely slow, almost static sections for a cappella chorus alternate with four much more fluid solo bass flute sections. In accordance with the work's title, the vocal writing is of unprecedented lucidity. A very limited number of pitches weave in and out of unison and every new pitch constellation is suspended in time, by means of an array of fermatas of different length (ranging from 2″ to 17″). As previously in *Fragmente – Stille, an Diotima*, suspended 'stillness' goes hand in hand with extreme quietude. Vocal dynamics very rarely rise to *mp*, *mf* or even *f*. Instead, the intense drama of this music takes place within a differentiated *p–pppppp*, 'tutto interno' (completely within).[89] As André Richard and Marco Mazzolini specify, these

> choral parts are not to be sung in a traditional manner. Rather, they require absolutely precise intonation and extremely soft pianissimi in order to suggest an air of 'fragility'. The quality of the unison in each part is therefore of fundamental importance: when the dynamic level is particularly delicate, the three voices must be able to sing a perfect unison, completely free of beats. This will produce a sound with few audible overtones, almost like a sine wave, so that all the intervals are as pure as possible. [. . .] An excessive variety of

87 Melkert, «*Far del silenzio cristallo*», 13–81; Edwards, 'Object, Space, and Fragility'; Durazzi, *Musical Poetics and Political Ideology*, 184–239; Dollinger, *unendlicher Raum – zeitloser Augenblick*, 27–80.

88 Nono initially considered three instrumental soloists (bass flute/piccolo, viola and trombone), percussion (including tubular bells and metal sheets), chorus and live electronics. Sketches further mention a tape of church bells (referred to as 'nastro campane'/ 'Freiburg campane') and another of Cacciari reading the text of *Das atmende Klarsein*, possibly with electronic modification. Sketch 45.07/20 indicates that Cacciari's spoken rendition was to be complemented by that of a female speaker, and fragments of both were to form a spoken 'continuo'. While this idea was dropped for *Das atmende Klarsein*, it clearly anticipates the use of two speakers (male and female) in *Prometeo*.

89 Richard and Mazzolini, preface to *Das atmende Klarsein*, score, xiii.

> timbres is incompatible with the aesthetic intentions of the composer. Young singers whose voices are not yet completely formed can most easily render the sound and 'fragile' feeling that Nono sought.[90]

This 'pure' and 'fragile' vocal sound is not only on the brink of silence but also wavers in between metered movement and timeless stasis. Temporal stasis is accentuated further by means of the live electronics. Throughout the piece the transmission of the voices remains static: the choral sound is consistently transmitted through the loudspeakers at the front and back (L1/L2 and L4/L5), and only the third choral section demands subtle live-electronic sound transformation. Two harmonisers here immerse the vocal parts in a microtonal haze, adding lower and upper quarter-tone transpositions in real time at a slightly quieter level. The live electronics thus subtly underline one of the principal compositional concepts: the process of losing the 'clarity' of the work's opening statement, this initial band of open fourths and fifths which very obviously stands for Rilke's 'atmendes Klarsein' and, on a more abstract, philosophical level, Cacciari's understanding of 'clarity' in language. The striking clarity of this opening chorus is gradually lost: with the introduction of tritones (T) and seconds, sevenths and ninths (2–7–9) in the second choral section, and electronic microtonal transposition in the third. After this technological 'impurification', the final chorus allows only a partial return to 'clarity': mediated, momentary glimpses of its origin.

If electronic mediation is kept to a minimum in the vocal sections, it is practiced in abundance in the bass flute sections. As Durazzi and Dollinger have shown, flute and chorus share largely the same material.[91] Through the prism of extended avant-garde flute techniques, however, this material appears in a totally new, often barely recognisable guise. The first bass flute section is an example in point. It begins with the pitches of the opening chorus in retrograde. With a high degree of breath noise and percussive key action, these pitches are merely hinted at, absorbed into the sound of their production. Even further removed from the conventional flute sound is the fragile and naturally microtonal universe of multiphonics that is to follow. Unlike the chorus, the bass flute here immediately plunges into the full interval spectrum, including microtones, and explores it with maximum contrast of dynamics, speed, articulation and register. Is this, perhaps, part of the Promethean '*Flucht* [flight] – NOT towards *Gestein*

90 *Ibid.*, xiii.

91 Durazzi, *Musical Poetics and Political Ideology*, 204–25; Dollinger, *unendlicher Raum – zeitloser Augenblick*, 60–79.

[rock] (the "solid", unalterable NOMOS), but towards *Fruchtland* [harvest land]'? The notion of evading 'all that is solid' is certainly enhanced by the use of two halaphones, electronic spatialisers which set the live bass flute sound into motion to encircle the audience in two extremely slow moving trajectories (clockwise and anti-clockwise through all six loudspeakers).[92] Yet even this electronically enhanced 'flight' allows glimpses of 'clarity'. Natural harmonics momentarily evoke past eras with their quasi-tonal structure and extremely quiet non-vibrato sound. As Durazzi observes, these magical *lentissimo* moments were fairly late additions and, not by coincidence, they are again primarily based on 'open-string' pitches – one of the *ad libitum* dimensions of the quartet.[93]

The flute's quest for 'clarity' continues in its subsequent sections. Pitch is much more clearly defined in the second flute section, and techniques such as vibrato, addition of breath noise and whistling are now employed not to distract or submerge, but to differentiate the slow and sustained pitch development. As shown by Durazzi and Dollinger, the pitch structure of this section derives from a quarter-tone version of the familiar all-interval series from Nono's works of the late fifties.[94] The extended quarter-tone wedge is now used to gradually reduce the ambitus of this section from a minor seventh down to unison. This development is not linear, however, but proceeds in four waves. Beginning with the minor seventh C♯–B, the first wave narrows down chromatically to the tritone E♭–A. The second expands outward again from the quarter-tone fifth D–A ¼↑ to the sixth C–A ¾↑, then settling on the fifth C–G ¼↑. The process continues with two similar waves in part B. Again the first makes use of diatonic pitches only, moving from E–G♯ down to the chromatic cluster G–F♯–F. The second moves in quarter-tones from the fourth D–G ¾↑ down to F–G ¼↑ and finally resolves into unison F. This pitch development is perceived as intervallic (and not just as a solo line) because of the use of two simultaneous delays of 3″ and 3.5″. The polyphony of these delays creates increasing friction between the differentiated playing techniques and the added chromatic and quarter-tone neighbour-note

92 On the variation in speed 'from static (almost motionless) to (very) slow to (very) fast' see Richard and Mazzolini, preface, xvii–xviii. The halaphon (named after Hans Peter *Ha*ller and Peter *La*wo) was developed in 1971; Haller, *Das Experimentalstudio*, I, 77–79.

93 Three of the lentissimo passages make use of the 'open-string' fundamentals C, D, E and G; on one occasion, Nono also adds D♭ and F.

94 Durazzi, *Musical Poetics and Political Ideology*, 210–12; Dollinger, *unendlicher Raum – zeitloser Augenblick*, 72–73.

pitches.[95] Live electronics thus provide the principal compositional idea with a spatial dimension. The same idea would later attain crucial significance in *Prometeo*. On a far larger scale, the 'Hölderlin' section of Isola 2° represents an equally narrowing 'funnel': the sound of two solo sopranos is subjected to much longer delays with feedback and set into contrary motion, resulting in an all-encompassing spiral or vortex in which the multiplied waves of the gradually narrowing pitches become all the more effective.

The more modest polyphonic funnel in *Das atmende Klarsein* serves to draw the listener's attention to minute microtonal deviation and thus presages the electronically mediated, microtonal fuzziness of the following movements. Like the chorus, the bass flute, too, is subjected to microtonal clouding, and this precisely when its sound is at its most 'natural' and 'pure'. The entire third flute section consists of natural harmonics only. With an extremely slow and open airflow the flautist produces a mere shadow-sound of the fundamentals indicated, occasional aeolian harmonics in the middle register as well as exceedingly pure and quiet whistle tones that naturally cascade through the higher end of the harmonic series. The score here merely presents a rough guide, since aeolian harmonics and whistle tones will happen more or less by chance. The flautist is asked to enter a shadowland between sound and silence that is for the most part beyond his or her exact control. The distinctive presence of the flute sound of the previous section thus dissolves into a virtual non-presence of sound, a 'void' between shadows of low fundamentals and fluctuating high harmonics, so quiet that they are only really perceived when amplified (as is the case). The natural purity of these aeolian sounds is furthermore steeped in a haze as live electronics subject the flute to the same microtonal harmonisation as that which is applied to the singers in the preceding choral section.

This 'void' on the verge of silence is followed by a final improvisation on Fabbriciani's and Nono's last tape from the Studio di Fonologia, which takes the performing flautist through a kaleidoscope of contemporary flute techniques. Despite minimal editing, this tape of duration approximately six minutes has an astonishingly convincing shape. At the start, tongue rams and *aria intonata* (breath noise with a hint of pitch) are surprisingly tonal and even include a C-major scale. However, submerged in the surprising sound of its production, pitch is clearly secondary here. When pitched sound eventually emerges from *aria intonata* after a passage of rapid tongue and finger clicks, it clearly delineates a tritone (F♯–C). This brief exposition

95 Also see Haller, *Experimentalstudio*, 125–26. Haller mentions delays of 1.5″ and 3″, yet Richard confirms that this was later changed.

of 'normal' flute sound is followed by a passage of high whistling that breaks off with a rhythmic intervention of key clicks and leads into a long stretch of almost inaudible whispering (2′50″–3′21″). The incredible tension which builds up in this vortex of inaudibility is followed by the most virtuosic, fast and furious *fffff* outburst through the entire range of the bass flute, which few flautists will be able to match. After this energetic climax the tape concludes with brief fragments of earlier materials: key and tongue clicks, multiphonics, whistling, *aria intonata* and the initial tongue rams.

In performance, the sound of this tape is set in motion by the two halaphones and moves clockwise and anti-clockwise through all six loudspeakers at variable speeds (the dynamics and speed are determined by the person controlling the sound projection). The improvised live sound of the performing flautist, however, does not move and is transmitted through the front speakers (L1 and L2) throughout. When Fabbriciani himself performs this final improvisation, he more or less duplicates what he recorded on tape. The moving tape sound is thus given a core mirror image that creates deliberate confusion between live and recorded sound. According to Richard, however, Nono himself had a very different kind of interaction in mind and wanted the performing flautist to choose and superimpose material from the first flute section *ad libitum*. The latter approach not only vastly extends the range of possibilities, but also provides a much more unified ending to the work as a whole. The final outburst of individuality would thus be firmly grounded in the materials of the composition itself – certainly a much better option for any flautist other than Fabbriciani, who will find it difficult to emulate Fabbriciani's virtuosic agility in this, his very own territory.

Nono's compositional concept of interlocking waves of sound is perhaps nowhere as clear as in *Das atmende Klarsein*, where two such waves are consistently assigned to and represented by two distinct forces: the chorus and the solo bass flute. The two waves are generated from the same pitch material, but each wave is placed in its own time zone and follows a structurally different course. The choral wave begins with the purest and most archaic interval category (IV/V), the slowest of speeds (♩ = 30) and a minimum contrast of dynamics (*pp*, *ppp*, only once rising to *p*). This initial equilibrium is disrupted by the much more energetic surge in the second section, the longest and most varied of the four. Enveloped in two additional interval categories (2–7–9 and T), the vocal sound now rises and recedes with the greatest variety of speeds (♩ = 66, 54, 44, 30, 40, 46 and 36) and maximum contrast of dynamics (*pppp* to *f*). It continues to recede in the third and fourth sections, through an added microtonal haze at first, but ultimately without microtones. The vocal wave thus gradually returns to the slowest speed (♩ = 30, via 44 and 52) and fades into increasing quietness (*pppppp–mf* in section III, *pppppp–mp* in section IV) without ever regaining its initial crystalline purity.

As soon as the bass flute enters, it is clear that this complementary instrumental wave of sound moves with a much higher level of agility, contrast and rhythmic punctuation. Unlike the chorus, the flute immediately makes use of the full interval reservoir, including microtones, with contrasting speeds (♩ = 60, 72 and 92) and dynamics (*pppp* to *ffff*) and continues to invert the course of the vocal wave in its subsequent sections. Speeds calm down to a steady ♩ = 88 in section II and further to ♩ = 72 in section III. The dynamics recede accordingly: *p–mf* in section IIa, *pp–p* in section IIb, followed by the extreme but lively quietude of shadow-sounds and aeolian sounds in section III. The flute then logically returns to its initial state of contrast and variety, which it supersedes with the most energetic section of all: the improvised finale.

Not only do the vocal and instrumental waves interlock in alternation but also, as previously in *Fragmente – Stille, an Diotima*, there is a central crossover point marked by a high degree of assimilation. The nodal point here is the final resolution of the flute's polyphonic funnel, the unison F that is then almost seamlessly incorporated into the fourth C–F of the female voices. As in the quartet, Nono also introduces the all-encompassing microtonal 'haze' at precisely this point. *Das atmende Klarsein* is, however, also markedly different from the quartet, especially regarding its use of text. Words are now actually set, and, despite the many layers of Cacciari's trilingual collage, Nono no longer assigns specific scala enigmatica segments to specific layers of text. Musical layers are clearly distinguished by different forces and the text is an intrinsic element of the vocal layer alone.

On the use of the Rilke texts, Cacciari initially wrote to Nono that

> They are fragments [. . .] a bit like the verses of Hölderlin in your quartet. I conceived them primarily with this function in mind. Even if you can "use" them as *text*.[96]

The same letter also makes clear that Rilke fragments were originally intended to link the 'episodes' of the *Prometeo* 'tragedy'. This function was later taken on by the *Maestro del gioco*.[97] *Das atmende Klarsein*, however, was written at a stage when Rilke was still very much at the heart

[96] Cacciari, letter to Nono, 19 August 1980 (Cacciari/M 80–08–19 m; ALN 45.01.01/01).

[97] 'Rompi gli episodi!!!/ con Benjamin/ Rilke/ anche rompendo Episodi' (Break up the episodes!!!/ with Benjamin/ Rilke/ also breaking up episodes), Nono writes on ALN 51.17.01/07. For the prologue Nono notes 'Allora: II da solo Forse + 1° Rilke' (ALN

of *Prometeo*. Sketches for *Das atmende Klarsein* contain a fascinating early outline, entitled 'Frammenti – Klarsein – studi – schizzi per *Prometeo* – 1981' (partly reproduced in Figure 7.1).[98] This outline shows that the episodes of the Promethean 'tragedy' were already firmly in place, but still linked to Rilke and Nietzsche's Wanderer. Nono was at this stage thinking of a work in three parts. Part [A] includes a 'Prologo' and two episodes entitled 'Prometeo' and 'Io'. Quite obviously with Rilke's *Duineser Elegien* in mind, Nono annotates the 'Prometeo' episode with 'striscia di terra/ torrente – pietra/ fruchtlands/ menschliches'.[99] The 'Io' episode is summed up in similar fashion with the words 'violenza – eros – Io' and 'ascolta'. A second part, Part [A′], begins with an episode entitled 'EKO – FINE UTOPIA/ ACHILLE – ANTICIPA WANDERER'. This 'Achilles' episode, too, is associated with a line of Rilke: 'oltre le porte dei morti' (beyond the doors of the dead).[100] After this crucial 'end of utopia', the philosophical framework takes on primary importance over the tragedy. For the concluding two episodes of Part [A′] Nono notes 'un attimo . . . χαίρε – herrlich – / Ulisse – mare – eros – libera'[101] and finally (without further reference to Greek mythology) 'Klarsein – ins freie/ un attimo/ Wanderer'.[102] The work was to conclude with an exodus: Part [A″] 'Esodo come eko di tutto e wanderer'.

Annotations on possible forces and the use of live electronics underline the centrality of the Prometheus, Io and Achilles episodes and the crucial concept of the renunciation of the utopia of liberation at the heart of Prometheus' decision to prophesy. As in *Das atmende Klarsein*, the forces envisaged for these central episodes are two-fold, divided into singers and wind instruments. For 'Prometeo' Nono specifies 'ottavino [piccolo] + audio computer'. With several underlinings he then adds 'con soprani (utopia)', bringing to mind the four sopranos who so potently sang of revolutionary utopia in *Al gran sole carico d'amore*. An arrow connects these utopian sopranos to the following 'Io' episode for which Nono notes the forces 'fl. basso + trb + coro = fiati'. The 'Fine Utopia/Achilles' episode is finally envisaged without the sopranos, for the two low wind instruments and live electronics alone. Indications regarding the already-familiar

51.17.01/01). From then on Parts I and II of the Prologue are associated solely with stanzas I and II from *Il Maestro del gioco* (ALN 51.17.01/02).

98 ALN 45.04/02r.

99 ALN 45.04/02r. Nono's Rilke citations correspond to Cacciari's first draft for *Das atmende Klarsein* (ALN 45.02.01/04r & 05).

100 ALN 45.04./02r. This line from Rilke's *Sonette an Orpheus* (VII) is included in Cacciari's first draft for *Das atmende Klarsein* (ALN 45.02.01/05) but was later discarded.

101 'a moment . . . rejoice – magnificent – / Ulysses – sea – eros – free', ALN 45.04/02r.

102 'clarity – into the open/ a moment/ Wanderer' (ALN 45.04/02r).

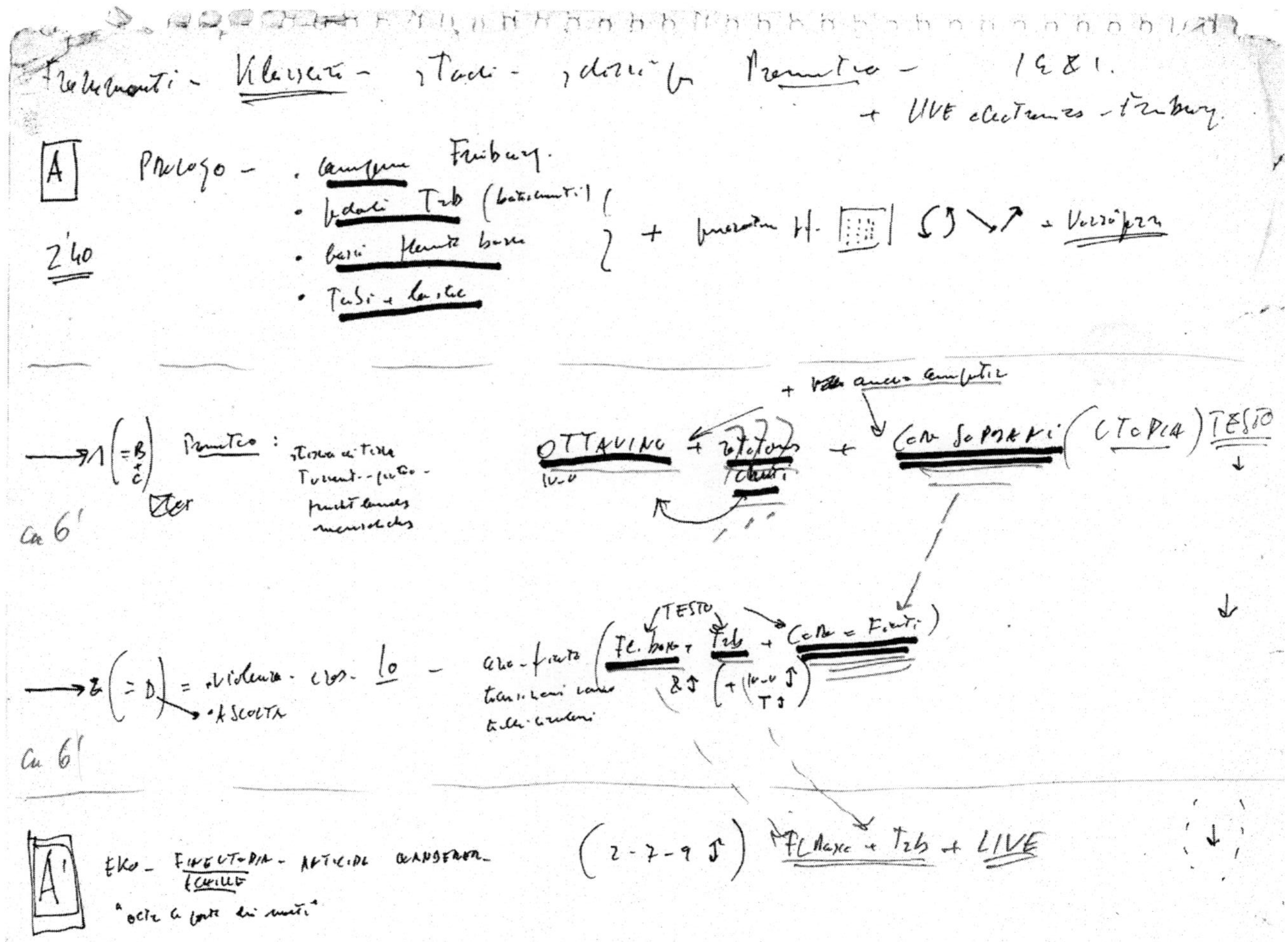


**Figure 7.1** 'Frammenti – *Klarsein* – studi – schizzi per *Prometeo* – 1981' (ALN 45.04/02r).

interval categories underline the progression from 'utopia' to 'fine utopia': the 'pure' category 'IV–V' is reserved for 'Prometeo', 'Io' is marked '8↕ (+ IV–V↕/ T↕)' and the most dissonant category of all, '2–7–9↕', is assigned to 'Achilles'.

This fundamental 'end of utopia' episode in turn initiates a process that is to lead *Prometeo* back 'into the open' as the Nietzschean 'Wanderer', the solitary free spirit who (like Ulysses before him) seeks 'the philosophy of the morning' and 'takes pleasure in change and transience'. This progression towards Rilkean 'Klarsein' implies that, from the very outset, *Das atmende Klarsein* was most probably conceived as one of the concluding pieces of *Prometeo*, either as the final episode, here marked 'Klarsein – ins freie/ un attimo/ Wanderer', or even as the 'Esodo', as which it was still performed (at least in part) at the Venice premiere of *Prometeo* in 1984. After all, Cacciari speaks of a concluding 'pezzo di Mnemosine' in his early notes on Rilke, a 'brano dell'ATTIMO' (piece of the MOMENT) in which all strains of the Promethean 'tragedy' and its commentary were to come together as a

> true FINAL TOLL – a toll (like those in *Sofferte onde . . .*): where you say 'einen unseren Streifen' – where Klarheit is gained (have you seen the Klarheit in *Dallo Steinhof* [*Posthumous People*]) on the event which 'precipitates' the Exodus . . .[103]

'Mnemosyne' is again the subject of a much later letter (4 July 1984), beginning with the words 'Gigi, this is for the Exodus'. 'We, the living', Cacciari here reflects, 'praise *Mnemosyne* – Memory of the atemporal – Memory of what we have not experienced – Memory of a path we have *not* taken. *This* is the Memory you will have to make heard!' As already mentioned in Chapter 2, Cacciari recognised a similar concept of memory in *Il canto sospeso*, where 'grief was the Memory of an atemporal – insolvable – grief'. For the 'Esodo' he thus suggests

> A large initial chorus that divides, comes back together 'joyously' (as a kind of *Song of Songs*) and then re-divides and returns again 'in one voice' [*Kol Nidre! Or the *Survivor* – but, above all, the Hebrew chant of the 17$^{th}$ century which you made me listen to!], which will have to match the other 'finales' of the pieces which you already have.[104]

How Nono himself imagined the Exodus is shown in Figure 7.2.[105] The key figures 'Mnemosyne', the 'Wanderer' and the 'Angel' are here associated

[103] Cacciari, 'da Rilke, *Duineser* ' (ALN 45.01.01/03).
[104] Cacciari, letter to Nono, 4 July 1984 (Cacciari/M 84–07–04 m; ALN 51.07.02/07).
[105] ALN 51.03.07/03–04.

with the fundamental concepts of listening and the 'moment'. With no further mention of Rilke, Nono refers only to the Benjaminian 'moment that shatters the duration' and 'blasts out an era'. This sketch is therefore unlikely to refer to *Das atmende Klarsein* as 'Esodo'. The 'power of singing', however, now clearly associated with Benjamin's 'messianic force', is already encapsulated in suspended, duration-shattering moments of

(a)

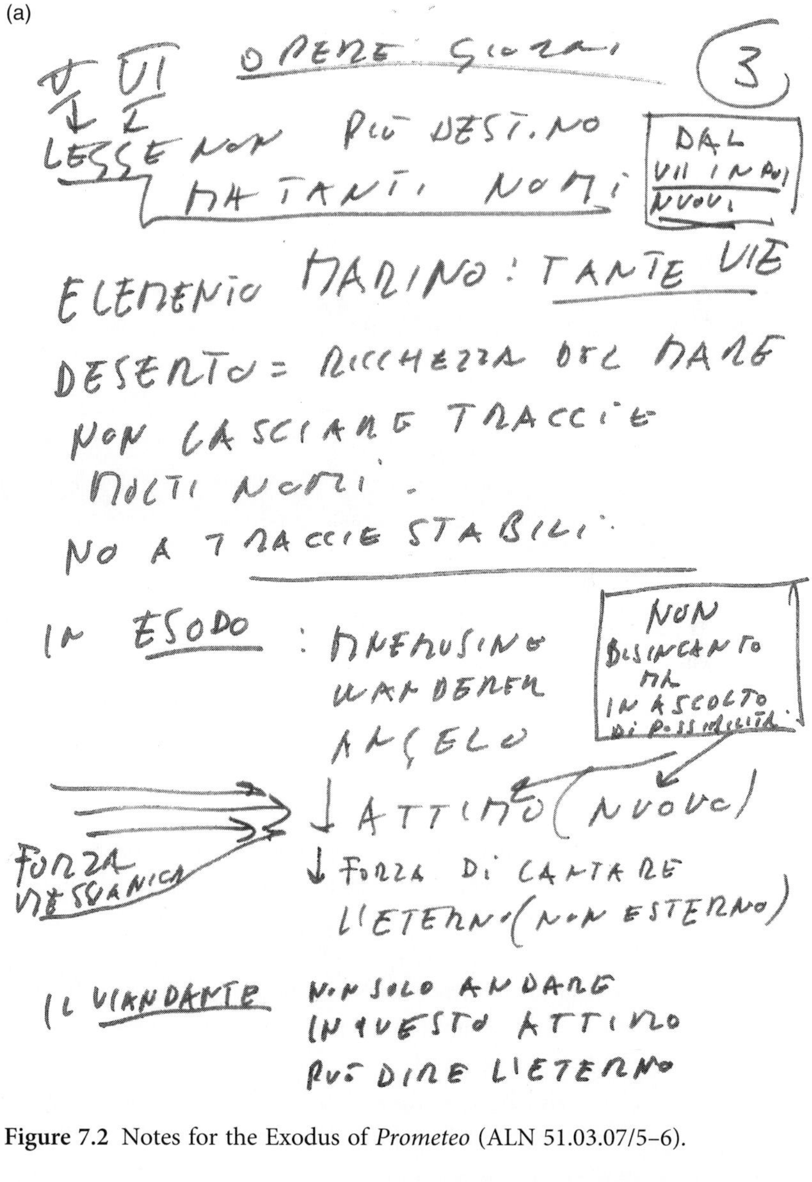


**Figure 7.2** Notes for the Exodus of *Prometeo* (ALN 51.03.07/5–6).

(b)

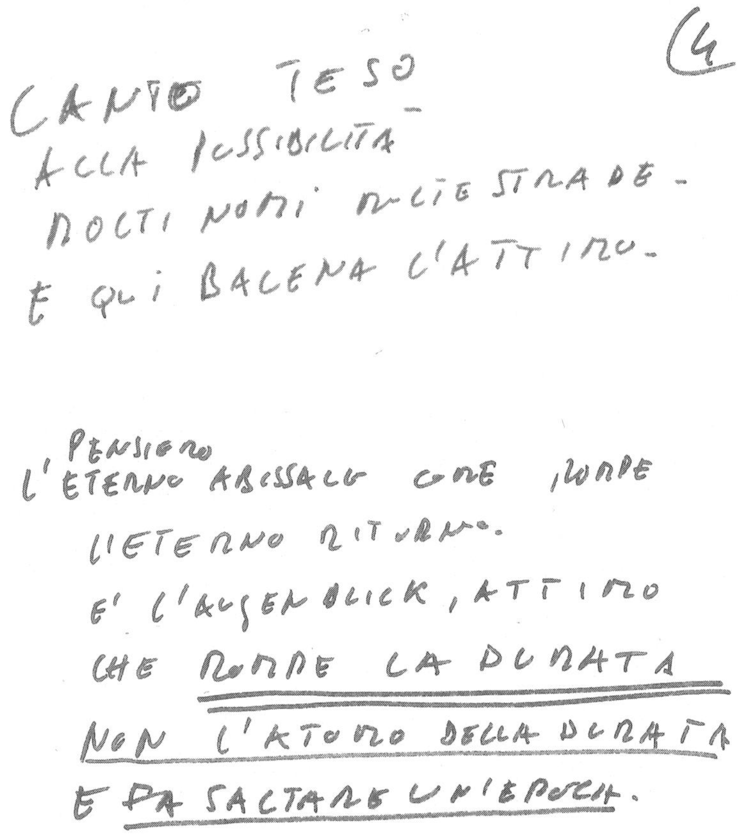


**Figure 7.2** (*cont.*)

*drân* in this preliminary 'pezzo di Mnemosine' – the reason, perhaps, why Nono regarded *Das atmende Klarsein* as a true breakthrough for *Prometeo* and still used it as 'Esodo' in 1984. Precisely because Nono did not merely set a text in *Das atmende Klarsein*, but developed a musical language, the work still encapsulated the philosophical ground of the project as a whole.

Contrary to Cacciari's suggestion on the use of Rilke, Nono's approach is completely different from the use of Hölderlin in *Fragmente – Stille, an Diotima*. The multi-layered text collage is no longer assigned independent musical layers. Instead, Nono fragments the text further, extracts the key words and strings them into one kaleidoscopic, translucent band of suspended moments of 'pure' vocal sound, a 'narrow strip of harvest land' which slowly meanders through the prism of the predetermined interval categories. Special emphasis, in terms of intelligibility, is given to words of appeal: *Dí*, *Siehe*, *EIΠEIN* and *Ascolta* (say, see, listen). These are the first words to be singled out for syllabic analysis and, together with 'Aus Lust ins Freie' (out of desire into the open) and 'KPHNA' (spring), among the very few words which are meant to be understood.[106] Much more important than the intelligibility of the text, I believe, is the perceptibility of the 'moment' of *drân* as an instant of total presence and awareness, true human Being, the unmediated 'clarity' of which is reserved for the human voice alone.

## Reflections on the harmonic system

Sketches for *Prometeo* show that Nono marked and numbered each individual 'moment' of the vocal parts of *Das atmende Klarsein* and also selected parts of *Io, frammento dal Prometeo* for possible reuse.[107] How these individual units or 'moments' of vocal music were to reappear in *Prometeo* with different texts and in completely new contexts has been analysed by Melkert.[108] Many of the direct quotations from *Das atmende Klarsein* were integrated at a very late stage, during the substantial revision between the Venice premiere and that of the final version in Milan (1985). *Das atmende Klarsein* no longer served as 'Esodo' but, as Nono told Richard at the time, was scattered and interspersed instead. Closer scrutiny of the score of *Prometeo* will quickly lead to the realisation that – whether quoted, altered or new – the same pitch sets occur in ever-changing, truly kaleidoscopic combinations, which are indeed best described as 'constellations'.

Continuous reshuffling of compositional units of this kind was possible because the parameters Nono set for the composition of *Das atmende Klarsein* were later extended, but not fundamentally altered.[109] In other words, *Das atmende Klarsein* was the first manifestation of a system conceived to serve the composition of *Prometeo* as a whole. What, then, constitutes this all-encompassing compositional system and how does it relate to the scala enigmatica material which, as Nono always insisted, remained fundamental? The much-cited list of scala enigmatica transpositions from

[106] ALN 45.02.03/01–02.

[107] The first two vocal sections of *Das atmende Klarsein* are segmented and numbered 1–51 (ALN 51.17.03/01–12r). Similarly, bars 60–95 of the first movement of *Io, frammento dal Prometeo* are segmented, arranged in reverse order and numbered 1–21 (ALN 51.17.04/01–06).

[108] Melkert, «*Far del silenzio cristallo*», 118–94.

[109] Such play with a limited number of constellations already happens within *Das atmende Klarsein*: vocal sections III and IV derive from material exposed in sections I and II; Melkert, «*Far del silenzio cristallo*», 37–50.

the time of the quartet shows that Nono did indeed return to this material for *Prometeo* (Figure 6.2). The sketches Nono himself chose to publish on the inside covers of *Verso Prometeo* (1984) and the programme for the Festival d'automne (Paris, 1987) demonstrate that the pitch organisation was to make use of the same scale segmentation as employed in the quartet. Figure 7.3 shows that the ascending scala enigmatica on C is once again divided into the familiar segments C–C♯–E, E–F♯–G♯–B♭ and B♭–B–C, now labelled A, B and C. In addition, Nono notates a further pitch category 'T': two sets of chromatically interlocking tritones on E. All four pitch cells are explicitly linked to matters of content:

| *Mythos* | | | | |
|---|---|---|---|---|
| Gea | Dei | Uomini | Una | *Mythologia* |
| [T] | [B] | [C] | [B+C] | [A] |

This schematic disposition is obviously tied to Cacciari's reading of the Prometheus myth. Under the heading *Mythos*, the first to appear is Gea (Gaia), the primordial goddess and common mother of god and man, whose power exceeds that of all those born to her. This primordial power is assigned the category 'T'. This category T is fundamentally independent of the scala enigmatica, and yet its core intervals (8, T, IV–V, 2–7–9) are also mapped onto the scale. Two segments from the scala enigmatica on C are then assigned to Gaia's descendents: segment B (the basis for the 'Diotima' layer in the quartet) is assigned to the race of gods (Dei) and segment C (the basis for the quartet's '*Tiefe*' layer) to the race of men (Uomini). The combined segments B + C are further coupled with 'Una', a reference to Cacciari's original starting point in Pindar as it was to appear at the end of 'Hölderlin': 'Una dell'Uomo/ Una del Dio/ la stirpe/ Del Dio/ fratelli infelici'. With its very different, commentary function, the *Mythologia* is set apart from the principal players of the *Mythos* and coupled with segment A (the basis of '*Stille*' and '*Unruhe*' in the quartet).

In *Prometeo* this scale segmentation no longer gives rise to distinct compositional layers. The limits of these were perhaps explored to the full in the quartet. According to my understanding, the scala enigmatica on C is now conceived as a fixed harmonic field from which certain tonal centres are derived in loose accordance with this initial dispositon of material and content. Not unlike the all-interval row Nono used for almost all of his works of the mid and late 1950s, the scala enigmatica on C thus becomes a constant point of reference for a myriad of possible pitch constellations (and I firmly believe that the scala on C is the only transposition Nono uses for the whole of *Prometeo*). In contrast to the all-interval

**Figure 7.3** Reflections on the pitch material for *Prometeo*.

series, however, this scale is not twelve-tone and contains only eight pitches (including the F from the descending scale, which Nono adds for a further tritone relationship).[110] The full chromatic total is thus spanned not by the scala enigmatica material, but by the other harmonic category T. This category, too, has its precedent in the string quartet, where open strings and tritones were added *ad libitum*. Sets of interlocking tritones (or fifths/fourths, depending on one's perspective) are now much more prominent and constitute the true harmonic backbone of *Prometeo*. As Nono remarked in several interviews, they were also deeply rooted in the music of Varèse, Scriabin and Schoenberg:

> The music of Varèse in particular was a formidable innovation by virtue of this projection of the harmonic space, with the octave, the fifth and the tritones, which in a very similar manner is found also in Scriabin and Schoenberg.[111]

A further important model is mentioned in conversation with Restagno:

> The famous interval of the fifth and the tritone, which Scriabin uses in his Sonatas, is also typical of Schönberg and of Varèse: the octaves in Varèse, those superimpositions of octaves which are reminiscent of the beginning of Mahler's first symphony where spaces are defined, sudden openings, which now recur to me emphatically.[112]

The beginning of Mahler's first symphony fascinated Nono. With the performance instruction 'Wie ein Naturlaut' and the single (tuning) pitch A, Mahler immediately spans the entire registral space from the lowest octave up to the highest harmonics. To Nono, this mysterious 'natural' opening represented 'not a beginning', but a truly spatial sensation, where 'one immediately finds oneself drawn into the large breathing space of an infinite valley'.[113] The sensation of being drawn into the sound, of being within the sound and becoming part of the sound space was also the ideal for *Prometeo*, Nono's very own 'Lied von der Erde'. Not surprisingly, the Mahlerian instruction 'Wie ein Naturlaut' appears in association with 'Gea' and its related category T, which was clearly designed to allow such 'sudden openings', not into octaves but into fifths, and those on 'natural' open strings in particular.

Nono thus thought of Gea and the assigned category T in both spatial and intervallic terms. The characteristic intervals of this category (8, IV–V,

110 ALN 51.21.02/01. 111 Nono, 'I futuri felici' (1987), *Scritti*, II, 410.
112 Nono, 'Un'autobiographia', *Scritti*, II, 496.
113 Nono, 'Verso *Prometeo*', *Scritti*, I, 394.

T and 2–7–9) then also 'govern' the harmonic sphere assigned to god and man. As can be seen in Figure 7.3 (and another sketch with the added F), these intervals are systematically mapped onto the scala enigmatica on C, and it is with these that Nono will determine the large-scale compositional processes of the work. Microtonal extension is further applied to both harmonic categories. In terms of the relation between material and content, this initial set-up is extremely clever. As in the reading of the myth, Nono works with different 'laws' on two levels. The omnipotent natural forces, Gaia–Themis–Ananke, are assigned the simpler and more 'primordial' material which reigns *Ekdike*, above the laws of god and man, with the entire pitch spectrum. Its sets of interlocking tritones/fifths are designed to span the chromatic total and are deliberately restricted in terms of intervallic content. The subordinate laws of god and man lie within this 'natural' cycle, but are clearly emancipated and demarcated in the form of the more sophisticated scala enigmatica on C. Because the tragedy of Prometheus is generally marked by the gods' absence, I believe that the scala enigmatica on C primarily came to represent the *Grenzen der Menschheit*, the 'Limits of Humanity' which are to be transcended and overcome. In terms of the relation of material and content, it is therefore extremely fascinating to see what lies within the scala enigmatica and what lies without. Not by chance do the four pitches which lie outside the scala enigmatica (G–D–A–E♭) comprise the three 'natural' open-string pitches which are common to violin, viola and cello. Furthermore, Gaia's sets of interlocking tritones are often based on these four pitches. The overriding use of the interval categories of the Gaia material, however, also ensures that a genuine dialectic between the two types of material ensues. It is with their compositional application that Nono controls the large-scale processes and allows for total assimilation as well as maximum contrast, sudden openings into Rilkean *Klarsein* and truly disconcerting clouds of microtonal tension.

By means of a few key examples I will now show how I understand the harmonic system for *Prometeo* to function in detail. Seamless fusion of the two types of harmonic material is practiced to great effect in the opening choral section of *Das atmende Klarsein*, for example. In concordance with the opening text, 'Nach spätem Gewitter, das atmende Klarsein', Nono selects the 'purest' and most 'natural' of his interval categories: 'IV–V'. Example 7.1 shows the 'narrow strip' of interlocking fourths and fifths that forms the basis of this opening choral wave. The wave begins and ends on the octave dividing F♯ of the scala enigmatica on C and meanders solely through open fourths and fifths. These interlock either by means of a tie, or in steps of a semitone or tone. The entire range of fourths and fifths is taken from either the ascending scala enigmatica on C or the category T on

**Example 7.1** (a) Category T on D. (b) Scala enigmatica on C. (c) *Das atmende Klarsein*, reduction of the opening choral section.

D. Each of these categories contains four different fourths/fifths, one of which they share. In my reduction of the section, all fourths/fifths from the category T on D are marked in round brackets and the common fourth/fifth C♯–G♯ in square brackets. The two categories are used in exactly equal measure: the sphere of man is in equilibrium and complete harmony with that of nature. Still, the scala enigmatica is given precedence as Nono begins and ends with the material from the scala enigmatica on C. The last two fifths, A–D and B–F♯, are further coupled with the all-important word 'Klarsein'. With this symbolic 'meaning', the final fifth B–F♯ (from the sphere of man) later serves as a kind of tonal centre for the whole of *Prometeo*.

If the beginning of *Das atmende Klarsein* is an example of completely balanced and homogeneous fusion, a chord from the Finale of *Io, frammento dal Prometeo* (IX) demonstrates that the two pitch categories can also clash and negate each other. The text of the Finale of *Io* is identical to that of the first Stasimon in *Prometeo* and stems from Euripides' *Alcestis*. In *Prometeo*, this Stasimon is placed after the irrevocable split between god and man (at the end of 'Hölderlin'), when man finds himself alone in the face of Ananke, the subject of this text by Euripides. The Stasimon ends

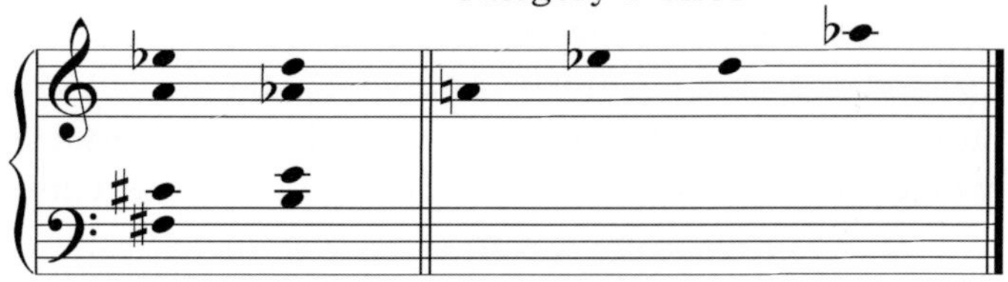


**Example 7.2** The 'Manfred' chord.

with the line 'Inaccessa ha la cima' (Inaccessible she holds the summit). Example 7.2 shows the first chord of this last phrase as it was set in *Io, frammento dal Prometeo* (bar 508). The male voices, who represent Prometeo in much of the latter work, are here assigned the two fifths F♯–C♯ and B–E from the scala enigmatica on C. These fifths are now drawn into a dissonant chord with a second set of pitches from the category T on A in the female voices. 'Gaia' here clearly denies access to the 'clarity' of its peaks. As Melkert has shown, precisely this chord was later coupled with the syncopated rhythm of the opening of Schumann's *Manfred Overture* to form the violent, microtonally enriched orchestral flashes which Nono inserted in the final 1985 version of *Prometeo*.[114] Overpowered by the beauty of inaccessible summits at dawn, Byron's *Manfred*, too, is forced to recognise the '*Grenzen der Menschheit*' in the face of Ananke:

> I lean no more on super-human aid,
> It hath no power upon the past, and for
> The future, till the past be gulf'd in darkness,
> It is not of my search. – My mother Earth![115]

An example in which the Gaia material does indeed span the chromatic total is found in the music of the Third Island in the intertwined *3°–4°–5° Isola*. Again the two harmonic categories come together here, but each

[114] Both Jeschke and Melkert regard this chord as a conglomeration of fifths; Jeschke, *Prometeo*, 149–51; Melkert, *«Far del silenzio cristallo»*, 114, 174–75. Melkert traces the chord back to the Finale of *Io, frammento dal Prometeo* (*ibid.*, 175). The way the chord is spaced and distributed in the male and female voices in *Io, frammento dal Prometeo*, however, suggests that Nono was thinking not of fifths alone, but of two distinct harmonic categories.

[115] Byron, *Manfred*, 282.

follows its own compositional laws and is clearly distinguished by means of different forces. The dramatic situation is the following: Prometheus is reconciled with Zeus and sets sail for Athens, assured that no god will take the fire from him. Cacciari's text describes this tragic journey to Athens from the slightly different perspectives of Prometeo and the commentating Mitologia. Nono does not distinguish Cacciari's two columns of text, but merges them into a single vocal and instrumental layer: the female soloists (SSAA) accompanied by the solo wind and string trios (who double, take up or anticipate the pitches of the singers). Example 7.3(a) shows that this vocal layer strictly adheres to the pitches of the scala enigmatica on C (with the exception of the last two entries). Nono begins with the first four pitches of the scale (C–C♯–E–F) or scale segment 'A' (initially assigned to the Mitologia) coupled with the F from the descending scale for a further 7+ relationship. This symmetric pitch cell then expands outwards in chromatic steps on either side until all pitches of the scala enigmatica on C are in play in the third block and the layer continues to play through the pitches of the scale with a predominant focus on the inherent 2–7–9 relationships. Only at the very end do the four remaining pitches from the Gaia material seep in to form perfect Gaia formations (chromatically interlocking fifths).

The scala enigmatica pitches in the vocal layer are gradually enveloped by a mysterious and ever denser orchestral texture (marked 'sempre *ppppp*'). The pitches of this expanding orchestral layer are notated in the double system below the vocal layer in Example 7.3(a). The orchestras begin on the fundamental pitch C, spaced out in truly Mahlerian fashion: a 'sudden opening' spanning five octaves and rendered by violins and trombones in anti-clockwise motion from opposite poles in space (orchestras I/II–IV/III–II/I). Over ten block entries, the remaining eleven pitches and one more C are gradually added to build up a porous twelve-tone texture, stacked in fifths and spanning the entire orchestral register. Example 7.3(b) shows this twelve-tone chord in fifths (with its three Cs notated separately) and Example 7.3(c) summarises the principle of pitch addition which, once again, recalls Nono's all-interval row of the fifties. If Prometheus' journey is conditioned by the 'Limits of Humanity', it also leads over the all-encompassing sea of the natural forces which gradually pervade the entire registral and auditory space.

These few examples suffice to show that the two harmonic categories allow for total assimilation but can also be diametrically opposed. As previously in the quartet, the two categories are linked to content, but the boundaries are much more fleeting, being controlled by a choice of intervals that apply to both. In terms of intervallic content, Gaia's category 'T' is more limited, but also much more spacious and 'open'. The scala enigmatica on C then

(a)

**Example 7.3** (a) '3°–4°–5° Isola', pitch reduction of the Third Island. (b) Twelve-tone chord in fifths. (c) Principle of pitch addition.

(b)

(c)

**Example 7.3** (*cont.*)

provides Nono with manifold possibilities for filling – populating – these earthly spaces. However, when reduced to the intervals it shares with the Gaia material, it can also be completely assimilated. In philosophical terms, Gaia is, of course, also the symbol for the unattainable origin, and the scala enigmatica is the means to move away from the 'clarity' of this origin. Yet it also carries within it the possibility of returning to this clarity.

## *Prometeo* (1985)

In the following overview of the final 1985 version of *Prometeo* I will focus on how these harmonic categories are used to dramatise and elucidate Cacciari's reading of *Prometeo*. I will look at their distribution between the forces and examine the large-scale processes in particular. Two days of intensive discussions with André Richard further allow me to show how *Prometeo* is set up electronically and how this tragedy of listening unfolds in space.[116] Nono himself always emphasised the importance of adapting

[116] There is hardly any information about the use of live electronics in the printed manuscript score. Without André Richard's invaluable information on all matters

to the acoustics of each new venue. However, there is also a more or less fixed choreography of sound that has to be realisable in each performance space. Certain elements of the set-up are consistently adhered to by the team of the Experimentalstudio and may thus be regarded as the pillars of the spatial dramaturgy. These 'pillars' take the layout of Renzo Piano's 'struttura' into account, yet no longer physically make use of it. Abandoned, too, was the computer system 4i, references to which are still found in the score. Nono explored this advanced IRCAM technology together with Alvise Vidolin at the Centro di Sonologia Computazionale (CSC) in Padua and used it for added synthesised sounds in the Venice premiere in 1984. The results cannot have been entirely satisfactory, however. Its use was already much reduced in Milan and synthesised sound was dispensed with for good thereafter.[117]

Elements of Nono's original spatial vision remain of great importance, however. As Richard explains, each set-up for *Prometeo* should take the height of Piano's ark as a model. With a height of 2.4 m for each of the three tiers, Piano's performance space in the church of San Lorenzo rose to a height of almost 10 m, with a further extension for the highest of the loudspeakers. Within this extremely high and multi-levelled space, no source of sound was or should be placed at the same height. This rule applies just as much to the disposition of the musicians as it does to that of the loudspeakers. Since the 1987 Frankfurt performance there has been a consensus as to how the various sound sources should be placed in relation to the central control panel. While exact locations for the musicians and loudspeakers have to be determined anew each time, there is actually not as much freedom to the arrangement as one might have thought. In other words, the set-up has to allow a spatial choreography that is more or less

regarding the set-up, the use of live electronics and the movement of sound in space I would not have been able to discuss *Prometeo* in this way. The insights I gained from this intensive and extremely enlightening encounter with Richard have corrected many of my all-too-academic misconceptions, raised my own listening awareness and helped me to understand much of what is written in this text. For this I am immensely grateful. I also want to thank André's wife Danièle for her friendship and hospitality during those extremely long days (20–21 March 2009).

117 On Nono's use of the computer system 4i see Zattra, 'Il Centro di sonologia computazionale', in Durante and Zattra (eds.), *Vent'anni di musica elettronica all'Università di Padova*, 41–102 (66–71). Vidolin recounts that the 4i system was employed for the Prologue, Isola 1° and Interludio 2°, but he too emphasises that its use was marginal; Sassanelli, 'Intervista ad Alvise Vidolin', *ibid.*, 114–19 (118). Vidolin further kept an informative diary, cited in Zattra, 'Utopia e realtà nella ricerca informatica del Prometeo', unpublished paper presented at the conference The Dramaturgy of Sound in the Music of Luigi Nono (Venice, 13–15 June 2009).

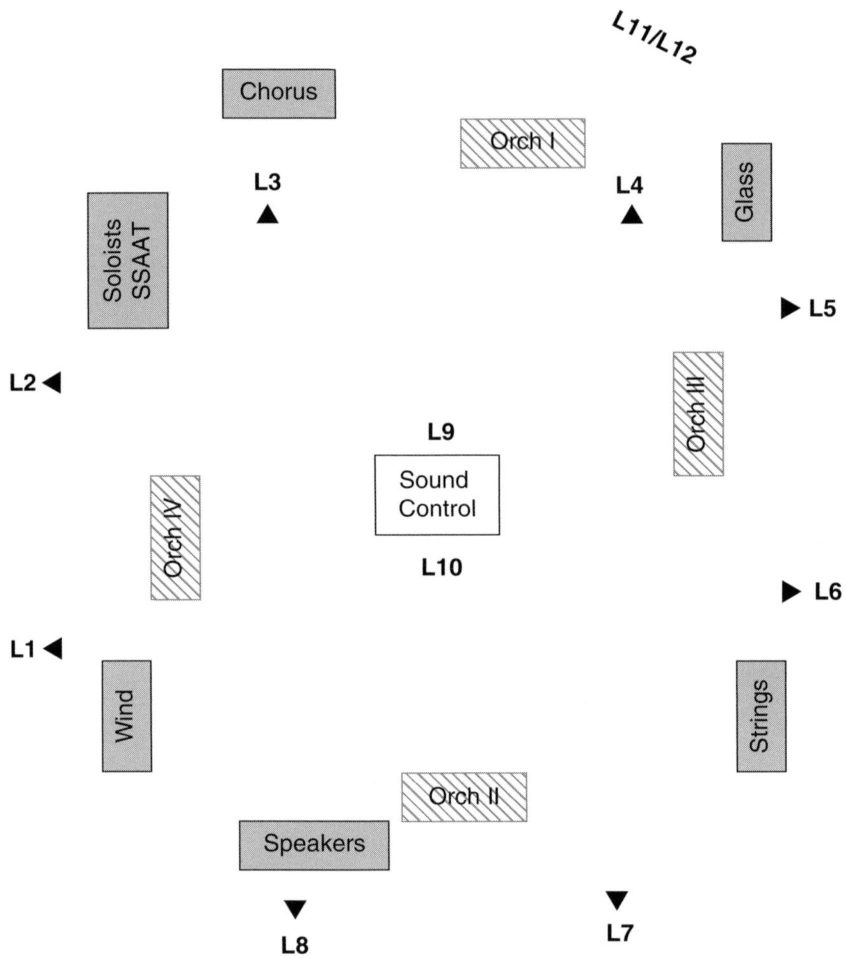


**Figure 7.4** *Prometeo*, spatial disposition of forces and loudspeakers.

fixed and indeed an inherent part of the composition (although it is not notated and became established solely in performance practice).

According to Richard, the ideal set-up of the sound sources is arranged as shown in Figure 7.4. The four orchestras are positioned around the audience at different heights to form a lopsided circuit of their own. The orchestras are generally not subjected to live-electronic sound transformation and thus form a 'natural' basis of surround sound. Their orbit is evident from the score in which they are notated in anti-clockwise order (I–IV–II–III). In addition, *Prometeo* requires six groups of vocal and instrumental soloists: a chorus of twelve, five soloists (SSAAT), two speakers, a wind trio (bfl/fl/picc, cbcl/cl/E♭ cl, tb/euph/trb), a string trio (vla, vcl, db) and three percussionists on glass bells. These six groups are all subjected to live-electronic sound transformation and placed around the audience with as much difference in height as possible. The greatest fluctuation in height, however, is reserved for the distribution of the twelve loudspeakers. Beginning with L1 near the wind trio, eight of the loudspeakers form a clockwise loop around the audience. The lowest loudspeaker (L3) is near the chorus and faces the audience, the highest (L8) is located near the speakers behind the audience and all others are placed at irregular heights in between. As indicated in Figure 7.4, this loop of loudspeakers is linked to that of the six solo groups, but there should, of course, be sufficient difference in height to avoid interference between the live sound and its electronically transformed transmission. Four additional loudspeakers are placed outside this loop: L9 and L10 are suspended high above the central control panel, while L11 and L12 are placed either at the far front or at the rear to transmit sound indirectly from the floor or ceiling. With this template, I will now go through the final version of *Prometeo*, section by section, to examine the large-scale developments of the drama and its spatial dramaturgy.

## Prologo (*ca.* 20′)

Orchestras I–IV, chorus, soloists (SAT), speakers, solo wind, solo strings, glass

Ancient Greek text: Hesiod, *Theogony*; Hesychius, *Lexicon*; Aeschylus, *Prometheus Bound*; Sophocles, *Trachiniae*

Italian text: Cacciari, *Il Maestro del gioco* I and II (based on Benjamin's Theses II and IX)

The Prologue alone makes use of all available forces. The scene for the drama is set with Gaia emerging from Chaos as the powerful, all-encompassing origin. Fragments of Hesiod's *Theogony* and various other Greek sources then serve to trace the common genealogy of god and man up to the birth of Prometheus. On a second textual level, Nono makes use of Cacciari's *Maestro del gioco* to ask his audience to 'listen' to the fragments of ancient Greek as a sound of the distant past that continues to resonate in the present:

> The past carries with it a secret index by which it is referred to redemption. Doesn't a breath of the air that pervaded earlier days caress us as well? In the voices we hear, isn't there an echo of now silent ones? Don't the women we court have sisters they no longer recognize? If so, then there is a secret agreement between past generations and the present one. Then our coming

> was expected on Earth. Then, like every generation that preceded us, we have been endowed with a *weak* messianic power, a power on which the past has a claim. Such a claim cannot be settled cheaply. The historical materialist is aware of this.[118]

The first two stanzas of Cacciari's *Maestro del gioco* are inspired primarily by this second Thesis, in which Benjamin introduces the concept of *Erlösung* (redemption). The term *Erlösung* was most probably taken from Franz Rosenzweig's *Der Stern der Erlösung* (a book of great importance also to Cacciari and Nono).[119] Benjamin associates this term with remembrance. In the service of historical materialism, Benjamin assigns 'a redemptive theological quality to remembrance' that is capable 'of "making into something incomplete" the apparently "complete" suffering of the victims of the past'.[120] In this sense, remembrance is 'one of the tasks of the theological dwarf hidden in materialism' – the *Maestro del gioco*. However,

> neither the remembrance and contemplation in consciousness of past injustices nor historical research are sufficient in Benjamin's eyes. For redemption to take place, there must be reparation – in Hebrew, *tikkun* – for the suffering and grief inflicted on the defeated generations, and the accomplishment of the objectives they struggled for and failed to attain.[121]

Precisely for this reason we humans are 'endowed with a *weak* messianic power, a power on which the past has a claim' and which 'cannot be settled cheaply':

> Messianic/revolutionary redemption is a task assigned to us by past generations. There is no Messiah sent from Heaven: we are ourselves the Messiah; each generation possesses a small portion of messianic power, which it must strive to exert.[122]

The idea of a human 'messianic power' (heretical from the standpoint of orthodox Judaism) is also found in the work of Martin Buber, another of the central-European Jewish intellectuals read by Cacciari and Nono.[123]

In conversation with Kropfinger, Nono would later emphasise the importance of Benjamin's *Theses* and the 'weak messianic power' in particular:

[118] Benjamin, *On the Concept of History*, Thesis II, Löwy, *Fire Alarm*, 29–30.

[119] Nono refers to Rosenzweig as 'the great master of Benjamin' ('Un'autobiografia', *Scritti*, II, 497) and credits Cacciari for introducing Rosenzweig in Italy ('. . . kein Anfang – kein Ende . . .', *Scritti*, II, 456). Cacciari wrote on Rosenzweig in *Icone della legge*.

[120] Löwy, *Fire Alarm*, 31. [121] Löwy, *Fire Alarm*, 32. [122] Löwy, *Fire Alarm*, 32.

[123] Like Rosenzweig, Buber is referred to frequently in Nono's texts and interviews of the 1980s.

> You see, *Prometeo* is a combinatorial composition by Massimo Cacciari with various texts from Aeschylus to Benjamin. He took twelve fragments from Benjamin's *Theses on the Concept of History*, which, from beginning to end, are set against other texts in a contrapuntal way. The central word in *Prometeo* also stems from Benjamin: 'the weak messianic power'; the 'messianic' – that is the power of non-violence.[124]

The Prologue homes in on this central 'messianic power' with the second stanza of Cacciari's *Maestro del gioco*. Stanza I initially evokes the mysterious – redemptive – vibrations of our 'secret agreements' with the past. A brief allusion to the 'Angelus novus' then links past and present in stanza II. Nono consistently marks these first two stanzas of the *Maestro del gioco* with the words 'past' and 'present', and this division essentially determines the Prologue's bipartite form.

Another concept, which is not yet present in the text but almost immediately of relevance to the music, is Benjamin's distinction between 'homogeneous, empty time' (which he associates with the continuous, chronological and merely accumulative methods of universal historiography) and 'now-time' (which, 'as a model of messianic time', is associated with the methods of the true historical materialist who seeks to seize and take hold of 'a revolutionary chance in the fight for the oppressed past'). In addition to the textual layers, Nono also introduces two independent time layers, each of which requires its own conductor. Throughout the prologue, one of the layers moves at the slowest speed of all (♩ = 30). This extremely slow and 'homogeneous' layer of time is consistently linked to the 'narration' of Hesiod's genealogy. The other, much more varied and dramatic, layer surges out of this continuum with speeds ranging from ♩ = 30 to ♩ = 152 and is assigned to the *Maestro del gioco*. As is evident from Nono's notes, this 'Master of the Game' was to represent the

| | |
|---|---|
| Tema dell'attimo | Theme of the moment |
| Nuova terra | new land |
| Nuovo tempo | new time[125] |

With the comment 'Like X/ Like a psalm against the idols'[126] Nono further specifically refers to Benjamin's Thesis X, and it is hard not to read this as a response to the political situation in Italy at the time:

> The themes which monastic discipline assigned to friars for meditation were designed to turn them away from the world and its affairs. The thoughts we

[124] Nono, '. . . kein Anfang – kein Ende . . .', 168; *Scritti*, II, 456. [125] ALN 51.06.04/06.
[126] 'Come X/ Come salmo contro gli idoli', ALN 51.06.04/06.

> are developing here have a similar aim. At a moment when the politicians in whom the opponents of Fascism had placed their hopes are prostrate, and confirm their defeat by betraying their own cause, these observations are intended to extricate the political worldlings from the snares in which the traitors have entangled them. The assumption here is that those politicians' stubborn faith in progress, their confidence in their 'base in the masses', and finally, their servile integration in an uncontrollable apparatus are three aspects of the same thing. This consideration is meant to suggest the high price our customary mode of thought will have to pay for a conception of history that avoids any complicity with the concept of history to which those politicians still adhere.[127]

As a 'Psalm against the idols', the *Maestro del gioco* is to break with our 'customary mode of thought' also in music. The associated keyword 'recitativo biblico' reveals that Nono, too, assigned 'a redemptive quality to remembrance' in order to achieve this goal. The Evangelist of Bach's passions is named as another model.[128] And Nono's gaze goes back even further into the musical past, to the music of Josquin, Machaut, Vittoria and Dowland (some of the composers named in the sketches). The relics of this musical past, however, are always used in view of the music of the future, reflected through the prism of Nono's own harmonic system and subjected to the most avant-garde techniques of sound emission and transformation available to him at the time.

Of overriding importance in the Prologue is the 'Gaia' material. In this sense, it is indeed Gaia who 'gives birth' to all that follows. In the tradition of Greek tragedy, the drama begins with the commentating chorus as a distant 'coro lontanissimo'. Throughout the first part of the Prologue, the function of this 'distant chorus' is to draw some of the otherwise spoken names of Hesiod's genealogy into song and the first name to be sung is that of Gaia. This name alone is rendered a cappella, and the score alone does not do justice to the magic of this opening statement in the female voices. Notated is a progression of fifths linked by a tone. The live electronics simultaneously echo these choral pitches a tritone below. There is no indication of dynamics, but, according to Richard, it is of the utmost importance that this first choral statement comes into being almost imperceptibly from silence. As shown in Figure 7.5, the extremely quiet vocal sound is transmitted through loudspeakers L11 and L12, which do not project the sound directly towards the audience, but rather reflect it off the walls or the ceiling of the hall. This

[127] Benjamin, Thesis X, in Löwy, *Fire Alarm*, 68.

[128] 'Quasi Evangelista di Matteo Giovanni' ALN 51.17.01/06.

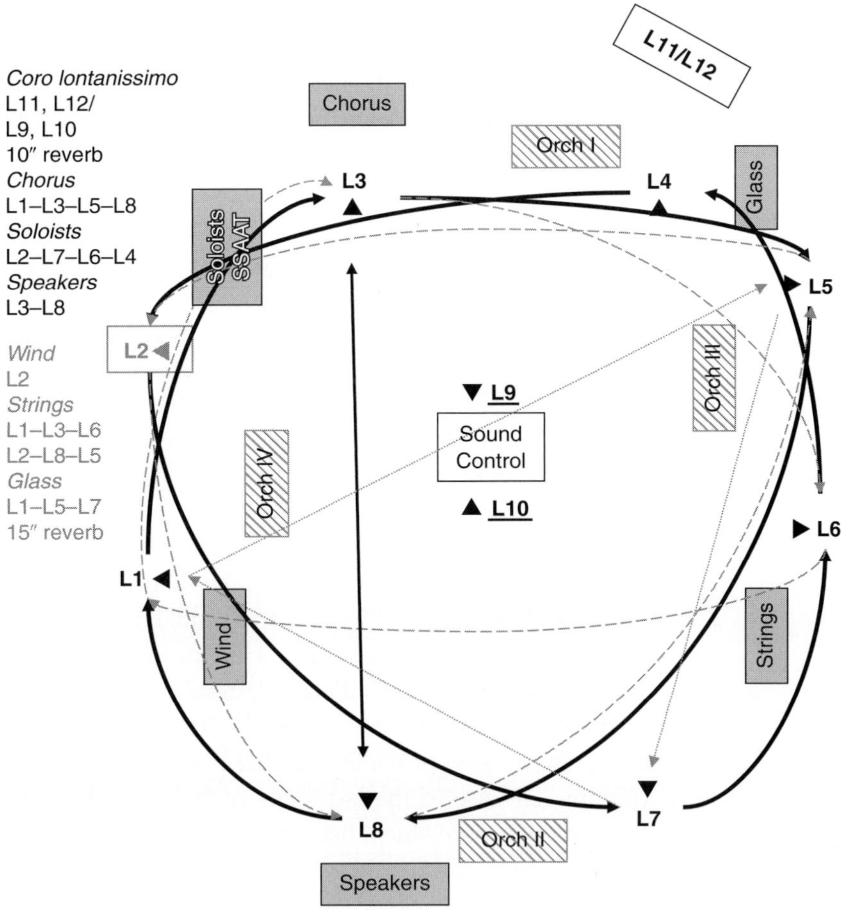


**Figure 7.5** *Prometeo*, spatial set-up for 'Prologo' I.

creates the unsettling sensation of an as yet undefined, 'yawning' space, which is further enhanced by a large reverb of 10″.

In terms of pitch, this opening statement is once again an equilibrium of the scala enigmatica and 'Gaia' materials: the initial fifth F–C and its tritone echo B–F♯ are both inherent in the scala enigmatica on C, whereas the fifth D–A with its A♭–E♭ echo belongs to the category T on D (the same pitch set is also the 'Gaia' component of the 'Manfred' chord shown in Example 7.2). The electronic tritone echo, of course, turns the whole statement into the category T format. This live-electronic echo gradually fades out on the suspended fifth D–A, thus allowing a final glimpse of the purity of *Das atmende Klarsein* from which this opening statement is actually taken. As Melkert has shown, the sung names of the 'coro lontanissimo' were added during the final revisions of *Prometeo* and mostly stem from *Das atmende Klarsein.*[129] Not all interventions of the 'coro lontanissimo' are quotations from *Das atmende Klarsein*, however. 'Klarsein' is ultimately reserved for the names of 'Gaia', 'Ouranos' and 'Oceanos' (Earth, Sky and Sea) and for Prometheus and his parents, the Titan Iapetos and the Oceanid Clymene. In contrast, the lineage of the gods is far less 'clear'. The two other sung names, Cronos and Rhea, are not quotations from *Das atmende Klarsein*, and the name of their son Zeus is not even lifted into the realm of song. In spatial terms, the sung names certainly stand out. When almost all other musical layers are kept in constant flux and motion, they cut through the spatial commotion as moments of Benjaminian 'Stillstellung' (arrest of happening), transmitted through either the indirect loudspeakers (L11 and L12, like 'Gaia') or those above the central control panel (L9 and L10, like 'Ouranos', bars 22–24), or both (L9–L12, like 'd'Ourea' (the mountains), bars 32–33).

Before man's '*Flucht* ' (flight) towards 'Fruchtland' can begin, however, the omnipotent Gaia–Themis has yet to appear. 'GAIA–GEA–THEMIS–OCEANINA–CLIMENE' Nono writes in sketches for the Prologue, and thus focuses on Gaia as the natural power through which the knowledge of the possible fallibility of Zeus is transmitted to Prometheus. Sea and Sky, too, are immediately associated with this power and poetically circumscribed with the words 'ondate – desteso' (waves – aroused) and 'venti – e sospeso' (winds – and suspended).[130] The recurring term 'URANO STELLATO' (starry sky) provides a further poetic image of vast natural *Klarsein* (reminiscent also of the last scene of Dallapiccola's *Ulisse*). So how does this natural origin which, like Ananke, rules outside and above the laws of god and man, first manifest itself in Nono's music? I firmly believe that, with all its philosophical connotations, 'Gaia' is assigned not only the interval category T (outside and above the scala enigmatica material) but also, and much more perceptibly so, her very own instrumental force: the four orchestras. In spatial terms alone, the orchestras are clearly a force apart. They form their own spatial orbit and follow their own 'natural' laws in regard to the motion of sound. With one exception, they are also the only source of sound which is not subjected to live-electronic sound transformation, i.e. the only truly 'natural' source of sound.[131]

After 'Gaia' has been announced by the coro lontanissimo, the strings of the four orchestras take up the 'Gaia' component of this opening chorus:

[129] The quotations are identified in Melkert, «*Far del silenzio cristallo*», 122–25. The opening fragment is taken from the third choral section, bars 11–12 ('di cielo [stellato]' (of the [starry] sky)).

[130] ALN 51.14.04/11.

[131] Four orchestral instruments are exceptionally singled out for amplification in the First Island.

the fifth D–A. On the brink of audibility this fifth is diffused microtonally and used to branch out into ever higher and lower octaves, gradually seeping into all registers and the entire performance space. The influence of Mahler's 'wie ein Naturlaut' is undeniable here. With slow, sweeping bow strokes that make use of the entire hair surface, one is perhaps drawn not so much 'into the large breathing space of an infinite valley', but into the 'magic vibration' of a large breathing forest. Nono often spoke of his fascination with the Black Forest, in the midst of which he resided while working in Freiburg, and openly attests to 'a relation between the Black Forest and the extreme pianissimo, on the brink of audibility' in his compositions of the 1980s.[132] Discussing Mahler's 'Naturlaut', Cacciari also draws in the idea of the primordial origin:

> The nature of the «Ur», of an *arché* in which there would reside the original, essential sense of the object, of the sound, is not certain . . . but is instead silence: there where you really find yourself in silence, you will start to hear the nature of the sound . . .[133]

'This is just the *discovery* I was talking about', Nono replies, 'in Germany, in the Black Forest: music from nature, based on resonant silences of inaudibility . . .'[134]

With an increasingly dissonant agglomeration of microtonally enriched fifths and tritones in all instruments and registers, the resonant open forest soon contracts into a dense crackling thicket. The next entry of the coro lontanissimo, setting the word 'egeinato' (bore) is entirely embedded into this disquieting orchestral texture like a central focal point, the sound of which is heard through loudspeakers L9 and L10 high above the central control panel. The sung pitches are now a full category T on C and mirrored by their lower tritone echo. The chromatically related fifths C–G and F♯–C♯ are once again taken up by the strings and tied in with the fifth D–A in yet another chromatic (and microtonal) relationship. The opening hint of 'purity' is thus increasingly concealed.

At the 'homogeneous' speed of ♩ = 30, the two speakers (one female, one male) now begin to recite fragments of the Greek genealogy.[135] The many names and attributes are spoken in ancient Greek and the text is also slightly phased, so that true intelligibility is virtually impossible. During the course of the Prologue this interwoven and archaic stream of ancient Greek

[132] Nono, 'Intervista di Philippe Albèra', *Scritti*, II, 427. Nono stayed at the Hotel Halde outside Freiburg, surrounded only by forest and mountains.

[133] Cacciari, in Nano, Cacciari and Bertaggia, 'Verso Prometeo' (1984), *Scritti*, II, 349.

[134] *Ibid*., 349. [135] The speed indication is missing in the score.

forms an A–B–A′ pattern: names and attributes are recited separately in section B (bars 85–91 and 99–106) and brought together again in a more fragmented and shortened A′ section along with the *Maestro del gioco* II. Cacciari's already fragmented choice of text from Hesiod and other Greek sources is thus reshuffled and fragmented even further by Nono. The intelligibility is also deliberately reduced by means of the live electronics. As Richard explains, the spoken text fluctuates between live transmission and its subjection to various filters. Filtered speech immediately loses its intelligibility. The filter programme thus literally 'ruins' the steady flow of ancient Greek and has to be used sparingly and with great flexibility. The dialectic between 'whole' and 'broken' speech is further accentuated spatially: the unaltered live sound is heard through the lowest loudspeaker, L3, and clashes with the 'ruined' filtered speech transmitted through the highest loudspeaker, L8, at the back.

This deliberate fragmentation and electronic destruction of the ancient Greek text brings to mind the many photographs of temple ruins in Nono's sketches for the Prologue.[136] Single-word annotations such as 'Nomos', 'Prologo', 'Unruhe', 'ondate esterne', 'ondate interne' and 'Wanderer' are written in large capitals over these images of the ruined past. With 'I Ascolta' and 'II Germogliano' Nono specifically refers to the first and second stanzas of the *Maestro del gioco*.[137] Photomontage is also experimented with: ruins of Greek temples are linked to a war scene and a medieval figure of an angel gazes upon the ruins of the Parthenon.[138]

In *Prometeo*, the spoken 'ruins' of ancient Greek are soon joined by the quietest and perhaps most mysterious force of all: the solo strings. As in Dessau's operatic vision of the underworld,[139] Nono excludes the violin and makes use of the three lower string instruments only (viola, cello, double bass). The solo strings are consistently assigned the longest durations and sustain one or few chosen chords over a substantial period of time. At their first entry in the Prologue, for example, they take up the pitches C, C♯ and F♯ from the 'egeinato' cell (C–G–C♯–F♯) which this category T shares with the scala enigmatica on C. The trichord is built up and sustained for over 6 bars, which, at ♩ = 30, translates into about 50″. The sustained textures of

[136] Images from Charbonneaux, Martin and Villard, *La Grecia arcaica* and Lloyd, Müller and Martin, *Architettura mediterranea preromana* (ALN); partly reproduced in Cecchetto and Mastinu (eds.), *Diario di bordo*, 73–81.

[137] ALN 51.09.04/1–11. The word 'germogliano' stems from the line 'germogliano intese segrete' (secret agreements germinate), the first line of the *Maestro del gioco* II, which was later dropped. 'I Ascolta' has now become the trademark image of the Fondazione Archivio Luigi Nono.

[138] ALN 51.10.05/1–3.

[139] Dessau, *Die Verurteilung des Lukullus* (1949–51).

the string trio are never static, however, but (as previously in the quartet) enlivened by a great variety of playing techniques. For this first entry Nono marks 'crini sul tasto/ con rumore' and also specifies a change in bow position, from the more muted sound on the fingerboard to the metallic sound at the bridge and back to the fingerboard. With each reiteration of the chord, the texture is further broken up by small accents. Playing techniques later include also the use of the mute, 'battuto legno e crini', 'arco saltato' and 'arco mobile'. Throughout the Prologue this low 'continuo' reveals itself as a mysterious, underlying 'force of disquiet'.

The most atmospheric feature of this disconcerting presence of string sound, however, is again not notated in the score. Like the spoken text, it is transformed by means of electronic filters. In this case, however, this does not have a destructive effect. Instead, the filters extract frequencies of the whole-tone scale on C up to the highest perceptible register $c^6$–$d^6$–$e^6$–$f\sharp^6$–$g\sharp^6$–$a\sharp^6$ (note the strong overlap with the scala enigmatica). The filter setting Nono chose is a combination of the lowest and highest frequencies (leaving out the middle range). For the most part, the frequencies extracted are present merely as overtones in the live sound. These filtered frequencies alone are then moved around the audience by two halaphones. As indicated in Figure 7.5, the first loop moves clockwise through loudspeakers L1, L3 and L6, the second anti-clockwise through L2, L8 and L5 (loop I moves slightly slower than loop II). The audience is thus slowly encircled by a ghostly 'vibration' of overtones. Successful rendition of this mesmerising sound is extremely difficult because the filtered frequencies are, of course, an inherent part of the live sound and will easily be subsumed by it, even when amplified. It is thus of utmost importance that the live sound is as quiet as possible, indeed on the brink of inaudibility. According to Richard, Nono was extremely tough on his string players, who were often unable to deliver the required degree of quietude.[140]

Into this ghostly string texture the coro lontanissimo announces 'Ourano' from high above the control panel (L9 and L10). Holding on to F♯–C♯, the Gaia material has meandered to include the fifth C♯–G♯ (again all pitches coincide with the scala enigmatica). The orchestras take up the

140 The string trio was first used in this fashion in *Guai ai gelidi mostri* (1983), and Haller describes the 'difficult' and 'time-consuming' search for this 'new quality of sound': 'The transmission of the filtered sound together with the live sound results in [. . .] *Phasing*. This effect becomes all the more characteristic when a delay is added to the filtered sound, with feedback at times. Nono also experimented with different techniques of phasing until he found his special, great *Klangkontinuum* [sound continuo], his *Chor-effekt* [choral effect].' Haller, *Experimentalstudio*, II, 135.

central C♯ in a faint pointillist whirl around the audience. To this brief appearance of the natural forces, Nono now adds a much more futuristic 'wind': the solo wind trio. With three exceptional players, Fabbriciani on bass flute (flute and piccolo), Ciro Scarponi on contrabass clarinet (clarinet and E♭ clarinet)[141] and Giancarlo Schiaffini on tuba, trombone and euphonium,[142] Nono had ample opportunity to study and experiment with a broad spectrum of extended wind techniques. Throughout *Prometeo*, the solo wind trio is thus assigned the most 'utopian' avant-garde sounds. Here in the Prologue, Nono focuses on breath sounds in particular, beginning with the exceedingly quiet 'aria intonata' (breath with just a hint of pitch) in bass flute and contrabass clarinet. The wind sound, too, is constantly kept in flux with a great variety of performance instructions, in this case 'poco soffio' (very little air) and 'frullato' (flutter-tonguing). Nono later also differentiates between 'frullato labbra' (lip), 'gola' (throat) and 'lingua' (tongue), and frequently adds 'aperiodico' to give rise to a maximum of disquiet. Just as aperiodic, fleeting and inherently unpredictable are the high aeolian sounds Nono demands of all wind in the Prologue.[143] These glistening textures of high harmonics and their shadowy fundamentals are among the most mysterious sounds, and it is surely no coincidence that precisely these surround the name Prometeo when it is sung by the coro lontanissimo (bars 99–101). 'Prometeo is Angel', Cacciari writes in his notes for the libretto – 'not rebel, but prophet'. And the solo wind in particular will play an important part in Prometeo's prophecy.

141 Ciro Scarponi (1950–2006) performed with the Solisti della Filarmonica Romana, the ensemble Musica Oggi in Rome and his own Quintetto Scarponi (cl/str), and taught at the conservatory in Perugia. Numerous new works were written for him by Bussotti, Donatoni, Nono, Rihm and Sciarrino, amongst many others.

142 Giancarlo Schiaffini (b. 1942), a trained physicist, began his performing career with the Gruppo Romano Free Jazz in 1960. In the 1970s he studied electronic music with Franco Evangelisti, joined the Gruppo di Improvvisazione di Nuova Consonanza and taught at the conservatory in Pesaro. His performing and composing career included intensive collabarotion with Nono throughout the 1980s. His treatise on contemporary trombone techniques *Il trombone: Estensione delle possibilità tecnico-espressive* was in Nono's possession.

143 Bar 136 of the *Maestro del gioco* layer is a good example. For bass flute and contrabass clarinet Nono here specifies 'suoni eolien acutissimi mobili mikro/ con suono ombra' (extremely high, mobile, micro-aeolian sounds/ with shadow sound) and 'suoni armonici akutissimi mikro mobili/ strumento chiuso/ molta ancia sopra i denti incisivi/ andando verso la punta del bocchino' (extremely high, mobile, micro-harmonics/ instrument closed/ a lot of reed on the [lower] incisors/ moving towards the tip of the mouthpiece). The tuba is required to play 'eolien akutissimi mobili micro/ con base' (extremely high, mobile, micro-aeolian sounds/ with the fundamental). For tuba and trombone Nono later also notes 'suoni tibetani' and 'tibetano eolien'.

If Nono largely avoids normal pitch production for the wind in the first part of the Prologue, live electronics enhance this effect with upper and lower quarter-tone transpositions. Because breath sound and any other unpitched 'noise' is not transposable, this procedure primarily results in white noise. When a pitch does emerge, however, the transposition is all the more perceptible. Throughout Part I, the solo wind sounds are consistently transmitted through loudspeaker L2. At their first entry, with the tuba's breathy pedal note C, they are further steeped into the nebulous resonance of the three glass bells. The glass, too, is not exactly pitched but simply notated as high, medium and low.[144] Live electronics add a long reverb of 15″ and transpose the sound almost two octaves down. This results in a mysterious low drone in simulated spatial vastness. Throughout *Prometeo* this spacious low drone descends upon the audience from the rear, through L1, L5 and L7.

The 'homogeneous' web of the distant past is now fully exposed, and its elements are clearly designed to create maximum 'Unruhe'. The ancient Greek text is spoken, not sung, and deliberately 'ruined' by means of filters. The low strings provide porous harmonic textures and their almost inaudible ghosts spiral slowly around the audience. With only a hint of pitch, the wind add a shadowy 'Hauch der Luft' (breath of air) and occasionally escape into aeolian heights. Reminiscent of the low drone in the music to *Die Ermittlung*, the glass adds yet another sinister dimension to this truly disconcerting soundscape.

Man and Earth (the two forces which live on in the present) dramatically rise from the interlocking constellations of this fragmented, 'ruined' past. In 'non-homogeneous' time the phrases of the *Maestro del gioco* I and the remaining names of the coro lontanissimo surge out of the underlying continuum in typical, wave-like fashion. The speeds of this second, non-homogeneous time layer are closely graded (♩ = 30, 44, 54, 56, 60, 64, 66, 68, 76 and 82) and only the 'Manfred' chord in Part II of the Prologue stands out with a much faster speed of ♩ = 152. The dramatic impact of the

[144] According to Richard, Nono initially planned to use eight glass bells. A prototype was blown in Murano, but broke on its first test. Together with Haller, Nono went shopping in Freiburg instead. He bought five glass bowls and cheese domes at a houseware store and tested their sound at the studio. Hard crystal glass turned out to sound best, so Nono chose to work with three crystal bowls. These crystal 'bells' have been used for *Prometeo* ever since, but unfortunately one of them broke at a performance in Schwaz (Austria). Richard, who had, luckily, recorded the pitch of the original glass bells, toured houseware stores all over Europe to find a suitable replacement. A bowl with approximately the same sound turned up in Basle, but it is far less resonant than the original. The search for suitable Promethean crystal thus continues.

wave-like vocal phrases is enhanced spatially as two more halaphones move the sound of the chorus and the soloists clockwise and anti-clockwise around the audience (see Figure 7.5). Although they are part of the layer of non-homogeneous time, the sung names of the coro lontanissimo (with their slower speeds of ♩ = 30, 40, 56 and 60) are exempt from this spatial motion and continue to be transmitted through the indirect and/or central loudspeakers L9 to L12.

The dramatic nature of the commentating layer of song is much increased by the orchestras, which generally take up the vocal pitches in order to dynamically embed and extend them. This function is evident immediately in the phrase 'Ascolta' with its short coro lontanissimo intervention 'd'Ourea' (bars 28–39). The tritone F–B is central to this phrase, but Nono also branches out into the adjacent semitones C and C♯. Chorus and soloists do not sing above *p*, yet the orchestra dramatically accentuates all vocal pitches with *sff*, *mf*, *f*, *ff* and *fff* and, at times, also diffuses them microtonally. Another extremely dramatic example of orchestral extension can be found at the end of the phrase 'respirava il passato' (breathed the past) (bars 81–86), where trumpets, flutes and trombones take up the seventh C–B of the chorus, extend it microtonally and gradually go full circle, building up an increasingly dramatic cluster, which finally breaks off simultaneously in all four orchestras with *sffff*. Another such violent outburst appropriately accompanies the name of Kronos, Zeus' father and one of the most violent gods in Hesiod's genealogy.

On very few occasions the orchestras also appear as an autonomous force. These brief orchestral interventions are marked in double bars and occur after the first 'Ascolta' (bars 40–41), after 'Non vibra qui ancora un soffio dell'aria che respirava il passato' (Does not still resonate here a breath of air that the past breathed) (bars 64–66) and again after 'Non resiste nell'eco la voce' (Does not endure in the echo the voice) (bar 97). These short orchestral fragments are pure 'Gaia' material: microtonally enhanced interlocking fifths F–F♯–C–C♯ (bars 40–41), C♯–G♯ (bar 97) and E♭–F–F♯–B♭–B (bars 64–66). As will be shown in detail, the latter set is a constellation of particular consequence in the First Island and beyond.

Taking up the last chord of the *Maestro del gioco* I (E–B–F♯–C♯), the orchestras eventually fade out on pure fifths in violins and violas, which clash with the increasingly affirmative category T G♯–D–D♯–A in the solo strings. This simultaneous fade out and fade in marks a complete change of scene and the beginning of Part II. In this second part, the orchestras no longer support and dramatise the sung passages. From the dense disquiet ('Unruhe') of Part I, in which all forces are heard and moved simultaneously at times, Part II emerges with otherworldly calm ('Ruhe') and with a strong focus on the vocal line. The soloists of Part I (SAT) are replaced by the two solo sopranos, who will later render Hölderlin's *Schicksalslied.* Here they blend with the choral voices, who now sing with their hands folded over their mouths and extremely close to their microphones. The result of this unusual performance instruction is a much more intimate 'internal' choral sound with few overtones. The use of live electronics, too, is completely altered. The chorus is no longer embedded in its tritone echo. Instead, the soloists are immersed in upper and lower quarter-tone transpositions (as was the wind previously). When vocal phrases end in unison, as is often the case (e.g. the very first phrase, 'Vibrano intese segrete' (Secret agreements resonate)), the 'impure' sound of the soloists beautifully resolves into the 'pure' sustained choral sound.

Drama is replaced by reflection also in terms of spatial projection. The vocal sound no longer moves, but is heard stereophonically from opposite sides of the hall, with the soloists transmitted through L2 and the chorus through L6 (possibly also through L9 and L10, depending on the acoustics of the hall; see Figure 7.6). Only the wind are now moving in the familiar

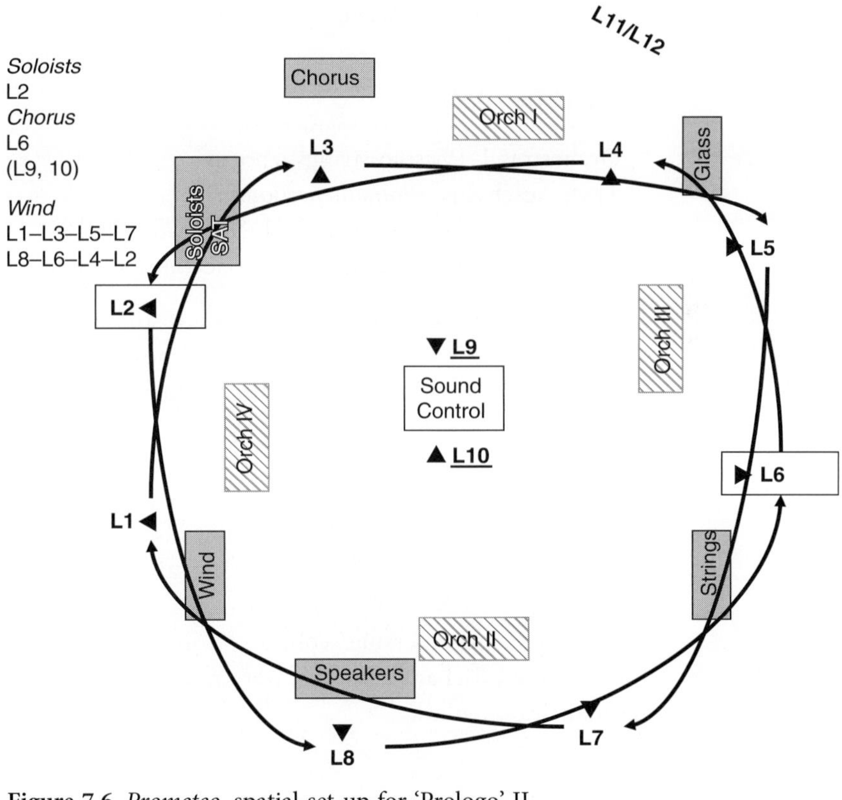


**Figure 7.6** *Prometeo*, spatial set-up for 'Prologo' II.

concentric circles. No longer transposed, they emerge perceptibly out of largely unpitched breath noise into a much more defined realm of pitch, taking up the pitches of the vocal phrases with occasional additions of aeolian harmonics in whole-tone series. Together with the text's first reference to the 'angel', the wind and glass now fully come to the fore as the most 'messianic' and 'prophetic' of the instrumental forces. In contrast, the solo strings and speakers enter much more sporadically, and the orchestras too seem to have vanished from the scene altogether. 'Gaia' does appear again, however, with an extremely quiet reference to the beginning fifth D–A, now expanded inwardly (D–E♭–E–G–A♭–A plus microtones), followed by a clashing agglomeration of fifths in low register (bars 183–87). This mesmerising orchestral texture prepares the phrase 'Questa debole forza c'è data' (This weak force is given to us). When this text is sung once more by the voices alone (bars 198–201), it is framed by much more violent orchestral interventions, including the first bolt of the 'Manfred' chord with its characteristic rhythm borrowed from Schumann's *Manfred Overture*. This stark contrast between orchestral violence and vocal calm homes in on Benjamin's 'weak messianic power' and reveals it as a truly non-violent 'power of singing'.

## Isola 1° (*ca.* 23′)

Orchestras I–IV, solo strings, chorus
Text: Aeschylus, *Prometheus Bound*
Mitologia: Questions with which Nono and Cacciari distance themselves from the idea of Prometheus as revolutionary rebel

If Part II of the Prologue is marked by a distinct absence of the orchestral forces, the music of the First Island is now utterly dominated by the orchestras and their very own spatial domain. Nowhere else in *Prometeo* is the orchestral writing of such variety and on such a grand scale. Within the austere limits of the 'Gaia' material, Nono here creates a vast and truly desolate soundscape lasting for well over twenty minutes, which revels in intensely quiet microtonal textures, but also periodically breaks out into blocks of extreme violence. 'Durissimo' and 'drammatico' Nono notes in preliminary sketches and 'contrarre–rovesciamento/ scontro/ agonismo è visibile' (tensing–reversing/ collision/ conflict is visible).[145] These orchestral extremes, Richard recounts, were never more gripping than in Piano's resonant wooden ark.

[145] ALN 51.06.04/02; ALN 51.14.04/10.

The scene (as is clear from the inserted text) is that of the opening of *Prometheus Bound*: on 'a rocky mountain top, within sight of the sea,' the absent Zeus governs with Kratos (Strength) and Bia (Violence).[146] His willing executioner, Hephaestus, is endowed with the thankless task of having to nail Prometheus to the rock. In Aeschylus, Hephaestus fulfils this task reluctantly. Cacciari simply states the harsh punishment Efesto (Hephaestus) is about to inflict on Prometeo and ends with the following warning:

> Know:
> it is hard to calm
> the heart of Zeus
> dispenser of fates

Efesto's words are juxtaposed with those of Prometeo, the farsighted 'champion of the human race'[147] or, as Nono repeatedly annotated his copy of the play, of the working class. Prometeo's words stem from the magnificent monologue addressed to the 'Chorus of the Daughters of Oceanus' in which he praises and defends his many achievements for mankind, his 'techne'. Four lines of this truly defiant speech impressed Nono to such an extent that he referred to them repeatedly, as in his tribute to Berlinguer:

| | |
|---|---|
| Pur vedendo non vedevano | They had eyes, but sight was meaningless; |
| pur udendo non udivano | heard sounds, but could not listen |
| gli uomini | ephemeral |
| effimeri | Man[148] |

Through Prometheus, his cunning and his techne, 'ephemeral man' is made aware of the true meaning of seeing and listening. With his techne, Prometheus enlightens and illuminates, yet also effects man's irreversible, 'technological' break with Gaia–Themis, 'the natural law, his origin'. It is precisely this break with Gaia–Themis that constitutes in Cacciari's thought the human 'guilt-of-existence' for which we are forever punished.[149]

Cacciari's text, however, is deliberately not set. 'NEVER read out the added text', Nono writes in the score,

146 Aeschylus, *Prometheus Bound*, 20. 147 Aeschylus, *Prometheus Bound*, 20.

148 Aeschylus, *Prometheus Bound*, 34–35; Nono, 'Le sue parole', *Scritti*, I, 397.

149 Cacciari, preliminary notes A, ALN 51.02.05/3.

**Example 7.4** Pitch reduction of the amplified instruments in the First Island.

> BUT listen to it (and make it 'felt') in the 4 orchestras, in the 3 solo strings: nature – stones – affirmations – questions – inner problems – externalised by means of the possible 'answers' in the 4 orchestral groups, the silence of the pauses.

Whenever text is added, be it that of Prometeo or Efesto, it is simply associated with a recurring type of sound. This type of sound emerges from within the four orchestras, but is clearly distinguished in terms of pitch and instrumentation and, exceptionally so, by means of live electronics. For the first and only time in *Prometeo* live electronics are employed for selected instruments of the orchestras. Only one instrument of each orchestra is singled out for amplification: a solo violin in orchestras I and II, a horn in orchestra IV and a trumpet in orchestra III. With slow, sustained and always varied combinations of the interlocking fifths B–F♯ and B♭–F (plus interim quarter-tones), this spatially separated instrumental quartet repeatedly halts the flow of the otherwise much rawer and more monumental textures. Example 7.4 shows the pitch development of these thirteen interruptions (including one silence). Their associated text fragments are listed in Table 7.1.

The development begins in middle register on the single pitch F♯, the central pitch of the scala enigmatica on C. To this F♯ on violin Nono then adds the lower B on horn. The fifth B–F♯, exposed here in linear fashion, will gradually manifest itself as the 'tonal centre' of the whole of *Prometeo*.

Table 7.1 *Unperformed text in the First Island*

| Bar | Character | Text (written into the score but *not* to be performed) | Instrument [Orchestra] |
|---|---|---|---|
| 11–13 | Prometeo | Know, they had eyes, but sight was meaningless/ Heard sounds, but could not listen | vln [1], hrn [4], vln [2] |
| 22–23 | | . . . ephemeral man . . . | vln [1/2] |
| 29 | | like shapes in dreams . . . they lived in holes, like swarms of ants | hrn/trp [4/3] |
| 34 | | till I taught them to determine when stars rise and set . . . | hrn/trp [4/3] |
| 43–44 | Efesto | You, son of Tethys, I shall bind | hrn/trp [4/3] |
| 46–50 | Prometeo | I, was the first to harness beasts under a yoke, to take man's place under the heaviest of burdens, discovered the sailor's wagon – flax winged craft that roam the sea | All |
| | Efesto | You, with inextricable knots | |
| 78–84 | Prometeo | I, invented for them the number | All |
| | Efesto | You, onto this immobile rock | |
| 94–98 | Prometeo | I, what crafts, what methods I devised | hrn [4]/trp [3], vln [1/2] |
| | Efesto | You, will wither in the blazing sun | |
| 140 | Prometeo | I, was the first to tell from dreams | hrn [4]/trp [3], all |
| 145 | | . . . the flights . . . | Silence |
| 201–205 | Efesto | Know, it is hard to calm the heart of Zeus, dispenser of fates | vln [1]/hrn [4], all, vln [2]/trp [3] |
| | Prometeo | I, was the first to tell from dreams, the flights, the voices | |
| 221–23 | | the omens, the encounters, the customs, | All |
| 226 | | Love | All |

This very fifth will eventually bring the work to its conclusion in the absolute 'clarity' it first attained in *Das atmende Klarsein*. Here in the First Island, however, this fifth emerges tentatively from the surrounding natural forces with equally tentative amplification. As Richard explains, the amplification of the four orchestral instruments is applied irregularly, being increased and decreased with caution and sensitivity. Expanding into higher and lower registers, Nono gradually adds the chromatically related pitches of the second fifth B♭–F and soon also moves on to microtonal inflection. With the perceptible support of technology, Nono thus gradually breaks away from man's 'natural origin' and thereby 'sets' the central idea of Promethean TECHNE – 'TEKNAI' as Nono himself jots down in a preliminary draft.[150] The pitch development ends with a final juxtaposition of the central fifth B–F♯ and the now extremely spaced-out fifth B♭–F. These two fifths, both inherent in the scala enigmatica on C, rise out of the Gaia material and break away without ever actually contradicting it. The scala enigmatica material is thus once again part of 'Gaia' but also clearly distinguished from it. Within the limits of this pitch range Prometeo's techne breaks through the harsh and overpowering 'natural' surroundings in quietly fluctuating moments of calm and reflection. 'Striscia di terra/ torrente – pietra/ fruchtlands/ menschliches' Nono jotted down in early sketches for this scene, and later, 'Catastrofe: flessione del destino/ della necessità/ con dentro la speranza' (Catastrophe: flexion of destiny/ of necessity/ with hope therein). At this point in the drama, this hope still comprises 'la speranza del ribelle', the revolutionary hope of the fire-bringer and rebel.[151]

The reflective, philosophical dimension of the First Island is enhanced by means of the exceptionally pure and stunningly beautiful choral statements of the 'Mitologia' as well as the continued underlying presence of the solo string trio. The use of the solo strings and the coro lontanissimo audibly harks back to the mysterious, disconcerting presence of the past in the Prologue. Again, the solo strings move independently in their own homogeneous layer of time at the slowest of speeds (♩ = 30) and continue to encircle the audience with quiet and sustained configurations of the Gaia material. Their sound is filtered as before, but Nono now adds two delays and feedback. As shown in Figure 7.7, the first halaphone moves the filtered string sound clockwise with a delay of 4″ and feedback, whereas the second moves it anti-clockwise at a different speed with a delay of 8″ and feedback. The textural sonority thus builds up to denser clouds of string sound, which, in its quietude, is often drowned out by the mightier orchestral forces and mostly comes to the fore together with the amplified orchestral quartet which generally assimilates the same slow speed and with which it is heard in ever-changing constellations.

This underlying, electronically multiplied presence of the Gaia material in the strings is only ever cut off in the few instances when the Mitologia calls on Prometeo. The Mitologia is the only 'character' of the First Island whose text is actually voiced.[152] Its function, according to one of Nono's sketches, is to 'interrogate Prometeo on the sense of it all' and, with an allusion to Mahler, the composer poetically adds 'Fragenlied klagendes'.[153]

150 ALN 51.14.04/10. 151 ALN 51.03.07/01.

152 This was not yet the case in the 1984 version; see Melkert, «*Far del silenzio cristallo*», 157–59.

153 ALN 51.06.04/02.

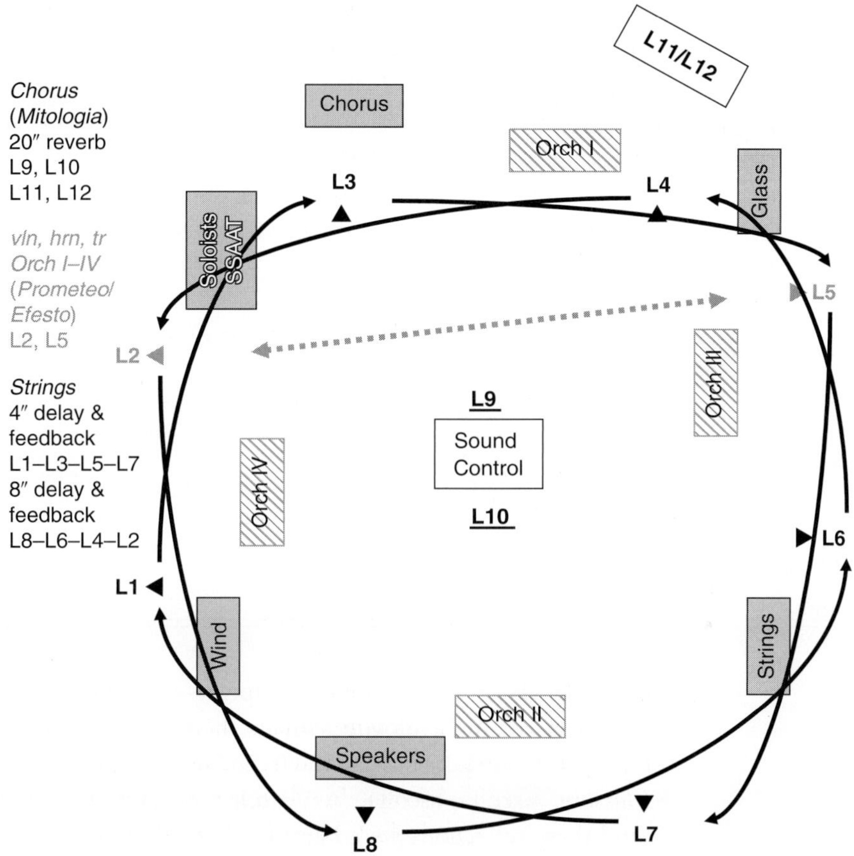


**Figure 7.7** *Prometeo*, spatial set-up for 'Isola 1°'.

Like the names in the Prologue, the text of the Mitologia is sung by the coro lontanissimo. With an even larger reverb of 20″ (though no tritone echo), the distant sound of the chorus is again transmitted indirectly through loudspeakers L9/L10 and L11/L12. The Mitologia enters six times in the latter half of the Island. The first and last time it is embedded in orchestral textures. Otherwise it is heard a cappella. As Melkert has shown, these four a cappella fragments stem from *Das atmende Klarsein*.[154] In the 1984 version the part of the Mitologia was vocalised and (like the orchestral quartet) merely associated with the text. In contrast, the final version questions Prometheus' revolutionary utopia in fully articulated 'clarity'. Only the names 'Gaia', 'Iapetus' and 'Clymene' were previously exposed in such pure a cappella fashion and, of course, they too stem from *Das*

[154] Melkert, «*Far del silenzio cristallo*», 154–57.

Table 7.2 *Interventions of the Mitologia in the First Island*

| No | Bars | Text | Pitches |
|---|---|---|---|
| I | 111–12 | Prometeo | F/C, B/F♯ |
| II | 121–22 | Questa speranza liberarsi del Dio<br>This hope of freeing oneself from the god<br>[*Das atmende Klarsein*, choral section II, bars 20–21] | B♭–E♭, F/C, B–F♯ |
| III | 163–66 | Sei come un nuovo signore<br>Are you like a new master<br>[*Das atmende Klarsein*, II, bars 43–44] | C♯/G♯, F♯/C♯ |
| IV | 175–80 | Ascolta, ascolta<br>Listen, listen [jealous and troublesome]<br>[*Prologo*, bars 106–11; *Das atmende Klarsein*, II, bars 40–42] | F/B, C♯, E♭, B♭/F |
| V | 236–41 | Credi onnipotente il tuo fuoco<br>Do you believe your fire is omnipotent<br>[*Das atmende Klarsein*, II, bars 30–31, 46] | G/D/A, A/E, D |
| VI | 254– | Chiami verità [quella] stretta radura<br>Do you call [this] narrow clearing truth | F/C, B/F♯ |

*atmende Klarsein*. The music of 'Iapetus–Clymene' reappears exactly as it was heard in the Prologue with its memorable whole-tone ascent. Now, however, Nono goes back to the fragment's original text from *Das atmende Klarsein*: 'ascolta, ascolta'. As Cacciari explains in his preliminary notes (and these reflections were later highlighted by Nono),

> Here, the mother of Prometheus is Clymene, Oceanid, daughter of Oceanus and Tethys – and therefore part of the Aeschylean Chorus! – the Chorus is the *Mother* of Prometheus in Aeschylus! – there, in other stories, it is Gaia herself (Gea, Earth), or Themis (in Aeschylus)[155]

No wonder, then, that 'Clymene' should become part of the commentating Chorus here in the First Island. The primordial 'mother' Gaia–Themis is present, too, in the form of the pure and open fifths and fourths, the interval category which once again determines these choral interventions. Table 7.2 lists the six fragments of the Mitologia with their respective text and pitch sets. The first and last fragments are heard through the enveloping sounds of the orchestras and solo strings and make use of the same two fifths from the scala enigmatica on C (F–C and B–F♯). The central four fragments are performed a cappella and all stem from *Das atmende Klarsein*.

[155] Cacciari, preliminary notes A, ALN 51.02.03/01.

In terms of pitch and interval structure, the reused Iapetus–Clymene fragment (IV) stands out for its exceptional use of the tritone F–B. It is the only fragment not to move exclusively in fifths and fourths, and also deviates from Cacciari's libretto text. Exceptional, too, is fragment V with its troubling question 'Do you believe your fire is omnipotent?' This fragment alone is marked '*Das atmende Klarsein*' and moves entirely out of the realm of the scala enigmatica by making use of open-string fifths only. The fifths and fourths of all other fragments are firmly rooted in the scala enigmatica on C. Omnipotence is thus musically associated with the powers that rule 'Ekdike', pure and essentially unattainable, outside the laws of the harmonic sphere of god and man.

## Isola 2°: Io–Prometeo (*ca.* 17′)

*Io*: female soloists (SSAA), chorus, bass flute
*Prometeo*: solo tenor, chorus, contrabass clarinet
Orchestras I–IV, solo strings
Text: Aeschylus, *Prometheus Bound*

> After having been possessed by Zeus, Io is persecuted by Hera and arrives in front of the chained Prometheus. She too is therefore a creature forced to wander, pursued by nagging worry. She too struggles with the divinity, and in some way wills the struggle, the persecution. But above all she is for Prometheus the troubled mirror of his Eros, it is she who forces him to become aware of it. Io's disquiet reveals itself as the disquiet of Prometheus. And, if you like, this is the disquiet of softness, of tenderness. It happens in life that there are moments of incredible amazement, of wonder, which make one rediscover the beauty of ecstasy, of meditation. Not in a consoling sense, but rather as an explosion of uncontrollable inner urgency [. . .] Why feel ashamed of our fragility? It is what characterises us most as human beings, what makes us worthy of living. The manifestation of force is nothing other than the mask of him who has no other reason for asserting his humanity.
>
> Nono, 'Ecco il mio Prometeo'[156]

Nono's portrait of the figure Io in this interview with Dino Villatico (on the occasion of the 1981 premiere of *Io, frammento dal Prometeo*) is among the composer's most detailed statements with regard to subject matter, though here, too, the tragedy's political core argument is stubbornly avoided. In Cacciari's notes, the figure of Io is tied to the concept of Prometheus as Angel: 'Prometheus is Angel' because he announces the

[156] Nono, 'Ecco il mio Prometeo', *Scritti*, II, 260–61.

'liberation from the jealous and subversive god' Zeus. This 'great impossible utopia' would also 'put an end to the Kratos and Bia of Zeus', the 'same forces that persecute Io [. . .], the feminine, maternal figure, who is so "essential" to Prometheus that he prophesies the whole story' to her.[157] Yet the 'great impossible utopia' at the heart of this story, that Zeus will 'be deposed from sovereignty [. . .] by his own foolish purposes', through 'a union that will turn to his undoing' and 'a son more powerful than his father',[158] is alluded to only in the vaguest of terms in Cacciari's final libretto text. 'Il NUME sempre violento', the 'always violent', 'jealous and troublesome' Divinity is Zeus, of course, but the 'great impossible utopia' of his downfall is merely hinted at with the last two lines of Prometeo's prophecy: 'Amare nozze le sue/ Sempre violento' (His are bitter weddings/ Always violent).

Nonetheless, Nono's and Cacciari's conception of the Second Island, and *Prometeo* as a whole, largely depends on this 'utopia' and its tragic impossibility. If there is indeed a 'single, irretractable decision' or 'drân' that underlies and determines this entire tragedy of listening, it is Prometeo's decision not to rebel, but to prophesy. And Prometeo comes to this irretractable decision in the Io episode. This episode is thus not just 'the story of Io', but the all-important link between the 'utopia' of Prometeo and the 'end of utopia' with Achilles and, as such, defines *Prometeo* as 'drân dell'ascolto'. The scene was of such importance to Nono that *Io, frammento dal Prometeo* (1981) became the second milestone after *Das atmende Klarsein*. And this work, too, was still conceived entirely in the context of Rilke, not Benjamin. Cacciari's understanding of 'drân' as 'the tragic theory of the moment of decision' and 'the moment of most intense suffering that the hero cannot escape' is here initially developed in the context of the symbols of transcendence in Rilke's *Duineser Elegien*: young heroes, lovers and the angel.

'Violenza – eros – Io' Nono notes for the Io episode on the early draft of 1981 and 'ascolta' (Figure 7.1). Violent oppression and love are, of course, familiar antipodes in Nono's oeuvre as a whole. Already in *Intolleranza 1960* the protagonist's journey towards greater political awareness reaches new heights in the struggle for a more humane and just society when he encounters his 'comrade' in the solo soprano. Together they are eventually engulfed and swept away by the apocalyptic flood that concludes this existentialist *azione scenica*. In *Prometeo*, the 'catastrofe: flessione del destino' has already occurred when the persecuted kindred spirit Io

[157] Cacciari, preliminary notes A, ALN 51.02.05/06–07.
[158] Aeschylus, *Prometheus Bound*, 42–43.

appears in front of the bound Prometheus. 'Io Klagende Lied' and 'Voce disparata contra il Destino' Nono notes in later sketches.[159] In *Io, frammento dal Prometeo*, this 'disparate voice against destiny' was initially scored for three sopranos. Especially the high first soprano takes vocal intensity to dramatic extremes, repeatedly soaring up to an $E^4$, $F^4$, $F\sharp^4$ and even $G^4$ at the seemingly impossible dynamic *ppp*. The 'Chant of Io' is imagined here as 'dramatic in cold desperation, wild-eyed desolation, violated eroticism, enforced wandering, inexorable persecution'.[160] Completely absent, in this desolate first version of the episode, is the solo tenor who takes on the voice of Prometeo in the finished work. Yet Nono has already assigned the bass flute to Io and the contrabass clarinet to Prometeo. These two instrumental characters then join forces with two of the solo sopranos for a preliminary version of Hölderlin's *Schicksalslied*.[161] In the movements with chorus, Io is represented by the female voices, Prometeo by the male voices. Already in this first version, the collective choral sound is effectively employed to merge the two characters into one – Rilke's 'Lovers'.

The Io episode in *Prometeo* focuses far more on this element of assimilation. Gone is the desparate dramatic exaltation of the high solo soprano. Io is now represented by two solo sopranos and two solo altos, supported by the female voices of the chorus, branching out into full chorus at times. Prometeo's part, in turn, is rendered by the solo tenor, the male choral voices and the full chorus at times. The boundaries between the two vocal characters are thus much more fleeting, and Nono deliberately exploits the similarities of the two vocal 'collectives', merging them into one at times. In terms of ambitus, the soloists hardly exceed the boundaries of the choral sound: firmly grounded in middle register, they do not rise above B. Instead of a high soprano, the predominant soloist is now the tenor. The tenor's lines, Prometeo's all-important prophecy to Io, often begin and lead into collective vocal statements of varying length and density (less often, they also emerge out of them). Occasionally, the character of Io is also heard in isolation. Especially towards the end, when, despite Prometeo's prophecy (and in contrast to Aeschylus), Io falls victim to resignation, the vocal interventions become ever shorter and eventually fade out in the female soloists alone.

In the final version of *Prometeo*, this crucial 'Io–Prometeo' episode evolves in twenty-seven vocal moments. Most of these are 4–6 bars long,

[159] ALN 51.06.03/1–9. [160] As quoted in *Io, frammento da Prometeo*, score, viii/xviii.

[161] Movement VI of nine. As in *Prometeo*, Hölderlin's *Schicksalslied* is assigned to the commentating 'Mitologia'.

some are longer (up to 9 bars) and quite a few are shorter (2–3 bars). As Melkert has shown, Nono selected these moments from movements 1, 3, 5 and 7 of *Io, frammento dal Prometeo*, but then completely reordered them and reassigned the text.[162] Considering this radical segmentation and re-contextualisation, it is fair to say, as Nono himself implies in a letter to Piano, that this is no longer quotation, but the reuse of existing material for the composition of something entirely new:

> Prometeo will be new – I will use very little of what has already been composed [. . .] new skies/ new stars/ new seas/ new abysses/ new walls of water/ new planets/ new black holes/ new catastrophes/ new innovative types of chaos/ instinct – viscera – heart – emotions – non-illusionist asystematic reason/ *designing the undesignable*/ not static/ not resolved/ Air – fire – earth – water – This is contemporary technology projected towards the future[163]

Truly new in this episode of *Prometeo* is the much more radical focus on the fragment as a singular moment and the role of the chorus in defining these decisive moments of Rilkean awareness as 'drân' in music. To Villatico, Nono speaks of the disquiet and inner urgency that is conveyed to Prometeo through Io.[164] This disquiet is now evoked primarily by the chorus, the force that effectively merges and unites the two characters. These fragments are not just exceedingly quiet constellations of few notes. The twelve singers of the chorus are asked to use their hands as a mute, but with swift outward movements they also momentarily assume megaphone position to errupt into loud and violent shouts of 'Hu!' and 'Ha!' and thus dramatically evoke Io on the brink of madness, persecuted and tormented by the ghost of the many-eyed herdsman Argus and the continuous stings of a gadfly. 'Unruhe' is further created by means of improvisation. Parts of the chorus are notated only in outline, as a rough guide for hummed and muted improvisation in middle register. The effect of this is a deliberate impurification of the fully notated vocal parts, similar to live-electronic phasing, but far stronger than that. The choral disquiet is underlined by the fluctuating sound transmission, which constantly shifts between a 'fast' and 'nervous' movement in centre space (L1–L5–L2–L6) and static transmission from behind and above (L7, L9 and L10; see Figure 7.8).

A similar kind of 'Unruhe' is added to the lines of the female soloists by means of improvised live-electronic transposition: the choice of the

[162] Melkert, «*Far del silenzio cristallo*», 160–73.

[163] Nono, letter to Piano (Piano/R 83-12-06 d, ALN), in *Diario di bordo*, 102–103.

[164] Nono, 'Ecco il mio Prometeo', *Scritti*, II, 260–66.

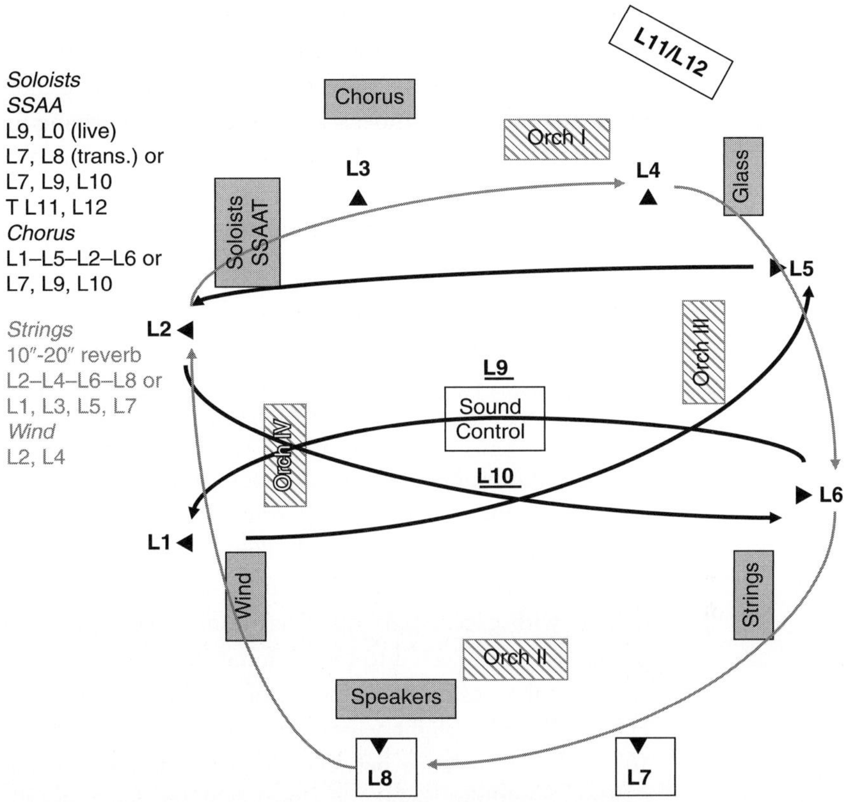


**Figure 7.8** *Prometeo*, spatial set-up for 'Isola 2°, Io–Prometeo'.

transposition interval is left entirely up to the person in charge of sound projection. Nono thus introduces yet another kind of phasing, and Richard recalls how this *ad libitum* transposition was performed with maximum variety and occasional 'terror' by the so-called 'infernalista' during the first performance in Venice. Vidolin also discusses this improvised phasing and stresses that

> It is important to remember that the transposed sound is not always present, but added [. . .] in support of the vocal articulation and for additional vocal expression. Towards the end of a crescendo, for example, an added transposition provides maximum force and tension. And on a sustained vocal pitch, modulation of the transposition and its intensity introduces ambiguous transformations of timbre which may seem like veiled progressions from a single voice to a choral chord.[165]

[165] Vidolin, 'Il suono mobile', in Doati (ed.), *Con Luigi Nono*, 43.

The 'drân' which determines the course of this tragedy thus comes from within the vocal sound, its unpredictable, sometimes violent and always deeply unsettling core. The episode as a whole is dominated by these moments of vocal disquiet. Compared with the driving force of the orchestras in the First Island, this highly fragmented dialogue between Io and Prometeo clearly takes place in another realm, far removed from the 'natural forces' whose role is now reduced to an absolute minimum.

| | |
|---|---|
| Es wäre ein Platz | Suppose there's a place |
| den wir nicht wissen . . . | we don't know of . . . |
| Zeigten die Liebenden | Lovers could show |
| ihre Türme aus Lust | their towers of ecstasy |
| wo Boden nie war . . . | where there was never any ground . . .[166] |

Rilke's unknowable place 'where there was never any ground' is magically evoked by the accompanying solo instruments (bass flute, contrabass clarinet and the solo strings).[167] Throughout this episode, the solo strings leave their usual 'ground' of bass foundations behind and rise up to angelic heights with exceedingly quiet harmonics. The glassy sound of the string harmonics is subjected to two different live-electronic programmes: subtle microtonal phasing to achieve the desired 'choral effect' described by Haller,[168] and a slight variant of this phasing together with a reverb of 10″–20″. The balance between these two types of sound transformation (with and without reverb), Richard explains, has to be shimmering ('schillernd'). Like that of the chorus, the transmission of the string sound further alternates between movement (clockwise through L2–L4–L6–L8) and stasis (L1, L3, L5 and L7; see Figure 7.8), creating yet another layer of fertile uncertainty 'between stream and rock'.

Truly 'unknown' sonorities come into play, however, with the solo wind, the precariously unpredictable universe of bass flute multiphonics in particular. Annotations in Nono's copy of Pierre-Yves Artaud's *Flûtes au présent* show that these multiphonics were carefully selected with the harmonic system and its interval categories 8, 4/5, T and 2–7–9 in mind.[169] As anyone who has ever worked with multiphonics will know, however, the defining characteristic of these multiple sonorities is not so much their intervallic structure, but rather their inherent unreliability, inaccuracy and utterly surprising timbral quality, features Nono will have revelled in,

[166] Cacciari, 'da Rilke, *Duineser* ', Fifth Elegy, *Gesammelte Gedichte*, 461; *Duino Elegies*, 56.

[167] Nono further noted 'venti Alvise', probably an indication that the 4i computer was to provide atmospheric wind sounds in this scene (ALN 51.24.01/02).

[168] See note 140. [169] Artaud, *Flûtes au présent*, ALN.

especially in the context of this scene in which uncertainty and in-between states are of the utmost importance. Whether tonal or microtonal, in pure quietude or buzzing friction, immediate simultaneity or fluctuating instability, multiphonics have a beguiling richness of timbre that totally matches the idea of Prometeo as Angel and Wanderer. Not surprisingly, fragments of these quietly prophetic wind parts in 'Io–Prometeo' will later reappear in '3 Voci a' together with another layer of 'angelic' string harmonics, this time on the orchestral violins. Here in 'Io–Prometeo', these surprising wind sonorities encapsulate the 'softness', 'tenderness', 'incredible amazement' and 'wonder' which, according to Nono, enable us to 'rediscover the beauty of ecstasy, of meditation'. Unlike the 'shimmering' transmission of strings and chorus, the transmission of the wind sound is not subjected to fluctuation. The live electronics do not add disquiet, but introduce textural fuzziness and its resolution into the live sound. This subtle clarifying effect is achieved by means of two extremely short delays of 150 ms and 220 ms. The first filters the sound and transmits it through L2. Milliseconds later, the unaltered live sound then follows through L4 (see Figure 7.8).

Despite the tantalising surge into the high atmosphere of solo strings and wind, this decisive encounter between Io and Prometeo is not entirely detached from Gaia. As Cacciari warns in his preliminary notes with a quote from Goethe's *Grenzen der Menschheit*,

| | |
|---|---|
| Denn mit Göttern | For against gods |
| Soll sich nicht messen | No man alive |
| Irgendein Mensch. | Should measure himself. |
| Hebt er sich aufwärts, | If he rises up |
| Und berührt | And with the crown of his head |
| Mit dem Scheitel die Sterne, | touches the stars, |
| Nirgends haften dann | Nowhere then do the groping |
| Die unsichern Sohlen, | Soles of his feet adhere, |
| Und mit ihm spielen | But clouds and winds |
| Wolken und Winde. | Make him their game.[170] |

Orchestral interventions are kept to an absolute minimum in this episode, and many were yet to be crossed out in the finished score, particularly those which merely take up the pitches of the vocal layer. On the few occasions when the orchestras do come into play, however, they bring us back to earth primarily with the category T on A (A–E♭–E–B♭), but also

170 Goethe, *Grenzen der Menschheit* (*ca.* 1780), in *Poems and Epigrams*, 26–27; ALN 51.02.05/11.

F♯–C–B–F from within the scala enigmatica.[171] In addition to these mostly exceedingly quiet Gaia formations, the orchestras also interrupt the scene with five violent bolts of the 'Manfred' chord. To Nono, the story of Io was, after all, also a potent symbol of the repressed struggle of the oppressed.

## Isola 2°: Hölderlin (*ca.* 8′)

2 Solo sopranos, 2 speakers, bass flute, contrabass clarinet
Text: Hölderlin, *Schicksalslied*; Cacciari, allusion to Pindar's *Nemean Ode* VI

The extremely fragmentary and non-developmental moment structure of 'Io–Prometeo' is answered with 'Hölderlin', the second section of the Second Island, which is just over eight minutes long and presents us with one of the most stringent and clear-cut compositional processes of the work as a whole. The idea for this drawn-out process can be traced back to Nono's early *Prometeo* draft of 1981 (Figure 7.1) and its fundamental concern with '*the impossible utopia* in mythical–tragic Greek thought' which, 'as only Hölderlin understood', is concealed in the figure of Achilles. Nono here maps out the process from 'utopia' to the 'end of utopia', moving from the heights of 'ottavino + con soprani (utopia)' in the 'Prometeo' episode via 'Fl basso + trb + coro = fiati' in the 'Io' episode to the depths of low wind and live electronics alone in the (later discarded) 'Fine utopia – Achilles' episode. Roman numerals further indicate the interval categories for each of the episodes. Moving from pure fourths and fifths in 'Prometeo' to tritones and microtonal inflection in 'Io' and '2–7–9' in 'Fine utopia – Achilles', it is clear that Nono had a progressive loss of 'clarity' in mind.

Although eventually composed on a much smaller scale, 'Hölderlin' realises some of the key elements of this progression from 'utopia' to the 'end of utopia' as it was first imagined. Above all, the section stands out for its prominent and truly utopian use of the solo sopranos. Never before or after are the two singers given such exposure. Again, much more is heard than what is notated. Two delays and feedback continuously multiply and superimpose the sound of this closely interwoven duo. The vocal lines are

[171] A–E♭–E–B♭ occurs most frequently, always varied in instrumentation and register, at bars 48–49 (vla/bsn), 69 (hrn/trb), 73 (fl/vln), 78–81 (vcl/trb), 94 (db/hrn), 124–27 (db/hrn/trb). Melkert regards these orchestral interventions as quotations from *Io, frammento dal Prometeo*; *«Far del silenzio cristallo»*, 165–66. Given their substantial re-instrumentation and rhythmic variation, they are perhaps simply manifestations of the category T, which was already in use for *Io, frammento*.

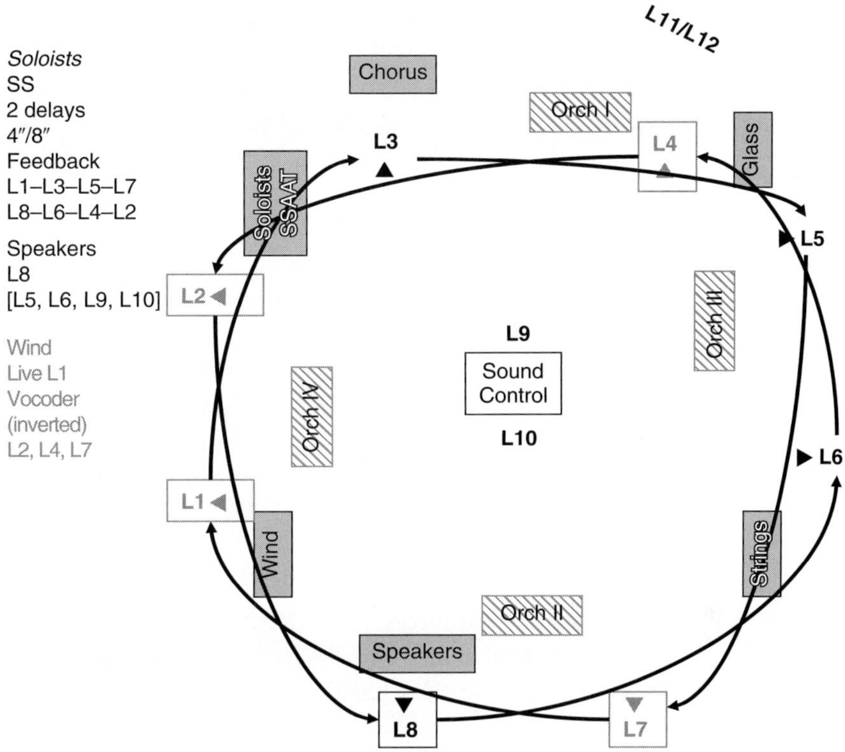


**Figure 7.9** *Prometeo*, spatial set-up for 'Hölderlin'.

thus layered and slowly grow into an ever denser chorus of soprano voices. This growing polyphony of live and played-back vocal sound slowly encircles the listener in the familiar fashion: clockwise and anti-clockwise at different speeds (see Figure 7.9).

'Oltre le porte dei morti' (Beyond the doors of the dead) is the poetic image from Rilke's *Sonnets to Orpheus* Nono first associates with the planned 'Fine utopia – Achille' episode. 'Achille/ solo soprano/ altri voci senza testo' (Achilles/ solo soprano/ other voices without text) he notes on another early sketch.[172] With the composition of *Io, frammento dal Prometeo* (1981), it must have become clear, however, that the hidden concept of the end of utopia should not be laid bare and that the process from 'utopia' to the 'end of utopia' was best subsumed into a setting of Hölderlin, the poet who 'alone' understood the full significance of Achilles. Like the impossible utopia itself, the figure of Achilles is thus 'mere memory', a case of 'Hölderlinian *Andenken*' (as Cacciari notes in his initial notes).

172 ALN 51.14.03/04

More important than the end of the utopia of liberation, after all, is its consequence: the retreat of the god, which leaves the human race to an uncertain fate on Earth. Without further mention of Achilles, the envisaged musical process from 'utopia' to the 'end of utopia' is thus encapsulated in an extended version of Hölderlin's *Schicksalslied*, the very poem which, together with *Brod und Wein*, most clearly speaks of the 'tragic awareness' of 'the "retreat" of the god' which both Cacciari and Heidegger saw as a defining feature not merely of Hölderlin's poetic thought, but generally of any creative endeavour in modern times, our very own 'dürftige Zeit'.

As shown by Jeschke, Nono first envisaged encircling the audience with Hölderlin's *Schicksalslied* throughout the entire course of *Io, frammento dal Prometeo* (1981).[173] For this continuous, work-encompassing spiral the composer initially intended to use two sopranos and piccolo, precisely the forces he associated with 'utopia' in his 1981 draft of *Prometeo*.[174] This plan was never realised, however, and Hölderlin's *Schicksalslied* was first embedded into *Io, frammento dal Prometeo* as movement VI. This first setting is scored for two solo sopranos, bass flute and contrabass clarinet, the instrumental forces associated with Io and Prometeo. The text stems from the third stanza and the focus is, once again, not on the gods (who dwell 'fateless' in their heavenly abode), but on the human race alone:

| | |
|---|---|
| DOCH . . . | YET |
| uns ist gegeben | to us is given |
| auf keiner Stätte | no place |
| zu ruhn . . . | to rest . . . |
| | |
| es schwinden | they disappear |
| es fallen | they fall |
| die leidenden | the suffering |
| MENSCHEN | PEOPLE |
| | |
| blindlings | blindly |
| wie Wasser | like water |
| von Klippe | from cliff |
| zu Klippe | to cliff |
| | |
| ins Ungewisse | into uncertainty |
| | |
| hinab . . . | downward . . . |

173 Jeschke, *Prometeo*, 223/24.

174 See the preliminary sketch for *Io* published in Jeschke, *Prometeo*, 224.

For the first version in *Io, frammento dal Prometeo* the closely intertwined soprano lines are already multiplied and give rise to an ever more unstable polyphony of live and 'recorded' vocal sound by means of a long delay (14″) with feedback. When the sopranos cease to sing, the wind instruments continue to play their independent parts from opposite corners of the performance space while the still circulating feedback of the vocal sound gradually fades into silence. The envisaged process from 'utopia' to the 'end of utopia' is thus composed in a nutshell. Not unlike the second flute section of *Das atmende Klarsein*, the two 'utopian' sopranos trigger waves of sound demarcating the boundaries of the vocal register (rising up to C♯ and descending to middle D) and then descend to ever lower depths. As I will show in more detail for the second version, the process begins with open fifths and fourths but quickly loses its purity as the open intervals are increasingly filled out with tritones, tones and semitones. The final descent is then markedly chromatic, and this chromaticism is greatly enhanced by means of the electronic multiplication. After a brief last recourse to 'pure' Gaia formations, only the microtonal 'depths' of the wind soloists and the fading echo of the vocal 'utopia' remain.

More important than the process of 'falling' (which Jeschke focuses on in her comparative analysis with Brahms's *Schicksalslied*)[175] is the tightening grip of the perceptibly denser and ever more dissonant progression from 'utopia' to the 'end of utopia' that will continue into microtonal pitch differentiation in *Prometeo*. For this extended 'Hölderlin', Nono more or less reuses the original soprano parts from *Io, frammento dal Prometeo* (with only a few, mostly registral changes). The wind parts are newly composed, however, and now coordinated with the sopranos. The use of live-electronics, too, is considerably altered. Crucially, Hölderlin's *Schicksalslied* is now continued with Cacciari's allusion to Pindar's sixth *Nemean Ode*, which goes to the heart of the work's conception. To interconnect Hölderlin and Pindar, Nono adds the two speakers. The section is thus not merely a second setting of the *Schicksalslied*, but a continued concern with the process from 'utopia' to the 'end of utopia' which began with 'Hölderlin' in *Io, frammento dal Prometeo* but is then considerably altered and extended for *Prometeo*.

Above all, the two shorter delays of 4″ and 8″ now result in a much tighter multiplication of the soprano lines. Greater vocal intensity is further created by an increase in speed (from ♩ = 72 to ♩ = 84).[176] With sustained

[175] Jeschke, *Prometeo*, 212–43.

[176] The score notates ♩ = 72. According to Richard, Nono later changed the speed to ♩ = 84.

**Example 7.5** Pitch reduction of 'Hölderlin'.

durations and extremely slow harmonic change, the effect of this change is one of urgency rather than speed. Two halaphones move the soprano sound clockwise and anti-clockwise around the audience at two different speeds (see Figure 7.9). Example 7.5 outlines the oscillating pitch progression of the sustained and almost continuous vocal band. Fourths, fifths and tritones are notated as dyads and the fields of 2–7–9 relationships with which they are linked, filled out and extended are bracketed. Bearing in mind that all pitches are continuously delayed and overlapped, this outline is by no means to be read as a linear process. Instead, it indicates the nature of the pitch fields with which Nono gradually moves from purity to microtonal impurity, from wide oscillations to ever tighter 'uncertainty'.

Each of these fields is given a harmonic centre, ambitus and direction (ascending or descending). Usually they begin and end on a single pitch, the feedback of which is then carried over into the next field of pitches. In other words, the shape of these fields is clearly conceived with the electronic sound transformation and spatialised polyphony in mind. Each field is meant to trigger a wave of pitches, of which the listener is to perceive the direction and the widening and contracting ambitus, as well as its inner density. The effect of the relentless electronic layering is all the more intense the narrower the ambitus of the field, and this gradual intensification is further underlined with a steady increase in dynamics to *f–ff e più* in Part I.

Part II continues the concerns of Part I with slightly altered parameters. The ambitus of the vocal lines is now considerably narrower. Yet the inner pitch spectrum is just as rich, with the sopranos branching out into microtones. Microtonal tension peaks in the passage setting the text 'Una del dio', the ambitus of which also happens to fit neatly into the scala enigmatica segment Nono first associated with the gods (E–F♯–G♯–B♭). But the fields of this second part, too, open out into fourths and fifths, most notably the pure 'Gaia' fifth D/A. All openness and purity is inevitably lost, however, in the surrounding haze of increasingly microtonal feedback into which the god 'retreats'. On a par with fourths and fifths is the interval of the tritone. Much more prominently than in Part I (where the tritone A–E♭ twice sets the words 'die leidenden Menschen' (suffering humanity)), the tritone F–B frames Part II and thus takes on the function of the V–IV formations at the beginning and end of Part I. With microtonal deviation similar to that of the amplified instruments in the First Island, the interval of the tritone now comes to stand much more explicitly for the 'unhappy' union of god and man in this second stage of the progression from 'utopia' to the 'end of utopia'.

The third stage of this progress (originally envisaged for low wind and live electronics alone, with a focus on the 2–7–9 intervals) is realised in the new wind parts which atmospherically underline and continue the progression from 'purity' to 'impurity' and total pitch effacement. Throughout Part I the wind parts are pitched and by no means confined to the interval category 2–7–9. After a deceptively tonal beginning in F♯ minor, this interval category predominantly defines the relationship between the vocal polyphony and the increasingly more violent and dynamically accentuated interventions of the wind. The multiphonics on bass flute provide additional impurity and an unpredictable flux of timbres. By means of a vocoder the bass flute also regulates the sound of the contrabass clarinet: with an inverted vocoder setting, the lower frequencies of the flute sharpen the high frequencies of the contrabass clarinet.[177] The sound of the clarinet is further modified with the addition of pink noise. As Nono told Haller, the sound of the two wind instruments is to become so harsh that it seems 'as sharp as a blade'.[178] In contrast to the spiralling soprano sound, the transmission of the wind is static throughout (L1, L2, L4 and L7; see Figure 7.9). Like the cliffs in Hölderlin's text, the instruments thus offer a rough, rugged and increasingly harsh resistance to the cascading lyricism of the sopranos.

The impurity grows with the entry of the two speakers, who render the *Schicksalslied* twice more. In its spoken rendition the text is interlocked and superimposed, and thus loses much of its intelligibility. Both sopranos and speakers are asked to articulate and accentuate the consonants. In the sung layer, this accentuated articulation effectively marks the pitch changes, though, overall, the long durations of the interwoven sopranos primarily sustain and highlight the vowel structure of the text. The harsh articulation of the consonants is much more pronounced in the spoken parts. As Nono instructs in the score, the text should be 'murmured *on top* of the microphone, very articulated: *consonants as articulated as possible*: explosive – dental/labial – guttural *as harsh as possible*'.[179] Like the wind sound, the transmission of this guttural spoken layer is static, heard through either the highest loudspeaker behind the audience or the speakers on the right and above the control panel (L8 or L5, L6, L9 and L10). As Hölderlin moves into the realm of speech and Cacciari's allusion to Pindar is microtonally phased in by the spiralling sopranos, the wind instruments similarly retreat into increasing pitch uncertainty: a dynamic cloud of 'aria intonata' (breath noise with only a hint of pitch) and fluttering noises on the mouthpiece of the contrabass clarinet. The wind only gain their footing in pitched terrain again as the sopranos cease to sing. Very quietly they bring the progression from 'utopia' to the 'end of utopia' to a close with a few final 2–7–9 relationships while the fading feedback of the sopranos eerily disperses in space.

## Isola 2°: Stasimo 1° (*ca.* 8′)

Soloists (SSAAT), chorus, orchestras I–IV
Text: Euripides, *Alcestis*

[177] On the vocoder and its use for 'Hölderlin' see Haller, I, 65–66; II, 128–29; and Jeschke, *Prometeo*, 226–27.

[178] Haller, II, 129.

[179] 'mormorato *sul* microfono molto articolato: *consonanti articolatissime*: esplosive – dentali/labiali – gutturali *durissime*', *Prometeo* (1985), 143.

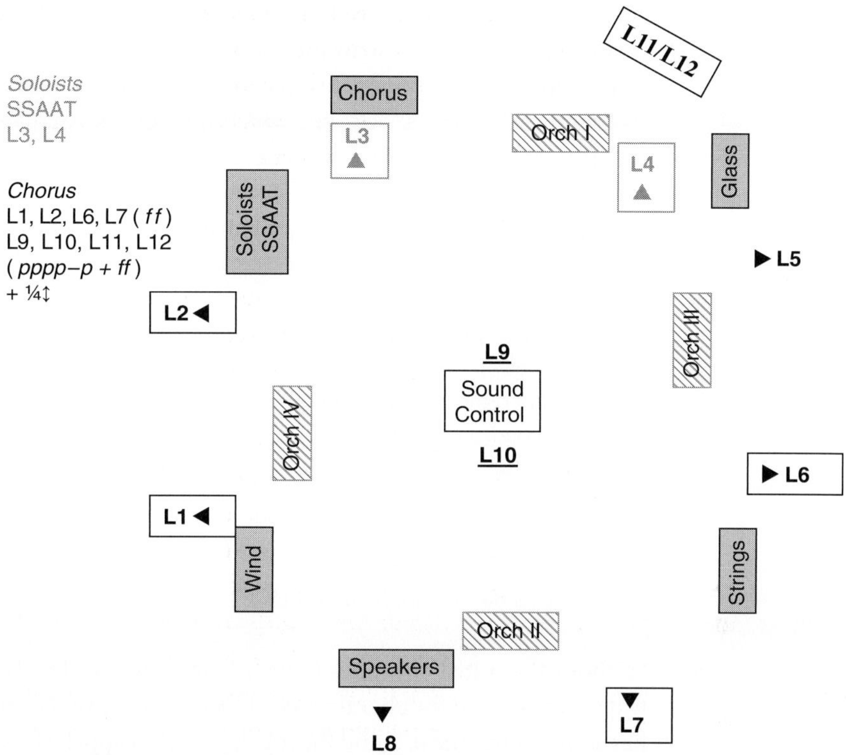


**Figure 7.10** *Prometeo*, spatial set-up for 'Stasimo 1°'.

Of all sections in *Prometeo*, the First Stasimon has received the most detailed analytical attention. Much of Jeschke's pioneering study is dedicated to this central turning point, and Melkert has shown how it was reworked from the last movement of *Io, frammento dal Prometeo.*[180] I will supplement these analyses by adding some reflections on the Gaia material as the underlying harmonic system.

The First Stasimon particularly appeals to the analyst because Nono here clearly harks back to the Renaissance and the music of 'few notes' he so admired. For the first time in *Prometeo*, the spatial set-up is used in truly antiphonal fashion, in a manner reminiscent of the Venetian 'cori spezzati' and their use during ceremonial services in St. Mark's. Throughout this section, the vocal and orchestral sound comes from fixed points in space, and spatial movement is deliberately halted (see Figure 7.10). This is after all a 'stasimon', a choral song in lyric metre, which, in Greek tragedy, is inserted between episodes to momentarily interrupt the dramatic action

[180] Jeschke, *Prometeo*, 99–163; Melkert, *«Far del silenzio cristallo»*, 112–16/173–83.

with a collective, poetic reflection. Stasima were deliberately set apart in performance and sung with the entire chorus 'standing in one place'.[181]

The form corresponds to Cacciari's choice of text from the fourth stasimon of Euripides' *Alcestis*, which introduces Ananke (Necessity) as a superior power on a par with Gaia:

> [and having touched on many arguments
> I found nothing stronger than Necessity]
>
> Neither Thracian enchantment,
> Nor the voice of Orpheus,
> Nor the remedy of Phoebus,
> Nor blood sacrifice,
> Nor statue,
> Nor altar calms her
> Nor Chalybean iron bends her
> She knows no shame
> Inaccessible she holds the summit.

Without the initial two lines (which Nono reserves for 'Interludio 1°'), this text was first set in the choral finale of *Io, frammento dal Prometeo*. As Melkert has shown, both the text and the music of this a cappella finale were reused for *Prometeo*. With the four orchestras, chorus and all five soloists, the 'Io episode' here concludes on a much grander scale. At its core, however, this version too is essentially 'choral song'. In the manner of the 'cori spezzati', the music proceeds in extremely clear-cut micro-polyphonic blocks of contrasting instrumentation, dynamics and density. The great majority of these blocks are sung and the vocal layer is predominantly led by the chorus. The soloists mostly double the choral parts, only rarely taking on an independent role. Much more extraordinarily, however, the 'choral song' also extends to the orchestral musicians who sing and play their parts whenever they accompany the vocal forces.[182] To indicate this avant-garde playing and singing technique (unique to 'Stasimo 1°'), Nono makes use of the performance instruction 'a sonar e cantar' which, in Renaissance times, indicated the possible addition of instrumental forces to a vocal composition and is perhaps best known from Giovanni Gabrieli's madrigal 'Lieto godea'.[183] While Renaissance composers

[181] Howatson (ed.), *Oxford Companion to Classical Literature*, 577.

[182] The instrumentalists were at first expected to sing text; Jeschke, *Prometeo*, 117.

[183] 'Lieto godea' carries the direction *per cantar et sonar* and was published together with two similar *arie di sonar* ('Fuggi pur se sai' and 'Chiar' angioletta') in the secular section of the *Concerti* (1587).

added instruments for additional contrast and grandeur, Nono uses this instruction to almost opposite effect. In asking the musicians to sing and play at the same time (higher or lower octaves if necessary), even to sing into the instrument (in the case of the wind), the orchestral textures provide a mysterious and almost mystical aura – 'quasi eco' as Nono notes in the score. This 'natural' vocal haze in the orchestras is further complemented in the vocal layer with subtle microtonal phasing of the chorus (the sound of which is transposed by about a sixth of a tone up and down).

After the retreat of the god and the loss of all certainty in 'Hölderlin', the dramatic thread of the tragedy thus momentarily comes to rest in the microtonal haze of Gaia, the origin. This is, after all, the tragic moment in which man finds himself abandoned on Earth, alone in the face of Ananke. Without the tyrant Zeus, this is also a moment of great possibility, the dawn of a new era. Nono beautifully captures these dawning new possibilities by drawing the human voice and the orchestras together into song. There is unsung orchestral violence too, however, in the recurring 'Manfred' chord. And the orchestras also recede into exceedingly quiet 'ricordi lontanissimi', distant memories of the hazy microtonality with which Gaia first emerged from Chaos: 'wie ein Naturlaut' not yet ruled by Kratos and Bia.

In recognition of the higher laws of Gaia and Ananke, it is hardly surprising that all three compositional elements should derive from the Gaia material alone. Both Jeschke and Melkert have shown that the vocal and orchestral blocks are composed in sets of fifths and include some very overt examples of the category T which Nono himself linked to Gaia.[184] I will offer another view of these sets of fifths and propose a possible generative system for the use of the Gaia material in this section.

In my reflections on the harmonic system, I have already cited the 'Manfred' chord as an example of dischord between the harmonic categories of Gaia and its descendants (Example 7.2). As shown by Jeschke, the 'Manfred' chord attains its greatest prominence in the First Stasimon. Despite its choral origin in *Io, frammento dal Prometeo*, it is assigned only to the orchestras in *Prometeo*, extended microtonally, and used for sudden disruptive and extremely violent outbursts that occur only during the first half of the work. These orchestral outbursts are repeatedly (but not always) also charged with the characteristic syncopated rhythm of the opening motif of Schumann's *Manfred Overture* and assigned the fastest speed by

[184] Jeschke mentions the category T and draws the link to Gaia; *Prometeo*, 107–116; Melkert details the sets of fifths for movement IX of *Io, frammento dal Prometeo* and shows the link to 'Stasimo 1°'; Melkert, «*Far del silenzio cristallo*», 112–16/173–83.

far (♩ = 152).[185] In the First Stasimon the chord also appears with a much slower speed (♩ = 63) and a quiet dynamic (*p*). In this unique double guise, the bold intervention is particularly reminiscent also of its precedent in *Fragmente – Stille, an Diotima*. '... Wenn in einem Blick ... und Laut ...' (... when with one glance ... and sound ...) is the Hölderlinian title assigned to the strikingly similar gesture in the quartet. Here too, this 'motif-like' fragment bursts in with an extremely fast and characteristic syncopated rhythm and is coupled with a textural manifestation of the same material at a more moderate speed and dynamic. The material itself relates to the later category T in *Prometeo*, since both 'Blick' and 'Laut' are essentially composed of chromatically interlocking tritones.

Both Jeschke and Melkert have shown that the 'Manfred' chord attained its motivic function and characteristic association with Schumann's overture only in the final version of 1985. However, among preliminary reflections on various possible materials, Nono had already jotted down 'As cues: mutation of the basic material of the *Tritone*'.[186] With its characteristic rhythmic structure and fixed set of tritones, the 'Manfred' chord stands out as the most recognisable mutation of this category T. A further clue as to how this material may have been organised is found in the same group of preliminary sketches. Nono here notates two sets of whole-tone scales: an ascending lower set on C and C♯ and a descending higher set on D and E♭.[187]

With these preliminary sketches and the use of tritones in the quartet in mind, the following disposition of the Gaia material allows the deduction of all the compositional blocks of the 'First Stasimon'. Making use of the whole-tone scale on C, I have divided the cycle of fifths into two groups: A and B in parts (a) and (b) in Example 7.6. According to Nono's own reflections, Group A is notated in the bass clef and comprises the upper fifths of the ascending whole-tone scale on C. Group B is notated in treble clef and contains the lower fifths of the descending scale on C. The fifths of each group are then chromatically interlocked. For Group A the ascending whole-tone scale on C is intertwined with that on C♯ and upper and lower fifths are added respectively. The six fifths of Group A are thus duplicated and interlocked in semitone and tritone relationships. The same procedure is applied to Group B, on the basis of the descending whole-tone scales on E♭ and D (again following Nono's own specifications).

185 Since Jeschke first revealed this association, the chord has generally become known as the 'Manfred' chord. On its repeated occurrences see Jeschke, *Prometeo*, 150.

186 'Per battute: spostamento di Base del *Tritono*' ALN 51.14.01/07.

187 ALN 51.14.02/06.

**Example 7.6** (a) Pitch Group A. (b) Pitch Group B. (c) Pitch reduction of 'Stasimo 1°'.

It now becomes clear that the agglomerated fifths of the 'Manfred' chord (M) can be seen to belong to Group A of this disposition. With the exception of the five 'ricordi lontanissimi', all the building blocks of the First Stasimon can now be explained in this way. Example 7.6(c) notates all blocks of interlocking fifths in the manner of my proposed disposition of the Gaia material. The 'Manfred' chord with its four fifths from Group A is marked M and the 'ricordi lontanissimi' are italicised (*RL*). Table 7.3 provides details on the length of each block, its text (if applicable), forces, dynamics and speeds. Only the blocks with text carry the performance instruction 'a sonar e cantar' in the orchestras. All others are purely instrumental (the 'ricordi lontanissimi' are further marked 'solo sonar'). Unlike Jeschke, I do not regard the bars of silence as independent entities.[188] Together with the many

[188] See Jeschke, *Prometeo*, 106.

Table 7.3 *Stasimo 1°*

| Bar | Group | Text | Forces | Dynamics | Speed | P |
|---|---|---|---|---|---|---|
| 1 | A (4V) | | orch. I–IV | *f–sfff* | 44 | |
| 2 | B (3V) | Né incantamento tracio | *chorus* | *P* | 34 | |
| | | Né voce d'Orfeo | vlc/db/hrn/trb | *ppp–pppp* | | |
| | | Né rimedio di Febo | (+ vln/bs orch. II) | | | |
| 6 | Rla | | vln/fl/cl | *ppppp* | 56 | |
| 9 | B (3V) | Tracio/Orfeo/Febo | *chorus* | *P* | 34 | |
| | | | vcl/db/hrn/trb | *ppp–pppp* | | |
| 11 | Rla′ | | vln/fl/cl | *ppppp* | 56 | 1″ |
| 15 | B (2V) | La placa | *soli/chorus* | *mf, f–ppp* | 46 | 3″ |
| | | | female voices | | | |
| 19 | B (3V) | La placa | *chorus* | *p, fff >* | 60, 30 | |
| | | ['. . . ins Weite | vln/fl/cl/tr/hrn | *mixed* | | |
| | | verfliegend . . .'] | (I/III) | *ppp–sfff* | | |
| | | | vln/bs/hrn/trb | | | |
| | | | (II/IV) | | | |
| 23 | RLb | | vln/vla | *ppppp* | 30 | |
| 25 | A (4V) | Né altare né statua | *soli/chorus* | *p–pp* | 34 | 3″ |
| | | Né sanguinante offerta | vcl/trb | *pp–pppp* | | |
| | | Né ferro Calibe | | | | |
| 29 | A (M) | | orch. I–IV | *p–f* | 152 | 3″ |
| 30 | A (2V) | La piega | *soli* (SSAA) | *pp, mf, ff* | 44 | 5″ |
| | | ['. . . ins Weite | vln/vla/fl/cl | > | | |
| | | verfliegend . . .'] | | *mixed* | | |
| 35 | A (M) | | orch. I–IV | *f–fff* | 152 | 3″ |
| 36 | B (2V) | Ignora | *soli/chorus* | *ppppp* | 30 | 3″ |
| 38 | A (M) | | orch. I–IV | *p* | 63 | 3″ |
| 39 | A (3V) | ΑΙΔΩΣ | *chorus* | *pppppp* | 30 | 7″ |
| | | | vla/vcl | | | |
| 41 | A (M) | | orch. I–IV | *f–sfff, p* | 152, 63 | 7″ |
| 44 | A (M) | Inaccessa/U | *chorus* | *mixed,* | 56–72, | |
| | | | mixed (orch. I–IV) | *ppppp* | 54 | |
| 50 | RLc | | Fl/cl/vla/db | *pppp* | 54 | |
| 51 | B (2V) | Ha | *soli/chorus* | *ff* | 76 | |
| | | | *mixed (orch.* I–IV) | *ff–sfff* | | |
| 52 | RLd | | vla/vcl/db/tr/hrn/ | *pp, pppp* | 44, 30 | 4″/8″ |
| | | | trb/bs | | | |
| 55 | A + B | La cima | *soli* (SSAA)/*chorus* | *fpp–pppp* | 46 | 7″ |
| | (2 + 2V) | | orch. I–IV | *sfppp, pppp* | | |

fermatas, they provide extra time and space for this 'choral song' to resonate. The durations of these punctuating moments of silence gradually increase and are listed in the last column of the table under the heading 'P' (for pause).

In terms of pitch, Nono works with sets of two to four fifths from Group A and sets of two and three fifths from Group B. The movement begins with maximum density: a set of four fifths from Group A. Like the 'Manfred' chord, this set is rendered by the four orchestras (strings and brass) and used for a dramatic opening blast that charges in from all sides. The pitch material for the entire first 'stanza' then stems from Group B. Interspersed with the first 'ricordo lontanissimo', a span of five interlocking fifths is gradually covered in blocks of three and two (3/3/2/3) whereby the set of three fifths remains the same throughout. This 'choral song' begins in still quietude. At the static dynamic *p*, the sound of the chorus is transmitted through the indirect loudspeakers only (L9 to L12, see Figure 7.10). Its orchestral 'aura' echoes the choral sound in the lowest of registers. Led by cello, double bass, horn and trombone, the mysterious mixture of sung and instrumental sound seems to surge up from Hölderlinian depths ('. . . Wenn aus der Tiefe . . .').

As Jeschke and Melkert have shown, each set of fifths gives rise to a tight-knit polyphonic texture in which some instrumental players double the vocal parts while others render the remaining parts from the equivalent section of the finale of *Io, frammento.*[189] In the first choral block, for example, the instrumentalists of orchestra I play and sing the parts of the chorus in retrograde while selected instruments of the other three orchestras double the choral parts in their original form. All other instruments render the remaining parts from *Io, frammento*. The part allocation for this first vocal block is detailed in Table 7.4.

In comparison with the original choral passage in eight parts, the vocal forces are now compressed into a three-part nucleus in middle register. The instrumentalists not only echo the voices (O/R) but also add the remaining five parts from *Io, frammento dal Prometeo*. The result is a denser and much more diffuse field of sound with a firm vocal core. Sound diffusion is further enhanced by the singing of the instrumentalists and the microtonal transposition of the choral sound. In this fashion, *Io, frammento dal Prometeo* serves as a compositional basis for the entire stasimon. From the original choral composition in four to twelve parts, Nono consistently selects three to four parts (and a maximum of six at the very end).

[189] The contrapuntal structure is analysed in Jeschke, *Prometeo*, 107–19. Melkert compares the blocks with their original form in the finale of *Io, frammento dal Prometeo*; 175–78.

Table 7.4 *Stasimo 1° – first choral block*

| *Io, frammento dal Prometeo*, IX (bars 489–92) | *Stasimo 1°* (bars 2–5) |
|---|---|
| Soprano 1 | Double bass IV |
| Soprano 2 | Horn IV |
| Mezzo soprano 1 | Soprano & alto (chorus) |
| | Cello IV, violin & bassoon II (O) |
| | Cello I (R) |
| Mezzo soprano 2 | Tenor (chorus) |
| | Trombone IV, cello III (O) |
| | Trombone I (R) |
| Alto 1 | Horn II |
| Alto 2 | Bass (chorus) |
| | Cello II, horn III (O) |
| | Double bass I (R) |
| Tenor 1 | Trombone III |
| Tenor 2 | Double bass III |

If vocal register and density were used to maximum effect in *Io, frammento dal Prometeo*, they are now clearly stabilised in the middle register and it mostly falls to the singing instrumentalists to differentiate the music in terms of density, ambitus and colour.

Already for *Io, frammento dal Prometeo* Nono had rearranged Cacciari's text into a clear A–A′–B form. Text and music are now reused in the same tripartite form:

| | | | |
|---|---|---|---|
| **A** | né voce di Orfeo | no voice of Orpheus | *Pitch Group B* |
| | né incantamento Tracio | no Thracian spell | |
| | né rimedio di Febo | no remedy of Phoebus | |
| | la placa | calms her | |
| **A′** | né altare né statua | no altar or statue | *Pitch Group A* |
| | né sanguinante offerta | no blood sacrifice | |
| | né ferro Calibe | or Chalybean iron | |
| | la piega | bends her | |
| **B** | Ignora | she knows no | *B* |
| | ΑΙΔΩΣ | Shame | *A* |
| | Inaccessa | Inaccessible | *A* |
| | Ha | she holds | *B* |
| | la cima | the summit | *A + B* |

The first choral block sets the first three lines of the text with a set of three fifths from Group B in low register. The second vocal block extracts and repeats the mythological names, homing in on them with the same set of fifths, in the same register, dynamics and core instrumentation as the first block of text. The next vocal block is marked by a harmonic shift to the adjacent upper category T, thins down to just four parts and is set for the female voices alone, again in very low register. This a cappella use of the vocal forces is exceptional and occurs just twice. Much more so than in *Io, frammento* (where this moment is rendered by baritone and bass), Nono now underlines the connection to Io's repeated plea 'placa-mi', also sung by the female soloists, with exactly the same pitch set (and framed by the 'Manfred' chord) in the 'Io–Prometeo' section (bar 105). The 'la placa' is now longer and much more stoical. It comes from all sides, fairly loudly, before receding into indirect transmission (see Figure 7.10). Even here Nono maintains the idea of core and aura: the sound of the soloists is transmitted in all purity from the front, while the choral voices are heard from the side and rear, discretely steeped in microtonal haziness.

The next vocal block draws the words 'la placa' into the initial block of three fifths. The familiar set is once again rendered by the full chorus. With a slightly enlarged group of instrumentalists (including violins, flutes, clarinets and trumpets), this final block of section A rises into a much higher register. The orchestral aura, too, is substantially altered. As before, the musicians play and sing, but their accentuated single beats no longer echo and embed the vocal parts. These instrumental 'shouts' shatter and disperse the pitch set very much in the manner of the irregular 'spiccato–sautillé' articulation 'con possibile pause' which Nono makes use of for the fragment '... ins Weite verfliegend ...' (... dispersing into the distance ...) in *Fragmente – Stille, an Diotima*. A similar dispersal of sound is later found in Nono's last orchestral work, *No hay caminos, hay que caminar ... Andrej Tarkowskij* (1987). In all three cases, the device is used to mark the end of a section or block sonority in order to make way for new materials and developments.

Similar text gives rise to similar music in section A′, but this much shorter middle section is also a central turning point and initiates new developments. It begins with a dense field of four fifths, the same set as that of the orchestral opening (Example 7.6(c)). The central chromatic link (ascending F–F♯–G–A♭) is also closely related to that of the block of three fifths in section A (descending G♯–G–F♯). The chromatic core of section A is simply extended at the lower end and flipped into its harmonic opposite (using the fifths of Group A rather than those of Group B). The effect of this is magical, and is underlined by a subtle change in balance between the vocal and instrumental forces. The soloists now join the chorus in four parts. The other four parts are covered by the singing instrumentalists, but Nono radically reduces the instruments to cello and trombone only. In low register and with equally quiet dynamics, the similarities to the first stanza are evident and yet 'choral song' now quietly gains the upper hand. All song is rebuffed, however, by the first appearance of the 'Manfred' chord. Like the orchestral opening, it is a dense blast in the middle register that will steadily gain in force before it, too, becomes the basis of a vocal block. The tentative first 'Manfred' intervention is followed by 'la piega', the corresponding block to the 'la placa' settings in section A. With two fifths from Group A, Nono homes in on a second category T. This Gaia formation is not sung a cappella, however. Instead, the female soloists and a group of mellow strings and woodwind (fl/cl/vln/vla) immediately surge into the higher middle register to mark the end of this much tighter section A′. Flutes and violas echo and embed the vocal lines, and only the violins and clarinets break up and disperse the sound.

As the 'Manfred' chord bursts in once more and increases to *fff*, it reveals itself as an independent compositional means of maximum contrast. After this sudden outburst, the next category T is all the more effective. The set is again a chromatic extension of the previous vocal block and flips into the complementary set of fifths (Group B). The four parts are rendered a cappella by all available vocal forces at the impossibly quiet dynamic *ppppp* and the slowest of speeds. In great stillness, this restrained vocal setting of the word 'ignora' reveals itself as the focal point of the stasimon.[190] On the verge of audibility, this moment of calm provides a tentative glimpse of the Promethean transgression and the 'weak messianic force' to come in the second half of *Prometeo*. After this brief glimpse of purity, the instrumental aura emerges in force to envelop and encompass the vocal nucleus, in a manner not dissimilar to that disquieting 'thicket' into which the 'coro lontanissimo' first placed the word 'egeinato' (bore). This final development begins exceedingly quietly. Even the 'Manfred' chord has momentarily been tamed to the dynamic *p* and the slower speed of ♩ = 63. As detailed in Example 7.6(c), the pitch sets of the vocal blocks now alternate between Groups A and B, and the progression culminates in a combination of the two groups.[191] As the 'Manfred' chord makes its last and most forceful appearance, it is assimilated back into its origin, the

190 See Jeschke, *Prometeo*, 115.

191 Hence the ending on the diminished third C♯–E♭, which Jeschke regards as 'unusual'; Jeschke, *Prometeo*, 116.

setting of the word 'inaccessa', which is now all the more dramatic on account of its use of mixed instrumentation (primarily wind) and contrast in dynamics. Thereafter, the last blast is of a very different nature: the word 'ha' is sustained and dispersed at maximum dynamic by the full vocal and orchestral forces as if to show that a new era has indeed begun.

In this new era, the 'Manfred' chord is no longer relevant and makes way for 'ricordi lontanissimi'. Much has already been written on the introduction of these distant memories.[192] Jeschke argues that they refer back to passages of the 1984 version of the First Island that are no longer present in the 1985 version, and this argument has not been disputed since.[193] I cannot believe, however, that Nono would refer back to a sound that lies outside the realm of experience for the listener in this tragedy of listening. It is much more plausible that these distant memories do not have an exact equivalent, but simply refer back to a similar type of sound with a similar pitch set. After all, it is in the nature of memories to blur and become less exact over time. The most productive way of looking at these 'ricordi lontanissimi', it seems to me, is to strip them of their chromatic and microtonal haziness and reduce them to their core pitch and interval content as shown in Example 7.6(c). Jeschke herself produces a similar reduction, but fails to recognise that Nono here refers back to precisely the fifth with which Gaia first emerged from Chaos in the Prologue and the fifths B–F♯ and B♭–F which, throughout the First Island, stood for man's emancipation from nature. The extremely quiet and purely instrumental 'ricordi lontanissimi' may thus be regarded as momentary glimpses of the lost origin: distant memories of the opening orchestral sound, 'wie ein Naturlaut', not yet ruled by Kratos and Bia, as well as man's quest for his very own 'strip of harvest land between stream and rock'.

## Interludio 1° (*ca.* 7′)

Solo alto, solo wind (flute, clarinet, tuba)
Text: Euripides, *Alcestis*; Cacciari, *Maestro del gioco* IV/V

Listening to the stones, the red bricks. Listening to the darkness, listening as if the sky were a creature of the stones, the bricks, the water. Knowing how to see and listen to the invisible and the inaudible. Attaining the minimum degree of audibility, of visibility.

Nono, *Ascoltare le pietre bianche. I suoni della politica e degli oggetti muti*

[192] Jeschke, *Prometeo*, 124–42; Melkert, 182; Mast, *Luigi Nono «Io, Prometeo»*, 110–14.
[193] Jeschke, *Prometeo*, 124–33. Neither Melkert nor Mast disputes Jeschke's findings.

That which transgresses most severely

That which recasts most harshly

'Whereof one cannot speak, thereof one must be silent' *Wittgenstein*

But that which you cannot express in speech, you must not for that reason absolutely 'silence'. *Cacciari*

Nono, sketches for *Prometeo*[194]

With the instruction 'always as *pppppp* as possible on the verge of audibility or inaudibility' this First Interlude goes to the very heart of Nono's 'tragedy of listening'. As the composer told Jürg Stenzl, it is the 'axis of the work' and the 'narrow gateway towards a "new Prometeo"'.[195] One of Nono's preliminary outlines graphically illustrates this nodal point: two lines intersect over a section entitled 'soli', the only musical term within a wide range of other keywords relating only to matters of content.[196] A very large part of Nono's time at the studio was devoted to the realisation of these 'soli'. As André Richard recounts, Nono conducted the most intensive experiments with Fabbriciani, Scarponi and Schiaffini to pave the way for this spiritual centre of the work. Nono himself describes this acoustic research.[197] With the help of the sonoscope, the team set out to explore the register in which all three instrumentalists could come together at the brink of audibility, a zone in which the instrumental timbres would become almost indistinguishable. They eventually settled on three extremely narrow instrumental spans just above and below middle C:

Fabbriciani in the register [$c^1$–$f^1$] on the flute
Scarponi in the register [d♭–a♭] on the clarinet
Schiaffini in the register [f–$f^1$] on the tuba[198]

Walking this tightrope at the very centre of our Western harmonic system, Nono's wind players were able to produce 'true sine waves *without overtones*' at such an exceedingly quiet level of dynamics that it was no longer possible to distinguish who was playing what and where the sounds were coming from. The idea was to create maximum

194 Wittgenstein, *Tractatus*, 150; 'Ma ciò che non puoi esprimere parlando, non per questo devi in assoluta "tacerlo". Cacciari'; ALN 51.04.05/01.

195 Stenzl, *Luigi Nono*, 111. 196 ALN 51.14.04/10.

197 Nono, 'Verso *Prometeo*', *Scritti*, I, 393–94.

198 *Ibid.*, 393. The low flute and clarinet registers are easy to render quietly. The range of the tuba, however, is extremely high and difficult to play quietly. For *Prometeo* it is thus of utmost importance to find a performer who, like Schiaffini, is capable of extreme quietude in high register.

assimilation to the point of confusion. In this way, the three performers would allow the listener to experience

> a spatial listening without origin and without orientating source. [. . .]
> perceiving not only the spatial mobility of the 'breathed' sounds, their 'non-origin', but also an extremely strange diversity of mobile micro-intervals for a single pitch, even almost a memory of 'melody', almost an effect of *phasing*.
> It is the inaudible or the unheard which does not merely slowly fill the space, oh no, *but discovers it*, reveals it.[199]

The minute 'spatial mobility' of these drawn-out pitches at the abyss of nothingness is completely different from the characteristic 'suono mobile', the wide spectrum of highly unpredictable avant-garde techniques with which the solo wind players established themselves as a force of 'Unruhe' throughout the first part of the work. If, in the quartet, 'Stille' gives rise to 'Unruhe', exactly the opposite is the case at this point in *Prometeo*: 'Unruhe' is distilled into 'Stille', with all the German term's connotations of quietude and stillness. In this new and no less disquieting territory, the 'prophetic' power of the wind instruments is inextricably bound to that of the human voice.

The solo alto part is placed in the same octave as the tuba and was written for the natural, low alto voice of Susanne Otto, who is still performing this part with total commitment today. The text for this spine-tingling solo is once again a montage of ancient Greek, Italian and German and, for the first time since the *Prologo*, Nono returns to *Il Maestro del gioco*. Only the most essential fragments of text from stanzas IV and V are intertwined with the as-yet unset opening verse of the fourth stasimon of Euripides' *Alcestis*:

| | |
|---|---|
| Non sperderla | Do not lose it |
| questa debole messianische Kraft | this weak messianische Kraft |
| non a noi soli | not to us alone |
| resiste | endures |
| l'eco | the echo |
| silenzi trascorsi | past silences |
| attimo | moment |
| | |
| kai pleistôn | having touched |
| hapsamenos logon | on many arguments |
| chreisson | nothing |
| ouden | stronger |
| Anankas êyron | than Ananke I found |

[199] *Ibid.*, 393–94.

It is here in the First Interlude (not in the First Stasimon as envisaged by Cacciari) that Ananke is recognised as the most powerful force of all. With these remaining lines from Euripides, Nono goes straight to the heart of Cacciari's conception: the affirmation of a cosmic law that governs *ekdike*, above and beyond the *dike* of the rulers. Precisely this affirmation effects the conciliatory 'pact' that seals man's 'harsh' independence from Zeus. 'There is no joy–liberation in this!', Cacciari writes in his notes for Nono, and 'this will have to be "heard"!' As the highest of ethical principles (Cacciari speaks of the '"purest" concept of God' and thus draws the link to Schoenberg's Moses), this cosmic law does not 'indicate hope' ('no Achilles – no liberation from the god') but demands total submission at the 'most elevated level of spirituality'. It evolves 'in the wasteland' and depends on the 'wonders of the wasteland' to be recognised and affirmed. Without ever appearing, it is the foundation of 'the *techne*, the work, the life of man' and is therefore 'necessarily *political*'.

Nono's and Cacciari's 'new' Prometheus is born out of this demand for 'most sublime abstraction' – 'not Mysticism, not Rebellion'. In Cacciari's preliminary notes, *Prometheus Unbound* is understood

> no longer as mere prophet of the death of the god – as if the death of the god were equivalent to the 'liberation' of man – but as the problem of the liberation of man: the relationship between 'spirituality' and 'politics' in man's liberation – the painful sentence to the wandering and techne of Ulysses, above all – like Moses who is constantly constrained by Aaron [. . .] – 'tragic construction' of a dwelling of one's own.
>
> But doesn't all this also mean: fallibility, indeterminacy, impossibility of theorising this 'dwelling' and its relationships to Zeus and Dike as 'well-grounded'? Is this relationship not a 'conglomeration of fractures'? And is it not thus possible, a priori, that all this is 'deception' – that the 'feast' of conciliation itself is deception? Techne, work, etc., where are they 'well-grounded'?[200]

It is hardly surprising, therefore, that Nono set himself the 'harshest' of laws and sought inspiration in the austere spirituality and 'sublime abstraction' of the music of Machaut for this 'narrow gateway' towards the 'new Prometeo'. 'Machaut monovalori', Nono notes at the top of a sketch for the First Interlude reproduced and discussed by Jeschke.[201] Along with this brief reference to Machaut one finds the following:

| | | | |
|---|---|---|---|
| A = | lunghi | = 10 valori | (A = long = 10 values) |
| B = | lunghi | = 15 valori | (B = long = 15 values) |

[200] Cacciari, preliminary notes B, ALN 51.02.05/31.
[201] ALN 51.07.12, reproduced in Jeschke, *Prometeo*, 63.

As shown by Jeschke, the ten duration values of A are used for a rhythmic structure of five bars and the fifteen values of B are drawn into a structure of seven bars. In both the duration values are separated by rests. Each of the two structures then serves as a basic collection from which a systematically varied selection of 'monovalori' (single values) is chosen for the six manifestations of each structure in the more extensive 1984 version of this interlude.[202]

At the present stage of sketch studies, it is clear that Nono simply makes use of the same duration system as previously for *Con Luigi Dallapiccola* and *Fragmente – Stille, an Diotima*. The two rhythmic structures identified by Jeschke are in fact sub-collections of the much larger collections of duration values which Nono first refers to as 'A veloce' and 'B calmo' in sketches for *Con Luigi Dallapiccola*.[203] Structure A makes use of the ten longest duration values from 'A veloce' while B comprises the fifteen longest durations from 'B calmo'. 'A veloce' and 'B calmo', too, are collections of single duration values separated by rests. And these 'monovalori' are now cast into a system of five bars (A veloce) and seven bars (B calmo) with six 'parts' each.

Without being able to explain Nono's use of 'A veloce' and 'B calmo' in full, I suspect that 'Interludio 1°' is not exceptional in its predetermination of the parameter of duration but presents us with a particularly transparent manifestation of the much more comprehensive underlying system that governs the rhythmic structure as a whole. The idea for this interludio, as Nono reminds himself with Machaut, was simply to single out the longest duration values from both collections and to merge them at the very outer limit of the time scale (tempo ♩ = 30 throughout). All other parameters (pitch, register, dynamics and density) are cast into equally 'narrow' bounds. Much more exceptional than this quasi-serial predetermination of the material (practiced with various degrees of strictness throughout Nono's career) is the introduction of chance procedures into the compositional process itself. As Jeschke discovered, an envelope with snippets of parametric information shows that Nono determined the combination of pitch, instrumentation, density and duration for each of the compositional units of this interludio by drawing lots. With this extraordinary move, Nono is willing to relinquish complete compositional control and thus radically questions the very foundation of his aesthetics.

[202] On the two duration funds see Jeschke, 64–66.

[203] ALN 43.03.02/06 ('A veloce') & 43.03.02/07 ('B calmo').

'To put chance and its automatic acoustic effects as *knowledge* in place of one's own decisions', Nono famously asserted back in 1959, 'can only be the method of those who fear their own decisions and the liberty they entail.'[204] To take chance and improvisation for artistic freedom, Nono argued very forcefully at the time, is 'spiritual suicide' and such 'aesthetes of liberty' know nothing 'of the true concept of creative freedom as the capacity, attained through knowledge and consciousness, to take the necessary decisions within and for one's own time'. Yet, even at the height of his strictest integral serialism, Nono concedes that the 'panacea' of chance may be of interest amongst composers, as long as it is understood and used only as 'a means of expanding one's empirical horizon, a path towards extended knowledge'.

When, more than twenty years later, Nono allows chance into the compositional process itself, his 'empirical horizon' has indeed expanded vastly (through his experience with electronic music in particular) and the move is now 'theoretically grounded' in the philosophical thought of Musil and Wittgenstein:

> In the spirit of Musil, if there is a sense of reality, there must also be a sense of probabilities. It is not true that that which one has chosen is unique and right; perhaps that which wasn't chosen is more adequate. Working in the studio, with electronic music, one experiences this. There are many unforeseens, chance events, errors – errors that have a great importance, as theorised by Wittgenstein.
>
> Because error is that which breaks the rules.
>
> Transgression.
>
> That which opposes the establishment.
>
> That which strives towards other spaces, other skies, other human feelings, internally and externally, without dichotomy between the two, as the banal and manichean mentality still claims today.[205]

'Error as Necessity', Nono's aesthetic manifesto of the early 1980s, makes clear that the composer's decision to engage with chance is by no means at odds with the fundamental belief he expressed back in 1959, that 'music will always remain a historical presence, a testimony of human beings who

[204] Nono, 'Geschichte und Gegenwart in der Musik heute' (1959), in Stenzl, *Texte*, 40; 'Presenza storica nella musica d'oggi' (1960), *Scritti*, I, 53. The various versions of this controversial lecture (ghostwritten by Lachenmann), including the poor English translation in *The Score* 27 (1960), are listed in *Scritti*, I, 563–64.

[205] Nono, 'L'erreure comme nécessité' (1983), *Écrits*, 257. Nono refers to Musil's *The Man Without Qualities* (Chapter IV) and the discussion of error in Wittgenstein's 'Notes on Frazer's Golden Bough'.

consciously address the historical process and who, in every moment of this process, decide with the full clarity of their intuition and logical reasoning and take action because of the vital need for new structures, in order to open up new possibilities'.[206] The moment Ananke (Necessity) is recognised as 'cosmic law' and the new Prometheus emerges as no less than the 'problem of the liberation of man', Nono decides to expose the harshest of compositional predetermination to the rule of chance as if asking himself Cacciari's question 'but doesn't all this also mean: fallibility, indeterminacy, impossibility of a "well-grounded" theoretical basis?' The once 'well-grounded' dwelling of serial theory, it seems, is deliberately undermined to reveal itself as a 'conglomeration of fractures' at the abyss of nothingness.

At the 'most elevated level of spirituality' this moment of 'sublime abstraction' is not mere submission to the 'cosmic law' of Ananke, however, but, crucially, also marks the return to Benjamin's Marxist–messianic concept of history. Once again, the philosophical dimension is drawn into the context of the myth to consciously address the historical process from the perspective of the historical materialist. The principle of text fragmentation and text reduction is thereby taken to the absolute extreme. In complete disregard of the poetic structure of Cacciari's *Maestro del gioco*, Nono simply homes in on some of the key terms of Benjamin's *Theses* and, with the words 'non sperderla/ questa debole messianische Kraft' (do not lose it/ this weak messianische Kraft), picks up the thread exactly where he had left it in the Prologue. The 'weak messianic power', the term Nono later regarded as 'the central word in *Prometeo*', returns together with the concept of the 'echo' of 'past silences', of the silenced voices of the past which it is up to us and every present generation to remember and redeem. 'Beyond the doors of the dead' was the Rilkean image Nono first associated with the opening of the second part ('EKO – FINE UTOPIA/ ACHILLE – ANTICIPA WANDERER').[207] And this image is by no means lost as the idea of the 'echo' receives its full Benjaminian appropriation in conjunction with the term of the 'moment':

> The true image of the past flits by. The past can be seized only as an image which flashes up at the moment of its recognizability and is never seen again. [...] For it is an irretrievable image of the past which threatens to disappear in any present that does not recognize itself as intended in that image.

[206] Nono, 'Geschichte und Gegenwart in der Musik heute', 40. On Nono's controlled use of chance further see Stenzl, 'Improvisation im Schaffen Luigi Nonos', 36–43.

[207] ALN 45.04./02r.

> Articulating the past historically does not mean recognizing it 'the way it really was'. It means appropriating a memory as it flashes up in a moment of danger. Historical materialism wishes to hold fast that image of the past which unexpectedly appears to the historical subject in a moment of danger.[208]

No moment in *Prometeo* is more precarious than this tightrope walk between audibility and inaudibility, and it is precisely this 'moment of danger' which leads us to the most attentive and perceptive kind of listening. As music, this First Interlude is essentially about recognition. At the very heart of the 'tragedy of listening', myth and philosophy converge and completely penetrate each other to lead us to this heightened state of awareness. Past and present are no longer cast into independent compositional layers (as was the case in the Prologue), but all strains of thought are now merged to the point of confusion. At the verge of intemporality, all parameters (including the two layers of text) are reduced to the extreme, almost to the point of erasure, and subjected to the same 'harsh laws' and chance procedures. Drawing lots as to how to combine the strictly predetermined parameters is precisely the radical move with which Nono here breaks with progressive–constructive reasoning and anticipates the Nietzschean 'Wanderer'. Tied to Wittgenstein's concept of language as a continuous and non-progressive struggle to unearth that which lies beyond the utterable, Nono ensures that this precarious musical tightrope walk arrives at no final destination, but only leads 'from chance to chance, from event to event' – 'irgendwohin' (some place). Linear movement is also deliberately abandoned in the spatial dimension: each 'monovalore' of the solo alto voice is transmitted through a different loudspeaker, chosen at random and on the spur of the moment (see Figure 7.11). Meanwhile, the movement of the sound of the wind instruments is kept to a minimum, such that in the spatial dimension, too, the idea of the 'Wanderer' is brought together with Benjaminian 'arrest of happening'[209] to consciously break with progressive thinking in order to move 'beyond the doors of the dead'. And thus the key concept – '"the weak messianic power"; the "messianic" – that is the power of non-violence' – reveals itself as that which 'recasts' and 'transgresses' in the face of the omnipotent 'cosmic law' of Ananke.

[208] Benjamin, Theses V and VI, in Löwy, *Fire Alarm*, 40, 42.

[209] Benjamin uses the term 'Stillstellung' (Thesis XVII); Nono and Cacciari consistently speak of 'Stillsetzung'.

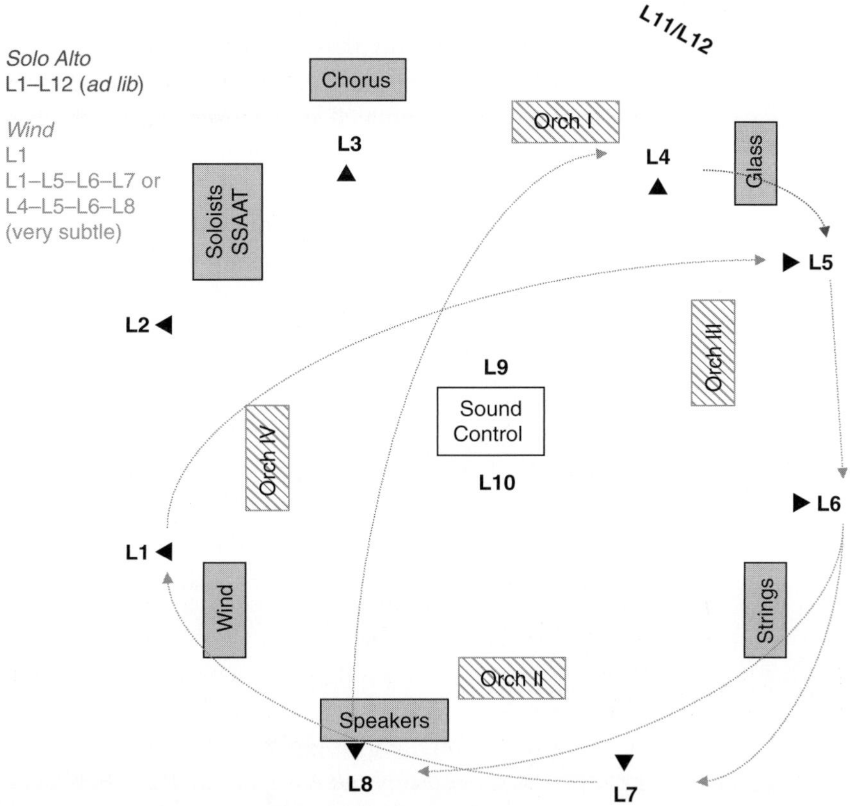


**Figure 7.11** *Prometeo*, spatial set-up for 'Interludio 1°'.

## 3 Voci a (*ca.* 13′)

Soloists (SAT), solo wind (bfl, cbcl, euphonium), glass, orchestras I–IV (violins only)
Text: *Maestro del gioco* VII/VIII/IX

Ein jeder Engel ist schrecklich.
Every angel is terrible.

Rilke, *Duineser Elegien*, I

With '3 Voci a' Nono returns to compositional layers and progressive development. The three 'acoustic levels' of this movement are identified as

(a) the three soloists
(b) euphonium
(c) strings 'sempre *pppp*'[210]

[210] Nono, *Prometeo*, score, 164.

With an underlined 'non unificarli' Nono further stresses that no attempt should be made to unify these acoustic levels.

The dominating and most extraordinary of these three 'voices' is that of the euphonium. Its notated part moves exclusively in fifths and yet this compositional layer is hardly one of great purity. The hastily notated dyads (lacking all indications of dynamics and many ties) hardly convey the skill and stamina this part demands. To render the sustained 'monovalori' of up to twelve crotchet beats and a maximum duration of more than 16″, the performer plays the lower pitch and sings the upper pitch into the instrument. Such simultaneous playing and singing is very unlikely to result in pure and stable fifths but invariably leads to microtonal interference. The live electronics enhance this empirical imprecision: the live sound is transposed twice, by a fifth and two fifths down, and a 10″ reverb is added (see Figure 7.12). The euphonium sound is further subjected to two delays with feedback (4″ and 8″) and two halaphones ensure that the growing polyphony of fifths slowly encircles the audience in contrary motion at different speeds. Stacked fifths are also the fundamental basis for the

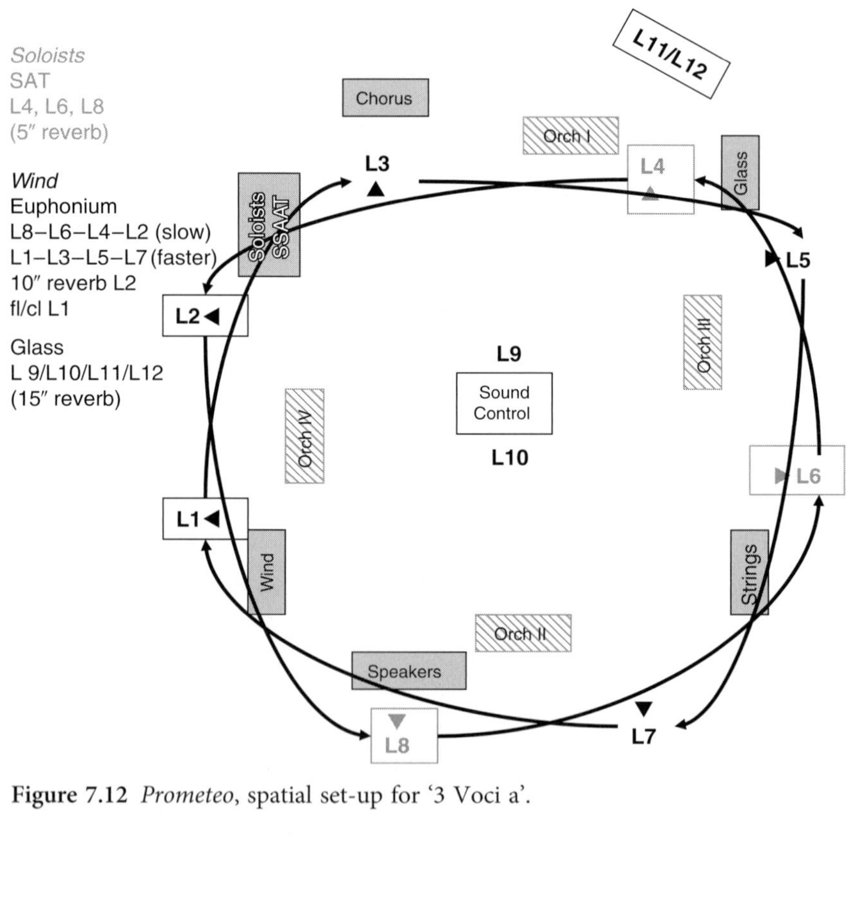


**Figure 7.12** *Prometeo*, spatial set-up for '3 Voci a'.

**Example 7.7** (a) '3 Voci a', harmonic fields of the euphonium layer. (b) Pitch reduction of the string harmonics.

notated euphonium part. Within the range that allows simultaneous playing and singing (played B to sung f♯[1], bearing in mind that this part was written for Schiaffini), Nono meanders quite systematically through the chromatically adjacent blocks of fifths shown in Example 7.7(a). The complete circle of fifths is thus gradually encompassed twice, with less systematic extensions at the beginning and end of the movement. Once again it is clear that Nono simply sets up harmonic fields in which the spatial polyphony is to take shape with maximum effect.

The score alone does not convey the storm that ensues with these sustained and carefully spaced out 'monovalori' in performance. The euphonium player begins as quietly as possible and gradually increases the sound to maximum force. As he gets louder and louder and the overlapping layers of impure fifths become denser and denser, the spiralling polyphony builds up to a threatening roar similar to that of fighter planes. At the centre of the movement, the process is reversed and the sound begins to decrease again. As the last remaining 'voice', the euphonium finally fades out on B–F♯, exactly the fifth with which Prometheus first emancipated himself and mankind from nature with his techne. The drama and atmosphere of the entire movement are thus governed by a single-minded, linear process that spins out of control but remains within clear-cut boundaries, in this case a simple arch form. The passing storm is coupled, at times, with the sinister low drone of the glass. Precisely this fusion of progressive–constructive thought and technical progressiveness with the most spiritual sonorities is what is truly disconcerting here, bringing to mind the image of Benjamin's 'Angelus Novus':

> [. . .] This is how the angel of history must look. His face is turned towards the past. Where a chain of events appears before us, *he* sees one single catastrophe, which keeps piling wreckage upon wreckage and hurls it at his feet. The angel would like to stay, awaken the dead and make whole what has been smashed. But a storm is blowing from Paradise and has got caught in his wings; it is so strong that the angel can no longer close them. This storm drives him irresistibly into the future, to which his back is turned, while the pile of debris before him grows towards the sky. What we call progress is *this* storm.[211]

Nowhere in Benjamin's *Theses* is the critique of progress as emphatic as in this famous evocation of the angel of history. Nowhere in the music of *Prometeo* is Nono's dialectical use of progressive means as prophetic as in '3 Voci a'. With the tempestuous 'voice' of the euphonium and its electronic transformation, progress and progressiveness are audibly represented in space as an 'inevitable' process – 'something that automatically pursue[s] a straight or spiral course'.[212] While the low drone of the glass adds to the growing feeling of doom, Nono also harks back to another of the characteristic sonorities in the 'Io–Prometeo' episode, the tragedy-defining prophecy, to extrapolate this process into the 'angelic' realm of the highest register.

A continuous texture of shimmering string harmonics quietly builds up and recedes in the registral stratosphere. To take us to these extreme heights, Nono no longer makes use of the string trio (as in 'Io–Prometeo'), but moves on to larger, more conventional forces: the orchestral violins. Their 'natural' surround-sound is composed of five extremely high harmonics and four slightly lower sets of fourths. Example 7.7(b) shows the simple principle of addition and subtraction with which these harmonics enter and recede. Both euphonium and violins begin on the pitches E♭ and B♭, but the progressions of fifths and fourths soon diverge as the texture of violin harmonics builds up markedly faster and reaches its maximum density before the peak of the euphonium's polyphony of fifths. The string texture is further differentiated by means of articulation, beginning with 'arco crini tasto', changing to 'crini legno tasto' at maximum density (bars 34–88) and receding with 'crini legno al ponte'. In addition, it is of a

[211] Benjamin, Thesis IX, in Löwy, *Fire Alarm*, 60–61.
[212] Benjamin, Thesis XIII, *ibid.*, 85.

shimmering inner mobility: with every new entry the spectrum of harmonics is redistributed among the twelve violin parts (four per orchestra). The spatial constellation of these glistening harmonics thus constantly changes and adds to this fleeting mobility. This most atmospheric and 'angelic' of 'voices' not only harks back to the 'continuo' of Prometeo's prophecy, but also gives the progressive storm of the euphonium an aura that basically adheres to tested conventions of 'celestial' music. With this bold combination of avant-garde and tradition, Nono's critique of progress and progressive thinking comes to the fore in truly dialectical fashion, though stripped of Hegelian synthesis. It is surely no coincidence that the two contrasting layers of progressive–constructive thought in this movement also hark back to the instrumental forces that quietly emancipated themselves with the help of modern technology in the First Island (2 violins, 2 brass).

Dialectics is taken much further with the third 'voice'. With three soloists (SAT), the tightrope walk of the 'new Prometeo' continues. They, too, proceed without goal, from moment to moment, with dynamics ranging from *ppppp* to *ppp*. The text from stanzas VII, VIII and IX of the *Maestro del gioco* is now charged with the Benjaminian concept of *Jetztzeit*: 'now-time, which, as a model of messianic time, comprises the entire history of mankind in a tremendous abbreviation' and allows us 'to blast open the continuum of history' with a 'tiger's leap into the past'.[213]

| | | |
|---|---|---|
| IX | Ascolta . . . | Listen . . . |
| VIII | Cogli quest'attimo | Seize this moment |
| | Balena un istante | An instant flares up |
| | un batter [del] ciglio | a blink of an eye |
| | un istante | an instant |
| VII | Non dire dell'ieri | Do not speak of yesterday |
| | Oggi il sole lancia | today the sun casts |
| | il laccio dell'alba, | the lace of dawn, |
| | Oggi il sole alba | the sun dawn today |
| | qui vibrano | Here resonate |
| | intese segrete | secret agreements |
| VIII | Al colmo | At the peak |
| | del pericolo | of danger |
| | deserto | wasteland |
| | Stendi le ali | Spread your wings |
| | intesa segreta | secret agreement |
| | trascini | to sweep along |

213 Benjamin, Theses XIV and XVI, *ibid.*, 86, 93.

| | | |
|---|---|---|
| IX | Irrompono Angeli | Angels burst in |
| | a volte | at times |
| | Angeli | Angels |
| | cristallo del mattino | crystal of morning |
| | Battono ali di porpora | Purple wings beat |
| VII | la misura del tempo si colma | the measure of time peaks |
| IX | Ascolta | Listen |

As these shards of text crystallise into the familiar constellations of tritones, fourths, fifths, semitones and tones, Nono consistently and stubbornly works against the idea of progress and progressive thought in music. Without live-electronic transformation of any kind (apart from the possible addition of a 5″ reverb), the vocal moments are designed to shine through the other 'voices' in pronounced stillness and transparency. In truly kaleidoscopic fashion, they capture the core ideas of Benjamin's *Theses* 'as though they were all simply views of one object seen from different angles'.[214] Other contexts are also touched upon: the poetic image 'crystals of morning' from Baudelaire's 'Le vin des amants', for example, briefly alludes to the profound influence of *Les Fleurs du mal* on Benjamin's *Theses*. The whole aura of 'dawn' which, to Ramazzotti, is rooted in the poetry of Pavese,[215] is clearly also a sign of Nietzsche's Wanderer, the free spirit who seeks the 'philosphy of the morning' and who, in Cacciari's political writings, stands for none other than the 'unpolitical', the radical critique of the state as 'political totality'.[216]

If Cacciari's text is virtually subsumed, the philosophical and political discourse these fragments allude to is not. By means of extreme fragmentation the continuum of this discourse is perceptibly blasted wide open ('Testo tutto/ frammenti miei/ frammenti di Massimo' Nono tellingly jots down in regard to the possible uses of text).[217] Rilke's angels, too, burst in again in the form of the fundamental idea of *Klarsein* – precisely the 'clarity' which, according to Cacciari's reading of Wittgenstein, does not lie in progressive and constructive reasoning, but 'means to render transparent the very foundation of construction, to constantly return to that same thing, constituted by its problem, to render its non-constructive

[214] Wittgenstein, *Culture and Value*, 7.

[215] Ramazzotti, 'Il dubbio, la lotta, la speranza', 195–96.

[216] Cacciari, 'Nietzsche and the Unpolitical', in *The Unpolitical*, 92–103. Similarly to Heidegger's interpretation of the Hölderlinian terms 'dichterisch' and 'undichterisch', Cacciari's 'unpolitical' is not opposed to but transcends the 'political'.

[217] ALN 51.07.05/04.

foundation evident'.[218] Filled to the brim with existence ('Hiersein ist herrlich'), only such momentary glimpses of the origin are capable of turning our gaze – which, like that of Benjamin's Angel, is 'as though reversed' and forever facing the past – into 'das Offene' (the open), 'das Freie' (freedom). Precisely this is the function of the vocal layer. Together with direct quotations from 'Io–Prometeo' ('ricordi lontanissimi') on bass flute and contrabass clarinet, it is once again 'suspended song' that conditions us to perform the 'tiger's leap into the past' and thereby takes us ever closer to true 'dialectical listening'.[219] For it is the deliberate juxtaposition of progressive and non-progressive musical thought with which the critique of progress is represented here in its most angelic form.

## 3°–4°–5° Isola (*ca.* 18′)

Isola 3: female soloists (SSAA), solo wind, solo strings, orchestras I–IV
Text: Sophocles, *Oedipus at Colonus*
Isola 4: soloists (SSAAT), solo wind (fl, cl, high trb), solo strings
Text: Sophocles, *Oedipus at Colonus*; Hölderlin, *Kolomb*, *Achill*; Schoenberg, *Moses und Aron*; Hesiod, *Works and Days*
Isola 5: solo wind (picc, E♭ cl, tuba)
Text (unperformed): Schoenberg, *Das Gesetz* op. 35, II; Aeschylus, *Prometheus Bound*; Nietzsche, *The Wanderer*; Hölderlin, *Das Nächste Beste*; Trakl, *Psalm*
Eco lontana (dal Prologo): chorus, orchestras I–IV (low instruments only)

Je suis des grans folz navigans
Sur la mer du monde parfonde
Pierre Rivière, paraphrase of Brant, *The Ship of Fools* (1497)

With the conjoined Third, Fourth and Fifth Islands, the mythological core of this tragedy presents itself in the most fragmentary form. Led by the overall principle 'rotto tutto' (everything torn apart),[220] text and music are extremely fractured and the splinters of all three islands are interwoven in a manner reminiscent of the tormented 'Zerrissenheit' (rupturedness) of the string quartet. Owing to the much more heterogeneous forces, the

218 Cacciari, 'A Critique of the Modern', in *Posthumous People*, 30; Wittgenstein, *Culture and Value*, 7.
219 Also see Vieira de Carvalho, 'Towards Dialectic Listening'.
220 A sketch with the remark 'tutto rotto' is reproduced and discussed in Haller, *Das Experimentalstudio*, II, 131/157.

difference between the three layers is now much easier to perceive. And yet, in this case too, there are unifying factors at work, which, to some extent, undermine the idea of constant fragmentation and separation. Common to all three islands is the sonority of the 'utopian' wind trio. Solo strings and soloists are added in the Third and Fourth Islands, but only the Third Island is supported by the orchestras. In the Third and Fourth Islands the sound of the vocal soloists is uniquely dependent on that of the solo instrumentalists. Not only is the vocal layer completely embedded into the pitch sets of the solo wind and strings, but, also, the instrumentalists regulate the sound and spatial transmission of the singers via four electronic gates. As Haller explains, not only are the instrumentalists thus in charge of their own parts, but also their rendition controls and regulates the dynamics and spatial distribution of the sound of one of the soloists.[221] The coupling of instrumental and vocal parts is constantly varied, and the four gates are used to weave a fluctuating, porous net of interdependence and shared responsibility.[222] The transmission, too, is constantly varied, and two halaphones add subtle movement in space at times. In the Fourth Island, the live electronics also add microtonal transposition to two of the vocal statements. While the music of the Third Island forms part of this fluctuating band of instrumental and vocal 'song', it is gradually enveloped by an ever-expanding orchestral texture, which eventually encompasses the entire circle of fifths (see Example 7.3). In stark contrast to these diffuse textural blocks, the music of the Fifth Island stands out at the brink of inaudibility in 'sublime' instrumental abstraction.

Nono's use of the forces is clearly linked to the degree of abstraction in the increasingly philosophical collage of text. The dramatic situation is that of *Prometheus Unbound*: the 'new Prometheus' is about to set off over the sea. Relying on a single ancient Greek source, Sophocles' *Oedipus at Colonus*, the Third Island describes this imminent journey in the most concrete form. With unusual consensus the protagonist and the commentating 'Mitologia' speak of Prometeo's journey home to Athens and the feast of conciliation with Zeus which forever secures the illuminating fire for mankind. Prometheus' homecoming is still given a concrete purpose here.

The Fourth Island takes up the idea of the sea journey and refracts it on a much more abstract level. In doing so, Cacciari indulges in a wealth of allusions. Established sources include Hölderlin's poems *Kolomb* (column

221 Haller, *Das Experimentalstudio*, I, 68–69.

222 The instrumentalists control the vocal lines throughout, except in the a cappella bars 189–91 (4° Isola), where A1 controls S1 and A2 controls S2.

I)[223] and *Achill* (column II),[224] Schoenberg's *Moses und Aron* (column I), and Hesiod's *Works and Days* (column III).[225] Other references are much more concealed and thus of far greater ambiguity. 'The voice of the crane' in column III, for example, may have its origin in Hölderlin's *Der Archipelagus*,[226] but could just as well be an allusion to Schiller's *Die Kraniche von Ibykus*. Likewise, the image of 'the open blue of the sky' through which Prometheus hears his calling not only brings to mind the poem *In lieblicher Bläue* (accredited to, but perhaps not written by, Hölderlin), but also recalls the context of Rilke's 'das Offene' and 'das Freie'. The laughing monster, on the other hand, whose lie severely threatens this freedom, is surely another reference to Nietzsche's 'new idol':

> The state is the coldest of all cold monsters. Coldly it lies, too; and this lie creeps from its mouth: 'I, the state, am the people.'[227]

The binding poetic image which holds all of these fragmentary allusions together is that of the sea. Like Ulysses, Prometheus essentially embarks on an odyssey. And it is only 'the wasteland of the sea' that allows Prometheus to reach out for the stars and to listen to the 'blue of the sky'. It is only *unbound* at sea that Prometheus turns hero and is able to keep the laughing monster at bay. For it is on the 'open sea', Cacciari argues with reference to Carl Schmitt, that 'all norm is no longer valid'.[228] Norms and

223 'Wünscht ich der Helden einer zu sein/ Und dürfte frei es bekennen/ So wär es ein Seeheld.' Hölderlin, *Kolomb*. Cacciari: 'Se ti è dato essere eroe/ solo del Mare lo puoi.' (If it is given to you to be a hero/ you can only do so at Sea.)

224 'Und die Mutter [Thetis] vernahm die Wehklage des Jünglings/ Stieg vom Grunde der See,' Hölderlin, *Achill*. Cacciari: 'Sopraggiungi al pianto del figlio/ Sali dal fondo del Mare.' (Arrive at the weeping of your son/ Rise from the bottom of the Sea.)

225 'First build a house and get an ox for the plow, and a woman', Hesiod, *Works and Days*, 77 (405); 'Beware of this month and its frosts/ that grip the earth when the gusty north wind/ stirs the broad sea and blows through Thrace', *ibid.*, 79 (505–507); 'And if longing seizes you for sailing the stormy seas,/ when the Pleiades flee mighty Orion/ and plunge into the misty deep/ and all the winds are raging,/ then do not keep your ship on the wine-dark sea/ but, as I bid you, remember to work the land./ Haul your ship onto land and secure it to the ground/ with stones on all sides to stay the blast of rain and wind,/ and pull out the plug to avoid rotting caused by rain water.' *Ibid.*, 82 (618–26).

226 'Kehren die Kraniche wieder zu dir, und suchen zu deinen/ Ufern wieder die Schiffe den Lauf?'; Hölderlin, *Der Archipelagus*.

227 Nietzsche, 'Of the New Idol', in *Thus Spoke Zarathustra*, 75. The same passage features in *Guai ai gelidi mostri* (1983).

228 Cacciari, 'Erinnerung an Karneval', 41. Cacciari refers to the opening of Schmitt's *The Nomos of the Earth*. Cacciari's Schmitt reception was first discussed by Mast, *Luigi Nono «Io, Prometeo»*, 137–55. It is absurd, however, and a sign of the implausibility of Mast's Freudian misreading of *Prometeo*, to associate Cacciari and Nono with Italy's *Nuova destra* (New Right); *ibid.*, 163–67. Precisely because of Schmitt's controversial alliance

laws are essentially tied to the Earth: '"iustissima tellus" ("die wohlbegründete, dauernde Erde" of Goethe)'.[229] The sea, however, is free: 'No field will be forged and cultivated here, no trace remains behind, no city can be erected here.'[230] This perilous freedom and 'inquietum' (disquiet) of the sea is metaphorically associated with the courage and knowledge of 'madmen':

> To Foucault, the tree of knowledge grows on the *Ship of Fools* by Bosch [. . .] Only madmen can defy the danger of the sea. But these madmen *know* and hold the course. They are madmen to those who remain in the old harbour, those who are therefore not aware of the imminent catastrophe that awaits them. But subjected to the greatest of dangers these madmen become experts at sea. They forge through the sea on their way to the new, promised land (where, as it says in the Revelation of the New Jerusalem, there will be *sea no longer*).[231]

As already discussed by Jeschke and Nanni, Nono, too, was extremely taken by the idea of the *Narrenschiff* and referred to the renowned satire by Sebastian Brant in conversation with Restagno:

> Think of the mad text, of extraordinary gaiety, from the great German literature of the 15th century, *Narrenschiff*, the ship of fools. The ship sails about on the Rhine, turned away from all moorings, because it is crowded with 'authorities', with freethinkers, with those considered mentally insane, thus bearers of disorder, even plague. The *Narrenschiff* persecutes with various methodologies: so many Pontormos have been confined on it! So many Schumanns! So many Hölderlins! So many Gramscis! So many Giordano Brunos! So many Rosa Luxemburgs! So many Rudi Dutschkes! So many Ulrike Meinhofs! So many Antonin Artauds! So many Andrei

with the Nazis, his demand for legal immunity in a political 'state of emergency' (Schmitt's so-called *decisionism*) continues to give rise to debate across the political spectrum, most recently in the aftermath of 9/11. As Nanni has shown, Cacciari clearly distinguishes between Schmitt's *nomos* and Rosenzweig's *law* in *Icone della legge* (1985); Nanni, 'Politica come silenzio', 227–31. Nono does not seem to have read Schmitt, though he did own a typescript of *Icone della legge*. On the Schmitt reception further see Staff, *Staatsdenken im Italien des 20. Jahrhunderts* and Laudoris, *Konterrevolution von links*.

229 Cacciari, 'Erinnerung an Karneval', 41.

230 'The *sea* knows no such apparent unity of space and law. [. . .] On the sea, fields cannot be planted and firm lines cannot be engraved. Ships that sail across the sea leave no trace. "On the waves, there is nothing but waves." The sea has no *character*, in the original sense of the word, which comes from the Greek *charassein*, meaning to engrave, to scratch, to imprint. The sea is free.' Schmitt, *The Nomos of the Earth*, 42–43.

231 Cacciari, 'Erinnerung an Karneval', 42; the reference to the *Ship of Fools* stems from Foucault, *History of Madness*.

> Tarkovskys! In recent times it has assumed also the form of psychiatric hospitals.[232]

The idea of the *Narrenschiff* was an important influence, too, on the design of Piano's ark.[233] The audience would enter this highly symbolic vessel to face and to listen to *Prometeo* as 'inquietum'. And as such, the work was to exude the notion of 'Hölderlinian Andenken' (remembrance).

Cacciari's preliminary notes speak of 'Andenken hoelderliano' in connection with the figure of Achilles. 'As a mere memory', Achilles encapsulates the '*death* of the utopian myth' which, to Cacciari, gave rise to none other than 'the world of *thought*'.[234] Without actually naming Achilles, Cacciari later alludes to Hölderlin's poem *Achill* in column II of the Fourth Island. Thetis here rises 'from the bottom of the sea' to listen to 'the weeping' of her son. The 'mute soul', however, is that of the poet himself who, up to 'his fleeing day' seeks to emulate Achilles' unconsolable lament. And the poet's 'Muse' is none other than Mnemosyne, the goddess of memory. From her silent 'source' alone springs forth the 'inquietum' that allows the poet to defy and 'chase the lie' of the laughing monster in the 'world of thought'. It is of this 'pile of memories' that he should 'speak to the Angel'.

The image of the sea thus attains an utterly metaphorical dimension that is undoubtedly influenced by Heidegger's reading of Hölderlin.[235] In his interpretation of the poem *Andenken* (*Remembrance*), Heidegger delves deep into Hölderlin's poetics to come to an understanding of the concept of *Andenken* (literally 'thinking-of'). On the 'sea' of poetic representation, poets are understood to set sail as 'mariners', Hölderlin's 'essential word' for the poet according to Heidegger. These mariners are swept along 'toward the origin of their own being' by the northeast wind, the wind that 'clears the sky' and brings 'sharp clarity':

> [T]his wind, through its blowing, makes clear for the poet the location and the time of his poetic vocation; it brings about that he must *think of* what has been and *of* what is coming. Indeed he is to think of what has been *as* what is to come [. . .] All at once this remembrance must think of what has been, as something which is not yet unfolded.[236]

[232] Nono, 'Un'autobiografia', *Scritti*, II, 525; Jeschke, *Prometeo*, 206; Nanni, 'Politica come silenzio', 227.

[233] See Jeschke, *Prometeo*, 206.

[234] Cacciari, preliminary notes, ALN 51.02.05/10; Cacciari's emphasis.

[235] Heidegger, *Erläuterungen zu Hölderlins Dichtung* (1981); *Elucidations of Hölderlin's Poetry*.

[236] Heidegger, 'Andenken', *ibid.*, 123.

The experience of the 'wide open spaces' of the sea is necessary in order for poets to recognise their 'historical destiny'. Only the unbounded 'wealth' and 'openness' of the sea 'takes and gives memory' and thus conditions the mariner to think-of what is 'still coming into presence from afar' as 'what is yet to come'. Through 'Andenken' the mariner's gaze is turned from the past into the future. In this sense, the 'sea voyage' is also a 'homecoming' to the foundation of man's dwelling through the poet's very own being.[237] In essence, the mariner's voyage is therefore nothing other than the 'founding' and 'sustaining ground' of man's *Works and Days*. Hesiod's epic poem is drawn into the context of this 'sea voyage' for this very reason. In other words, the ancient Greek poem, too, is to 'come into presence from afar' as 'homecoming': to reveal poetry as the essential ground of man's dwelling on Earth, the *Fruchtland* of our historically determined existence.

Traces of Heidegger's poetics are more obvious still in the text of the Fifth Island. With the term 'UNDICHTERISCH' Cacciari returns to the concept of dwelling poetically. Inasmuch as Cacciari's concept of the 'unpolitical' is rooted in and extends the boundaries of the political, Heidegger's concept of 'dwelling poetically' is anchored in Hölderlin's notion of the word 'undichterisch' (unpoetic). This uncommon negation in a late fragment entitled *Das Nächste Beste* (*The Next Best*) is cited repeatedly by Heidegger:

offen die Fenster des Himmels
Und freigelassen der Nachtgeist
Der himmelstürmende, der hat unser Land
Beschwäzet, mit Sprachen viel, *undichtrischen*, und
Den Schutt gewälzet
Bis diese Stunde
Doch kommt das, was ich will, . . .

open are the windows of the sky
And set free is the spirit of the night,
He who storms the heavens, and addresses our land,
in many languages, *unpoetic ones*, and
shifts through the rubble

[237] Heidegger repeatedly turns to the poem *In lieblicher Bläue* to define his concept of 'poetic dwelling': 'Voll Verdienst, doch dichterisch, wohnet der Mensch auf dieser Erde' (Full of merit, yet poetically,/ Man dwells on this Earth), e.g. in Heidegger, 'Remembrance', 113–14; 'Das Wohnen des Menschen' (1970), in *Denkerfahrungen 1910–1976*, 153–60.

to this very hour
Yet there comes that which I want, . . .[238]

In the manuscript, Hölderlin piles the variants 'unending', 'unpeaceful', 'unbinding' and 'unrestrained' over the word 'unpoetic'. To Heidegger, Hölderlin's 'poetic' therefore defines itself out of the 'unpoetic' as 'the bond which binds together all that is unbound' and 'that which is full of measure'.[239] 'Unpoetic' are the many languages of the 'spirit of the night' who rebels and storms the heavens. In 'miserable times', after the retreat of the god, the concept of 'dwelling poetically' takes root in the recognition that our presence on this Earth is fundamentally 'unpoetic', that the Earth itself 'can provide no bounds, but rather sweeps us away into boundlessness'. The 'escape route into seemingly reconciling dialectics' is insufficient, Heidegger concludes at the end of 'The Dwelling of Man':

> All too hastily we still think past the secret of the 'not' and nothingness.
> We do not yet experience with sufficient clarity what is suggested to us in withdrawal, because withdrawal itself, the poetic within the unpoetic, is not yet known to us.[240]

With its repeated imperative 'bedenke' ('consider', literally 'think about'), the text of Schoenberg's *Das Gesetz* (*The Law*) from the *Six Pieces for Male Chorus* op. 35 serves as a blueprint for Cacciari's reflections on the omnipotent natural law of Ananke. And again these reflections on law and measure are drawn into the underlying Heideggerian discourse in a highly allusive manner. The capitalised references to the poetry of Georg Trakl, too, form part of this foundational *Denkerfahrung* (thought experience). Trakl is explicitly named in an early libretto draft and linked to the words 'azzurro silenzio'.[241] The image of 'blue silence' stems from Trakl's second *Psalm* (1914),[242] but Cacciari also speaks of the 'truth of blue', 'the blue tolling of passing away' and 'the truth of the blue silence'. These poetic conjunctions are again best understood in the context of Heidegger's philosophical interpretation of Trakl and Cacciari's response in *Posthumous People*.[243]

238 Heidegger, 'Das Wohnen des Menschen', 157; 'Remembrance', 148 (amended).
239 Heidegger, 'Remembrance', 149. 240 Heidegger, 'Das Wohnen des Menschen', 160.
241 ALN 51.03.03/23.
242 'Wenn es Nacht wird siehest Du mich aus vermoderten Augen an,/ In *blauer Stille* verfielen deine Wangen zu Staub.' Trakl, *Psalm* (1914, first publ. 1949), in Trakl, *Dichtungen und Briefe*, I, 346.
243 Heidegger, 'Die Sprache im Gedicht'; 'Language in the Poem'. 'The intersection of the lines of Rosenzweig and Heidegger at their point of origin, in Wittgenstein, leads to that

In Trakl's 'blue' Heidegger discovers a very different 'spirit of the night', one that is inherently linked to Nietzsche's philosophy of the morning: a spiritual twilight that encompasses both decline and dawn. And the truth it conceals in its depth is none other than the 'holy':

> The holy shines out of the blueness, even while veiling itself in the dark of that blueness. The holy withholds in withdrawing. The holy bestows its arrival by reserving itself in its withholding withdrawal. Clarity sheltered in the dark is blueness. 'Clear' originally means clear sound, the sound that calls out of the shelter of stillness, and so becomes clear. Blueness resounds in its clarity, ringing. In its resounding clarity shines the blue's darkness.[244]

Only in this spiritual twilight, Cacciari argues with Heidegger, 'is the possible still unrevealed' and 'that is why the madman heads towards twilight. He seems mad because he tears away towards death. But only where the sun shines can there be a way through to the sweet song of the dawning day, of the revived.' Heidegger's interpretation of Trakl is crucial to Cacciari at this particular point in *Prometeo*,

> because it reinterprets the entire course of Trakl's lyrics as the destiny of contemporary lyric poetry. Lyric cannot be understood only in Benjamin's terms of urban dilation of intellect, much less as thinking of decline and ruin, but rather as the plane in which the road through a radical poverty of experience intersects thinking on the eternal return.[245]

Nono's intertwined setting of the Third, Fourth and Fifth Islands of *Prometeo* is, in my opinion, profoundly influenced by the Heideggerian discourse that seeps through these extremely allusive and fragmentary texts. Together with Nietzsche and Wittgenstein, Heidegger was one of the key thinkers discussed by the Italian left in the wake of Cacciari's 'negative thought', the anti-dialectical critique of Marxist idealism the philosopher developed in his influential books *Krisis* (1976) and *Pensiero*

area of Georg Trakl's poetry about which Heidegger wrote a definitive essay.' Cacciari, 'Abendland', in *Posthumous People*, 102.

244 'Aus der Bläue leuchtet, aber zugleich durch ihr eigenes Dunkel sich verhüllend, das Heilige. Dieses verhält, während es sich entzieht. Es verschenkt seine Ankunft, indem es sich in den verhaltenden Entzug verwahrt. Die ins Dunkel geborgene Helle ist die Bläue. Hell, d.h. hallend, ist ursprünglich der Ton, der aus dem Bergenden der Stille ruft und also sich lichtet. Die Bläue hallt in ihrer Helle, indem sie läutet. In ihrer hallenden Helle leuchtet das Dunkel der Bläue.' Heidegger, 'Die Sprache im Gedicht', 44; 'Language in the Poem', 165.

245 Cacciari, 'Abendland', 105.

*negativo e razionalizzazione* (1977).[246] Nono once credits Cacciari for bringing Heidegger to the attention of the Italian left, but generally refrains from discussing the politically controversial philosopher.[247] His avid interest in Heidegger is evident, however, from the many annotated volumes preserved in his library.[248] The *Erläuterungen zu Hölderlins Dichtung* were of particular relevance, but Nono clearly also focused on Heidegger's reflections on thought as such. In the light of his enduring fascination with 'wandering', also in the context of the later *Caminantes* series, thoughts such as the following for René Char must have had particular appeal:

| *Ortschaft* | *Abode* |
|---|---|
| Die das Selbe denken<br>im Reichtum seiner Selbigkeit,<br>gehen die mühsam langen Wege<br>in das immer Einfachere, Einfältige<br>seiner im Unzugangbaren<br>sich versagenden Ortschaft. | Those who think of the same<br>in the wealth of its sameness,<br>tread the long and arduous paths<br>Into ever greater simplicity, the simpleness<br>of the abode that denies itself<br>in the inaccessible.[249] |

Nowhere in *Prometeo* is the 'wealth of sameness' as apparent as in the combined Third, Fourth and Fifth Islands. With relentless perseverance, it seems, Nono here embarks on 'the long and arduous paths into ever greater simplicity'. For musicians and listeners alike, this section is undoubtedly the toughest of all. Not that it is more difficult to play; the

246 The journal *Nuova Corrente* subsequently published special issues on Nietzsche (1976), Wittgenstein (1977) and Heidegger (1978); reviewed by Dario Borso in *L'Unità* (20 February 1978). A seminar, 'Heidegger e il problema della tecnica', took place in Naples (April 1978) with Cacciari, Hans-Georg Gadamer (Heidelberg), Karl-Heinz Ilting (Saarbrücken) and Kostas Axelos (Paris). On the Heidegger reception in Italy also see Mandarini, 'Beyond Nihilism'.

247 Nono, '... kein Anfang – kein Ende ...', *Scritti*, II, 456. Nono mentions a newspaper article published shortly after Heidegger's death, probably refering to Cacciari, 'Heidegger: noi, i soggetti', *Rinascita* (2 July 1976).

248 Nono annotated the following books by Heidegger: *Erläuterungen zu Hölderlins Dichtung* (1971), three copies; *Schellings Abhandlung über das Wesen der menschlichen Freiheit* (1971); *Was heißt Denken?* (1961); *Zur Sache des Denkens* (1976); *Gelassenheit* (1979); *Aus der Erfahrung des Denkens* (1981); *Die Technik und die Kehre* (1982); *Denkerfahrungen* (1983); *Die Selbstbehauptung der deutschen Universität* (1983); *L'abbandono* (1983); *Ormai solo un dio ci può salvare* (1987). He further annotated Cacciari's essay 'Salvezza che cade. Saggio sulla questione della tecnica in M. Heidegger' (1982), as well as Levinas's article on the philosopher's controversial Nazi past, 'Heidegger e il nazismo'.

249 Heidegger, 'Gedachtes' (1970), in *Denkerfahrungen*, 163. On Nono's fascination with 'wandering' also see Esterbauer, *Eine Zone des Klangs und der Stille.*

difficulty presents itself solely in aesthetic terms: in the anti-dialectical juxtaposition of three layers or 'waves' and their extreme resistance to any kind of 'narrative' development. Like the text, the fragmented waves of sound are momentary manifestations of three different states of one and the same phenomenon. If Cacciari's text reflects Prometeo's final odyssey in increasingly philosophical terms, Nono's 'pensiero musicale', too, effectively draws on the Heideggerian notion of withdrawal to home in on the 'sublime abstraction' of the law.

The 'natural forces' of Gaia are present only in the music of the Third Island, the section's mythological core. Departing from the pitch C (the anchor of the harmonic sphere of man), this 'natural terrain' gradually floods the entire harmonic, registral and performance space (see Example 7.3). As the orchestras build up this all-encompassing 'sea' of sound, the mythological core is gradually engulfed and deliberately concealed. Notably, the text is rendered by the female soloists who, back in the Second Island, represented Io with similar emphasis on the '2–7–9' interval relationships. As a 'metaphor' for the repressed struggle of the oppressed, Io is also at the very heart of Prometeo's departure over the sea. Embedded into the supporting pitch fields of the forces of 'disquiet', Prometeo embarks on this final odyssey in memory of Io as the seafaring 'madman' he himself is to be remembered as.

The highly metaphorical vocal core is stripped of all natural surroundings and granted a far higher degree of 'clarity' in the music of the Fourth Island. Unconcealed and with the addition of the solo tenor, Prometeo the 'mariner' is here literally 'blown' along by the utopian continuo. The sounding control lines are almost exclusively rendered by the solo wind in middle register (flute, clarinet and alto trombone), while the solo string players mostly control the vocal lines by blowing into their microphones. With all four gates in use throughout and an ever-changing allocation of instrumental and vocal lines, the spatial transmission is kept in constant flux. For the first and only time in *Prometeo*, it is futile to summarise the spatial processes in graphic form.

In contrast, the music of the Fifth Island is marked by the Heideggerian concept of withdrawal. As is evident from the manuscript score, the text was at first envisaged to be spoken. However, Nono eventually decided to go beyond *Moses und Aron* with a purely instrumental setting. Compared with the close embrace of the instrumental and vocal dimensions in the Third and Fourth Islands, it is as if the vocal core is sucked into a gaping hole of 'nothingness' in the Fifth Island. Not by chance is this one of the instrumental combinations first employed for *Guai ai gelidi mostri*, Nono's and Cacciari's Nietzschean attack on the state. Here as there, the 'law' to subversively undermine the 'coldest of monsters' shines through the extremely unpredictable and fragile sounds of E♭ clarinet and piccolo, the instrument Nono first associated with 'utopia'. It is this allusive, politically charged fragility which takes us to the heart of the 'secret of the "not" and nothingness' and allows us to glimpse the 'poetic within the unpoetic'.

But this is not all. As previously in *Fragmente – Stille, an Diotima*, the three layers or waves are consciously torn apart, juxtaposed and interlocked in an expanding web of ever-changing constellations. Each of the waves forms an undercurrent of the 'wasteland of the sea' that gradually unfolds in this section. 'Contemplation of the sphere [. . .] in which existing beings [das Seiende] reveal themselves', Heidegger argues in *Was heißt Denken?* (*What Is Called Thinking?*), 'stands on the side of rupturedness [Zerrissenheit] – that is, of consciousness. As a result of its rift [Riß], this rupturedness is open to the admission of the Absolute.'[250] In this case, rupturedness is clearly designed to admit Hölderlinian 'Andenken'. From the 'wealth' and 'openness' of the consciously ruptured 'wasteland of the sea' remembrance arises in the form of seven 'echoes'. With the exception of the last, each of these echoes is entitled 'eco lontana (dal Prologo)' (distant echo (of the Prologue)). All seven echoes are rendered by the chorus and the four orchestras (predominantly lower strings and brass). Though without text, the chorus thus resumes its function as the commentating 'Mitologia'. As in the Prologue, the First Island and the First Stasimon, it is coupled with the orchestras and now rises out of the diverse undercurrents with singular, almost narrative directiveness. In terms of sound transmission, the chorus is partly heard as 'coro lontanissimo' through the indirect loudspeakers (L11 and L12), but also directly through L6 at the rear.

Both Jeschke and Melkert have argued that these distant echoes of the Prologue refer back to the 1984 version in which the chorus also sang without words.[251] However, on locating these reference points in the final 1985 version, Melkert then also lists the text they had, by then, been assigned.[252] The echoed fragments, it turns out, are not only part of the sung elevation of ancient Greek names, but also frame the following phrase of the *Maestro del gioco*:

| | |
|---|---|
| non vibra qui ancora un soffio dell'aria | does there not still resonate a breath of air |
| che respirava il passato? | that the past has breathed? |

[250] 'Die Besinnung auf den Bereich [. . .], worin das Seiende sich zeigt [. . .], steht auf der Seite der Zerrissenheit – nämlich des Bewußtseins. Dieses Zerrissene ist durch seinen Riß offen für den Einlaß des Absoluten.' Heidegger, *Was heißt Denken?*, 34.

[251] Jeschke, *Prometeo*, 142, n. 94; Melkert, «*Far del silenzio cristallo*», 183–85.

[252] Melkert, *ibid.*, 184.

Table 7.5 *The seven distant echoes of the Prologue in 3°–4°–5° Isola*

| Echo | Pitches | Chorus | Orchestras I–IV | Prologo (1985) |
|---|---|---|---|---|
| **(a)**<br>42–44 | A, B♭, E | *ppp* | lower strings (vla/vcl/db)<br>*pppppp* | 52<br>*Non* [vibra qui ancora un soffio dell'aria/ che respirava il passato?] |
| **(b)**<br>62–65 | B♭, E♭, F♯ | *ppp*,<br>*mf–ppppp*,<br>*pppp*,<br>*ppp>* | lower strings & brass<br>(vla/vcl/tr/hrn/trb)<br>*ppp>*, *sfff–pppp*, *sff*, *p–f* | 99–103<br>*Rhea Cronos* |
| **(c)**<br>101–103 | A, B♭, E | *mf–pppp*,<br>*<mf >* | lower strings (as before)<br>*pppppp* | 52 (a) |
| **(d)**<br>131–37 | B, C | *pppp–ff*,<br>*ppppp–mf*,<br>*ppppp* | wind (tr/fl/trb)<br>*ppppp–ff*, *ppppp–sfff*, *sff*,<br>*sfff* | 84–85 (3×)<br>[pass-]*ato* |
| **(e)**<br>172–76 | F, B, C, C♯ | *p–mffff*,<br>*p–pppp*,<br>*pppp*<br>*ppppp–fff* | lower strings & lower wind<br>(vla/vcl/db/bs/hrn/trb)<br>*ppp–sfff*,<br>*ppp–sfff quasi grido* | 28–34<br>*Ascolta/d'Ourea* |
| **(f)** | B, F | *ppp–pppp* | strings (vln/vla/vcl/db)<br>*pppp* | 32–34 (e)<br>*d'Ourea* |
| End | A, B♭, E | *ppppp* | lower strings (as before)<br>*pppppp* | 52 (a) |

Is the 'coro lontanissimo' here not given a new guise as the force of Mnemosyne, remembrance in the sense of Hölderlinian 'Andenken'? Without words, this chorus no longer remembers ('thinks of') specific names, but allows us to replace these names by those that befit our very own 'historical destiny' much in the way Nono himself continues the list of 'freethinkers' in his statement on Brant's *Narrenschiff*.

Table 7.5 charts the characteristics of each of the seven echoes and their origin in the Prologue, summarising much of the information listed by Melkert, yet with additional emphasis on the crucial changes in dynamics. In terms of pitch and instrumentation, the third and final echoes are a repeat of the first, a hidden allusion, perhaps, to the 'secret' of the 'not'. The final pitches of the fifth echo are repeated in the sixth; the contrast in instrumentation and dynamics could not be greater, however. This is precisely the level on which these echoes take on their completely new guise. With ever greater dynamic range and contrast, they surge out of the surrounding currents to culminate in one of the most dramatic moments of *Prometeo* as a whole: a repeated and extremely menacing crescendo by the a cappella chorus, extended to full power by the surrounding orchestras. 'Quasi grido' (almost screaming) is Nono's performance instruction at this dynamic climax. Reading Heidegger's *Was heißt Denken?*, one cannot but associate this instruction with the 'scream' of Nietzsche's *Thus Spoke Zarathustra* which Heidegger turns to time and again: 'The wasteland grows: woe to him who harbours wastelands!'[253] With this 'scream' the forces of Mnemosyne not only recollect themselves, but indeed 'think of what has been *as* what is to come'. They alone will now turn to and reflect Benjamin's *Concept of History* in the subsequent movement.

## 3 Voci b (*ca.* 6′)

Chorus (SATB)
Text: Cacciari, *Il Maestro del gioco* X, XI, XII

> Thinking involves not only the movement of thoughts, but their arrest (*Stillstellung*) as well. Where thinking suddenly comes to a stop in a constellation saturated with tensions, it gives that constellation a shock, by which thinking is crystallised as a monad. The historical materialist approaches a historical subject only where it confronts him as a monad. In this structure he recognises the sign of a Messianic arrest of happening, or, to put it differently, a revolutionary chance in the fight for the oppressed past. He takes cognizance of it in order to blast a specific era out of the homogeneous course of history; thus he blasts a specific life out of the era, a specific work out of the lifework. As a result of this method, the lifework is both preserved and sublated *in* the work, the era *in* the lifework, and the entire course of history *in* the era. The nourishing fruit of what is historically understood contains time in its *interior* as a precious but tasteless seed.
>
> Walter Benjamin, *Theses on the Concept of History*, XVII[254]

After the expansive wanderings of the intertwined Third, Fourth and Fifth Islands, the sudden focus on the human voice alone in '3 Voci b' is truly arresting. From the movement's opening appeal 'ascolta' through to its final demand to 'listen' to the weak messianic power that is given to us, this

[253] Nietzsche, *Thus Spoke Zarathustra*, 315 (trans. amended). This title is repeatedly referred to as Nietzsche's 'scream' in Heidegger's *Was heißt Denken?*.
[254] Benjamin, Thesis XVII, in Löwy, *Fire Alarm*, 95.

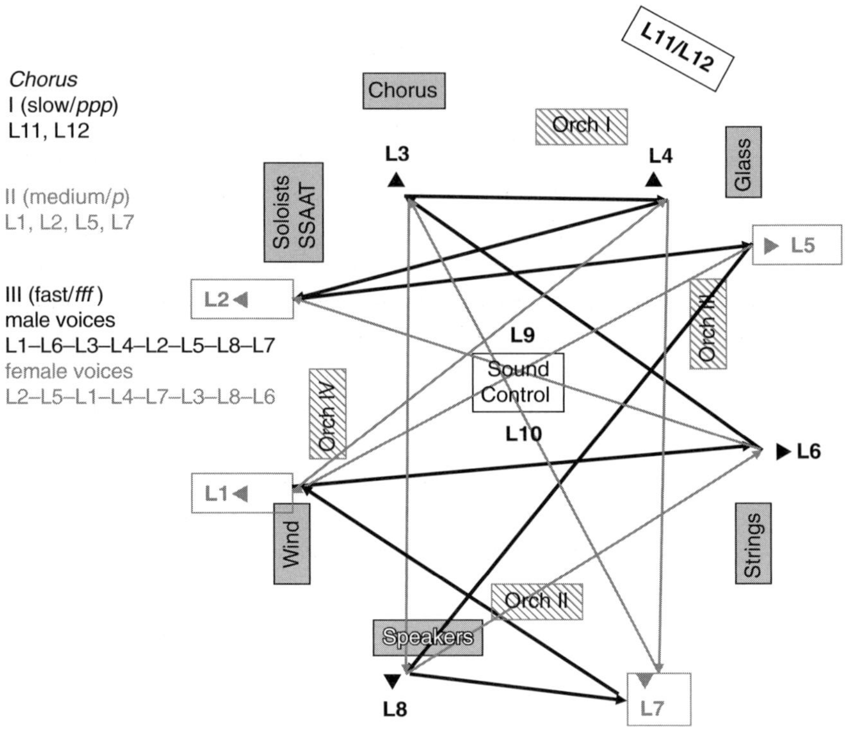


**Figure 7.13** *Prometeo*, spatial set-up for '3 Voci b'.

a cappella section is directly addressed to the listener. In this sense, it is indeed comparable to the moment in *Intolleranza* when the chorus suddenly turns to the audience with the words: 'And what about you? Are you deaf? [. . .] Megaphones! Amplify this shout! Before slander twists it and indifference chokes it!'[255]

According to Richard, '3 Voci b' was of far greater violence still in the 1984 version. In its final form, the chorus asserts its powerful presence in three contrasting 'voices'. All three 'voices' are rendered by the four-part chorus (SATB), and each voice is clearly demarcated in terms of speed, dynamic and spatial transmission. The movement begins with the slowest voice, which is also the softest. Throughout the movement it is assigned a speed of ♩ = 30 and the dynamic *ppp*. Like the 'coro lontanissimo', it is consistently transmitted through the indirect loudspeakers L11 and L12 (see Figure 7.13). The clearly articulated demand 'ascolta' is thus itself perceivable as 'a breath of air' from the past. The crystalline clarity of this

[255] See Chapter 1, n. 67.

**Example 7.8** (a) '3 Voci b' and 'Interludio 2°', core pitch constellation. (b) Pitch constellations of '3 Voci b'.

distant opening appeal is deliberately shattered with the second choral block, which bursts in at the fastest of speeds (♩ = 120), the maximum dynamic (*fff*) and with an entire line of text piled into its three-syllable dictum. Not only do the twelve singers here resume the intensity of the 'quasi grido' in the previous section, but, furthermore, their renewed and much more persistent outcries now fill the entire performance space and bounce off all sides in extremely agitated, unsettling zig-zag movements. Between these extremes, the intermediate voice moves calmly (*p*) at the medium speed of ♩ = 60, and this much more ordinary middle ground is perceived in straightforward stereophonic fashion (employing L1, L2, L5 and L7; a transmission similar to that of the louder choral passages in the First Stasimon).

Despite the immense contrasts in speed, dynamics and transmission, the musical and textual materials of these three voices are in fact one and the same. As shown in parts (a) and (b) of Example 7.8, Nono here returns to the core pitch constellation of the euphonium part in '3 Voci a': central stacks of fifths as in Example 7.7(a). Now, however, this constellation no longer gives rise to linear development, but instead the chromatic and tritone relationships of these adjacent stacks of fifths are explored in truly kaleidoscopic fashion: selected pitches of these sets continuously reveal the intervallic tensions and the combinatorial potential of this core constellation from within. This creates a musical situation in which 'thinking suddenly comes to a stop in a constellation saturated with tensions'. And by means of three widely contrasting time scales, it is given a shock in truly non-homogeneous time.

Once again, Nono goes to the core of Benjamin's *Theses on the Concept of History* in music, and not merely by setting Cacciari's *Maestro del gioco*. Each of the three voices is assigned fragments from all three remaining stanzas, but intelligibility is near zero. What is important is not so much the actual presence of this text, but the key concepts it entails. Once again the 'weak messianic force' reveals itself as a non-violent 'power of singing'. The 'central word' is sung three times (*pppp* and *p*). What is new is the concept of 'Stillstellung', the 'messianic arrest of happening' which is to be seized as a 'revolutionary chance in the fight for the oppressed past'. With this key term, Mnemosyne is now clearly put to the service of the oppressed. For only remembrance can halt our thinking in that brief, fulfilled instant of 'now-time' in which 'the whole tradition of the oppressed is concentrated, as a redemptive power' to blast through the 'homogeneous course of history' in order to grant us a glimpse of 'the universal history of saved humanity'.[256]

As a constellation saturated with tritone, whole-tone and semitone tensions dispersed in three extremely non-homogeneous zones of time and space, this arresting choral movement reveals itself as a Benjaminian monad in music alone. And as the lowest instruments of the orchestras quietly assume the final pitch set of the chorus, 'the nourishing fruit of what is historically understood' is about to fall on equally nourishing soil.

## Interludio 2° (*ca.* 5′)

Orchestras I–IV (bass instruments only: vcl, db, bs, hrn, trb), glass

If the bass instruments gave their all in the Third, Fourth and Fifth Islands to extend and spatialise the 'scream' of the chorus, they now echo the vocal force of Mnemosyne in a much more subdued way. 'Suono fermo/ non vibrare!' (closed sound/ no vibrato!) and 'tutti *ppppp* possibile' are the two performance instructions which head this movement in the score. A reminder of the quarter-tone notation points to a further characteristic: the seething microtonal tension which marks this final return to pure 'Gaia' terrain. The harmonic category T is, of course, already at the heart

[256] Löwy, *Fire Alarm*, 100.

of the preceding choral movement, and Nono also makes use of some of its most basic formations in this movement, notably at the very end (see Example 7.8(b)).

Almost unnoticeably, the very last pitch set of the chorus is taken up three octaves lower by the double basses, who fade in, one after the other, in anti-clockwise motion and with extreme quietude. At the bottom end of the registral scale, the fifths of the choral setting are inverted into fourths, and the set is gradually shrouded in adjacent quarter-tones by the horns and trombones. Throughout the movement, Nono once again focuses on an extremely narrow set of pitches, concentrating on chromatically adjacent Gaia formations throughout. Beginning and ending in the same harmonic region, the progression takes on a simple arch form. In contracting and expanding waves of varied densities the bass instruments slowly meander in and out of the chromatically adjacent sets with various degrees of microtonal inflection (including none at all, bars 13–26). The tritone is no longer the central interval here, but this ominously low band of sound seethes with chromatic and microtonal tension. The tempo changes are seamless and no longer designed to blast through homogeneous time, with speeds ranging from ♩ = 30 to ♩ = 72. Punctuation is achieved by means of complete silence as well as the occasional accumulation of shorter durations, with dynamics momentarily swelling up to *mf* and *f*. At its centre the movement briefly contracts into a dense quarter-tone cluster (bar 27), only to expand outwards again and meander back to the opening pitch set. At the brink of silence, this eerily atmospheric Second Interlude eventually fades out on the pitch G and its adjacent quarter-tones, dispersed in space by the double basses.[257]

In atmosphere, this dark orchestral soundscape suggests the best of Anselm Kiefer's barren, earthy backgrounds to the reflection of his mythical, historical and politically charged subject matters. Just like Kiefer, whose art Nono admired, the composer subtly combines and accentuates this furrowed 'natural' ground with an extremely allusive and historically charged element: the resonant low drone of the three glass bells (transmitted, as before, through loudspeakers L1, L5 and L7). No other instrument in *Prometeo* is so charged with spiritual connotations. With the collective tolling of the church bells of Venice in mind, many have noted the

[257] This microtonally inflected, spaced-out G is later the basis of *«No hay caminos. Hay que caminar» ... Andrei Tarkowskij* (1987). The connotations this pitch acquires in *Prometeo* provide the most plausible starting point for Nono's radical focus on the pitch G in this later homage to Tarkovsky. For other reasons see Esterbauer, *Eine Zone des Klangs und der Stille*, 76–79.

particularly Venetian character of this unique instrumental group. In the light of what I have written so far, I cannot but understand this electronically transformed bell sonority in much more abstract, philosophical terms. Electronically concealed in their own darkness, these tolling bells resonate with the mysticism of Heidegger's late philosophy. It is as if the 'blue tolling of passing away' and 'the truth of the blue silence', Cacciari's enigmatic allusions to Heidegger's essay on Trakl, find their ideal musical expression in this Second Interludio. Nowhere is Nono's preoccupation with 'concealment' as apparent as in this seething low ground of the 'natural' forces in combination with the resonant drone of the bells. Cacciari's notes for *Das atmende Klarsein* show that the concept of concealment in *Prometeo* is fundamentally linked to Heidegger's understanding of truth as *a-letheia* (un-concealment). From our limited, historically and culturally conditioned 'horizon of disclosure', as Julian Young explains, truth can never be fully disclosed and will forever remain shrouded in the mystery of its originating region (*Herkunftsbereich*):

> [I]n addition to what is intelligible to us, reality possesses an indefinitely large number of aspects, a 'plenitude' (*Vollzähligkeit*) of 'sides' or 'facets' [. . .] which would be disclosed to us were we to inhabit transcendental horizons other than the one we do, horizons which, however, we can never inhabit or even conceive. Truth, then, is concealment, ultimate truth concealment of the, to us, *ineluctably* mysterious. In 'The Origin of the Work of Art' Heidegger calls this 'region' [. . .] 'earth' (*Erde*). 'World' (in the ontic sense) is the intelligible in truth, that which is 'lit up'; as Heidegger calls it, 'the clearing' (*Lichtung*). 'Earth', on the other hand, is 'the not ['linguistically'] mastered [. . .] [the] concealed, the disconcerting (*Beirrendes*)' (OWA p. 55), the dark penumbra of unintelligibility that surrounds (and in an important sense [. . .] grounds) our human existence.[258]

In this Heideggerian sense, the Second Interludio is, like the first, a response to Wittgenstein's 'Whereof one cannot speak, thereof one must be silent' with Cacciari's afterthought 'But that which you cannot express in speech, you must not for that reason absolutely "silence".'[259] The dark and truly disconcerting 'penumbra of unintelligibility' that surrounds and grounds our human existence is expressed here with both the material and the 'deepest' forces of Gaia alone. Within this barely audible ground and shrouded in the mystery of their own resonant darkness toll the three glass bells. No sonority could come closer to representing Trakl's 'Blue', which,

[258] Young, *Heidegger's Later Philosophy*, 9.

[259] ALN 51.04.05/01; as quoted in my discussion of 'Interludio 1°'.

for Heidegger, conceals the 'holy' at its core.[260] Only with the addition of this most mystical sonority of the utopian 'forces of disquiet' does this narrow strip of barren ground disclose itself as true 'harvest land': a dark and fertile ground for the remembrance of the voiceless voices of the oppressed past.

## Stasimo 2° (*ca.* 9′)

Soloists (SSAAT), solo wind, solo strings
Text: fragments from Aeschylus, Cacciari and Schoenberg

> The antidialectic nature of mysticism insists everywhere on these terms: detachment, leap, decision, in other words, everything that exceeds the norm, the linearizing violence of the law. While the *Recht* [law] has to sacralize every state reached and sacralize its overall movement in as much as progress of mankind in history, justice [*Gerechtigkeit*] sees in this time always more secularized idolatry [. . .] Therefore, the critique of mysticism functions, on one hand, as powerful force from within that deconstruction of the law, of which Schmitt spoke of in rigorous legal-institutional terms, and, on the other, as idea of the possible break away from the ground of the law, of the theological, of progress, from their ground as such, as idea of the decision from it.
>
> Cacciari, 'Law and Justice'[261]

Cacciari's text for the final movement of *Prometeo* carries the title *Nomos* – Law. With the opening quotation from *Prometheus Bound*, Cacciari immediately points to the cosmic nature of this law:

> My mother, Themis, or Earth *one person, though of various names*,
> Had many times foretold to me, that not brute strength,
> Not violence, but cunning must give victory
> To the rulers of the future.[262]

Among the many names for the cosmic 'Gestalt' (form) of Gaia is, of course, also that of Ananke. In terms of subject matter, the Second Stasimon is thus intrinsically linked to the first. However, there is a world of difference between these two movements of the same name.

[260] See my discussion of the '3°–4°–5° Isola'. On Heidegger's concept of the 'holy' see Young, *Heidegger's Later Philosophy*, 12–25.

[261] Cacciari, 'Law and Justice', 185–86.

[262] Aeschylus, *Prometheus Bound*, 27 (Cacciari's quotation in italics).

In the First Stasimon, Nono makes use of the performance instruction 'sonar e cantar' to give rise to a mysterious, if not mystical 'aura' that is simultaneously played and sung by the forces of Gaia. 'Choral song' is thereby effectively concealed and the resulting 'mystery' conveys both man's uncertainty in the face of Ananke and the dawn of a new era after the retreat of the god. In stark contrast, the Second Stasimon leaves concealed darkness behind for lyric song to come into true Being. In other words, from the 'dark penumbra of unintelligibility which grounds our human existence' emerges the final 'clearing'. The forces of Gaia are no longer present in this 'world' of intelligible truth, and the instruction 'a sonar e a cantar' now applies to the soloists and the utopian continuo alone. In 'choral song' these musical protagonists now truly become one.

The Second Stasimon once again evolves in sets of extremely 'few notes'. The chosen Gaia formations clearly revolve around the tonal centre C and are thus placed in the combined harmonic spheres of the Mitologia and man. Throughout the movement, the solo instrumentalists discretely double the pitches of the five vocal soloists 'sempre il piú *pppppp* possibile'. Depending on the acoustics of the hall, some of these doublings may also be omitted. As in the First Stasimon, the vocal core is thus echoed, but this instrumental echo is now entirely in harmony with the singers and does not withdraw into microtonal haziness. With a 10″ reverb the vocal sound is transmitted from above and indirectly through loudspeakers L9 to L12. The long reverb is further combined with a subtle 4″ and 8″ delay of all forces (transmitted very quietly through L9/L10 (4″) and L11/L12 (8″)).

For the Exodus, Cacciari initially asked Nono to think of 'canto sospeso' in the sense of the 'Memory of the atemporal – Memory of what we have not experienced – Memory of a path we have *not* taken'.[263] This Heideggerian concept of remembrance also pervades Cacciari's compilation of the many 'names' of *Nomos*. If this cosmic 'Gestalt' took on the most mystic guise in the First Stasimon, it is now 'named' in all clarity and thus revealed – unconcealed – as the fundamental, yet eternally absent 'image of justice' Cacciari speaks of in 'Law and Justice'. Not the mystic 'Gestalt' of Nomos, but its many 'names', our grasp of this mystical ground in language is thus at the heart of this final 'canto sospeso'. 'No new laws', Cacciari argues,

> can be opposed to the golden chain of myth–theology–law, but the image of justice. No new states (always administered violence, always tending to serve and preserve the law), but the halting of that chain (of its eternal repetition) in

[263] Cacciari, letter to Nono, see n. 97.

> the pure language of justice (*Gerechtigkeit*), as 'principle of every divine finality'. [...] The conclusion of Wittgenstein's *Tractatus* could be reproposed in the light of these ideas. What is being sought there is the foundation of a just language (*lingua giusta*), a true and proper sphere of pure understanding, other with respect to the violence of law [...] And I believe that the sense of Gerechtigkeit should not be looked for in the biblical image suggested by Benjamin of 'pure divine violence,' instantaneous and *not* bloody, 'both sign and seal,' but in the idea of a language withdrawn from the discursive, from the theological, precisely, and constantly renewing itself to the fount of the 'just' word.[264]

'Not disenchanted but listening out for possibility', Nono himself noted for the Exodus (Figure 7.2). The composer, too, aimed to overcome the disenchantment (*Entzauberung*) of our secularised, modern and all too progressive world.[265] This 'canto sospeso' is indeed no longer the mere 'Memory of an intemporal – insolvable – grief' but manifests itself as 'the Memory of a path we have *not* taken' in serene moments of truly anti-dialectical song in which the 'weak messianic force' reveals itself as a fundamentally non-violent 'force of singing'. Calm and extremely focused, these seemingly intemporal moments of pure song put Rilke's 'Hiersein ist herrlich' (Being here is magnificent) centre stage (and literally at the centre of the performance space),

| | |
|---|---|
| eine Stunde war jeder, | where each has always |
| Vielleicht nicht ganz eine Stunde, | an hour, perhaps not even, |
| kaum Meβliches | hardly measurable |
| zwischen zwei Weilen | between two whiles |
| Alles | Everything |
| Die Adern voll Dasein ... | Veins filled with existence ...[266] |

Silence alone interrupts these moments of true Rilkean 'Klarsein' and stubbornly undermines linear process in sound and space. Precisely this is the clarity which 'argues with the semblance of progress' and 'slashes at its claims with pure crystal' to reveal the metaphysical gap between logos and 'aletheia' as 'a gap whose continual reformulation as a problem is a critique of "ratio typisch aufbauend"'.[267]

[264] Cacciari, 'Law and Justice', 183.

[265] The term 'Entzauberung' (disenchantment) was used by Max Weber 'to identify what he took to be the defining characteristic of modernity'; Young, *Heidegger's Later Philosophy*, 36.

[266] Rilke, *Duineser Elegien*, Seventh Elegy, as quoted by Cacciari, see n. 30.

[267] Cacciari, 'A Critique of the Modern', in *Posthumous People* 32.

'Do you call this narrow clearing truth?', the Mitologia asked with similar clarity back in the First Island, the dramatic situation of Prometeo's irreversible, progressive and increasingly destructive, technological emancipation of mankind from nature. But it is only at the very end of *Prometeo* that the fifth B/F♯, which first triggered this fateful emancipation, attains the clarity it was first granted in *Das atmende Klarsein*. After more than two hours, *Prometeo* fades out on this open fifth in the solo voices alone. The truly open end not only recalls the purity of the opening 'call' of Gaia, but summons it, in all clarity, into the harmonic sphere of man. Through listening alone we are led to the recognition that only such clarity is capable of turning our gaze, which, like that of Benjamin's Angel, is 'as though reversed' and forever facing the past, into 'das Offene' and 'das Freie' – the space in which *Prometeo* truly becomes 'invincible in the wasteland'. In the final instance, Prometheus' tragic decision to prophesy reveals itself as the foundation of a musical 'lingua giusta', a dramatic 'language' which consciously withdraws from the discursive, constantly renews itself 'to the fount of the "just" word' and thus cunningly seeks to undermine the 'linearising violence of the law'. In these politically charged final moments of serene clarity, the 'tragedy of listening' fully reveals itself as a 'psalm against the idols'.

# Bibliography


Adorno, Theodor W., *Minima Moralia: Reflections from Damaged Life*, trans. E. F. N. Jephcott (London: Verso, 1974).

*Negative Dialectics*, trans. E. B. Ashton (London: Routledge, 1990).

'Kulturkritik und Gesellschaft' (1949), first published in the Festschrift *Soziologische Forschung in unserer Zeit. Leopold Wiese zum 75. Geburtstag* (1951), later included in *Prismen* (Frankfurt am Main: Suhrkamp, 1955), 7–31; 'Cultural Criticism and Society', in *Prisms*, trans. S. and S. Weber (London: Spearman, 1967), 17–34.

'Das Altern der neuen Musik', broadcast April 1954, first published in *Der Monat*, 80 (1955), 150–58; expanded in *Dissonanzen: Musik in der verwalteten Welt* (Göttingen: Vandenhoeck & Rupprecht, 1956), 136–59; 'The Aging of the New Music', trans. R. Hullot-Kentor and F. Will, in Adorno, *Essays on Music*, ed. R. Leppert (Berkeley, CA: University of California Press, 2002), 181–202.

Aeschylus, *Prometeo incantenato,* in *Aeschylus. Le tragedie*, ed. C. Carena (Turin: Einaudi, 1956).

*Prometheus Bound*, trans. P. Vellacott (Harmondsworth: Penguin, 1961).

Allwardt, Ingrid, *Die Stimme der Diotima. Friedrich Hölderlin und Luigi Nono* (Berlin: Kadmos, 2004).

Anders, Günther, *Der Mann auf der Brücke. Tagebuch aus Hiroshima und Nagasaki* (Munich: Beck, 1959).

*Essere o non Essere – Diario di Hiroshima e Nagasaki*, trans. R. Solmi (Turin: Einaudi, 1961).

Aragona, Livio, '*Variazioni canoniche*: prime definizioni di una poetica', in A. C. Pellegrini (ed.), *Gli anni giovanili di Luigi Nono: Tre relazioni dal Convegno Luigi Nono. Musica e impegno politico nel secondo Novecento* (Venice, 3–4 December 2004), online publication (10 August 2006, rev. 1 February 2010), 25–41; accessible via the ALN website.

Artaud, Pierre-Yves, *Flûtes au présent: traité des techniques contemporaines sur les flûtes traversières à l'usage des compositeurs et des flûtistes/Present Day Flutes: Treatise on Contemporary Techniques of Traverse Flutes for the Use of Composers and Performers* [bilingual] (Paris: Editions Jobert, 1980).

Bailey, Kathryn, 'Work in Progress: Analysing Nono's *Il canto sospeso*', *Music Analysis*, 11:2–3 (1992), 279–334.

Baroni, Mario, and Rossana Dalmonte (eds.), *Bruno Maderna: documenti* (Milan: Zerboni, 1985).

Bassanese, Stefano, 'Sulla versione 1965 della *Composizione per Orchestra n. 2 (Diario polacco '58)*', in G. Borio, G. Morelli and V. Rizzardi (eds.), *La nuova ricerca sull'opera di Luigi Nono*, Archivio Luigi Nono, Studi, I (Florence: Olschki, 1999), 95–103.

Baudelaire, Charles, *Les fleurs du mal*, trans. W. Aggeler (Fresno, CA: Academy Library Guild, 1954).

Beauvoir, Simone de, *Force of Circumstance*, trans. R. Howard (London: Deutsch, 1965).

Behan, Tom, *The Italian Resistance: Fascists, Guerrillas and the Allies* (London: Pluto Press, 2009).

Benjamin, Walter, 'Über den Begriff der Geschichte' (1940), in *Werke und Nachlaß. Kritische Gesamtausgabe*, vol. 19, ed. G. Raulet (Frankfurt am Main: Suhrkamp, 2010); trans. C. Turner in M. Löwy, *Fire Alarm* (London: Verso, 2005).

Beumers, Birgit, *Yuri Lyubimov at the Taganka Theatre* (Amsterdam: Harwood Academic, 1997).

Biraghi, Marco, 'Entretien avec Massimo Cacciari', in *Luigi Nono: Festival d'automne à Paris 1987* (Paris: Contrechamps, 1987), 147–51.

Blumenthal, M. and Gorbey, K. (eds.), *Stories of an Exhibition: Two Millennia of German Jewish History*, trans. D. Wilkins (Stiftung Jüdisches Museum Berlin, 2001).

Borio, Gianmario, 'La tecnica seriale in *Studi per "Il processo" di Franz Kafka* di Bruno Maderna', *Musica/Realtà*, 32 (1990), 27–39; French trans. in G. Mathon, L. Feneyrou and G. Ferrari (eds.), *À Bruno Maderna* (Paris: Basalte, 2007), 25–37.

'L'influenza di Dallapiccola sui compositori italiani nel secondo dopoguerra', in M. De Santis and T. Pecker Berio (eds.), *Dallapiccola: Letture e prospettive* (Lucca: LIM, 1997), 357–87.

'Sull'interazione fra lo studio degli schizzi e l'analisi dell'opera', in G. Borio, G. Morelli and V. Rizzardi (eds.), *La nuova ricerca sull'opera di Luigi Nono*, Archivio Luigi Nono, Studi, I (Florence: Olschki, 1999), 1–21.

'Tempo e ritmo nelle composizioni seriali. 1952–56', in G. Borio, G. Morelli and V. Rizzardi (eds.), *Le musiche degli anni cinquanta*, Archivio Luigi Nono, Studi, II (Florence: Olschki, 2004), 61–115.

'«A Strange Phenomenon»: Varèse's Influence on the European Avant-Garde', in F. Meyer and H. Zimmermann (eds.), *Edgard Varèse: Composer, Sound Sculptor, Visionary*, Exhibition Catalogue (Woodbridge: Boydell Press, 2006), 361–70.

'Varèse und die Utopie der musikalischen Moderne', in G. Borio and H. Danuser (eds.), *Im Zenit der Moderne: Die internationalen Ferienkurse für neue Musik Darmstadt 1946–1966*, 4 vols (Freiburg im Breisgau: Rombach, 1997), I, 267–83.

Borio, Gianmario, and Hermann Danuser (eds.), *Im Zenit der Moderne: Die internationalen Ferienkurse für neue Musik Darmstadt 1946–1966*, 4 vols (Freiburg im Breisgau: Rombach, 1997).

Borio, Gianmario, Giovanni Morelli and Veniero Rizzardi (eds.), *La nuova ricerca sull'opera di Luigi Nono* (Venice: Olschki, 1999).

*Le musiche degli anni cinquanta*, Archivio Luigi Nono, Studi, II (Florence: Olschki, 2004).

Boulez, Pierre, 'Schoenberg is "dead"' (1952), in *Stocktakings from an Apprenticeship*, trans. S. Walsh, introduction by R. T. Piencikowski (Oxford University Press, 1991), 209–14.

Braun, Helmuth F., 'The Architectural Language of Daniel Liebeskind', in M. Blumenthal and K. Gorbey (eds.), *Stories of an Exhibition: Two Millennia of German Jewish History*, trans. D. Wilkins (Stiftung Jüdisches Museum Berlin, 2001), 176–81.

Breuning, Franziska, *Luigi Nonos Vertonungen von Texten Cesare Paveses* (Münster: LIT, 1999).

Brinkmann, Reinhold, 'Varèse in Darmstadt: Dokumentarischer Bericht und kurzer Kommentar', in R. Stephan, L. Knessl, O. Tomek, K. Trapp and C. Fox (eds.), *Von Kranichstein zur Gegenwart: 50 Jahre Darmstädter Beiträge zur Neuen Musik* (Stuttgart: DACO Verlag, 1996), 87–93.

Buchanan, Peter, *Renzo Piano Building Workshop: Complete Works*, vol. 1 (London: Phaidon, 1993).

Burian, Jarka, *The Scenography of Josef Svoboda* (Middletown, CT: Wesleyan University Press, 1971).

Byron, George Gordon, *Manfred*, in J. J. McGann (ed.), *Byron*, The Oxford Authors (Oxford University Press, 1986), 274–314.

Cacciari, Massimo, *Krisis. Saggio sulla crisi del pensiero negativo da Nietzsche a Wittgenstein* (Milan: Feltrinelli, 1976).

*Pensiero negativo e razionalizzazione* (Padua: Marsilio, 1977).

*Dallo Steinhof. Prospettive viennesi del primo Novecento* (Milan: Adelphi, 1980).

*Icone della legge* (Milan: Adelphi, 1985).

*Architecture and Nihilism: On the Philosophy of Modern Architecture*, trans. S. Sartarelli (New Haven, CT: Yale University Press, 1993).

*The Necessary Angel*, trans. M. E. Vatter (State University of New York, 1994).

*Posthumous People. Vienna at the Turning Point*, trans. R. Friedman (Stanford University Press, 1996).

'Abendland', in *Posthumous People. Vienna at the Turning Point*, trans. R. Friedman (Stanford University Press, 1996), 102–108.

'Erinnerung an Karneval', in *Zeit ohne Kronos*, ed. and trans. R. Kacianka (Klagenfurt: Ritter, 1986), 41–62.

'Per il «Prometeo»', in A. M. Morazoni (ed.), *Schoenberg & Nono* (Florence: Olschki, 2002), 341–44.

'Zeit, die bricht, reisst und teilt', in *Luigi Nono, Prometeo: Tragedia dell'ascolto*, programme book for *Prometeo* (Freiburg im Breisgau, 18 May 2003), 35–37.

'Verso Prometeo: Tragedia dell'ascolto' (1984), in S. Cecchetto and G. Mastinu (eds.), *Nono Vedova. Diario di bordo* (Turin: Allemandi, 2005), 125–30.

Libretto for *Prometeo*, in K. Pauler (ed.), 'Libretto & Listening score' trans. S. Lindberg, in Nono, *Prometeo, Tragedia dell'ascolto*, 2 CDs (col legno, 2007).
*The Unpolitical: On the Radical Critique of Political Reason*, trans. M. Verdicchio (New York: Fordham University Press, 2009).
(ed.), *Luigi Nono: Verso Prometeo* (Milan: Ricordi, 1984).
Calico, Joy H., *Arnold Schoenberg's A Survivor from Warsaw in Postwar Europe* (Berkeley, CA: University of California Press, 2014).
Calvino, Italo, *Il sentiero dei nidi di ragno* (Turin: Einaudi, 1964).
*The Path to the Nest of Spiders*, trans. W. Weaver (Hopewell, NJ: Ecco Press, 1976).
'Impiccagione di un giudice', in *Ultimo viene il corvo* (Milan: Garzanti, 1988), 224–33.
*Lettere 1940–1985* (Milan: Mondadori, 2000).
Carrera, Alessandro, 'On Massimo Cacciari's Disenchanted Activism', in *Cacciari, The Unpolitical: On the Radical Critique of Political Reason*, trans. M. Verdicchio (New York: Fordham University Press, 2009), 1–44.
Carroll, Mark, *Music and Ideology in Cold War Europe* (Cambridge University Press, 2003).
Cecchetto, Stefano, and Giorgio Mastinu (eds.), *Nono Vedova. Diario di bordo* (Turin: Allemandi, 2005).
Cisternino, Nicola, 'Con Luigi Nono . . . per rivedere le stelle. Conversazione con Massimo Cacciari', in G. Cresta (ed.), *L'ascolto del pensiero. Scritti su Luigi Nono* (Milan: Rugginenti, 2002), 23–35.
Comisso, Irene, 'Luigi Nonos *Prometeo. Tragedia dell'ascolto*. Rekonstruktion der Verarbeitung des Mythos anhand der Textentwürfe zum Libretto', in J. Kühnl, U. Müller and O. Panagl (eds.), *Musiktheater der Gegenwart* (Salzburg: Müller-Speiser, 2008), 439–67.
Conti, Luca, 'Le *Tre liriche greche* di Maderna e la prima dodecafonia italiana', in R. Dalmonte and M. Russo (eds.), *Bruno Maderna: Studi e testimonianze* (Lucca: LIM, 2004), 275–86.
Cooke, Philip, *The Legacy of the Italian Resistance* (New York: Palgrave Macmillan, 2011).
Dallapiccola, Luigi, 'Notes for an Analysis of the *Canti di liberazione*', trans. C. Stodt, *Perspectives of New Music*, 38:1 (2000), 5–24.
Dalmonte, Rossana, 'Letture maderniane del *Processo* di Franz Kafka', in R. Dalmonte and M. Russo (eds.), *Bruno Maderna: Studi e testimonianze* (Lucca: LIM, 2004), 9–40.
Dalmonte, Rossana, and Marco Russo (eds.), *Bruno Maderna: Studi e testimonianze* (Lucca: LIM, 2004).
Davismoon, Stephen (ed.), 'Luigi Nono: the suspended song (1924–1990)', *Contemporary Music Review*, 18:1 (1999).
'Luigi Nono: fragments and silence (1924–1990)', *Contemporary Music Review*, 18:2 (1999).

de Assis, Paulo, *Luigi Nonos Wende. Zwischen* Como una ola de fuerza y luz *und* . . . . . sofferte onde serene . . . , sinefonia, 2, 2 vols (Hofheim: Wolke, 2006).

de Assis, Paulo (ed.), *Luigi Nono – Escritos e Entrevistas*, trans. A. Morão, Casa da Música, Centro de Estudos de Sociologia e Estética Musical (Porto: Empresa Diário, 2014).

De Benedictis, Angela Ida, 'Gli equivoci del sembiante: «Intolleranza 1960» e le fasi di un'opera viva', *Musica/Realtà*, 19 (1998), 153–217.

*Radiodramma e arte radiofonica. Storia e funzioni della musica per radio in Italia* (Turin: EDT, 2004).

'Gruppo, linea e proiezioni armoniche', in G. Borio, G. Morelli and V. Rizzardi (eds.), *Le musiche degli anni cinquanta*, Archivio Luigi Nono, Studi, II (Florence: Olschki, 2004), 183–226.

'Luigi Nono et Cesare Pavese: miroir croisé', in P. Michel and G. Borio (eds.), *Musiques vocales en Italie depuis 1945. Esthétique, relations texte/musique, techniques de composition* (Paris: Millénaire III, 2005), 79–106.

'Omaggio a Emilio Vedova di Luigi Nono', in *Luigi Nono. Complete Works for Solo Tape*, CD booklet (Ricordi, Stradivarius 57001, 2006), 7–11; trans. A. Herklotz, 39–43.

'Intervals at the Service of Dramaturgy: The Conception of Character Rows in *Intolleranza 1960* by Luigi Nono', in G. Ferrari (ed.), *La musique et la scène: l'écriture musicale et son expression scénique au XXe siècle* (Paris: L'Harmattan, 2007), 49–68.

'*Intolleranza 1960* von Luigi Nono: Wandlungen eines Librettos', in H. Schneider and R. Musch (eds.), *Librettoübersetzung: Interkulturalität im europäischen Musiktheater* (Hildesheim: Olms, 2009), 305–27.

'The Dramaturgical and Compositional Genesis of Luigi Nono's *Intolleranza 1960*', trans. J. O'Donnell, *twentieth-century music*, 9/1–2 (2013), 101–41.

'*Nono, Luigi (Venezia, 29.1.1924 – Venezia, 8.5.1990)*', trans. M. Weir, Fondazione Archivio Luigi Nono onlus (website), Luigi Nono, biografia (2013).

De Benedictis, Angela Ida, and Giorgio Mastinu (eds.), *Intolleranza 1960 a cinquant'anni dalla prima assoluta* (Venice: Marsilio, 2011).

De Benedictis, Angela Ida, and Ulrich Mosch (eds.), *Alla ricerca di luce e chiarezza: L'epistolario Helmut Lachenmann – Luigi Nono (1957–1990)*, Archivio Luigi Nono, Studi, IV (Florence: Olschki, 2012).

De Benedictis, Angela Ida, and Veniero Rizzardi (eds.), *Luigi Nono: Scritti e colloqui*, Le Sfere, 2 vols (Milan and Lucca: Ricordi and LIM, 2001).

(eds.), *Luigi Nono: La nostalgia del futuro. Scritti scelti 1948–1986* (Milan: Il Saggiatore, 2007).

(eds.), *Nostalgia for the Future: Selected Writings and Interviews of Luigi Nono* [working title], trans. J. O'Donnell (Oakland, CA: University of California Press, 2016).

De Benedictis, Angela Ida, and Ute Schomerus, 'La lotta "con le armi dell'arte": Erwin Piscator e Luigi Nono. Riflessioni e documenti (II)', *Musica/Realtà*, 61 (March 2000), 151–84.

De Benedictis, Angela Ida, and Laura Zattra (eds.), *Presenza storica di Luigi Nono*, Quaderni di Musica/Realtà (Lucca: LIM, 2011).

Decroupet, Pascal, 'Gravitationsfeld Gruppen. Zur Verschränkung der Werke *Gesang der Jünglinge*, *Gruppen* und *Zeitmaße* und deren Auswirkung auf Stockhausens Musikdenken in der zweiten Hälfte der fünfziger Jahre', *Musiktheorie*, 12:1 (1997), 37–51.

'Aleatorik und Indetermination – Die Ferienkurse als Forum der europäischen Cage-Rezeption', in G. Borio and H. Danuser (eds.), *Im Zenit der Moderne*, (Freiburg im Breisgau: Rombach, 1997), II, 189–275.

Döpke, Doris, 'Fragmente – Stille, an Diotima', *Zeitschrift für Musikpädagogik*, 36 (1986), 10–24; Italian trans. in E. Restagno (ed.), *Nono* (Turin: EDT, 1987), 184–205.

Durante, Sergio, and Laura Zattra (eds.), *Vent'anni di musica elettronica all'Università di Padova*, Archivio musiche del XX secolo (Catania: CIMS, 2002).

Durazzi, Bruce, *Musical Poetics and Political Ideology in the Work of Luigi Nono*, PhD dissertation, Yale University (2005).

'Lugi Nono's *Canti di vita e d'amore*: Musical Dialectics and the Opposition of Present and Future', *The Journal of Musicology*, 26:4 (2009), 451–80.

Earle, Ben, 'Mario Zafred and Symphonic Neorealism', in R. Adlington (ed.), *Red Strains: Music and Communism outside the Communist Bloc* (Oxford University Press, 2013), 149–71.

Edwards, Peter Ivan, 'Object, Space, and Fragility in Luigi Nono's *Das atmende Klarsein*', *Perspectives of New Music*, 46:1 (2008), 225–43.

Eimert, Herbert, *Lehrbuch der Zölftontechnik* (Wiesbaden: Breitkopf & Härtel, 1950).

'Uraufführung von Nonos *Canto sospeso* in Köln', *Melos*, 23:12 (1956), 354.

Esterbauer, Erik, *Eine Zone des Klangs und der Stille. Luigi Nonos Orchesterstück 2°) No hay caminos, hay que caminar . . . Andrej Tarkovskij* (Würzburg: Königshausen & Neumann, 2011).

Fabbriciani, Roberto, 'Walking with Gigi', in S. Davismoon (ed.), *Luigi Nono: The Suspended Song*, Contemporary Music Review, 18/1 (1999), 7–15.

*Flauto in scena*, Quaderni di cultura contemporanea, 8 (Monfalcone: Teatro Comunale, 2007).

Feneyrou, Laurent, *Il canto sospeso de Luigi Nono* (Paris: de Maule, 2002).

(ed.), *Luigi Nono: Écrits* (Paris: Editions Bourgois, 1993).

Flamm, Christoph, 'Preface', trans. A. Davies, in *Il canto sospeso*, score (London: Eulenburg, 1995), iii–x.

Focardi, Filippo, *La guerra della memoria: La Resistenza nel dibattito politico italiano dal 1945 a oggi* (Bari: Laterza, 2005).

Foucault, Michel, *History of Madness*, ed. J. Khalfa, trans. J. Murphy and J. Khalfa (London: Routledge, 2006).

Franzoi, Umberto, and Dina Stefano, *Le chiese di Venezia* (Venice: Azienda Autonoma Soggiorno Turismo, 1975).

Frei, Norbert, 'Coping with the Burdens of the Past: German Politics and Society in the 1950s', in D. Geppert (ed.), *The Postwar Challenge: Cultural, Social and Political Change in Western Europe, 1945–58* (Oxford University Press, 2003), 27–40.

Frobenius, Wolf, 'Luigi Nonos Streichquartett «Fragmente – Stille, An Diotima»', *Archiv für Musikwissenschaft*, 54:3 (1997), 177–93.

Fučík, Julius, *Reportáž psaná na oprátce* (Zagreb, 1946).

*Reportage von unter dem Strang*, trans. F. Rausch (Berlin: Dietz, 1948).

*Scritto sotto la forca*, ed. F. Calamandrei (Milan: Feltrinelli, 1951).

*Report from the Gallows*, trans. and ed. S. Jolly (London: John Spencer & Co., 1957).

Garbato, Carla, and Mario Mastropietro (eds.), *Renzo Piano Building Workshop: Exhibit Design* (Milan: Lybra, 1992), 150–55.

Gargani, Aldo Giorgio, *Wittgenstein tra Austria e Inghilterra* (Turin: Stampatori, 1979).

Gennaro, Sara, 'Per un ritratto di Nono da giovane: sette interviste', in A. C. Pellegrini (ed.), *Gli anni giovanili di Luigi Nono: Tre relazioni dal Convegno Luigi Nono. Musica e impegno politico nel secondo Novecento* (Venice, 3–4 Decemeber 2004), online publication (10 August 2006, rev. 1 February 2010), 1–8; accessible via the ALN website.

Geppert, Dominik (ed.), *The Postwar Challenge: Cultural, Social and Political Change in Western Europe, 1945–58* (Oxford University Press, 2003).

Gerrero, Jeannie, 'Serial Intervention in Nono's *Il canto sospeso*', *Music Theory Online*, 12:1 (2006).

Ginsborg, Paul, *A History of Contemporary Italy* (New York: Palgrave, 2003).

Glancey, Jonathan, and Tudi Sammartini, 'Piano + Nono. Temporary auditorium, Venice', *Architectural Review*, 176 (December 1984), 53–57.

Goethe, Johann Wolfgang von, *Grenzen der Menschheit* (*ca.* 1780), in Goethe, *Poems and Epigrams*, trans. M. Hamburger (London: Anvill Press, 1983).

Gramann, Heinz, *Die Ästhetisierung des Schreckens in der europäischen Musik des 20. Jahrhunderts* (Bonn: Verlag für systematische Musikwissenschaft, 1984).

Grant, M. J., *Serial Music, Serial Aesthetics* (Cambridge University Press, 2001).

Guthrie, William K. C., *Orpheus and Greek Religion: A Study of the Orphic Movement*, 2nd rev. edn (London: Methuen & Co., 1952).

Haller, Hans Peter, *Das Experimentalstudio der Heinrich-Strobel-Stiftung des Südwestfunks Freiburg 1971–1989*, 2 vols (Baden-Baden: Nomos, 1995).

Heidegger, Martin, 'Die Sprache im Gedicht. Eine Erörterung von Georg Trakls Gedicht', in *Unterwegs zur Sprache* (Pfullingen: Neske, 1959), 55–82.

*Was heißt Denken?* (Tübingen: Niemeyer, 1961).

'Language in the Poem: A Discussion of Georg Trakl's Poetic Work', in *On the Way to Language*, trans. P. D. Hertz (New York: Harper & Row, 1971), 159–98.

*Erläuterungen zu Hölderlins Dichtung* (Frankfurt am Main: Klostermann, 1981).

*Denkerfahrungen 1910–1976* (Frankfurt am Main: Klostermann, 1983), 153–60.

*Elucidations of Hölderlin's Poetry*, trans. K. Hoeller, Contemporary Studies in Philosophy and the Human Sciences (New York: Humanity Books, 2000).

Henius, Carla, *Carla Carissima. Carla Henius und Luigi Nono: Briefe, Tagebücher, Notizen* (Hamburg: Europäische Verlagsanstalt, 1995).

Henze, Hans Werner, *Bohemian Fifths*, trans. S. Spencer (London: Faber, 1998).

Herrmann, Matthias, 'Das Zeitnetz als serielles Mittel formaler Organisation: Untersuchungen zum IV. Satz aus *Il canto sospeso* von Luigi Nono', in Wolfgang Budday (ed.), *Musiktheorie: Festschrift für Heinrich Deppert* (Tutzing: Schneider, 2000), 261–75.

Hesiod, *Theogony, Works and Days, Shield*, trans. A. N. Athanassakis (Baltimore, MA: Johns Hopkins University Press, 1983).

Hochhuth, Rolf, *Der Stellvertreter* (Reinbek bei Hamburg: Rowohlt, 1963).

*The Representative*, trans. R. D. MacDonald (London: Methuen & Co., 1963).

Hölderlin, Friedrich, *Gesammelte Werke*, ed. D. E. Sattler (Frankfurt am Main: Roter Stern, 1975–).

*Diotima e Hölderlin: lettere e poesie*, ed. E. Mandruzzato (Milan: Adelphi, 1979).

*Hyperion and Selected Poems*, trans. W. R. Trask and D. Schwarz, The German Library (New York: Continuum, 1990).

*Poems & Fragments*, trans. M. Hamburger, 3rd edn (London: Anvil Press, 1994).

Höss, Rudolf, *Commandant of Auschwitz: The Autobiography of Rudolf Hoess*, trans. C. FitzGibbon, introduction by Primo Levi, trans. J. Neugroschel (London: Weidenfels & Nicolson, 1959).

*Comandante ad Auschwitz: memoriale autobiografico di Rudolf Höss* (Turin: Einaudi, 1960).

Howatson, M. C., and Frisbee C. C. Sheffield, Glossary, in Plato, *The Symposium* (Cambridge University Press, 2008).

Howatson, M. C. (ed.), *The Oxford Companion to Classical Literature*, 2nd edn (Oxford University Press, 1989).

Huber, Nicolaus A., 'Luigi Nono: Il canto sospeso VI a, b', in *Luigi Nono*, ed. H.-K. Metzger and R. Riehn, Musik-Konzepte, 20 (Munich: edition text + kritik, 1981), 58–79.

Iddon, Martin, 'Serial Canon(s): Nono's Variations and Boulez's Structures', in L. Colton and M. Iddon (eds.), *Recycling and Innovation in Contemporary Music, Contemporary Music Review*, 29:3 (2010), 265–75.

*New Music at Darmstadt: Nono, Stockhausen, Cage and Boulez* (Cambridge University Press, 2013).

Idelsohn, Abraham Zvi, *Hebräisch-orientalischer Melodienschatz*, 10 vols (Leipzig, Jerusalem, Berlin and Vienna: Breitkopf & Härtel, Hofmeister and Harz, 1914–23).

Impett, Jonathan, 'Accelerated learning: Nono's years of study 1942–1950', unpublished paper read at the conference *From Fin de Siècle to Fascism: Music in Italian Culture, 1900–1950* (Oxford, 28–29 June 2004).

'The tragedy of listening: Nono, Cacciari, critical thought and compositional practice', *Radical Philosophy*, 125 (2004), 29–36.

Janiccy, Wacław and Lesław, *Dziennik podróży z Kantorem* (Kraków: Wydawnictwo Znak, 2000).

Jeschke, Lydia, *Prometeo: Geschichtskonzeptionen in Luigi Nonos Hörtragödie*, Archiv für Musikwissenschaft (Stuttgart: Steiner, 1997).

Jozefowicz, Nina, *Das alltägliche Drama. Luigi Nonos Vokalkompositionen mit Tonband* La fabbrica illuminata *und* A floresta é jovem e cheja de vida *im Kontext der unvollendeten Musiktheaterprojekte* (Hofheim: Wolke, 2012).

Junker, Joachim, 'Zum Verhältnis von Text und Musik in Luigi Nonos *Das atmende Klarsein*', in L. Holtmeyer, M. Polth and F. Diergarten (eds.), *Musiktheorie zwischen Historie und Systematik,* 1, Kongress der Deutschen Gesellschaft für Musiktheorie, Dresden 2001 (Augsburg: Wissner Verlag, 2004), 326–37.

Kafka, Franz, *Tagebücher 1912–1914*, ed. H.-G. Koch, M. Müller and M. Pasley (Frankfurt am Main: Fischer, 1990).

*Tagebücher 1914–1923*, ed. H.-G. Koch, M. Müller and M. Pasley (Frankfurt am Main: Fischer, 1990).

*The Diaries of Franz Kafka 1910–1913*, ed. M. Brod, trans. J. Kresh (New York: Schocken, 1948).

*The Diaries of Franz Kafka*, ed. M. Brod, trans. M. Greenberg and H. Arendt (New York: Schocken, 1949).

*Diari 1910–1923*, ed. M. Brod, trans. E. Pocar, 2 vols (Milan: Mondadori, 1953).

Kirchert, Kay-Uwe, *Wahrnehmung und Fragmentierung: Luigi Nonos Kompositionen zwischen «Al gran sole carico d'amore» und «Prometeo»* (Saarbrücken: Pfau, 2006).

Kolisch, Rudolf, 'Nonos Varianti', *Melos*, 24:10 (1957), 292–96.

Komar, Kathleen L., *Transcending Angels: Rainer Maria Rilke's Duino Elegies* (Lincoln, NE: University of Nebraska Press, 1987).

Kontarsky, Matthias, *Trauma Auschwitz: Zu Verarbeitungen des Nichtverarbeitbaren bei Peter Weiss, Luigi Nono und Paul Dessau* (Saarbrücken: Pfau, 2001).

'Stage Music for *Die Ermittlung* by Peter Weiss', trans. A. Herklotz, in *Luigi Nono: Complete Works for Solo Tape*, CD booklet (Milan: Ricordi, 2006), 43–46.

Kramer, Jonathan, 'The Fibonacci Series in Twentieth century Music', *Journal of Music Theory*, 17:1 (1973), 110–49.

Lachenmann, Helmut, 'Luigi Nono oder Rückblick auf die serielle Musik' (1969), in Helmut Lachenmann, *Musik als existentielle Erfahrung* (Wiesbaden: Breitkopf & Härtel, 1996), 247–57.

'Zur Analyse neuer Musik' (1971/93), in Helmut Lachenmann, *Musik als existentielle Erfahrung* (Wiesbaden: Breitkopf & Härtel, 1996), 21–34.

'Von Nono berührt' (1991), in Helmut Lachenmann, *Musik als existentielle Erfahrung* (Wiesbaden: Breitkopf & Härtel, 1996), 295–305.

'[Luigi Nono]', lecture at the Hochschule für Musik, Stuttgart (26 October 1960), in A. I. De Benedictis and U. Mosch (eds.), *Alla ricerca di luce e chiarezza: L'epistolario Helmut Lachenmann – Luigi Nono (1957–1990),* Archivio Luigi Nono, Studi, IV (Florence: Olschki, 2012), 219–32.

lecture at the Volkshochschule Ulm (16 November 1964), in *Alla ricerca di luce e chiarezza: L'epistolario Helmut Lachenmann – Luigi Nono (1957–1990)*, Archivio Luigi Nono, Studi, IV (Florence: Olschki, 2012), 244–59.

'Nono, Webern, Mozart, Boulez. Text zur Sendereihe *Komponisten machen Programm*' (1979), *Alla ricerca di luce e chiarezza: L'epistolario Helmut Lachenmann – Luigi Nono (1957–1990)*, Archivio Luigi Nono, Studi, IV (Florence: Olschki, 2012), 270–78.

Lammel, Inge, *Das Arbeiterlied* (Frankfurt am Main: Röderberg, 1973).

'Die beiden Berliner "Scherchen Chöre"', in *Arbeiterlied, Arbeitergesang: hundert Jahre Arbeitermusikkultur in Deutschland. Aufsätze und Vorträge aus 40 Jahren, 1959–1998* (Teetz: Hentrich, 2002), 72–114.

Laudoris, Leonard, *Konterrevolution von links. Das Staats- und Gesellschaftsverständnis der "68er" und dessen Quellen bei Carl Schmitt* (Baden-Baden: Nomos, 2007).

Levi, Primo, *Se questo è un uomo* (Milan: De Silva, 1947), 2nd edn (Milan: Einaudi, 1958).

*The Drowned and the Saved*, trans. R. Rosenthal (London: Joseph, 1988).

Liebknecht, Karl, *Ausgewählte Reden, Briefe und Aufsätze* (Berlin: Dietz, 1952).

'Trotz alledem!', *Die Rote Fahne* (15 January 1919), in *Gesammelte Reden und Schriften*, ed. W. Pieck (Berlin: Dietz, 1958), IX, 675–79.

Liebknecht, Karl, *Scritti politici*, ed. E. Collotti (Milan: Feltrinelli, 1971).

Linden, Walter, *Luigi Nonos Weg zum Streichquartett* (Kassel: Bärenreiter, 1989).

Lombardo, Patrizia, 'The Philosophy of the City', in Massimo Cacciari, *Architecture and Nihilism: On the Philosophy of Modern Architecture*, trans. S. Sartarelli (New Haven, CT: Yale University Press, 1993), ix–lviii.

Löwy, Michael, *Fire Alarm: Reading Walter Benjamin's 'On the Concept of History'*, trans. C. Turner (London: Verso, 2005).

Lucchesi, Joachim (ed.), *Das Verhör in der Oper: Die Debatte um die Aufführung 'Das Verhör des Lukullus' von Bertolt Brecht und Paul Dessau* (Berlin: BasisDruck, 1993).

Malcolm, Norman, *Ludwig Wittgenstein: A Memoir* (London: Oxford University Press, 1958).

Malvezzi, Pierro, and Giovanni Pirelli (eds.), *Lettere di condannati a morte della Resistenza italiana (8 settembre 1943 – 25 aprile 1945)* (Turin: Einaudi, 1952).

*Lettere di condannati a morte della Resistenza europea*, with a preface by Thomas Mann (Turin: Einaudi, 1954).

*Und die Flamme soll euch nicht versengen* (Zurich: Steinberg, 1955).

Mandarini, Matteo, 'Beyond Nihilism: Notes towards a Critique of Left-Heideggerianism in Italian Philosophy of the 1970s', in *Cosmos and History: The Journal of Natural and Social Philosophy*, 5/1 (2009), 37–56.

Mann, Thomas, 'Vorwort zu dem Buche *Briefe Todgeweihter*', in *An die gesittete Welt: Politische Schriften und Reden im Exil*, ed. P. de Mendelssohn, Gesammelte Werke (Frankfurt am Main: Fischer, 1986), 812–19.

'Die Lager' (1945), in *An die gesittete Welt: Politische Schriften und Reden im Exil*, ed. P. de Mendelssohn, Gesammelte Werke (Frankfurt am Main: Fischer, 1986), 698–701.

Marbach, Gertrud, 'Schlemmers Begegnungen mit Schönberg, Scherchen und Hindemith', *Neue Zeitschrift für Musik*, 123:12 (1962), 530–36.

Marx, Karl, foreword to the doctoral dissertation *The Difference Between the Democritean and Epicurean Philosophy of Nature* (March 1841), Karl Marx Internet Archive (2000).

Mast, Christine, *Luigi Nono «Io, Prometeo»* (Frankfurt am Main: Stroemfeld, 2008).

Mattis, Olivia, 'From Bebop to Poo-wip: Jazz Influences in Varèse's *Poème électronique*', in F. Meyer and H. Zimmermann (eds.), *Edgard Varèse: Composer, Sound Sculptor, Visionary*, Exhibition Catalogue (Woodbridge: Boydell Press, 2006), 309–17.

Maur, Karin von, *Oskar Schlemmer: Monographie*, 2 vols (Munich: Prestel, 1979), II, 271–77.

Maurer Zenck, Claudia, '«La di ella inaudita finezza». Zur Entstehung der «Varianti»', in A. M. Morazzoni (ed.), *Schoenberg & Nono: A Birthday Offering to Nuria on May 7, 2002* (Milan: Olschki, 2002), 267–315.

Mauser, Siegfried, '*An Diotima . . .*: Dichtung als Partitur', in O. Kolleritsch (ed.), *Die Musik Luigi Nonos* (Vienna and Graz: Universal Edition, 1991), 162–79.

Melkert, Hella, *«Far del silenzio cristallo» Luigi Nono: Chorkompositionen im Rahmen des* Prometeo (Saarbrücken: Pfau, 2001).

Metzer, David, *Musical Modernism at the Turn of the Twenty-First Century* (Cambridge University Press, 2009).

Metzger, Heinz-Klaus, 'Das Altern der jüngsten Musik' (1962), in *Musik wozu: Literatur zu Noten* (Frankfurt am Main: Suhrkamp, 1980), 113–28.

Meyer, Felix, and Heidy Zimmermann (eds.), *Edgard Varèse: Composer, Sound Sculptor, Visionary*, Exhibition Catalogue (Woodbridge: Boydell Press, 2006).

Meyer-Eppler, Werner (ed.), *Gravesano: Musik, Raumgestaltung, Elektroakustik* (Mainz: Ars Viva, 1955).

Mila, Massimo, 'La linea Nono', *La Rassegna musicale*, 30 (1960), 297–311; German translation in J. Stenzl (ed.), *Texte*, 380–93.

Misch, Imke, 'On the Serial Shaping of Stockhausen's *Gruppen für drei Orchester*', *Perspectives of New Music*, 36:1 (1998), 143–87.

*Zur Kompositionstechnik Karlheinz Stockhausens: Gruppen für drei Orchester (1955–57)* (Saarbrücken: Pfau, 1999).

Misch, Imke, and Markus Bandur (eds.), *Karlheinz Stockhausen bei den Internationalen Ferienkursen für Neue Musik in Darmstadt 1951–1996: Dokumente und Briefe* (Kürten: Stockhausen-Stiftung, 2001).

Morazzoni, Anna Maria (ed.), *Schoenberg & Nono: A Birthday Offering to Nuria on May 7, 2002* (Venice: Olschki, 2002).

Motte, Diether de la, 'Varèse, *Ionisation*: Europäische Erstaufführung am 20.8.1950 um 19 Uhr? – NEIN!', in H. de la Motte-Haber and K. Angermann (eds.), *Edgard Varèse 1883–1965: Dokumente zu Leben und Werk* (Frankfurt am Main: Peter Lang, 1990), 67; trans. H. Zimmermann, in F. Meyer and H. Zimmermann (eds.), *Edgard Varèse: Composer, Sound Sculptor, Visionary*, Exhibition Catalogue (Woodbridge: Boydell Press, 2006), 394.

Motz, Wolfgang, *Konstruktion und Ausdruck. Analytische Betrachtungen zu «Il canto sospeso» (1955/56) von Luigi Nono* (Saarbrücken: Pfau, 1996).

'Konstruktive Strenge und kompositorische Freiheit im ersten Satz des *Canto sospeso*', in G. Borio, G. Morelli and V. Rizzardi (eds.), *La nuova ricerca sull'opera di Luigi Nono*, Archivio Luigi Nono, Studi, I (Florence: Olschki, 1999), 53–66.

Musil, Robert, *The Man Without Qualities*, trans. S. Wilkins and B. Pike (New York: Knopf, 1995).

Nanni, Matteo, 'Bruch des ästhetischen Spiels. *Composizione per orchestra n. 2: Diario polacco '58* – Version mit Tonband (1965)', in T. Schäfer (ed.), *Luigi Nono: Aufbruch in Grenzbereiche* (Saarbrücken: Pfau, 1999), 25–35.

*Auschwitz: Adorno und Nono. Philosophische und musikanalytische Untersuchungen* (Freiburg im Breisgau: Rombach, 2004).

'Politica come silenzio/il silenzio della politica', in A. I. De Benedictis and L. Zattra (eds.), *Presenza storica di Luigi Nono* (Lucca: LIM, 2011), 205–37.

Nanni, Matteo, and Rainer Schmusch (eds.), *Incontri: Luigi Nono im Gespräch mit Enzo Restagno* (Hofheim: Wolke, 2004).

National Front of the GDR (ed.), *Brown Book: War and Nazi Criminals in West Germany, State, Economy, Administration, Army, Justice, Science*, Staatliche Archivverwaltung (Dresden: Zeit im Bild, 1965).

Navacchia, Stefania, 'La concezione drammaturgica dello spazio-tempo in *Composizione per orchestra n. 2 – Diario Polacco '58*', *Musica/Realtà*, 92 (2010), 105–14.

Neidhöfer, Christoph, 'Bruno Madernas flexibler Materialbegriff: Eine Analyse des *Divertimento in due tempi* (1953)', *Musik und Ästhetik*, 9:33 (2005), 30–47.

'Bruno Maderna's Serial Arrays', *Music Theory Online*, 13:1 (2007).

Nielinger-Vakil, Carola, 'Quiet Revolutions: Hölderlin Fragments by Luigi Nono and Wolfgang Rihm', *Music & Letters*, 81:2 (2000), 245–47.

'"The Song Unsung": Luigi Nono's *Il canto sospeso*', *Journal of the Royal Musical Association*, 131:1 (2006), 83–150.

'*Fragmente – Stille, an Diotima*: World of Greater Compositional Secrets', *Acta musicologica*, 82:1 (2010), 105–47.

'Between Memorial and Political Manifesto: Nono's Anti-fascist Works, 1951–1966', in A. I. De Benedictis and L. Zattra (eds.), *Presenza storica di Luigi Nono* (Lucca: LIM, 2011), 77–137.

Nietzsche, Friedrich, 'Of the New Idol', in *Thus Spoke Zarathustra*, trans. R. J. Hollingdale (Harmondsworth: Penguin, 1969), 75.

'The Wanderer', in *Human, All Too Human: A Book for Free Spirits*, trans. R. J. Hollingdale (Cambridge University Press, 1996), 203–204.

Nirenstajn, Alberto, *Ricorda cosa ti ha fatto Amalek* (Turin: Einaudi, 1958).

Nirenstein, Albert, *A Tower from the Enemy. Contributions to a History of Jewish Resistance in Poland*, trans. M. Savill (New York: Orion Press, 1959).

Noller, Joachim, 'La storia e la crisi della stampa musicale', in G. Cattin and P. Dalla Vecchia (eds.), *Venezia 1501: Petrucci e la stampa musicale* (Venice: Edizioni Fondazione Levi, 2005), 739–51.

Nono, Luigi, 'Luigi Dallapiccola e i *Sex Carmina Alcæi* ' (*ca.* 1948), in *Scritti*, I, 3–5.

'Über Anton Webern' (1953), in *Im Zenit der Moderne*, vol. 3, 63–64; H.-K. Metzger and R. Riehn (eds.), *Darmstadt Dokumente I*, Sonderband Musik-Konzepte (Munich: text + kritik, 1999), 69; in *Scritti*, I, 7.

'Zur Entwicklung der Serientechnik', *Gravesaner Blätter*, II:4 (March 1956), in *Texte*, 16–20; 'Sullo sviluppo della tecnica seriale'; in *Scritti*, I, 9–14.

'Die neue Kompositionstechnik. Bericht', *Gravesaner Blätter*, II:6 (December 1956), 19–20, in *Texte*, 146; in *Scritti*, I, 15.

'Die Entwicklung der Reihentechnik' (1957), *Darmstädter Beiträge zur neuen Musik*, 1 (1958), trans. W. Reich, in *Texte*, 21–33; 'Lo sviluppo della tecnica seriale' (1957), in *Scritti*, I, 19–42.

'*Composizione per orchestra n. 2 – Diario polacco '58* ' (1959), first published in *Blätter und Bilder* (1960), in *Texte*, 123–25; *Scritti*, I, 433–436.

'Testo – musica – canto', I (1960), in *Scritti*, I, 57–65.

'Text – Musik – Gesang', II (1960), ghostwritten by Helmut Lachenmann, in *Texte*, 48–60.

*Intolleranza 1960*, libretto, trans. H. Graham, CD booklet for the recording of the 1993 production at the Staatsoper Stuttgart, cond. Bernhard Kontarsky (Teldec, 1993).

'Appunti per un teatro musicale attuale' (1961), in *Scritti*, I, 86–95.

'Alcune precisazione su *Intolleranza 1960* ' (1962), in *Scritti*, I, 100–117.

'Possibilità e necessità di un nuovo teatro musicale' (1962), in *Scritti*, I, 118–32.

'Musica e Resistenza' (1963), in *Scritti*, I, 144–47.

'Viaggio attraverso la musica nell'URSS' (1963), in *Scritti*, I, 150–57.

'Lettera da Los Angeles' (1965), in *Scritti*, I, 177–81.

'Musica per "Die Ermittlung" di Peter Weiss', in *Scritti*, I, 450–451; original German in the programme, H. Goertz (ed.), *Die Ermittlung von Peter Weiss* (Berlin: Freie Volksbühne, 1965), 8–9; trans. A. Herklotz in *Luigi Nono: Complete Works for Solo Tape* (Milan: Ricordi, 2006), CD booklet, 47–48.

'Lettera di Luigi Nono agli operai dell'Italsider di Genova-Cornigliano' (21 November 1965), in *Scritti*, I, 186–88.

'Musica e teatro' (1966), in *Scritti*, I, 210–15.

'Josef Svoboda' (1968), in *Scritti*, I, 245–48.

'Saluto a Henze' (1968), in *Scritti*, I, 254–55.

'Gespräch mit Hansjörg Pauli' (1969), in H. Pauli (ed.), *Für wen komponieren sie eigentlich?* (Frankfurt: Fischer, 1971), 106–27; in *Texte*, 198–209; in *Scritti*, II,

23–33; partly translated by A. Davies in C. Flamm, 'Preface', *Il canto sospeso*, score (London: Eulenberg, 1995), ix.

'Gespräch mit Hartmut Lück' (1972), in *Texte*, 280–90; trans. P. Cavallotto, 'Compositore nella lotta di classe', in *Scritti*, II, 100–112.

'Intervista di Jean Villain' (1973), in *Scritti*, II, 129–43.

'Con Luigi Dallapiccola' (1979), in *Scritti*, I, 483–84.

'Intervista di Renato Garavaglia' (1979–80), in *Scritti*, II, 235–48.

'Das atmende Klarsein' (1981), in *Scritti*, I, 487.

'Ecco il mio Prometeo così pieno di dolcezza' (1981), in *Scritti*, II, 259–61.

'Solidarnosc elettronica. Intervista di Renato Garavaglia' (1982), in *Scritti*, II, 273–75.

'Anche la dolcezza è rivoluzionaria' (1982), interview with Philippe Albèra, in *Scritti*, II, 268–72.

'Per Helmut' (1983), in *Scritti*, I, 376–79; trans. B. Maurer, in Helmut Lachenmann, *Musik als existentielle Erfahrung* (Wiesbaden: Breitkopf & Härtel, 1996), xiii–xv.

'L'erreure comme nécessité' (1983), in L. Feneyrou (ed.), *Luigi Nono: Écrits* (Paris: Bourgois, 1993), 256–57; in *Scritti*, I, 522–23; in J. Stenzl (ed.), *Nono*, 105–106.

'Guai ai gelidi mostri' (1983), in *Scritti*, I, 491–92.

'Ascoltare le pietre bianche. I suoni della politica e degli oggetti muti', interview with Franco Miracco (1983), in *Scritti*, II, 287–307.

'Verso *Prometeo*. Frammenti di diari' (1984), in *Scritti*, I, 385–95.

'Prometeo' (1985), in *Scritti*, I, 493–94.

'I futuri felici' (1987), interview with Franck Mallet, in *Scritti*, II, 409–414.

'Intervista di Philippe Albèra' (1987), in *Scritti*, II, 415–29.

'Le sue parole e le sue grandi drammatiche solitudini' (1984), in *Scritti*, I, 397–99.

'Parte la nave di Prometeo', interview with Renato Garavaglia (1984), in *Scritti*, II, 332–34.

'Un'autobiografia dell'autore raccontata da Enzo Restagno' (1987), in *Scritti*, II, 477–568.

'. . . kein Anfang – kein Ende . . . Aus Gesprächen mit Luigi Nono', in conversation with Klaus Kropfinger, *Musica*, 42 (1988), 165–71; in *Scritti*, II, 451–62.

Nono, Luigi, and members of the LaSalle Quartet, 'Wie Hölderlin komponierte', conversation on occasion of the premiere of *Fragmente – Stille, an Diotima* at the 30. Beethovenfest Bonn (1 June 1980), in Kay-Uwe Kirchert, *Wahrnehmung und Fragmentierung: Luigi Nonos Kompositionen zwischen «Al gran sole carico d'amore» und «Prometeo»* (Saarbrücken: Pfau, 2006), 203–218 (including the WDR recording of this conversation on CD).

Nono, Luigi, and Massimo Cacciari (eds.), *Luigi Nono: Festival d'automne à Paris 1987* (Paris: Contrechamps, 1987).

Nono, Luigi, Massimo Cacciari and Michele Bertaggia, 'Verso Prometeo' (1984), *Scritti*, II, 338–58.

Nonnenmann, Rainer, *Der Gang durch die Klippen. Helmut Lachenmanns Begegnungen mit Luigi Nono anhand ihres Briefwechsels und anderer Quellen 1957–1990* (Wiesbaden: Breitkopf & Härtel, 2013).

Novati, Maria Madalena, 'The Tapes of the Archivio di Fonologia at the RAI in Milan', *Luigi Nono: Complete Works for Solo Tape*, CD booklet (Milan: Ricordi, 2006), 3.

Novati, Maria Madalena, and John Dack (eds.), *The Studio di Fonologia: A Musical Journey 1954–1983. Update 2008–2012* (Milan: Ricordi, 2012).

Ogborn, David, 'When they are dying, men sing . . .: Nono's *Diario Polacco n. 2* ', paper presented at the Electroacoustic Music Studies Network (Montreal, 2005).

Overy, Richard, *Interrogations: The Nazi Elite in Allied Hands, 1945* (Harmondsworth: Penguin, 2002).

Pavese, Cesare, *Disaffections: Complete Poems 1930–1950*, trans. G. Brock (Manchester: Carcanet, 2004).

Pellegrini, Alessandra Carlotta, 'Musica o diritto? La nascita di un compositore', in A. C. Pellegrini (ed.), *Gli anni giovanili di Luigi Nono: Tre relazioni dal Convegno Luigi Nono. Musica e impegno politico nel secondo Novecento* (Venice, 3–4 Decemeber 2004), online publication (10 August 2006, rev. 1 February 2010), 9–24; accessible via the ALN website.

Pestalozza, Luigi, 'Musica ispirata dalla Resistenza', *Il ponte*, 11:4–5 (1955), 687–95.

'La guerra civile spagnola e i musicisti italiani del dopoguerra', in A. Trudu (ed.), *Federico García Lorca nella musica contemporanea* (Milan: Unicopli, 1990), 12–23.

'Ausgangspunkt Nono (nach dem "Quartett")', in H.-K. Metzger and R. Riehn (eds.), *Luigi Nono*, Musik-Konzepte, 20 (Munich: edition text + kritik, 1981), 3–10.

Piano, Renzo '*Prometeo*. Uno spazio per la musica' (1984), in S. Cecchetto and G. Mastinu (eds.), *Nono Vedova. Diario di bordo* (Turin: Allemandi, 2005), 131–39.

*The Logbook*, preface by Kenneth Frampton (London: Thames & Hudson, 1997), 86–87.

Pindar, *Nemean Odes, Isthmian Odes, Fragments*, trans. W. H. Race, Loeb Classical Library, 485 (Cambridge, MA: Harvard University Press, 1997).

Piscator, Erwin, 'Anmerkungen zu einem grossen Thema' (October 1965), in *Schriften II: Aufsätze, Reden, Gespräche*, ed. L. Hoffmann (Berlin: Henschel, 1968), 321–25.

Pizzi, Emilio, *Renzo Piano* (Basel: Birkhäuser, 2003).

Plato, 'The Myth of Er', in *The Republic*, trans. F. MacDonald Cornford (Oxford University Press, 1945).

Quasimodo, Salvatore, *Lirici greci* (Milan: Mondadori, 1944).

Ramazzotti, Marinella, *Luigi Nono* (Palermo: L'Epos, 2007).

'Il dubbio, la lotta, la speranza: Nono legge Cacciari secondo Gramsci', in A. I. De Benedictis and L. Zattra (eds.), *Presenza storica di Luigi Nono* (Lucca: LIM, 2011), 165–204.

Richard, André, and Marco Mazzolini, Preface to Nono, *Das atmende Klarsein* (Milan: Ricordi, 2005).

Riede, Bernd, *Luigi Nonos Kompositionen mit Tonband* (Munich and Salzburg: Katzbichler, 1986).

Rilke, Rainer Maria, *Duineser Elegien*, in *Gesammelte Gedichte* (Frankfurt am Main: Insel Verlag, 1962), 441–82.

*Duino Elegies*, trans. D. Young (New York: Norton, 1978).

Rizzardi, Veniero, 'Verso un nuovo stile rappresentivo. Il teatro mancato e la drammaturgia implicita', in G. Borio, G. Morelli and V. Rizzardi (eds.), *La nuova ricerca sull'opera di Luigi Nono* (Venice: Olschki, 1999), 35–51.

"Nono e la 'presenza storica' di Schönberg", in A. M. Morazzoni (ed.), *Schoenberg & Nono: A Birthday Offering to Nuria on May 7, 2002* (Venice: Olschki, 2002), 229–50.

'La «Nuova Scuola Veneziana», 1948–1951', in G. Borio, G. Morelli and V. Rizzardi (eds.), *Le musiche degli anni cinquanta*, Archivio Luigi Nono, Studi, II (Venice: Olschki, 2004), 1–59.

Restagno, Enzo (ed.), *Nono* (Turin: EDT, 1987).

Romito, Maurizio, 'I commenti musicali di Bruno Maderna: radio, televisione, teatro', II, *Nuova Rivista Musicale Italiana*, 36:1 (2002), 79–98.

Rosenberg, Ethel and Julius, *The Rosenberg Letters* (London: Dennis Dobson, 1953).

*Lettere dalla casa della morte*, trans. R. Nicolai and G. Orlandini, Attualità politica, 5 (Rome: Edizioni di cultura sociale, Editori Riuniti, 1953).

Rufer, Josef, 'Arnold Schoenberg [1949]', in G. Borio and H. Danuser (eds.), *Im Zenit der Moderne*, III, 43–57.

Russell, Edward Frederick Langley, Second Baron of Liverpool, *The Scourge of the Swastika: A Short History of Nazi War Crimes* (London: Cassell, 1954).

Russell, Lord, *Il flagello della svastika: breve storia dei delitti di guerra nazisti* (Milan: Feltrinelli, 1960).

Sallis, Friedemann, 'Segmenting the Labyrinth: Sketch Studies and the *Scala Enigmatica* in the Finale of Luigi Nono's *Quando stanno morendo. Diario Polacco n. 2* (1982)', *Ex tempore. A Journal of Compositional and Theoretical Research in Music*, 13/1 (2006), 1–23.

Santini, Andrea, 'Multiplicity – Fragmentation – Simultaneity: Sound-Space as a Conveyor of Meaning, and Theatrical Roots in Luigi Nono's Early Spatial Practice', *Journal of the Royal Musical Association*, 137:1, 71–106.

Sartre, Jean-Paul, *Morti senza tomba/Le mani sporche* (Milan: Mondadori, 1949).

'Julius Fucik', *Les lettres françaises* (17–24 June 1954), in M. Contat and M. Rybalka (eds.), *The Writings of Jean-Paul Sartre: A Bibliographical Life*, trans. R. C. McCleary (Evanston, IL: Northwestern University Press, 1974), 301.

*Anti-Semite and Jew*, trans. G. J. Becker, preface by Micheal Walzer (New York: Schocken, 1995).

*What is Literature?*, trans. B. Frechtman, Routledge Classics (London: Routledge, 2001).

Sassanelli, Fiorella, 'Intervista ad Alvise Vidolin', in S. Durante and L. Zattra (eds.), *Vent'anni di musica elettronica all'Università di Padova*, Archivio musiche del XX secolo (Catania: CIMS, 2002), 114–19

Schäfer, Thomas (ed.), *Luigi Nono: Aufbruch in Grenzbereiche* (Saarbrücken: Pfau, 1999).

Schaller, Erika, *Klang und Zahl: Serielles Komponieren zwischen 1955 und 1959* (Saarbrücken, Pfau, 1997).

'L'insegnamento di Bruno Maderna attraverso le fonti conservate presso l'Archivio Luigi Nono', in R. Dalmonte and M. Russo (eds.), *Bruno Maderna: Studi e testimonianze* (Lucca: LIM, 2004), 107–16.

Scherchen, Hermann, 'I quattri pezzi sacri', *Il diapason*, 2:1 (1951), 13–15.

*Aus meinem Leben. Rußland in jenen Jahren*, ed. E. Klemm (Berlin: Henschelverlag, 1984).

*Werke und Briefe*, ed. J. Lucchesi (Frankfurt am Main: Peter Lang, 1991).

Schiaffini, Giancarlo, *Il trombone: Estensione delle possibilità tecnico-espressive* (Milan: Ricordi, 1980).

Schmidt, Christian Martin (ed.), *Moses und Aron: Oper in drei Akten. Entstehungsgeschichte, Texte und Textentwürfe zum Oratorium und zur Oper*, in *Arnold Schönberg: Sämtliche Werke* (Mainz and Vienna: Schott and Universal, 1998), III: 8,2b, 'Briefdokumente'.

Schmitt, Carl, *The Nomos of the Earth in the International Law of the Jus Publicum Europaeum*, trans. G. L. Ulmen (New York: Telos Press, 2006).

Schnebel, Dieter, 'Der körperliche Klang', in *Edgard Varèse. Rückblick auf die Zukunft*, ed. H.-K. Metzger and R. Riehn, Musik-Konzepte, 6 (Munich: text + kritik, 1983), 6.

Schoenberg, Arnold, *Six Pieces for Male Chorus* op. 35, no. 2, 'Das Gesetz', trans. D. Millar Craig and A. Weiss, score (Berlin: Bote & Bock, 1930).

Shore, Cris, *Italian Communism: The Escape from Leninism* (London: Pluto Press, 1990).

Smeliansky, Anatoly, *The Russian Theatre after Stalin*, trans. P. Miles, Cambridge Studies in Modern Theatre (Cambridge University Press, 1999).

Solza, Giorgio, and Mario De Michelis (eds.), *Canti della Resistenza italiana* (Milan: Avanti, 1960).

Soriano, Susana Moreno, *Arquitectura y Música en el siglo XX* (Barcelona: Fundación Caja de Arquitectos, 2008).

Spangemacher, Friedrich, 'Schönberg as Role Model . . . on the relationship between Luigi Nono and Arnold Schönberg', in *Contemporary Music Review*, 18:1 (1999), 31–46.

*Dialektischer Kontrapunkt: Die elektronischen Kompositionen Luigi Nonos zwischen 1964 und 1971*, 2nd edn (Saarbrücken: Pfau, 2006).

Spark, Edgard H., *Cantus Firmus in Mass and Motet 1420–1520* (Berkeley and Los Angeles, CA: University of California Press, 1963).

Spree, Hermann, *'Fragmente – Stille, an Diotima'. Ein analytischer Versuch zu Luigi Nonos Streichquartett* (Saarbrücken: Pfau, 1992).

Spruytenburg, Robert, *The LaSalle Quartet. Conversations with Walter Levin* (Woodbridge: Boydell Press, 2014).

Staff, Ilse, *Staatsdenken im Italien des 20. Jahrhunderts. Ein Beitrag zur Carl Schmitt-Rezeption* (Baden-Baden: Nomos, 1991).

Steinbacher, Sybille, *Auschwitz: Geschichte und Nachgeschichte* (Munich: Beck, 2004).

Stenzl, Jürg (ed.), *Luigi Nono: Texte, Studien zu seiner Musik* (Zurich: Atlantis, 1975).

'Luigi Nono und Cesare Pavese', in *Texte*, 409–433.

'Drammaturgia musicale', in E. Restagno (ed.), *Nono* (Turin: EDT, 1987), 169–83.

*Luigi Nono* (Reinbek bei Hamburg: Rowohlt, 1998).

'Improvisation im Schaffen Luigi Nonos', in T. Schäfer (ed.), *Luigi Nono: Aufbruch in Grenzbereiche* (Saarbrücken: Pfau, 1999), 36–43.

Stockhausen, Karlheinz, 'Musik und Sprache' (1957), first published in *Darmstädter Beiträge*, 1 (Mainz: Schott, 1958), revised version broadcast on SWR, published in *die Reihe*, 6 (1960), 36–58, and Karlheinz Stockhausen, *Texte*, ed. D. Schnebel (Cologne: DuMont, 1964), II, 58–68, 149–66.

'Music and Speech', trans. R. Koenig, *die Reihe*, 6 (1964), 40–64.

'About my Childhood' (1971), in *Stockhausen on Music*, ed. R. Maconie (London: Marion Boyars, 1989), 15–23.

Svoboda, Josef, *The Secret of Theatrical Space*, trans. J. Burian (New York: Applause, 1993).

Trakl, Georg, *Dichtungen und Briefe*, ed. W. Killy and H. Szklenar, critical edition, 2 vols (Salzburg: Otto Müller Verlag, 1969).

Trudu, Antonio (ed.), *Luigi Nono: Carteggi concernenti politica, cultura, e Partito Comunista Italiano* (Florence: Olschki, 2008).

Ungaretti, Giuseppe, *La terra promessa* (*The Promised Land* ), trans. M. Berridge, in *Luigi Nono: Choral Works*, SWR Vokalensemble Stuttgart, dir. Rupert Huber (Hänssler Classic, 2001), CD booklet, 8/16.

Valle, Andrea, Kees Tazelaar and Vincenzo Lombardo, 'In a Concrete Space. Reconstructing the Spatialization of Iannis Xenakis *Concret PH* on a Multichannel Setup', smcnetwork.org/files/proceedings/2010/40, accessed March 2014.

Varèse, Edgard, 'New Instruments and New Music' (1936), in E. Schwartz and B. Childs (eds.), *Contemporary Composers on Contemporary Music* (New York: Holt, Rinehart and Winston, 1967), 196–98.

'Rhythm, Form and Content' (1959), in E. Schwartz and B. Childs (eds.), *Contemporary Composers on Contemporary Music* (New York: Holt, Rinehart and Winston, 1967), 201–204.

Verzina, Nicola, 'Tecnica della mutazione e tecnica seriale in *Vier Briefe* (1953)', *Rivista Italiana di Musicologia*, 34:2 (1999), 309–345.

*Bruno Maderna: Étude historique et critique* (Paris: L'Harmattan, 2003).

'Musica e impegno nella *Kranichsteiner Kammerkantate* (1953): il tema della libertà', in R. Dalmonte and M. Russo (eds.), *Bruno Maderna: Studi e testimonianze* (Lucca: LIM, 2004), 199–225.

Vidolin, Alvise, 'Il suono mobile', in R. Doati (ed.), *Con Luigi Nono*, Festival Internazionale di Musica Contemporanea 1992/93 (Milan: Ricordi, Biennale di Venezia, 1992), 42–47.

Vieira de Carvalho, Mário, '*No hay caminos*? – Luigi Nonos Verhältnis zur Geschichte', in O. Kolleritsch (ed.), *Das aufgesprengte Kontinuum. Über die Geschichtsfähigkeit der Musik*, Studien zur Wertungsforschung, 31 (Graz and Vienna: Universal, 1996), 187–219.

'Towards Dialectic Listening: Quotation and *Montage* in the Work of Luigi Nono', in S. Davismoon (ed.), *Luigi Nono: fragments and silence, Contemporary Music Review*, 18:2 (1999), 37–85.

*A tragédia da escuta. Luigi Nono e la música do século XX* (Lisbon: Impresa Nacional, 2007).

'Idiom, Trauerspiel, Dialektik des Hörens. Zur Benjamin-Rezeption im Werk Luigi Nonos', in T. R. Klein (ed.), *Klang und Musik bei Walter Benjamin* (Munich: Wilhelm Fink Verlag, 2013), 179–99.

Vincis, Claudia, '"To Nono: a No" Luigi Nono and his Intolleranza 1965 in the U.S.', in F. Meyer, C. J. Oja, W. Rathert and A. Shreffler (eds.), *Crosscurrents: American and European Music in Interaction, 1900–2000* (Woodbridge: Boydell Press, 2014), 320–34.

Völker, Ernst-Joachim, 'Acoustical and electro-acoustic sound fields – The beginning in Gravesano 1954', in M. M. Boone (ed.), *International Conference on Acoustics: Rotterdam 23–26 March 2009*, 3 vols (Berlin: DEAG, 2009), I, 246–49.

Wagner, Andreas, (ed.), *Luigi Nono: Dokumente Materialien* (Saarbrücken: Pfau, 2003).

Wagner, Renata (ed.), *Karl Amadeus Hartmann und die Musica Viva* (Munich: Bayrische Staatsbibliothek, 1980).

Walbe, Joel, *Der Gesang Israels und seine Quellen* (Hamburg: Christians Verlag, 1975).

Weiss, Peter, *Die Ermittlung* (Frankfurt: Suhrkamp, 1965).

*The Investigation: Oratorio in Eleven Cantos*, trans. J. Swan and U. Grosbard, rev. R. Cohen, in Peter Weiss, *Marat/Sade, The Investigation and The Shadow of the Body of the Coachman*, ed. R. Cohen, The German Library, 92 (New York: Continuum, 1998).

'Meine Ortschaft', first broadcast under the title 'Auschwitz – 20 Jahre später', WDR (17 January 1965), in Christoph Weiß, *Auschwitz in der geteilten Welt: Peter Weiss und die 'Ermittlung' im Kalten Krieg* (St. Ingberg: Röhrig, 2000), II, 5–12; 'My Place', trans. C. Middleton, in C. Middleton (ed.), *German Writing Today* (Harmondsworth: Penguin, 1967), 20–28.

Weiß, Christoph, *Auschwitz in der geteilten Welt: Peter Weiss und die 'Ermittlung' im Kalten Krieg* (St. Ingberg: Röhrig, 2000).

Welsch, Helga, '"Antifaschistisch-demokratische Umwälzung" und politische Säuberung in der sowjetischen Besatzungszone Deutschlands', in K. D. Henke and H. Woller (eds.), *Politische Säuberung in Europa: Die Abrechnung mit Faschismus und Kollaboration nach dem zweiten Weltkrieg* (Munich: DTV, 1991), 84–107.

Wilcox, Dean, 'Political Allegory or Multimedia Extravaganza?', *Theatre Survey*, 37:2 (1996), 115–34.

Wismeyer, Ludwig, 'Wider die Natur!', *Neue Zeitschrift für Musik*, 118 (1957), 136–37.

Wittgenstein, Ludwig, *Tractatus Logico-Philosophicus*, trans. D. F. Pears and B. F. McGuinness (London: Routledge, 1974).

*Culture and Value*, trans. P. Winch (Oxford: Blackwell, 1980).

Woller, Hans, '"Ausgebliebene Säuberung"? Die Abrechnung mit dem Faschismus in Italien', in K. D. Henke and H. Woller (eds.), *Politische Säuberung in Europa: Die Abrechnung mit Faschismus und Kollaboration nach dem zweiten Weltkrieg* (Munich: DTV, 1991), 148–91.

Wörner, Karl H., *Schoenberg's 'Moses and Aaron'*, trans. P. Hamburger (London: Faber, 1963).

Young, Julian, *Heidegger's Later Philosophy* (Cambridge University Press, 2002).

Zattra, Laura, 'A colloquio con Roberto Fabbriciani', *Rassegna musicale*, 67:3 (September 2014), 45–51.

'Il Centro di sonologia computazionale (C.S.C.): l'istituzione, le strutture operative, la musica, la ricerca', in S. Durante and L. Zattra (eds.), *Vent'anni di musica elettronica all'Università di Padova*, Archivio musiche del XX secolo (Catania: CIMS, 2002), 41–102.

Zattra, Laura, Ian Burleigh and Friedemann Sallis, 'Studying Luigi Nono's *A Pierre. Dell'azzurro silenzio, inquietum* (1985) as a Performance Event', *Contemporary Music Review*, 30:5 (2011), 411–39.

# Index